D0406946

LOOK

L O

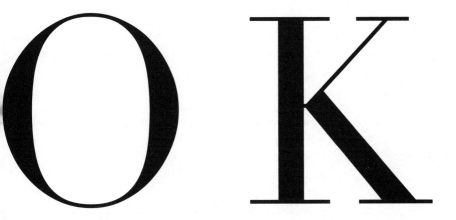

O K

How a Highly Influential Magazine Helped
Define Mid-Twentieth-Century America

Andrew L. Yarrow

POTOMAC BOOKS | AN IMPRINT OF THE UNIVERSITY OF NEBRASKA PRESS

© 2021 by Andrew L. Yarrow

All rights reserved. Potomac Books is an imprint
of the University of Nebraska Press.
Manufactured in the United States of America.

∞

Library of Congress Cataloging-in-Publication Data
Names: Yarrow, Andrew L., author.
Title: Look: how a highly influential
magazine helped define mid-twentieth-
century America / Andrew L. Yarrow.
Other titles: Look magazine.
Description: Lincoln: Potomac Books, an imprint
of the University of Nebraska Press, [2021] |
Includes bibliographical references and index.
Identifiers: LCCN 2021015704
ISBN 9781612349442 (hardback)
ISBN 9781640125100 (epub)
ISBN 9781640125117 (pdf)
Subjects: LCSH: Look magazine. | Popular
culture—United States—20th century. | United
States—Civilization—20th century. | BISAC: HISTORY
/ United States / 20th century | LANGUAGE ARTS &
DISCIPLINES / Journalism | LCGFT: Periodicals.
Classification: LCC PN4900.L6 Y37 2021 | DDC 051—dc23
LC record available at https://lccn.loc.gov/2021015704

Set in Sabon Next by Mikala R. Kolander.
Designed by N. Putens.

To the memory of Michael Rose

CONTENTS

ILLUSTRATIONS

PREFACE

The twenty-first century has not been a good time for magazines and newspapers or the people who read or write for them. When I left the *New York Times* in the 1990s, newspapers were thriving. By 2021 most print media that existed in the late twentieth century had folded or were barely hanging on. Circulation, the number of newsroom jobs, and ad revenues have plummeted, as all too many important stories and issues go uncovered. Instead, a torrent of "fake" news and generally thought-free, partisan commentary from tens of millions of sources inundate the Internet and cascade into the social media accounts of most Americans.

However, that is not what this book is about. That story—of what has happened to traditional media—has been told elsewhere.

Rather, this book tells the little-known story of *Look* magazine, one of the greatest mass-circulation publications in American history and the very different United States in which it existed. *Look*—which has slipped from national memory—had an extraordinary influence on mid-twentieth-century America, not only by telling powerful, thoughtful stories and printing outstanding photographs but also by helping to create a national conversation around a common set of facts, ideas, and ideals. It did not shy away from hitting hard when it came to exposing the country's problems, but it always believed that any problems could be solved. *Look* helped Americans feel that "we're all in this together," rather than seeing others as enemies, dissonant ideas as blasphemy, the present and future as entirely bleak, and government and other institutions as hopelessly flawed and evil.

Look was at once an astute observer and an influential player in American life. By providing a distinctive vantage point into the greatest era in U.S. history—from winning World War II and building immense, inclusive prosperity to celebrating grand technological achievements and advancing the rights of Blacks and women—*Look* offers new insights about our past and is a rich primary source that few historians have used. Because the magazine helped shape Americans' beliefs about their society and economy, politics and people, while guiding the country through a period of profound social and cultural change, this is also a story about how a long-gone type of journalism made the United States a better country and Americans better people. As such, *Look*, which published from 1937 to 1971, played a significant role in making the United States truly great and assuring readers that it could always be greater.

This is not to downplay the importance of *Life*, its better-known rival. *Life* published many great photos and also covered more than one-third of the twentieth century. Although I compare *Look* and *Life* in this book, I do not intend to diminish the importance or achievements of Henry Luce's magazine. Instead, I am telling a story that is largely unknown compared to that of *Life*, and explaining how *Look* differed from *Life* in so many ways.

As a historian of twentieth-century America, a journalist, and someone disappointed in many of the directions that the country has taken in recent decades, I find *Look* particularly appealing. It offers new information and perspectives on the United States in the middle of the last century. It is an outstanding example of how thoughtful journalism can reach far beyond elite audiences. And it viewed America hopefully, yet critically, rather than through the dark and distorted lenses of cynicism and take-no-prisoners bile.

It was also visually appealing in ways that no major publications—and very few websites, for that matter—are today.

Look, like any publication, was far from perfect. There were trivial and fluffy stories, and important stories that it missed or came late to cover. Yet, on balance, it was a remarkable magazine.

For those old enough to remember this glossy, eleven-by-fourteen-inch magazine, the stories and photos in this book undoubtedly will reawaken long-ago memories. Yet, more than just a trip down a beautifully illustrated memory lane, this book can also remind them of a time when Americans were optimistic and civic-minded, had broadly similar goals, and weren't browbeaten into believing that the country was a shambles and could only be magically returned to greatness by lashing out at other people, ideas, and institutions. For the majority of Americans, who have never seen an issue of *Look*, this book is intended to tell the story of a great American magazine during a momentous era in U.S. history and show that there are better alternatives to the politics, culture, and media of the twenty-first century.

It is impossible to talk about *Look* without discussing its photographs: color, black-and-white, occasionally enhanced, full page or a collage of smaller images, shots of newly prosperous and still poor Americans, beating hearts and Paris fashions, portraits of John Kennedy and Jackie Robinson, movie stars and sleek new technologies. Because of space limitations, this book could only include 61 of the 180,000 photos that the magazine published of the roughly 5 million held by the Library of Congress alone. That's a shame, given how evocative, surprising, and stunning so many were. There is no question that *Look* deserves big-format photo books and exhibitions of its most striking images.

The inaccessibility of *Look*'s photos is matched by the inaccessibility of its issues and articles. I had to pore through often damaged volumes of hard-copy issues at the Library of Congress and university libraries—none of which had a complete run of all *Look* issues. Some issues had disappeared even from the nation's largest library, and more than a few issues had pages torn out. Relatively few libraries even have *Look* on microfilm. I was fortunate to find a few dozen issues from *Look*'s last few years that my parents had saved and others for sale on websites like 2Neat.com.

Thousands of other publications have been digitized and are in databases or freely available to the public. *Life* can be found on the internet thanks to Google, which digitized every issue in the early 2000s. Making *Look* available online would not only enable readers to discover the magazine but also make it possible for scholars and students to delve into its riches.

*

After the introduction, the second and third chapters describe the eventful history of *Look*, from its founding during the Depression by Gardner Cowles Jr. until its demise after a tumultuous decade of cultural and political changes came to a close. How did *Look* grow from a lurid, widely panned Iowa tabloid in the late 1930s into a thoughtful, important national magazine with millions upon millions of readers? Who was Cowles and what made *Look*'s philosophy and approach to reporting and storytelling so distinctive? Even though *Look* did not really report the "news," it is too facile to call its varied content "feature" stories. They were "photo essays," idea-driven articles, guest-written opinion pieces, and more. As an exemplar of photojournalism, how did *Look*'s photos and writing work together in a way that few, if any, other print or broadcast media have accomplished? *Look* was not the pillar of the Establishment that the *New York Times* and *Time-Life* were, but how did it become so iconoclastic and even radical? It certainly had frills, but it was also dead serious. It was not the mouthpiece of a movement, but it clearly wanted its readers to be engaged with public life and informed about both contemporary life beyond America's shores and even some of the highpoints of Western civilization.

Chapter 4 introduces many of *Look*'s most prominent editors, writers, photographers, and business executives. Like Cowles, these men and women were colorful yet highly talented individuals who were the backbone of the magazine. Many were pioneers in their industry in what they covered and how they wrote about it.

The following nine chapters somewhat schematically explore *Look*'s coverage of major subject areas—civil rights, international relations, politics, families, technology, the economy, and popular culture. However, areas such as civil rights, foreign policy, economics, and politics fade into one another, and neither "politics" nor "families" nor "popular culture" quite embraces the ways in which *Look* covered changing social norms and values. These chapters will draw on noteworthy stories throughout *Look*'s history to show how the magazine approached a variety of topics and how its writing and perspectives on these topics changed over time. The magazine's content will be discussed against the backdrop of American history during the mid-twentieth century to illustrate how *Look* influenced that history by molding public opinion and uniting Americans around ideas of what should be considered "normal" and "good," as well as ideals like tolerance, optimism, and civic engagement. There is so much more that could be said about *Look*'s articles, photos, and impact, but this book aims to provide an introduction that will inspire others to further discover one of the most important periodicals in U.S. history.

ACKNOWLEDGMENTS

Michael Rose, my dear friend since the 1970s who died in September 2020, got me excited about *Look* as he and his wife, Carol King, developed King/ Rose Archives, which licenses great photos of the twentieth and twenty-first centuries. Many of the photos in this book are in their archives. He devoted countless hours to researching and discussing *Look*. Before his illness and death, Michael was to be my coauthor.

My editor, Tom Swanson at the University of Nebraska Press, has been strongly supportive and enthusiastic about this project and has provided many valuable ideas. His assistant at the press, Taylor Rothgeb, has been especially meticulous and thoughtful in the process of bringing this book to publication. Copyeditor Amanda Jackson did an excellent job of making the text more felicitously worded.

I am very grateful for the extremely valuable assistance of Claudia Frazer, archivist at Drake University, the principal repository for the papers of Gardner and John Cowles. Others associated with Drake who provided information and insight about *Look* include Patricia Prijatel, Herb Strentz, and Pat Dawson.

Several former *Look* staff members and their families took the time to provide me with a flavor of working at *Look* and insights about the magazine, tales of some of the magazine's remarkable articles, and information on *Look* writers, editors, photographers, and other staff. These include star-writer John Poppy; Patricia Carbine, *Look*'s executive editor in 1969 and 1970; Will Hopkins, *Look*'s final art director; Gilbert Maurer, a leader of Cowles Communications; Thomas R. Shepard III, son of *Look*'s last publisher; Patricia Fusco and Anthony Fusco, the ex-wife and son of brilliant photographer Paul Fusco; *Look* photographer Douglas Kirkland; Alan Waxenberg, a longtime *Look* advertising director; and Elizabeth Ballantine, granddaughter of John Cowles, who connected me with members of the Cowles family.

Staff at institutions other than Drake that hold resources related to *Look* were also very helpful in guiding me to materials. These include archivists at the Prints and Photographs Division of the Library of Congress, the Wisconsin Historical Society, and the George Gallup Archives at Columbia University, as well as staff at the Norman Rockwell Museum and the Richard Avedon Foundation, and Nadine Birner at the San Francisco Museum of Modern Art. A number of former *Look* readers told me of their memories of the magazine.

I also benefited from the valuable comments of my son, Richard Yarrow, and my partner, Jennifer Pettyjohn.

LOOK

1

A Forgotten, Misunderstood Magazine That Helped Define America's Golden Era

Those who remember *Look* magazine, or who know of it, are more than likely to think of it as a Middle American, middle-of-the-road, "middlebrow" publication with photos and not terribly memorable stories that played number two to archrival *Life* magazine during the prosperous and optimistic decades after World War II.

Other than being a magazine filled with dazzling photos, that perception is wrong. This is largely a function of the fact that *Look* has been all but forgotten, almost nothing has been written about it, and it can't be found online—only in research libraries.

In fact, *Look* was an iconoclastic—even radical—magazine that did path-breaking reporting and published essays by major public figures from the 1940s to the early 1970s. Yes, there were movie stars, photos of scantily clad models, and fluffy stories, but *Look* was also a pioneer in covering and advocating for civil rights and did some of the earliest and best stories about the threatening communist world. It was also the first major magazine to write positively about homosexuality, publish essays calling for an end to the white male dominance of American politics, and celebrate the cultural radicalism of the late 1960s.

Moreover, it actually outsold *Life* and every other magazine with original content during most of the 1960s. As one of the magazine's ads cleverly gloated: "*Look* is bigger than life."[1]

Baby Boomers and their elders may get a whiff of nostalgia when they happen on dusty, brittle copies of *Look* buried in basements or for sale at flea markets. But *Look* is so much more than a defunct mid-twentieth-century magazine that was once delivered to millions of doorsteps, or a vehicle to meander down memory lane, a reminder of a different time in American life and a different type of journalism.

Yet even that memory lane has been all but closed. It is highly unusual when once-mighty cultural institutions not only vanish but leave almost no traces. That's what happened to one of the most popular publications in history's most powerful country at the apogee of its power a mere fifty years ago. Almost nothing can be found on the internet about this one-time behemoth of American journalism.

Scholars ignore it, and it has become relegated to that periphery of historical memory that is literally the musty attic of aging Americans.[2]

Although the story and influence of *Life* have been extensively examined and its content repeatedly recycled by its publisher in "special issues" found at supermarket check-out aisles and in coffee-table books, the history, editorial and photographic content, and influence of *Look* have received scant attention. While Google hosts *Life*'s six million photographs online and has digitized *Life*'s more than 1,860 issues, *Look* is unavailable in digital databases, its articles are almost impossible to find, and approximately five million of its photos are hidden in the Madison Building of the Library of Congress in Washington DC, only a small fraction having been digitized. Another 250,000 images of New York are held by the Museum of the City of New York.[3]

However, *Look* was once ubiquitous and influential. It was in millions of homes and offices; readers waited expectantly for the magazine to arrive in their mailboxes every other Tuesday and many remember it sitting prominently in their living rooms until the next issue arrived. *Look* was neither didactic nor a strident crusader, yet it arguably had at least as great an impact on the mid-twentieth-century United States as Facebook or Twitter have had in the first decades of the twenty-first century.[4]

This book is the first time that *Look*'s story—its thousands of impressive articles, spectacular photographs, talented journalists, business successes and failures, and engagement with leaders in virtually every field—has been told in any depth. This story goes far beyond a nostalgic, rose-colored recounting of an America that enjoyed broadly shared economic growth; where tidy homes with happy nuclear families saw the good life getting better; where the rights of the historically disenfranchised finally began to be realized; where a president could point to the moon and the country could land men there eight years later; where utopian ideas of limitless abundance and technological wonders were widely believed; and where a still-new "nation under God" spread its ideals throughout the world. *Look* also cast a light on complex, troubling issues of racial injustice, poverty, radically changing values, the downsides of technology, the Cold War, and environmental degradation, although, in general, it believed these were solvable problems.

Above and beyond its content, *Look* did something that is unthinkable in contemporary America. A rarely considered, yet critical difference between the post–World War II era and today is the pivotal role that mass media like *Look* played in forging unity of purpose, common dialogue, and hope in the United States. A few other titans of the era's media world—Henry Luce's Time-Life empire, *Reader's Digest*, the *Saturday Evening Post, Collier's*, and the three television networks—played somewhat similar roles. *Life*'s photos and articles were also a shared experience for millions of Americans. Yet *Look*'s readership arguably cut across class lines more than these other mass magazines.

Through its powerful photojournalism, wide-ranging and provocative reporting, educational features, and essays by prominent politicians and intellectuals, *Look* offers an important new way of understanding the nation's postwar successes. With every biweekly issue produced on six floors of the modernist Midtown Manhattan *Look* Building, the magazine could be found in living rooms, barbershops, doctors' waiting rooms, boardrooms, and halls of government. Its articles, essays, and photographs reached and helped shape the thinking of what is today an unimaginable amalgam of political leaders, intellectuals, and Americans from all walks of life. When *Look* serialized William Manchester's *The Death of a President*, the story of John Kennedy's assassination, in 1967, 9½ million copies of the magazine were sold and, by some estimates, 70 million Americans read at least some of the 80,000-word series. *Look* was not only on coffee tables in home after home, but it was the talk of Washington, the media world, and the advertising industry.[5]

Like a national playbook, it facilitated a conversation among tens of millions of people about the events, trends, and issues of the day, ranging from the fight for racial equality and the economy to popular culture and technological advances. Even if Americans disagreed on specifics, the magazine helped make possible a national discussion in which much of the public had access to the same facts and opinions—not just the generally one-sided, poorly reported-on assertions of today. A half century after the magazine's audience peaked, President Barack Obama spoke of the need for the kind of "common conversation" that *Look* facilitated.

Three men largely engineered the success of *Look*—whose paid circulation grew from seven hundred thousand in 1937 to nearly eight million in the late 1960s—founder and publisher Gardner (Mike) Cowles Jr., top editor Daniel Mich, and photo editor Arthur Rothstein. Beyond these three, the magazine was put out with a relatively small, but brilliant and quirky, staff of photographers, writers, editors, and art directors—many who stayed with *Look* for much of its history. Despite its huge circulation, it ceased publication in late 1971, the victim of declining advertising revenues in the mid-to-late 1960s and the rise of television and special-interest magazines.

An idealist as well as an optimist, Cowles believed that well-informed, engaged readers and citizens could help make America and the world better. *Look*'s editorial content would show "scrupulous regard for the truth," present the "deficiencies" and greatness in America and the world, and appeal to people's better angels—although not so true in its very early years.[6]

As the magazine's editors described its goals and philosophy:

Look is essentially a magazine for people who are more interested in tomorrow than in yesterday and who want to change things for the better ... *Look* has its own point of view, too, perhaps best described as tough-minded optimism. We believe that the problems confronting our civilization—peace, poverty, population and pollution, just to name a few—can and will be solved. But only if more people understand what's really going on around them and why ... *Look* is sometimes serious but never solemn, usually entertaining but never frivolous, sometimes angry but never bitter, always hopeful but never complacent.[7]

In addition to its photos and photo-driven narrative approach and frequently outstanding articles, one of the things that made *Look* distinctive in mid-twentieth-century America was its philosophy of bringing information and ideas to a mass audience, reporting objectively on a remarkable array of topics, and providing multiple points of view so that people could make up their own minds about issues.

Look's politics seem almost unfathomable in bitterly partisan twenty-first-century America—a liberal Republicanism with more than a dash of radicalism that almost always expressed a strong revulsion toward social injustice, whether racism and anti-Semitism in the United States or communism and dictatorships abroad. It treated many liberal Democrats as heroes, and was open-minded about, if not supportive of, birth control, hippies, the Black Panthers, all religions, and the new psychological movements of the late 1960s.

Mich, who ran the magazine for fifteen years, was "a crusader for the poor and the powerless, a foe of entrenched power," *Look* writer Leo Rosten recalled. "Intolerance of any sort infuriated him." One former staffer half-jokingly suggested that rightwing Republicans like Ronald Reagan in the 1960s thought that "*Look* was a mass-circulation spinoff of the *Nation.*" *Life* was less likely to report or analyze the country's problems.[8]

Cowles and most of his staff were idealistic internationalists, believing that all people on the planet were important and that Americans should learn more about and support other peoples and nations. A remarkable 1955 issue included seven articles on Africa on the eve of decolonization.

Just as all Americans weren't racists, as Soviet propaganda alleged, *Look* illustrated that there was much more to the typical Russian or Chinese than lockstep adherence to Stalinism or Maoism. Cowles was deeply influenced by his extensive global travel and liberal Republican Wendell Willkie's "one world" philosophy. He supported the United Nations and other international institutions, and praised Jean Monnet, the principal founder of what became the European Union. He called for expanding foreign aid and reducing trade barriers, and was a forceful advocate for peace, urging cooperation and détente with the Soviet Union and the communist bloc.[9]

Most writers and editors were left of center in their politics. Cowles, by today's standards, was also liberal, despite being a faithful Republican. *Look* espoused some conservative viewpoints—supporting the anti-labor Taft-Hartley bill, opposing too much expansion of government involvement in the economy, and generally backing Republican candidates. Political figures like Willkie and other liberal Republicans were close to Cowles, but so too were liberal Democrats like Eleanor Roosevelt, Adlai Stevenson, and Hubert Humphrey. Cowles and *Look* believed in respectful debate, publishing essays by noted conservatives and liberals.[10] Yet it took what were then radical opinions on issues such as civil rights, denouncing prejudice, and highlighting the plight of poor urban and rural Blacks as early as 1939. By its last years, *Look* could even sound politically and culturally quite leftwing.

Cowles and *Look* expressed the supremely optimistic view that all Americans and people everywhere could embrace similarly humane values if given enough information and perspective through words and images. In many ways it was a somewhat hyped-up version of what Godfrey Hodgson and other historians have called the postwar "liberal consensus"—support for social welfare and economic growth; expanding rights, especially for Blacks; being engaged with the world; and standing tall as the world's leader in fighting first Nazism and then communism. "Whether you look at the writings of intellectuals or at the positions taken by practicing politicians or at data on public opinion, it is impossible not to be struck by the degree to which the majority of Americans accepted the same system of assumptions," Hodgson wrote.[11]

Believing that differences in ideals and goals were withering away, prominent political scientists and sociologists declared that "the end of ideology" was at hand. Although the term was first associated with a 1955 paper by sociologist Edward Shils, it is best known in the work of Daniel Bell, an editor at *Fortune* magazine and later a professor at Harvard University. In his 1960 book, *The End of Ideology*, he wrote: "There is today a rough consensus among intellectuals on political issues: the acceptance of a Welfare State; the desirability of decentralized power; a system of mixed economy and of political pluralism." There was essentially a singular American credo and way of life. Woven into this was a belief that Americans' interests were in harmony as the country moved toward a happy, beneficent, colorblind, and classless society. By and large, differing opinions were respected.

People had faith that anything wrong with the country could be solved through technocracy—policymakers seeing flaws in American life as technical issues that could be remedied by drawing on the findings of social science to design and implement public programs. In many ways, this consensus—and the relatively respectful, often cooperative nature of politics—began with World War II and survived until it crashed and burned with the Vietnam War and the cultural radicalism of the late 1960s.[12]

Although *Look* criticized Eisenhower-era Cold War policies and U.S. involvement in Vietnam, Cowles, Mich, longtime star writer William Attwood, writer and editor Patricia Carbine, and *Look* itself were key players in forging the nation's liberal internationalism from President Franklin Roosevelt to President Richard Nixon. Indeed, these years of the postwar consensus were the very years that *Look* flourished. Perhaps Cowles's politics best aligned with Presidents Dwight Eisenhower and Lyndon Johnson (pre-Vietnam), as well as with the liberal, business-organized Committee for Economic Development (CED). The magazine conveyed the belief that the government had a crucial role in improving American life and that the United States could do much more to promote world peace.[13]

As a magazine of and for the people—not finely targeted slivers of the population—*Look* helped undergird the set of broadly shared beliefs and goals that was the postwar consensus. At least from the mid-1940s to the mid-1960s, Americans and their leaders across most of the political spectrum could largely agree on the problems of the time and work together to try to find solutions to them. Large majorities of the American people, as well as "liberal" and "conservative" leaders and much of business and labor embraced these beliefs and goals, enabling the U.S. economy, politics, and culture to function with unprecedented success. It meant:

- Economic growth and improving living standards should be in reach of the huge middle and working classes, as a truly "rising tide [would] lift all boats," and poverty could be eradicated;
- Science and technology could achieve wonders that both improved people's lives and buoyed the pride of the American people;
- Americans could disagree on many things, but they were generally united on advancing freedom, justice, and opportunity at home and abroad;
- Democracy and government worked, with Democrats and Republicans often working together for the betterment of all Americans; and
- The United States could "fight all foes" and stand tall in the world.

An ardent defender of a vigorous free press, Cowles strongly believed that an educated and enlightened public was essential—not only through schools and colleges and newspapers, magazines, TV, and radio but also through adult education, public forums, and discussion groups. "One of the attributes of a democratic society is its ability to examine itself critically so that it can eliminate its shortcomings," a 1959 *Look* promotional pamphlet declared. Cowles would have seconded the slogan the *Washington Post* adopted in 2017: "Democracy dies in darkness."[14]

The magazine had a philosophy and approach that distinguished it from other postwar media; one that made it especially consequential in defining the beliefs, aspirations, and mood of America during the nearly thirty-five years that it published from 1937 to the end of 1971.[15]

Cowles and Mich thought that stories—even about complex subjects like the changing family or racism—should be told through the lens of real people, "with warmth, understanding and wonder." "*Look* believes in people," the magazine declared in a mid-1960s memo. "We care. We believe that people move history, not that history moves people.... Our readers, we believe, are passionately curious about other people.... People want—and desperately need—enlightenment." By contrast, *Life* paid more attention to leaders and official sources. As a 1950s *Look* advertising slogan put it: "Bored with life? Get *Look*, the exciting story of people."[16]

For example, it humanized the Cold War with stories about a little boy whose street stopped at the Berlin Wall and Finnish reindeer herders whose flocks wandered into the Soviet Union. *Look* told of the lives of poor Appalachian families, making poverty more than an abstract, statistical construct. It treated World War II chiefly from the enlisted man's perspective. And the more subtle sides of racism were shown in stories like ones about white neighbors' reactions to Black families moving into their neighborhoods.[17]

Attwood expressed the belief that the information and analysis provided by good reporting and photography could lead Americans to "do something about" the nation's and world's problems. Going beyond the traditional journalistic pillars of who, what, why, when, where, and how, he spoke of "public service journalism" that "encourages concerned people to believe that activism can make a difference."[18]

Although the magazine maintained high standards for reporting and fact-checking, its goal to inform and make the nation better did not mean blind impartiality. When it came to covering tough issues, it took a stand by its choice of stories, photos, the nature of its reporting, and commentary. As Mich said in the wake of McCarthyism: "The hottest places in hell are reserved for those who, in times of moral crisis, maintained their neutrality."[19]

Mich restated the magazine's mission in a 1960 speech to advertisers: "*Look*'s primary responsibility is to report to the American People on subjects that touch their minds and their emotions, in such a way as to inform, enlighten, and provide guidance wherever possible." He went on to say that its articles aimed to have the flavor of "one individual talking to another," and that it "is a magazine with a 1st and 2d person point of view—edited with the 'I' of *Look* and the 'you' of the reader always definitely in mind."[20]

Mich was "among the first to recognize photographers and writers as equals," according to Rothstein. Mich expected both to tackle "the tough and controversial issues of our time." Not doing so was unacceptable.

Look also stood for a principle that the press has a duty to present the same meticulously reported and researched facts, even if some might be hard to accept. To paraphrase the late senator and social scientist Daniel

Patrick Moynihan: everyone is entitled to their own opinions, but not their own facts. In this spirit, Mich was cited by the Society of Magazine Editors in 1963 for raising "the standards of magazines as a medium of democratic discourse."[21]

Look stated its "editorial ideal" as "interpreting in depth and bringing into sharp focus the most meaningful events and issues of our time." *Harper's*, in 1963, said that *Look* had "a muscularity rare until recently in the mass-circulation field. . . . It brought to the mass-circulation field an important lesson gleaned from the success of the *New York Times*, *Harper's*, the *Atlantic*, and other quality publications . . . provocative articles on ethics and events of our times . . . that contrast sharply with the mind-numbing superficialities of television."[22]

Even though white, male, Protestant, well-to-do Americans controlled the country's many levers of power, *Look* pried open the door to a more diverse nation. Far beyond Washington, Wall Street, and Hollywood, the magazine told stories of America as it was and what it was becoming. It was there for the postwar economic boom, scientific breakthroughs and new technologies, the reconstruction of Europe, rock n' roll, movie stars, African wars, new foods and fashions, business leaders, the baby boom, hippies, activists, surfers, suburbanites, singles, and teenagers. *Look* had its blind spots and temporary prejudices, but its ability to be open to new ideas and tolerate, if not embrace, them is a far cry from the hardened beliefs espoused almost trance-like by most twenty-first-century media, politicians, so-called opinion leaders, and many Americans. At its peak in the mid-1960s, when the nation seemed to be on a glide path to ever-better tomorrows, *Look* was both one of the prime mirrors and makers of the American zeitgeist.

Look brought home a world that included people and events beyond U.S. shores, helping Americans understand, if not care about, a planet on which 95 percent of the people were not American. The magazine reported on newly independent India, Israel, and Ghana, and took its readers to South Korea and Taiwan. *Look* interviewed Chinese Premier Zhou Enlai and a Mau Mau rebel leader in Kenya and traversed the back roads of the Soviet Union and went behind enemy lines in Vietnam. Readers learned of strife and poverty in the developing world in photo essays on Congo, Algeria, India, Indochina, and elsewhere. The world—especially Europe—was also delivered to its readers as exciting, newly affordable travel destinations.

Look's success was also due to the mix of talent it had and its generally high morale, collegiality, and the enthusiasm and creativity of its editors, writers, and photographers. "People were unpretentious, and really dedicated to doing their work well," *Look* writer John Poppy recalled. "They were not the kind of people seeking to make a big splash in the world." Half a century after their days covering rock music, student demonstrations, flower children, and civil rights, Poppy said that he and George Leonard, his visionary California compatriot, would go to lunch near their office on Market Street in San Francisco and marvel at how "this was the best job we would ever have."[23]

*

The comparison between the *Look* era and the politics, outlook, and media of the early twenty-first century is stark. The political, economic, and cultural dysfunction and divisions of recent decades have stemmed from many factors, but one that has received surprisingly little attention is the disappearance of mass-audience media like *Look*. Instead of *Look*'s thoughtful, public-spirited journalism, we now live in a maelstrom of countless small-audience, online, broadcast, and print media. Instead of objectivity, presenting opposing viewpoints, and offering news and ideas about a broad range of topics, the Babel of early twenty-first-century U.S. media dishes out information of questionable veracity, with little context, and "alternative facts," a term coined in 2017 by Kellyanne Conway, a spokeswoman for President Donald Trump. "One of the biggest challenges that we have to our democracy is the degree to which we do not share a common baseline of facts," President Obama said the following year.[24]

Look offers a perspective on how a long-gone type of journalism and media helped stimulate discussion among elites and average citizens and forged broad agreement around a set of social, political, cultural, and economic ideas and goals that enabled the nation to thrive. If anything, today's plethora of niche media and social media largely do the opposite—dishing out ideologically slanted, often factually inaccurate "information" that stokes cynicism and anger, disparages common ground and compromise, and creates echo chambers that reinforce divisiveness. Instead of offering multiple perspectives, ideas, high-quality reporting and commentary, today's *Pravda*-like online and broadcast media largely toe party lines in which those who disagree are enemies or traitors. The few remaining media that offer both quality journalism and some diversity of commentary are ones like the *New York Times*, the *Economist*, or the *Atlantic*, which have no reach beyond relatively small, insulated intellectual elites.

Look provided thoughtful articles and photographs that reached thirty-five million Americans during its heyday in a country with a population that was just over half the size it was in 2021. By comparison, Fox News and MSNBC had 3.2 million and 3.8 million primetime viewers, respectively, in early 2021. Today, we have billions of websites, thirty-two million regular bloggers, forty-nine million Twitter users, and specialized media with thousands or millions of "followers" (not readers) that reinforce the beliefs, prejudices, and preconceptions of their audiences but leave the United States more splintered and Americans less informed. *Look*'s place and impact on American life and thinking now seem so alien that its significance is difficult to grasp in a society where blogs seek to attract thousands and TV shows become "hits" with a few million viewers.[25]

From the vantage point of the early 2020s, it is hard to imagine a time when the United States was not so fractured politically, economically, and socially, not so divided by age, gender, race, class, and sexual orientation, not so laden with anger and pessimism, and led by such ineffective government. By contrast, the mid-twentieth century is often seen as a golden age, with an increasingly prosperous middle class, a government that got big things done, a reasonably well-informed citizenry, and a belief in better tomorrows. We could solve problems and accomplish almost anything. This "golden age" trope is often exaggerated, but the postwar decades were certainly a time of progress, rising incomes, optimism, and faith in government.

Look magazine tracked America's rise to its zenith economically, geopolitically, and in fulfilling its core ideals. It discussed issues in a way that elite publications and other mass media like the networks or *Life* typically did not. Dwight MacDonald, the social critic who distinguished between "mass culture" and "midcult," may have seen *Look* and its peers as fostering "conformity," yet it also fostered common understandings among Americans that is hard to comprehend in the early twenty-first century.[26]

In its roughly 990 issues, *Look* helped reflect America during its golden years, and played a significant role in making those years all the more golden. It provided a comprehensive and evocative visual chronicle of what were some of the most crucial years in U.S. history. Its story is not only that of an influential magazine with a very distinctive approach to "covering" the United States and the world, but also one of how a great publication could be a major player in helping the nation succeed as few, if any, others have.

Look flourished after World War II but was often seen as a poor man's version of *Life*, in the words of staff photographer Charlotte Brooks. In fact, it conveyed a more inclusive image of the nation than its competitor. It was decidedly more populist, telling the story of the heartland as well as the coasts (perhaps stemming from publisher Mike Cowles's Des Moines roots), and less a mouthpiece of the "Establishment" than *Life* or the news magazines.

"*Life* was cool, *Look* was warm," George Leonard wrote. "Where *Life* passed judgments generally aligned with those of the power elite, *Look* raised questions the power elite never thought of. Where *Life* was consistent and predictable, *Look* was inconsistent and surprising."[27]

As another staffer said, while *Life* and the *Saturday Evening Post* generally stayed in a "safe" zone of content, *Look*'s articles ranged from "the pits of bad taste" to "the visionary." Unlike *Life*, *Look* did not have an editorial in each issue; it only published a few. The editorials in *Life*, however, tended to simply celebrate America, rather than also point to its problems. This difference may have made it seem that, as one writer said, "it's hard to know what *Look* stands for—except success." This was far from true.[28]

Look saw America as one people whose citizens were equal and deserved respect. It helped promote the idea of the United States as a middle-class nation. Even if social class didn't disappear in the 1950s and 1960s, it wasn't a fiction that the trend lines toward greater economic equality were moving in the right direction. *Look* celebrated American achievement—science and industry and hard work that seemed to make anything possible. Its writers and photographers also communicated respect for institutions—government, religion, business, and even labor unions—that knit people together.

In its coverage of the wonders of science and medicine, rising incomes and college enrollment, strong families, increasing tolerance, and expanding "infrastructure," *Look* subtly encouraged Americans to see these as being for the common good. In a retrospective issue released after the magazine folded, its editors wrote: "We dreamed of tomorrow, of a world in which the brotherhood of man would be fulfilled. We dreamed of greater things to come."[29]

Look was dedicated to a forward-looking vision of the United States. Each issue carried at least one story about an ordinary person, his or her work, family, and city or town. *Look* focused on the vast, expanding middle class, showing how people lived and worked, and captured changing American ways of life in photos and stories. The world, for *Look*, was not the patter of daily events covered by newspapers or television. Whereas *Life*, as a weekly magazine, covered the news and its photos were more news driven, *Look* stepped back to publish imaginative, insightful, and analytical feature stories. It did not shy away from controversial topics such as prejudice and segregation, the Vietnam War and America's military buildup, mental illness, sexual mores, women's changing roles, the 1960s youth rebellion, and homosexuality.

Look covered the major issues of the day, but it also had a healthy dose of Hollywood stars, new cars, and fashion. Critics like Macdonald may have deemed it "middlebrow," but *Look* nonetheless did more to bring the "highbrow" ideas of a remarkably diverse array of leading scholars and thought leaders to a mass audience than virtually any other popular magazine in U.S. history. These essays by and interviews with luminaries from politics, the arts, and academia, and the book excerpts that it published gave an intellectual patina to *Look* that is little remembered. Illustrative of its unconventional, thought-provoking approach, in 1971, it paired an essay by the young Gloria Steinem on why America needed a woman as president with one by William F. Buckley Jr., who wrote the intriguing and prescient piece "Why We Need a Black President."[30]

Look was also emblematic of a type of journalism—also largely missing in the early twenty-first century—that believed that spreading historical knowledge and ideas to as many Americans as possible strengthened democracy. Believing that information and opinions could make a great nation greater, its motto could have been *lux et veritas*. *Look* was a storyteller, a champion of what the Founders called civic virtue, and a potent agent of cultural and social change. It was a "booster" in the best sense of the term, celebrating American greatness and excoriating an America that it knew could be better.

Look's approach to producing a magazine was quite different from *Life*. Luce's magazine practiced a "production line" process involving a large number of people and resources, with its reporters ceding writing to an in-house team of researchers and editors, led by a more authoritarian management. By contrast, *Look* decried "impersonal, assembly-line journalism." It took more of an artisanal approach, in which one senior editor/writer oversaw each article from start to finish, with a photographer assigned to take hundreds of images. Whereas *Life* stories were so heavily edited that writers often could barely recognize what they had written, staffers and others considered *Look* to be one of the least edited magazines in the country. *Look*'s photo essays tended to be more visually subtle than *Life*'s. With a six-week lead time, *Look* could take more care with stories than *Life*, where many stories were determined by the prior week's news.[31]

Look's editors wanted writers to become immersed in their stories and "never questioned how long we spent on a story or how much we spent," writer Ira Mothner recalled. One memo, he jokingly remembered, told staff: "You cannot charter a plane with more than one engine without checking with New York."[32]

Look was always best known for its photographs, despite its many thought-provoking and challenging articles. Its photos were not just pretty pictures, as Rothstein considered photography to have a "great social responsibility." He believed that photographs "could be used to communicate ideas and emotions." This came with a responsibility to penetrate and probe "the problems of our times and communicate ideas, facts, opinions and emotions with inspirational vision." He wanted to make "photographs that had universal appeal—that were seen by a large audience—that informed, entertained or provoked."

Photos were intended to be central to an article's narrative. They were usually not posed. Often, photos would tell stories with minimal text, an approach known as the "picture-sequence" technique that was promoted by editor Vernon Pope. Images for *Look*'s feature stories arguably required more creativity and care by both photographers and photo editors than the news photos that dominated *Life*. Cowles said that *Life*'s "brilliant news pictures" had been overtaken by TV. Rothstein's systematic six-stage process for photo essays began with editorial discussion of possible topics, followed by background research, selection of the writer-photographer team, the actual reporting (with a loose photo script in hand), editing and laying out photos, and concluding with the writer drafting captions and other text.[33]

During its three and a half decades, more than 180,000 photos were published, and millions of others were taken but never used. In its later years, some eight thousand photos were considered for each issue. These included the well-known photos of President Kennedy's son playing in the Oval Office or one of the 1965 civil-rights march from Selma to Montgomery, Alabama, as well as historically quirky ones like a World War II–era shot of Mao Zedong and Chiang Kai-shek toasting each other, and surprising ones like the famous image of Che Guevara with his cigar in his mouth.[34]

Look's photojournalists took risks to ferret out guerrilla compounds in Cuba and Palestine, escape from threatening policemen while covering the civil rights movement, traipse the length of the Iron Curtain, hang out in communes, and wade through muddy rice paddies under fire in Vietnam. The magazine delivered 1950s suburbia, poverty in India, the first look at Communist China, the villages of the Soviet Union, a pugnacious Ernest Hemingway, America's astronauts, early computing, and many a spread on the Kennedy family and Marilyn Monroe.

Look writers and photographers worked as a team. For example, writer J. Robert Moskin worked with photographer James Hansen on more than fifty stories over the years. In a late 1960s promotional fact sheet, the magazine spoke with bravado about how its teams would "scramble over the deadly hills of Judea, . . . slog through the mud and buffalo areas of Vietnam, and careen over rutted back roads to a murderous attack by [U.S.] policemen trying to prevent a story being told . . . *Look* teams may strip themselves of inhibition to participate in sensitivity sessions in California, or arrange for a life-saving operation for a little Vietnamese boy with a congenital heart defect, or sit day after day with preschoolers while they experience the joy of learning."[35]

They would go on assignments from China and the Deep South to Hollywood and America's new suburbs. As Rosten recalled, they "half-froze in Tibet, pierced the Iron Curtain, cozened access to the private salons of Paris or Cambodia or the White House," were shot at in war zones, "fled goons who tried to smash their cameras" from Jordan to Watts, and drove frantically to escape "morons from the KKK or Southern sheriffs hell-bent on keeping a story from being told."[36]

"We weren't just reporters parachuting in," Poppy said. Teams would often spend weeks with their subjects, living with them and getting to know them. Photographer Douglas Kirkland recalled traveling with Judy Garland for three weeks and going with Paris bureau chief Leonard Gross to spend time with John Lennon in Spain: "The understanding was you didn't just spend a couple days doing efficient interviews, but rather that we'd hang out with them for a week, 10 days, to get a flavor of them, what made them worth knowing. You developed a sense of trust. That's part of what made the job attractive."[37]

Look also sought to provide its massive readership with foundational knowledge about Western civilization. To this end, it conducted "visits with" the likes of J. Robert Oppenheimer, Frank Lloyd Wright, Erich Fromm, and Edward R. Murrow to Marshal Tito, Vladimir Horowitz, and the Maharishi Mahesh Yogi. *Look* also played the pedagogue in a way that no contemporary medium would do. It published the series "They Made Our World," which profiled the likes of Saint Paul, Constantine, Machiavelli, Newton, and other seminal figures of Western civilization. It published two lengthy, critically acclaimed series on America's religions. Another series on "The Story behind the Painting" provided brief biographies of great artists from Rembrandt, Durer, and Caravaggio to Henri Rousseau and Modigliani, together with color reproductions of their paintings. Cultural travelogues of places in the United States and the world often appeared. *Look's* annual "All-America Cities" series provided an upbeat picture of life in cities and towns chosen for residents' civic engagement, innovative policies, and quality of life. Two other series tried to answer "How Much Do We Know about the World?" and "How Much Do We Know about Human Nature?" *Look* commissioned Norman Rockwell to create thirty paintings for the magazine—including a powerful image of a Black girl being escorted to school by U.S. marshals in Little Rock in 1957 and an iconic image of the 1969 moon landing.

*

The end of *Look's* spectacular run in many ways dovetailed with the end of the great postwar American success story. In *Look's* last years and shortly after it stopped publishing, the social turbulence of the 1960s and early 1970s brought the era's "consensus" to an end, the Vietnam War undermined Americans' faith in government, the eventually lost war in Indochina destroyed the belief in U.S. omnipotence, once-powerful industries began to waver, and economic troubles in the 1970s ushered in what was to be the beginning of a half century when real wages no longer rose for most Americans and inequality increased.

In the early twenty-first century, the United States is ever more divided, more hostile toward institutions, gloomier about its future, and angrier. With the disappearance of *Look* and many other print media, most Americans are less informed about and interested in their country and the world. The nation is no longer so optimistic—fearful that climate change cannot be reversed, medicine cannot permanently defeat deadly viruses, and wary of technology that can bring as many ills as benefits. People have become more inwardly focused, have attention spans shortened by the internet, and are more easily able to choose particular stories and opinions and shut out others. While there are many causes for these troubling phenomena, the virtual decimation of mass media is a major one.

First, we must understand what this extraordinary journalistic endeavor of the middle third of the twentieth century was about. Why did it develop the way it did and cover America and the world as it did? Why did such compelling journalism and stunning photojournalism attract such a huge and diverse audience? How did it both reflect and define an America that was willing to listen to opposing views, not disparage them, and reach compromises that, on balance, made the nation's politics, economics, and culture largely "work"? How too did it mirror and reinforce the sense of anything-is-possible optimism and abiding faith in almost limitless scientific, economic, political, and cultural progress?

In the chapters that follow, we will first discuss the history, philosophy, and people of *Look*. Then we will examine the magazine's coverage of the economy, science and technology, politics, civil rights, changing families and values, the Cold War and foreign affairs, popular culture, and its pedagogical series.

2

In the Beginning

More than three decades before *Look* was part of the commanding heights of America's culture industry, it got off to a rocky start as the brainchild of Mike Cowles, the publisher of the *Des Moines Register and Tribune*. His father had bought the paper in 1903, shortly after Mike was born. What became *Look* was initially a supplement to the Sunday *Register*, but Cowles[1] wanted to create a national, general-interest magazine that would compete with, but differ from, *Life*, which Time chairman Henry Luce had launched in 1936.[2]

Both magazines emerged and defined the golden age of photojournalism and mass-circulation magazines. *Collier's* and the *Saturday Evening Post*, like *Life* and *Look*, sold millions of copies by the early 1940s. Cowles, like Luce, had seen the success of photo-driven magazines of the 1920s like *Berliner Illustrirte Zeitung* and the *Arbeiter-Illustrierte Zeitung* in Germany, *Pour Vous* in France, and the *Illustrated London News* in England. Influenced by these magazines, *Look* sought to capture real life in action rather than just publishing posed photos. Like newspapers, radio, and later TV and the internet, American magazines followed the business model of making content inexpensive to readers while making money through advertising.[3]

In the early years after *Look* first hit the newsstands on January 5, 1937, the magazine was printed on cheap paper with poor color, presenting a mishmash of serious stories on social and geopolitical issues, make-up and fashion tips, actresses, photos with long captions, and lurid regular features like "Photocrime," a one-page story in pictures and words that invited readers to solve a real-life crime. Early issues also included "Confidentially," which generally featured sexualized images of women, men with "the finest physique," and sinister figures like Nazi foreign minister Joachim von Ribbentrop; quizzes about photos; and an end-of-magazine reader test, "What did you learn while reading this issue?" It ran a fair number of bizarre stories like one about the bride of Nazi leader Hermann Goering, and a happy family photo of Joseph Goebbels, Hitler's propaganda chief. The very first issue was a publishing disaster, with the cover depicting a woman tied to two poles, legs spread, and a back-cover head-and-shoulders shot of Greta Garbo that, when folded together, "looked like a female crotch." Cowles recalled unsold copies to the magazine's headquarters at 715 Locust Street in Des Moines, and there were widespread calls for *Look* to be shut down. Syndicated columnist Walter Winchell called the magazine obscene. John Cowles, Mike's older brother; Ray Larsen at Time Inc.; and Henry Luce, initially a friend of Cowles, suggested he restart the magazine with a different name a few years later. The *New Republic* called it "a morgue and dime museum on paper," and *Editor and Publisher* drily noted that "two newspapermen who have had no magazine experience announce a new publishing venture."[4]

Subtitled "The Monthly Picture Magazine," promising "200 pictures . . . [and] 1,001 facts," and selling for ten cents, the second issue wasn't much more edifying. It featured a two-page color centerfold of actress Dolores Del Rio, and photo-stories on Japanese prostitutes, murderers who were paroled, a racist story on Gypsies, a woman and her baby being killed by a car in Paris, and a visual re-creation of the seventeenth-century Black Death with many bare breasts. The third issue, in March, included burning buildings and sinking ships, crowds watching executions, and a color image of Myrna Loy in a bathtub. After a last proto-*Playboy* centerfold of Marlene Dietrich in the March issue, *Look* started to clean up its act, publishing more serious stories and replacing many of the photo spreads on actresses with ones on Gandhi, Henry Cabot Lodge, and FDR, although more than a whiff of tawdriness remained. Serious features included one by birth-control advocate Margaret Sanger, who made an impassioned plea for family planning. A 1938 issue whose cover had "the world's most beautiful Chinese girl" about to plunge a dagger into her chest also looked at Norman Bel Geddes's cities of the future and included FBI director J. Edgar Hoover telling readers that "Criminals are Rats." Articles on the plight of Spanish-Civil-War orphans and a surprisingly positive portrayal of the Soviet Union were sandwiched together with photo spreads on fashion and Hollywood stars and attempts at humor in "Grounds for Divorce," in one 1939 issue. Pirates, dating etiquette, the dog industry, quintuplets, and similar sensationalism, still prevalent that year, gave way to articles about organized labor and the Dies Committee (which became the House Un-American Activities Committee), and author John Gunther writing about Stalin in the first issue of 1940.[5]

Vulgar, peculiar, and risqué, the first issue—put out with a staff of seven—still sold more than 705,000 copies, more than doubling that number by May and outselling *Life* within a year. Despite the initial ostracism, Cowles pressed ahead. After the fiasco with the first issue, the second and third issues sold nine hundred thousand copies. *Look* started taking advertising after its sixth issue and began publishing every other week on May 11, 1937. It still relied heavily on photos and stories about movie stars, models, bathing beauties, and children, publishing a ten-part series provocatively called "Hollywood Uncensored." It was not uncommon to have covers like those with a blond, lipsticked, eighteen-year-old diving champion, a drum majorette headlined "Sex Appeal in Sports," Broadway beauties, and a dancing girl named Zorina in a tutu and leggings. *Time* magazine snidely and snobbishly dismissed *Look* as "barbershop reading," adding that it was for "your private secretary, for your office boy—a magazine mostly for the middle class and for ordinary lives."[6]

Cowles went on a hiring spree, seeking to upgrade *Look*'s quality and image. Harlan Logan, who was hired to be the magazine's "editorial adviser," was a Rhodes Scholar who Cowles called "a man of vision whose creative ideas converted the early *Look* of garish pictures into a family magazine of unquestioned respectability."[7]

Vernon Pope, who helped produce the first dummy versions of the magazine, and Donald Perkins were moved from the *Register* to become, respectively, *Look*'s editor and head of the advertising sales team. Also moved was Marvin Whatmore, who stayed with *Look* for its entire history, initially covered the East Coast, and was credited with improving the magazine's paper quality. Cowles established a one-man New York office with Jean Herrick, who was quickly moved to Hollywood, which he deemed more important. During its first year, he hired Daniel Mich, who was to be *Look*'s most renowned editor, from the *Wisconsin State Journal*, after meeting him at the American Society of Newspaper Editors annual meeting in Washington. Cowles also brought on a number of advertising, subscription, circulation, and other business staff, who mostly stayed with the magazine until the end.[8]

Cowles was drawn to George Gallup, the pioneering pollster whose PhD dissertation at the nearby University of Iowa focused on the public appeal of photographs in newspapers and magazines. Both young men, the two met in the mid-1920s. "Picture journalism became a consuming interest with me," Cowles recalled in his memoir. "My conviction that it could become the most dramatic and persuasive form of reporting a story was confirmed when I hired George Gallup to do a survey for me on what had the greatest appeal for our readers." He had *Register* reporters carry cameras and was the first to use a plane, the *Good News*, for aerial shots; the pilot would hurl film out the window to photo editors in the late 1920s.[9]

"Out of these studies subsequently grew *Look* magazine," Gallup recalled. "What Cowles discovered, I think before anyone else, is that you can actually tell stories with pictures." Indeed, this was one of *Look*'s most noted journalistic innovations and what set it apart from *Life*. Instead of using photos to adorn text, *Look* used pictures like words and combined photos and text to tell a story or present an idea.[10]

The Cowles Family Publishing Empire

The story of *Look* cannot be told without understanding its place—eventually as the crown jewel—in the publishing endeavors of the Cowles family. Mike Cowles's father, Gardner Cowles Sr., was the scion of what was one of the most prominent families in twentieth-century American journalism. The Cowleses were descendants of English immigrants who arrived in Massachusetts fifteen years after the *Mayflower*, and Mike's grandfather the Rev. William Fletcher Cowles was an abolitionist Methodist minister who was appointed by President Lincoln to be the Iowa district collector of revenues. The minister's son began his career as a rural postal deliveryman, enabling him to get to know every corner of Iowa, southern Minnesota, and South Dakota. Moving on to become a chicken farmer, school superintendent, and two-term Iowa legislator, he bought a part interest in two Iowa newspapers, the *Algona Republican* and the *Des Moines Register and Leader* with $300,000 made from real-estate deals and ten banks that he had acquired. Between his 1903 purchase and his death in 1946, he bought two other Des Moines papers and consolidated and expanded them into the *Register*, which became Iowa's dominant news medium and one of the nation's most respected newspapers.[11]

A strong supporter of civil rights, the League of Nations, and one of the first U.S. employers to provide his workers with health insurance, pensions, and stock options, Cowles Sr. imbued two of his sons, Mike and John, with the once-liberal Republican values of service and internationalism, inspired them to be inquisitive, and introduced them as children to prominent figures ranging from President Howard Taft and Populist leader William Jennings Bryan to Iowa Democrat Henry Wallace and evangelist Aimee Semple McPherson. He knew many presidents—as Mike and John later did—and served in one administration, as head of President Herbert Hoover's Reconstruction Finance Corporation.

Gardner Cowles, the youngest of six children, was born in 1903 and given his nickname (Mike) by his father, who purportedly thought he looked Irish. Mike knew by eighth grade that he wanted to follow his father as a journalist. Sometimes said to have been "born with a silver spoon," the younger Cowles went to Phillips Exeter Academy and Harvard University, where he became editor of the *Crimson*. Foreshadowing his lifelong efforts to expose injustices, he wrote an article for the *Crimson* on the Ku Klux Klan. Harvard president Laurence Lowell, who was considered a racist, summoned Cowles to his office, but the young journalist refused to name his sources. Soon after graduating, in 1925, he joined the family business, moving within a matter of years from being a *Register* reporter to city editor, executive editor, publisher, and chairman of the board.[12]

Mike had followed his older brother, John, to Exeter, Harvard, and the *Register and Tribune*, where John's journalistic career began in 1921. John, born in 1898, was the less flashy and flamboyant of the two. Whereas Mike was always pictured with his round glasses, a cigarette, and a twinkle in his eyes, John was more staid and serious looking. In contrast to the many women in Mike's life, John married Elizabeth Bates and stayed married for fifty-three years. As *Harper's* described them in 1963: "Mike is more impetuous, dramatic. John is more contemplative, more given to details."[13]

When their father bought the *Minneapolis Star* in 1935 for $1 million, John, Elizabeth, and their four children moved to Minneapolis to run the new Cowles newspaper, while remaining involved with the *Register*. Within four years, when John bought the *Minneapolis Evening Journal* and merged it with the *Star*, the paper had tripled its circulation. He also owned a number of smaller papers around the country. John and Elizabeth, like Mike and their father, were civic spirited, strongly supported civil rights, women's rights, and foreign aid, and fought racism, anti-Semitism, and the more virulent forms of anti-communism. He was appointed to advisory roles by the five U.S. presidents from FDR to Lyndon Johnson and became a director of the Ford Foundation. His paper was called the "red star" by critics for its progressive views. He and his wife were very active with civic and political causes. "As I've learned more," John said, "I've become more liberal." Just as *Look* was a pioneer in advocating for birth control, Elizabeth founded the Minneapolis's Maternal Health League, which later became the regional Planned Parenthood, and was vice chairman of the United Negro College Fund, the NAACP, the ACLU, the League of Women Voters, and the Minneapolis Society of Fine Arts.[14]

The Cowles brothers were pillars of society, at once "a dyed-in-the-wool newspaper family with an urge, above all, to produce a paper that would honor their craft," and "rich boys who had done what their father told them to do, and [had] done it well," as articles in *Fortune* in 1950 and *PM* in 1949 described them. The two collaborated on building the *Register* in the 1930s, but Mike soon became focused on *Look* and speaking to the world beyond Iowa, while John turned his attention to the *Star* and becoming an influencer and benefactor in Minneapolis and St. Paul. John severed his ties with Cowles Communications, which became Mike's parent company of *Look*, in 1953. John's son, also active in Minneapolis philanthropy and the arts, took over the helm of the *Star* in 1961, only to be fired by the board in 1983, after the paper had merged with the *Minneapolis Tribune*.[15]

The third brother, Russell, turned away from journalism, much to his father's consternation, studying at the Art Institute of Chicago and becoming an abstract painter in New York. With shaggy gray hair and without the shrewdness and polish of his brothers, Russell exhibited works that he painted in his East Sixtieth Street studio. Adopting some of the same liberal views of his father and brothers, he was among more than three hundred signatories to a 1949 letter calling for the abolition of the communist-baiting House Un-American Activities Committee.[16]

One of Mike's three sisters, Florence, married David Scholte Kruidenier, who largely ran the *Register* from the early 1950s to the early 1980s. In 1941 David's sister Nancy married Tom Shepard, who later joined *Look* and became its last publisher in the 1960s. In another marriage that linked family and *Look*, Mike's son Gardner Cowles III married the daughter of Marvin Whatmore, who became vice president and general manager of *Look* in 1961.[17]

Although the Cowles family was at the peak of their influence during the *Look* years, the only family member still in the newspaper business after the mid-1980s was one of John's daughters, Morley, who bought two papers in Durango, Colorado, with her husband in 1952. She was editor and chairman of the board until her death in 2009.[18]

Mike Cowles: The Man Who Made *Look*

It is hard to think of a man who played such a major role in American journalism history and who was such a larger-than-life figure during the mid-twentieth-century, yet more forgotten, than Mike Cowles. He was a brilliantly creative journalist. He always wanted to learn and to educate the American people. He was an idealist who was outspoken on foreign policy and civil rights. He hobnobbed with presidents, Hollywood stars, writers, artists, and foreign leaders. He took risks, some of which didn't go very well. Although *Look* was remarkably successful from the 1940s to the late 1960s, and Cowles became a very rich man, he had a mixed record as a businessman, happy with a level of profits that would get CEOs fired today. He married four times, lived with a Black man (Luther Brown) during his bachelor days in the 1920s, and was a fixture on the New York social scene. He was optimistic, fun loving, and jovial.[19]

Mike was of medium height, slender, had "iron gray" hair, and was soft-spoken, with a gravelly, bass voice. He was athletic, but didn't care what he ate. "Mike was always an alert, aggressive, thoughtful person," Gallup recalled. "I wouldn't call him intellectual, but I've never known a person in my life who was so willing to listen. . . . [He was] in a sense the best reporter I've ever known in my life."[20]

"The greatest editors I know are just like the greatest educators and are successful for the same reason," Cowles told a Simpson College audience in 1955. "They are thoughtful men with scrupulous regard for the truth. They are men who strive to stir the best in the human race, not pander to the worst. They are men who dare to lead, even when the direction is temporarily dangerous and unpopular."[21]

Although he enjoyed his influence in mid-twentieth century America as much as Henry Luce did, Cowles "wanted to turn out a good product and have fun doing it," according to Herbert Strentz, a former dean of Drake University's journalism school. "I have always had a lot of fun out of life," Cowles once said.[22]

"Mike was fun to be with, a great story-teller," Gilbert Maurer, who spent nineteen years with Cowles Communications Inc. (CCI, one of several names of Cowles's empire), recalled. "He overcame an early-life speech impediment to become a good after-dinner speaker. He grew up in an era of big men thinking about big things."[23]

Cowles hated injustice of any kind, a quality he attributed to his mother's influence, and which won him plaudits from civil-rights, Jewish, and women's organizations. In 1947 *Look* published a five-thousand-word excerpt of Laura Z. Hobson's *A Gentleman's Agreement*, the landmark novel exposing anti-Semitism in the supposedly liberal Northeast. He was active for many years in the CED, with his name on the cover of its 1958 two-volume report *Problems of United States Economic Development*. He attacked business groups to the right, such as the U.S. Chamber of Commerce and the National Association of Manufacturers, for their crude promotion of free enterprise. Always active in many causes, Cowles also worked to promote reading, declaring in a 1954 statement for the American Book Publishers Council: We must "keep books free, make them widely available, and encourage people to read them." Alluding to McCarthyite attacks on "subversive" books, he continued: "It is clearly within the public interest to expand the reading audience, to encourage the wiser and wider distribution and use of books, and to nourish the freedom to read."[24]

He was an ardent internationalist, calling for NATO to expand into cultural, economic, and political issues, and, perhaps naively, believed that U.S.-Soviet cooperation was possible. In a 1955 commencement address, he said: We "will not be able permanently to find a good life if the rest of the world slips deeper and deeper into squalor and tyranny." The FBI, which tracked Cowles from 1929 to 1954, concluded that "his loyalty to the U.S. in no way can be questioned," even though the bureau described him as "progressive" and "affiliated to an undetermined degree with various organizations which have since been cited as alleged subversives." The timing of *Look*'s 1954 book *Story of the FBI* coincided with the end of his surveillance.[25]

Most of the many people who worked for or knew Cowles found him likable and generous, and a striking number of his staff remained with him for decades. Some described him as a poor manager, who gave much leeway to his staff, but also as someone who wanted to be on equal terms with his employees. However, a labor dispute and the mismanagement that partly accounted for *Look*'s demise in 1971 irked many who lost their jobs. When he fired dozens of *Look* staff in 1946, the union went on strike and took out an ad in the *New York Times*, saying: "To the Readers of *Look*: Our publisher, Gardner Cowles Jr. has fired 56 *Look* employees." Noting that Cowles was studying labor relations for CED, the ad continued: "His study, like charity, should begin at home. . . . Remind him that employees of *Look*, the family magazine, have families too." When he demoted a fifty-six-year-old manager and replaced him with the husband of his favorite niece, Nancy, it also left bad feelings among staff.[26]

Before launching *Look*, Mike and John not only built up the *Register* but bought a number of radio stations in Des Moines and elsewhere, creating Iowa (later, Cowles) Broadcasting Co. Cowles is said to have given Ronald Reagan his first radio announcing job, in Iowa in 1933, although decades later he denounced Reagan's policies as president.[27]

A prankster, he bought the "Cardiff Giant," an oversized stone figure created by an anti-fundamentalist. He was given a jock strap from Bergdorf's by Danny Kaye for his fiftieth birthday and held a stag party at the 21 Club for his sixtieth birthday. He loved games like squash, tennis, and golf, as well as betting on politics and sports with the likes of Humphrey Bogart, Hollywood producer Dore Schary, and drugstore executive Justin Dart. Cowles had a penchant for aviation. He learned to fly, supported the building of the Des Moines Airport (for which he had bought the land), and was on the board of United Airlines. He was an inveterate traveler, often looking for a good story. He flew on the *Hindenburg* blimp a year before its 1937 disaster, took one of the first commercial around-the-world flights, on Pan Am in 1947, and was on the first flight of the Pan Am Stratocruiser in 1949. He made five trips to the Soviet Union, one as part of a thirty-one-thousand-mile, forty-nine-day around-the-world trip with 1940 Republican presidential candidate Wendell Willkie on behalf of President Franklin Roosevelt, and one for a three-hour interview with Nikita Khrushchev in 1962.[28]

Cowles knew every president from Hoover to Richard Nixon, frequently meeting in the White House. He was appointed by FDR in 1942 to be director of the Domestic News Division of the Office of War Information (a position he left after less than two years), hosted stag dinners at New York's Waldorf Hotel for Vice President Nixon, swam in the nude with LBJ, and cultivated close relationships with the Kennedys. In addition to the Manchester book and articles by the Kennedys, *Look* published several books on JFK. Cowles was especially fond of Willkie's politics and "one world" internationalism, playing a major role in his 1940 presidential campaign. Cowles met with world leaders from Stalin (at 4:00 a.m. in the Kremlin) and Churchill to de Gaulle, Chiang Kai-Shek, and the Duke and Duchess of Windsor, and hosted Khrushchev in Iowa to teach him about growing corn. Madame Chiang Kai-Shek told Cowles that if Willkie were elected, "then he and I could rule the world," Cowles recalled. He also cultivated friendships with some of the leading figures in Hollywood, including producers David O. Selznick, Sam Goldwyn, Louis B. Mayer, Cecil B. DeMille, and Daryl Zanuck, as well as actors Charlie Chaplin, Rita Hayworth, Marilyn Monroe, and Grace Kelly. Dinners at his home included Supreme Court justices, movie stars, European leaders, painters, poets, businessmen, musicians, ballet dancers, and writers. He also was friends with blue-blood families like the Vanderbilts, Whitneys, and Rockefellers. Cowles was close to other publishers, notably the Sulzberger family at the *New York Times*, as well as leading ad executives.[29]

He was on the boards of the *Times*, Macy's, and major journalism organizations like the American Society of Newspaper Editors, the Magazine Publishers' Association, and the advisory committee for the Pulitzer Prize. He was active in the Council on Foreign Relations and regularly spoke at an annual advertising-industry luncheon at the Waldorf, giving a sort of state of the world address, and gave speeches throughout the country at upper-crust clubs like San Francisco's Union Club and at many universities and conferences. He also addressed organizations ranging from the National Democratic Women's Club and the Russian Relief dinner, during the war, to the Anti-Defamation League and the NAACP. He received eleven honorary degrees and gave millions to charity, mostly to education and the arts, and led the fundraising drive to build a new building for the Museum of Modern Art.[30]

Cowles's first marriage, to Helen Curtiss, who John warned was "too old and too sophisticated" for him, ended in divorce in a year. He married Lois Thornburg, a reporter for the *Register*, in 1933 and they took their honeymoon in the USSR. They had four children together—Gardner III (Pat), Kate, Lois, and Jane—before they split up when she charged him with adultery, and he moved, with *Look*, to New York in 1940. There, in 1946, four months after his divorce from Lois, he married his most flamboyant wife, Fleur Fenton, who also had been married twice before, including to advertising executive Atherton Pettingell. One journalist described her as "an attractive Brooklyn-born woman whose own story, if found in fiction, would be labeled gaudy and preposterous." During Mike's nine-year marriage to her, Fleur assumed significant roles at *Look* and in the Cowles publishing empire and became a fixture in high society, chosen by President Eisenhower to represent the United States at Queen Elizabeth II's coronation. They divorced in 1955 and Fleur almost immediately married Tom Montague Meyer, another wealthy executive who she had met two years earlier, and went to live in a five-hundred-year-old Elizabethan estate in Sussex, England, painting and designing tapestries and china. Not missing a beat, Mike married Jan Hochstraser Cox, in 1956, who had just divorced her second husband, the publisher of the *Miami News*. Their honeymoon also took them to the Soviet Union. He remained with her until his death in 1985, and they had one child, Virginia, and he adopted Jan's son, Charles. Mike delighted in the fact that each of his divorces was front-page news in the *Register*.[31]

Between wives, he dated Joan Fontaine and at least one other actress. People "mistakenly thought Mike a playboy, because he loved parties and dancing," Leo Rosten recalled. He frequented the Stork Club, El Morocco, and the 21 Club in New York, attended the Bohemian Grove, the super-elite annual men's gathering in California, and belonged to clubs like the Links, the River, and the Racquet and Tennis Club. Yet, as Rosten said, "he was completely devoid of snobbery."[32]

Cowles lived in a townhouse at 47 East Sixty-eighth Street, before moving in 1957 to 740 Park Avenue, called "the richest apartment building in the world," where he had art by Renoir, Grant Wood, and Andy Warhol, among others. He bought homes in Weston, Connecticut, Southampton, New York, and in Indian Creek Island, Florida. Describing himself as "completely sold on Florida," Mike bought a 6,500-acre tract near Fort Pierce, Florida, which he developed under the auspices of the General Development Corp., as well as 182 acres near Key West and 500 acres in Puerto Rico. By the late

1950s, he would generally spend about two weeks a month in New York, ten days in Miami, and a few days in Des Moines, when he wasn't traveling the world. When he was still living in Des Moines, Mike and John bought a remote northern Minnesota hunting lodge, which they called Glendalough, where they frequently hosted hunting parties for influentials ranging from Nixon to Madison Avenue executives.[33]

Aside from his periodically poor business acumen and impetuousness, Mike Cowles was a man with the near-perfect combination of interests, values, and temperament to create and build a magazine that would interest everyone "from a teenager to a Harvard professor," as he once said.[34] Although he hired and depended on talented writers, editors, photographers, and business managers, *Look* was Cowles's baby.

Although *Life* debuted in 1936, a few months before *Look*, Cowles and Luce had discussed developing a photo magazine, and Gallup credited Cowles with probably having the idea first. Initially Luce saw no conflict between the two magazines, saying that *Life* was geared toward readers of the *New York Times*, while *Look* was aimed at *New York Daily News* readers. *Look* certainly was more populist than *Life* and more likely to tell stories of the common man and woman, but by mid-1938, the two publishers "realized there was a definite conflict between the two," Cowles said. And *Look*'s readership went far beyond the demographic profile of *Daily News* readers.[35]

3

Look's Thirty-Five Years in
Mid-Twentieth-Century America

Look: The Early Years

After its ill-fated launch in January 1937, *Look* was gradually transformed into what was to become America's largest-circulation magazine and one of the country's most influential publications in the twentieth century.[1]

The idea for the magazine came from both Gallup's research and Cowles's experience publishing a ten-part serialization of a photo book on World War I by Lawrence Stallings in the *Register* in 1935. The paper used high-quality photogravure printing for a Sunday section, which was popular with readers. "I became consumed by the idea of a picture magazine," Cowles recalled. "At that point, *Look* was born." After considering it as a Sunday supplement that could be sold to other papers, Cowles decided to make it a freestanding monthly magazine. He raised $25,000 for the launch from his father; his brother John; Fred Bohen, publisher of *Better Homes and Gardens*; and his own funds.[2]

By 1938, with the magazine selling about 1.7 million copies, Mich was made assistant managing editor, and bureaus in Washington, New York, and Hollywood had been established. Whether thanks to Logan, Mich, or Cowles, *Look* began interspersing its more tabloid stories with serious articles and "how-to" stories about everything from how to improve at bowling to how to be a better father. The November 22, 1938, issue—with the strange juxtaposition of actress Claudette Colbert doing the can-can on the cover and pictures of Hitler's girlfriends inside—also included reasonably thoughtful stories about the aviation industry and marijuana and graphic photos drawing attention to Japanese massacres in China. In addition to the articles on birth control and orphans of Generalissimo Francisco Franco's brutality in Spain, other late 1930s issues had stories about migrant laborers in the California fields, Father Coughlin's anti-Semitism, and columns by renowned newspaperman Drew Pearson. A good example of the strange editorial mix of the late 1930s is the October 14, 1939, issue with a cover photo of a drum majorette, which also included a sixteen-page spread on the early days of World War II, an interview with Al Capone in prison, an article on divorced women ("America's Misfits"), a belly dancer next to a camel in "Confidentially," and actress Ann Miller in a glittery short outfit. Although quasi-erotic photos remained after 1939, they tended to feature actresses like the leggy Cyd Charisse dancing or women supposedly illustrating some important issue, rather than a girl escaping from a flaming building.[3]

By the time Cowles made the decision to move *Look*'s headquarters to New York in 1940, the most garish content had begun to disappear. The staff expanded further, and the magazine's long-term goals, identity, and philosophy started to take shape. It explicitly stated that its aim was "the democratization of learning," an idea very much in line with writer Walter Lippmann's belief that true democracy is impossible without a well-informed citizenry. Cowles, Logan, and other staff believed that their mission was to teach Americans of all backgrounds the basics about politics, the world, social trends, injustice, art, sports, film, religion, and even the cultural history of the Western world. Cowles sought to make facts and ideas easily understandable.[4]

"I want to upgrade *Look*," Cowles said in 1941. "I am willing to pour a good deal of money into making it—well, respectable. I want to get the best writers, the best pictures. I want to publish articles as significant as any mass-circulation magazine in the country. I want to see *Look* on the coffee tables of the homes to which I am invited."[5]

The content mix continued to change as Cowles sought to differentiate *Look* from the fourteen other picture magazines that emerged in the wake of *Life* and *Look*. In 1940 attractive women were still on the cover of twenty-two of *Look*'s twenty-six issues. On one, there was a woman whose white dress had blown well above her knees, even though the major story inside the magazine was on "How Hitler Fools America." During the next two years, covers with starlets vied with ones on World War II, as two women in bathing suits adorned a 1941 issue with an in-depth story by John Gunther on South Africa, a 1942 issue with a bikini-clad blonde on the cover told the "Life Story of Stalin." By 1944 the girlie covers were largely gone, replaced by artists' renderings of FDR, Churchill, Roosevelt, Stalin, Generalissimo Chiang-Kai-Shek, General Eisenhower, and Admiral Chester Nimitz, as well as many soldiers and war scenes.[6]

After the war, amid a fair amount of fluff, penetrating articles became more common. In the November 9, 1948, issue, which came out just before the Truman-Dewey election, a story on a "White Child in a Negro World" was accompanied by another long piece by Gunther on life behind the Iron Curtain, a story on age discrimination, and dazzling photos from a V-2 rocket sixty miles above Earth. Similarly, the December 6, 1949, issue included photos and stories on Black life in Harlem, the dangers of the KKK, Franco's dictatorship, and a wholesome cover with President Harry Truman with his daughter, Margaret. As Cowles later said, it was "not until 1950 that *Look* began to reach the level of quality for which I had hoped."[7]

Nonetheless, in 1951 sixteen of the magazine's twenty-six issues had women's faces on the cover. During this one year, these included glamorous close-ups of actresses Elizabeth Taylor, Jean Simmons, Sonia Henie, Hedy Lamarr, Gene Tierney, Lily Pons, Marlene Dietrich, "Three Universal Starlets," Vivian Blaine, Jeanne Crain, Jane Russell, Marilyn Monroe, Elaine Stewart, Maureen O'Hara, Doris Day, and Ava Gardner. *Look*'s many swimsuit issues were another way to get titillating photos of young women on covers and in photo spreads. Other publications—down to the present—have taken a similar tack, but this was especially common in *Look*.

When the magazine left its Des Moines home, it took up residence on seven floors of the Postal Life Building at 511 Fifth Avenue in December 1940 and by 1948 had an editorial staff of 115. The mail subscription department remained in Iowa. Mich, who was managing editor under Pope, was named executive editor in 1942 when Logan fired Pope over differences. Four years later, Cowles dismissed Logan, who clashed with Mich, and Mich took over editorial operations. Whatmore became Cowles's right-hand man, more or less running day-to-day affairs by the late 1940s. Cowles and Mich appointed Henry Ehrlich as managing editor in 1947, after his predecessor, Jack Guenther, died in a plane crash. Mich left *Look* in 1950, clashing with Fleur Cowles. He returned to lead the magazine as editorial director in early 1954. Art director Merle Armitage pointedly told Cowles: "You must be feeling good these days and secure knowing that *Look* is back again in the hands of men who have the interest of you and the magazine at heart." Cowles responded: "I think there will be more drive and serenity on the 11th floor than we have had for a long, long time." William Arthur, who had reported from Washington since 1946, was promoted in 1949 to become assistant managing editor and managing editor in 1953, and the magazine's top editor after Mich died in 1965.[8]

By the end of the 1940s, *Look* had offices in twenty-five cities in the United States and Europe, with editorial staff in most of these. It was the second most-read magazine in the country, after *Life*, and was number eight in ad revenues.[9]

Many new staff writers, who were called "editors," joined *Look* in the 1940s. These included fashion, food, and special features writer Patricia Coffin; entertainment editor Jack Hamilton ("an encyclopedia of cinema history"); sportswriter Timothy Cohane; film and stage writer George Eells; science writer Matilda Smith; intellectual Leo Rosten; and writers Ben Kocivar, Joseph Roddy, Frank Latham, Woodrow Wirsig, Hope Beauchamp, Joseph Breed III, Olive Clapper, Lewis Gillenson, Harold Clemenko, William Houseman, Jonathan Kilbourne, Deb Wickersham, and Henriette Kish.[10]

Look began commissioning well-known figures to write for the magazine in the late 1940s, a practice it would step up in subsequent years. Gunther—the prolific author of *Inside the USA* (1947) and six other "Inside" books on

Russia and the major continents—was a frequent contributor, reporting from Europe, and boxer Joe Louis wrote about his "greatest fights."[11]

Whereas the magazine had largely used freelance photographers during its Des Moines years, *Look*'s first photographer, Marion Pease, came on board in the late 1930s. In 1940 the magazine hired Arthur Rothstein, a talented photographer who had worked for the New Deal's Farm Security Administration (FSA), as director of photography, and the photography staff expanded during the 1940s. (Fellow FSA veteran Walker Evans became a staff photographer for *Fortune* magazine.) A nine-person picture research department and six-person darkroom staff added to *Look*'s photographic heft. An art department, an editorial research department, and a library were created.[12]

Decisions about each issue's content would be made during a Wednesday editorial lunch, when senior editors would discuss ideas and mark up a "Story Idea" form with questions like: "Is the idea visual?" "Will it motivate the reader?" "Does it have wide family appeal?" "Is it entertaining?" "Is it informative?" "Will it be timely three months from now?" "Will it contain new information?" This Editorial Plans Board would consider 250 stories out of about 800 story ideas for a two-month period.[13]

Like other publications, writers both proposed stories and were assigned them. What was different about *Look* was that photographers were always part of the decision-making process and writers were almost always given free rein about what to write. Editors "never gave us marching orders," Poppy said. "We were never told to emphasize this or that or glorify things because Mike Cowles liked them." This was quite different from the hierarchical and more ideological *Life*, where decisions were made top down, and stories were more or less in tune with the thinking of Luce and even liberal Time-Life executives like longtime chairman, Andrew Heiskell.[14]

Look's Photo Department—together with Cowles, the managing editor, art director, photographer, and writer—would choose the images to be used. Based on these choices, writers would write their stories to fit the photos and layout. It was rare that stories were killed.[15]

Only in the late 1940s and early 1950s did tensions emerge between Cowles and his staff. The 1946 strike came in the wake of Cowles's decision to "eliminate or vastly curtail three fringe departments which were not essential." As *Look* grew and Cowles's ambitions expanded, many other "fringe departments" were launched, only to be eliminated soon after.[16]

Consequential and controversial editorial changes also occurred during this period, driven in large part by Cowles's marriage to Fleur. A profligate firebrand, she was invited to "watch" at a *Look* editorial meeting and instead blurted out that *Look*'s coverage of fashion and food were "awful; worse than awful. They make *Look* dowdy and old-fashioned to anybody with taste and discrimination." Within weeks of their marriage, his creative, blond third wife with what one staffer described as "a monumental ego," was named associate editor in charge of a new sixteen-person Women's Department. Its purview included fashion, food, home décor, travel, menswear, and art. Three times a year, she put together special packages on cheeses, beverages, and other categories of food. Within a few months, she assumed control over "special departments." Often dressed in a mink stole and long black gloves and adorned with expensive jewelry, Fleur cultivated the rich and famous, from President Eisenhower to Eva Perón. She bragged about her international awards, books, paintings, art patronage, and "multiple lives." She wrote staff memos on pink paper with blue carbon copies, and hand-wrote letters to readers in gold ink on royal blue paper.

Fleur antagonized John Cowles's wife, not to mention much of *Look*'s and even the *Register*'s staff, including Mich—who went to *McCall's* during the early 1950s—leading to a low point in morale at the magazine. "A good contrast is how Elizabeth Cowles approached life with how Fleur did," Herbert Strentz wrote. "One focused on helping others; the other on helping herself." She also burned through money with a magazine called *Flair*, one of Cowles's most dubious ventures. When she left, *Look* issued a press release that must have amused *Look*'s staff, in which Cowles said she "will be greatly missed by everyone at *Look*."[17]

Despite these problems, the magazine grew in audience, size, and stature during the 1940s. Circulation rose from 2.1 million in 1945 to 3.1 million in 1949, and *Look* claimed to have 18.5 million readers, based on the questionable multiplier of 5.8 readers per issue. Nearly two-thirds of copies were sold in areas with less than one hundred thousand people, with fewer than one in five sold in cities of five hundred thousand or more in 1951. Two-thirds to five-sixths of all copies were sold at newsstands after the war, whereas *Life* and *Collier's* had larger subscription bases. Half of its readers were in the top 60 percent of the income distribution, and more than 70 percent were in urban and suburban areas. Its readership was split evenly between men and women. Like other "mainstream" magazines at the time, it had few Black readers.[18]

Look also set a quota for 25 percent more editorial pages, as new features were introduced. The magazine grew from about seventy to ninety pages in its early days to close to two hundred by the mid-1950s. It started making newsreels in 1939 on World War II and published its first of about two dozen books in 1943, *Our American Heroes: A Pictorial Saga of American Gallantry on All the Fighting Fronts of the World, as Published in Look*. This was followed by another World War II book, *My Favorite War Story*, and a 394-page photo book on New York in 1948.[19]

The printing quality steadily improved, and the use of color and customized drawings and other art grew substantially. Whatmore introduced a "trail-blade" method of coating paper, creating smoother pages, and the so-called Look-Kromatic printing process that did not require printing plates and combined elements of rotogravure and letterpress techniques. Because *Life* used letterpress, its "reproductions were never as good as ours," asserted Will Hopkins, *Look*'s last art director. Multiple layouts would be presented to editors in the main conference room, and would be tinkered with and trimmed until deemed acceptable. As Hopkins recalled, unlike *Life*, "stories had to have a good layout, not just good text or pictures." Covers were carefully scrutinized by Cowles, who "always remembered the mistakes he felt he had made in *Look*'s infancy," Rosten said.[20]

Advertising expanded apace, with advertisers spending $15 million to promote 483 products in 1949. Blonds looking at their white teeth in a mirror for a Pepsodent ad. "More doctors smoke Camels." A day at the circus is better with Seven-Up. A Nash will take you six hundred miles on a gallon of gas. With Kodak, "your snapshots will always remember." There is "sheer magic" in GE's radios and phonographs. Santa holding a Parker 51, "the world's most wanted pen."

Although *Look* matched *Life* in ad pages per issue, it charged roughly three-fourths of what Luce's magazine did. In 1947, after refusing to take liquor ads because it was a "family magazine," *Look* reversed itself, telling readers: "Since it is used in millions of homes, if would be proper for us to accept a limited amount of such advertising." In addition to whiskey and rum, ads for Italian Swiss Colony Wines showed a couple in a dirndl and lederhosen toasting at an Alpine picnic, and the beer ads usually showed well-dressed men being served by women, although one titled "Thanksgiving Dinner" showed even grandma quaffing down a brew. As 1948 ushered in the magazine's long string of profitability, *Look* increased its ad pages by 310 during 1948 and 1949, while *Life* lost about 290 pages.[21]

Staff enjoyed raises and bonuses. Writers like Jack Hamilton were paid $131.50 per week in 1947, although a female writer like Helen Itria was paid $78 in 1948, and researchers like Gerald Rogavin made $68.75 per week. Benefits, a rarity at the time, were good.[22]

In 1949 Cowles moved *Look* into the tenth through thirteenth floors of the newly built, modernist twenty-one-story building at 488 Madison Avenue, which was just around the corner from St. Patrick's Cathedral in Midtown Manhattan. Designed by architect Richard Roth, the building also included the offices of *Esquire* magazine, Pocket Books, and industrial designer Raymond Loewy. *Look* later expanded its presence in the building. (The young Bob Dylan recorded "The Times They Are a-Changin'" there in the early 1960s.) In 1963 it expanded its office space by nearly 40 percent to more than two hundred thousand square feet, optimistically signing a twenty-four-year lease. When the magazine folded, the *Look* sign atop the building was taken down, although a shadow of the word could be seen for many years. In 2004 the building was listed in the National Register of Historic Places, but today nothing marks the fact that one of America's great magazines was produced there for twenty-two years.[23]

It brought the world into America's living rooms in a way that was more substantial than quick evening news clips and much more unvarnished than *National Geographic*. Readers weren't told what to think; rather, they were offered a number of different perspectives on issues. As Leo Rosten said: "[I know of] no magazine where the boss was less partisan, more reasonable, and more determined to publish the widest possible spectrum of opinion."[24]

The *New York Times* may have reported "all the news that's fit to print," but *Look* published features that were fit to help readers become well-informed, tolerant citizens. One issue might have stories on new health discoveries, abstract expressionism, the horrors of the Indochina war, Judaism in America, and its series on "Women Who Fascinate Men" (mostly movie stars) and "Men Who Fascinate Women" (including Graham Greene, Edward R. Murrow and more arcane choices like Italian writer and politician Luigi Barzini and Philippine president Ramon Magsaysay). Other issues included similarly diverse content—from interviews with Che Guevara or Picasso and the Berkeley student protests to lynchings, the "new" California, the Kennedy family, cellist Mstislav Rostropovich, girls frolicking on the beach, or the wedding of Nixon's daughter (reputedly to placate a president angry at *Look*'s Vietnam coverage).[25]

Look's covers may have treated women as eye candy, yet it also nurtured the feminist founders of *Ms.* magazine, Gloria Steinem and Patricia Carbine. Although it mostly criticized Truman and supported Ike, *Look* published an essay by socialist Norman Thomas in the midst of the McCarthy era. Its stories and essays demonstrated support for public investments, particularly in education and science, and the belief that government was, or should be, a force for the good. Its views on the family and the youth culture of the 1960s were complex and evolved with the times. Cowles, Mich, and others at *Look* implicitly and explicitly called for tolerance, if not support, for working women and single and divorced Americans and even wrote sympathetically about the first gay men to marry, in one of its last issues, nearly forty-five years before gay marriage became legal in the United States.[26]

Initially cool on rock and roll, by the late 1960s, *Look* published a remarkable psychedelically enhanced series of portraits of the Beatles by photographer Richard Avedon. The supposedly staid "Midwestern" magazine also became a booster of one of the ultimate counterculture institutions, the Esalen retreat center in Big Sur, California.[27]

The magazine's Cold War coverage was creative and daring. As U.S.-Soviet tensions were increasing, *Look* dispatched FDR's son, Elliott, to interview

Stalin in 1946 and Adlai Stevenson in 1952 to write ten articles, interview Khrushchev, and examine communism in India, Indochina, East Asia, and Europe. Twice, *Look* reporters and photographers spent weeks exploring Communist Eastern Europe. *Look* sent the first American journalist and photographer from a major publication to Communist China in 1956, and it covered the Cuban revolution from its jungle beginnings.[28]

Look's global coverage in the 1950s and 1960s brought countries, conflicts, and international issues to its mass audience that only elite media do in the twenty-first century. Its blend of photography, its people-oriented approach, its dash of commentary, and journalists writing in the first person would not have been found in the *Times* or *Life*. In a 1959 story on decolonization in Africa, Ernest Dunbar—the first Black reporter for a major U.S. magazine—told readers that he was the first Black American that most Africans had ever seen. A year earlier, writer Thomas Morgan and photographer John Vachon reported from Antarctica as negotiations ended on the Antarctic Treaty among twelve countries, playfully planting a sign, "*Look* Magazine Ross Ice Shelf Bureau."[29]

Look also did in-depth packages on places, like the 1959 issue on California that involved twenty-eight writers and photographers and included stories on braceros and "offbeat religions," political dynasties and intellectuals, "movie morals," and "beauties from two top campuses." Coffin put together similar packages on New York City, the Midwest, and New England. The magazine's "*Look* at America" series in the late 1940s and 1950s, edited by the magazine's longtime travel writer, Andrew Hepburn, included scores of four-page travel supplements with photos and maps, giving readers tips on U.S. destinations like Cape Cod, Washington DC, New York City, dude ranches, and Key West. In keeping with Cowles's belief that the future would only be better, the magazine did many stories that reflected the nation's economic growth and technological marvels. The 1968 *Look* book *Suburbia: The Good Life in Our Exploding Utopia* is illustrative of this buoyant optimism.[30]

Norman Vincent Peale, the prominent minister and best-selling author of *The Power of Positive Thinking*, began writing regular advice columns in *Look* in 1954. Harold Austin "Rip" Ripley's long-running "Photocrime" feature gave readers clues to solve murder mysteries in which celebrities enacted crime scenes; it was turned into a *Look* TV show in 1949. Another early short feature, "*Look* Applauds," celebrated the achievements of people from all walks of life. A regular page of light commentary, "Look on the Light Side," debuted in 1954 and was edited by J. M. Flagler. Not exactly up to *New Yorker* standards, these included not-very-funny cartoons, like one of a judge telling an author, "We didn't ban your book because it was pornographic; we banned it because it lacked realism," or another depicting two U.S. Customs officers looking at a sleeping dog, saying: "I think it's time that Rusty was relieved of marijuana duty." Fashion, food, and "home living" stories appeared with increasing regularity in the 1950s.[31]

William L. Shirer's *The Rise and Fall of the Third Reich*, Irving Stone's *The Agony and the Ecstasy*, staff writer Leonard Shecter's *Ball Four*, and a previously unpublished book by Sigmund Freud and William C. Bullitt on Woodrow Wilson, *Thomas Woodrow Wilson: A Psychological Study*, were among *Look*'s many book excerpts.[32]

Look's editorial content, its pioneering narrative juxtaposition of words and photos, and its philosophy contributed to making the mid-twentieth-century United States a more open-minded, informed, and optimistic nation. Many factors accounted for America's successes during this era, but *Look* was one that helped Americans understand their differences and, ultimately, their commonalities, enabling the country to evolve, be more or less united, and thrive.

In Cowles's September 16, 1971, statement on *Look*'s closing, he conveyed the same idealism that had characterized him, Mich, and much of *Look*'s staff during the middle of the twentieth century: "*Look* was edited for readers who see a better America being born out of the issues that now divide us. . . . The editors of *Look* believe that peace, poverty, pollution, and other problems could only be solved if people understood them."[33]

Look's Heyday in the 1950s and 1960s

From the late 1940s to the late 1960s, *Look* had one of the most impressive records in journalism history. With fewer resources and less than half the staff of *Life*, who some at *Look* regarded as "cocky and arrogant," Cowles's magazine's success was due to its being able to "outwrite, outphotograph, outedit, and generally outhustle *Life*," the publisher boasted. Its circulation, 1.9 million in 1944, doubled in a decade and topped 5.7 million by the end of the 1950s, passing *Life* in 1962 to become America's most read magazine for seven years, selling nearly 8 million copies per issue between 1965 and 1969. *Look*'s rate base—the minimum circulation it promised advertisers— peaked at 7.75 million between 1967 and 1970. Depending on the multiplier used, *Look* was read by 35 to 70 million Americans at a time when there were about 125 million citizens age eighteen and over and about 60 million households. A 1962 audience study found that it was read by 34 percent of American adults, and more than half of the adult population read at least one in three issues of *Look*. Its circulation benefited from the closing of two other venerable mass-circulation magazines. When *Collier's* folded in 1956, *Look* paid $1.6 million to buy its name, subscriber list, and liabilities. This lifted *Look*'s circulation to more than five million. The *Saturday Evening Post* hung on until 1969. With the possible exception of *Life* and the network TV news, no other medium in U.S. history reached such a broad swath of the American people.[34]

It recorded twenty-two straight years of profits, from 1948 through 1969, with advertising revenues hitting $80.2 million in 1966.[35] The newsstand price in the early 1960s was thirty-five cents, the same as *Life*'s. In 1962 it topped *Life* in ad revenue per issue. Cowles Communications Inc.— essentially *Look*—built up a staff of more than 200 full-time writers, editors, and photographers, more than 125 advertising and promotion staff, and several thousand circulation and other staff. Its photograph-laden articles made news, and were covered by the *New York Times* and other media big and small. It published freelance work by some of the most notable figures in American life. As its pages became ever more filled with thought-provoking stories on major political, economic, cultural, social, and other issues, the magazine won reporting, photography, and art awards, as well as awards from civil-rights, medical, education, religious, and other organizations. It bestowed awards not only to its "All-America" cities but also to college football players, teachers of the year, movies and TV shows, musicians, and aviators. Cowles Communications branched out into book publishing,

launched other magazines, acquired TV and radio stations as well as magazines and local newspapers, and developed new publishing technologies.[36]
The accolades came from many sources in addition to readers. From
1956 to 1959, the National Education Association bestowed its School Bell
Award on *Look*, and the Education Writers Association honored *Look* in
1962. The Anti-Defamation League (ADL) applauded *Look* for its 1959 "Jews
in America" article. Its 1956 story on "The South vs. the Supreme Court" won
a Benjamin Franklin Gold Medal for "the most distinguished and merito-
rious public service." *Look* also won awards from the National Conference
of Christians and Jews, the Albert Lasker Foundation, and the Freedoms
Foundation. NAACP president Roy Wilkins presented Cowles, who was
joined by legendary singer Marian Anderson, with an award for *Look*'s
civil rights coverage in 1959. *Look* won its first National Magazine Award
in 1966 for "its treatment of the racial issue." Kansas senator Frank Carlson
commended *Look* in 1956 for "exemplify[ing] the high sense of public
responsibility that is the hallmark of enlightened journalism." In 1970 it
won five Overseas Press Club awards and was represented by twenty-one
selections at the Art Directors Club of New York, in both cases, more than
any other magazine.[37]
Its dedicated readers were sending three to four tons of mail to the Des
Moines office every day by the end of the 1940s. Each issue included a half
page of readers' letters. Like other publications, some were from politicians
and other leaders, but most came from subscribers praising or damning
particular articles, often with clever twists. *Look* tried to a fault to be balanced. The letters published in response to a 1963 article on suppression
of the Black vote are indicative. One letter from an immigrant who said
he had waited ten years to become a citizen, said: "What is the waiting
requirement for those whose skin is not white?" Just below was a letter
from a Michigan woman who wrote: "Many of your lengthy articles have
been devoted to 'the poor Negro underdog,' but not one column could be
spared for the segregationist's view."[38]
Look's influence on civil rights and foreign policy certainly can be seen
from its many powerful articles that helped shape public debate. Members
of Congress who wrote for *Look* were writing for their colleagues as well

as constituents and *Look* readers. Several articles—including ones on the Middle East and Vietnam—were read into the Congressional Record. A 1965 story on a Seattle woman who went from welfare to get an education and become a psychologist led Vice President Hubert Humphrey to thank *Look* for showing that welfare could work. Its stories brought on the wrath of powerful figures like President Nixon; Wisconsin senator Joseph McCarthy; Alabama governor George Wallace; San Francisco mayor Joseph Alioto; Jackie Kennedy; a Tennessee judge; and the Irish government, not to mention Tass, the Soviet news agency. *Look*'s impact on American thinking also resulted from Cowles being a frequent guest of Presidents Eisenhower, Kennedy, and Johnson, as well as foreign leaders, and two of its writers were advisers and ambassadors to Kennedy and Johnson.[39]

Mike's Diversions: Other Ventures

The story of *Look* cannot be told without discussing Mike Cowles's many other, usually short-lived and unsuccessful, ventures. These included the magazines *Flair, Quick,* and *Venture*; book publishing and newsreels during World War II; 3-D photography; and newspapers. If *Look* was the cash cow, most of these were significant money losers.[40]

Certainly the most famous—or infamous—of these ventures was Fleur's folly, which Cowles enabled his wife to create in 1950, timed to kick off the second half of the twentieth century. She promised that her magazine would provide "the most delicious of all rewards—a sense of surprise, a joy of discovery." Stylistically daring, *Flair*'s expensively produced thirteen issues had holes in the cover, foldouts, half pages, and accordion inserts. One issue invited readers to light a match and hold the flame near the copy to make invisible ink appear. Underneath a double cover, the first issue proved its avant-garde bona fides by including a color reproduction of a painting by Lucian Freud and an essay by French writer Jean Cocteau. It also featured a short story by Tennessee Williams, a tale of a flight to Morocco, a fifteen-page fashion section, and a story about decorating the Paris home of the Duke and Duchess of Windsor, accompanied by a handwritten note from Fleur.[41]

Another issue had a rose fragrance, decades before scent strips became common. Others had pen-and-ink drawings of a state fair with circus freaks, a strip show, and an American flag surrounded by rings of circles. With more than one hundred pages and two dozen stories per issue, its stock-in-trade was high-end fashion, home décor, and travel, with a dash of art, entertainment, and fiction. Pretentious and geared to the rich, Cowles paid for *Flair* to hire staff and open bureaus in Rome and Paris, on the swanky Place Vendome. Despite its gold gift subscription cards and fifty-cent cover price, *Flair* never reached half its target circulation of two hundred thousand and lost seventy-five cents per issue. During its one-year existence, the *New Yorker* published several cartoons about *Flair* and much of the press lampooned it, with *Time* calling it "avant-gaudy," and the *Nation* saying that reading *Flair* "presents difficulties to anyone not equipped with an opposable thumb." Some speculated that Cowles bankrolled it to keep his extravagant wife away from *Look*'s staff.[42]

In 1949, shortly before *Flair*, Cowles introduced a pocket-sized weekly news digest called *Quick*, priced at ten cents. It provided the news in brief, along with stories on Roy Rogers, Albert Einstein, Jackie Robinson, and "Cooking with Ike." With its covers rotating among four colors, it sold as many as 1.3 million copies, mostly on newsstands, but it never attracted advertisers. It too was disparaged, as one critic said: "It makes *Reader's Digest* look like *Fortune.*" *Quick* folded in June 1953, as Cowles claimed the decision would draw *Quick* readers to *Look* to boost its circulation.[43]

The *Insider's Newsletter*, intended by Cowles to be another sophisticated newsletter, made its debut in 1959 and folded in 1968. Never selling more than 190,000 copies, it also drained the Cowles coffers.[44]

In 1964 Cowles launched yet another magazine, *Venture—The Traveler's World*, a glossy, bimonthly, initially hardcover travel magazine with 3-D photos on the cover. With 180 pages per issue and noted writers like Graham Greene writing about Goa, the magazine was initially something of a sensation with its XO-Graph photos that Whatmore developed with Kodak under a *Look* subsidiary, Visual Panographics. Selling for the then-unheard-of price of one dollar per copy, *Venture* built up its circulation to 150,000, helped by promotion from the American Express card. Gilbert Maurer was its publisher and it survived for seven years, serving as a precursor to Amex's *Travel and Leisure* magazine.[45]

Flush with cash from *Look*, Cowles went on a buying binge in the 1960s, acquiring *Family Circle*; the *San Juan Mirror*; *Modern Medicine*; a number of radio and TV stations; newspapers in South Dakota, Montana, Tennessee, New York, and Wisconsin, as well as several Florida papers. Believing that he could compete with *Newsday* on Long Island, he started the *Suffolk Sun* in 1966, handing control over to his son, Gardner Cowles III. Inauspiciously opening to picket lines, within three years it was losing up to $15 million per year, and the *Sun* folded. Cowles was "blinded by the majesty of the empire," Maurer said. "What's cooler than putting your son in such a position, but it was cruel to the son."[46]

Look published more than twenty coffee-table and other books, most of which were compilations of photos and articles from the magazine. These included the tome on New York City, coedited with Frederick Lewis Allen; the powerful 1945 anti-prejudice book, *One Nation*, edited with Wallace Stegner; the lavish 592-page *Look at America* in 1955, which the *Times* called "pictorial journalism at its best"; and *Our Land, Our People: People in Pictures from Look Magazine* in 1958. During the mid- to late 1940s, *Look* had a book department, spurred by Logan and headed by Harry Shaw. It published nine earlier volumes of *Look at America*, with photos, fold-out maps, and stories, as well as *How to Keep Your Family Healthy* (1946), but it was shut down in 1947 in the wake of disputes with Logan, a decision Cowles later regretted. *Look* published the highly regarded *A Guide to Religions in America* in 1955; *The Story Behind the Painting* in 1962, a photo book memorializing John Kennedy; and a series of travel books by travel editor Andrew Hepburn. *Look*'s 1968 book *Red Russia after 50 Years* drew on seventeen articles it had published in October 1967. Cowles launched the *Cowles Comprehensive Encyclopedia* and the Cambridge Book Company, and between 1959 and 1961, the company published brochures on social responsibility, health and medicine, and education.[47]

The Business of *Look*

Despite these many ego-driven failures, *Look* was extraordinarily successful as a business, thanks to its writers, photographers, advertising, circulation, and other executives. With revenues of $137 million in 1967 (equivalent to nearly $1.1 billion in 2021 dollars), Cowles Communications was listed by *Fortune* as the 449th largest U.S. corporation in 1967. That year it had four thousand employees, five times the number it had a decade before. As the most-read national magazine in the United States for the majority of the 1960s, *Look* was not only a cultural and journalistic success but also made a lot of money.[48]

In 1947, when *Look* was a private company, Cowles Magazines had 96,050 shares outstanding. Most were held by Mike and four other men—24,000 for Mike, 21,000 for John, 7,500 for Whatmore, 6,250 for longtime advertising manager James Milloy, and 5,000 for Donald Perkins. Fourteen years later, in 1961, Cowles Magazines and Broadcasting made its first public stock offering. Listed on the New York Stock Exchange, it was renamed Cowles Communications Inc. (CCI) in 1965.[49]

Its advertisers included scores of major American companies. Like most print media, its revenues from circulation were not the major source of the company's income. Whereas a copy of the magazine cost about eighty cents to produce in the late 1960s, it was discounting them to some subscribers for the equivalent of two to three cents per copy. The magazine promoted itself through print and TV ads, direct mail, and research. In its later years, it targeted about one thousand of the nation's richest zip codes in what was called its Top/Spot plan.[50]

The End and the Aftermath

The story of how television took away mass advertisers from so-called "general interest" magazines, and how special-interest magazines picked up advertisers and readers in the late 1960s and 1970s is familiar. So is the more recent tale of the internet—social media in particular—devastating approximately two thousand newspapers and countless magazines between 2004 and 2019 alone. The modus operandi of many internet "media" was to appeal to narrow interests and prejudices, substituting often fact-free opinions for the kind of relatively unbiased information for the masses that *Look* provided.[51]

The great economist Joseph Schumpeter talked about "creative destruction"—new industries replacing old ones—as essential for a vital capitalism, recognizing that there would be short-term casualties. The conventional wisdom is that TV, then the internet, were "advances" on mass-circulation print media. While Schumpeter was right in many ways about the dynamics of capitalism, he and others during the last seventy years bought into the facile fallacy of late twentieth-century and early twenty-first-century business that almost anything new is good, especially if it can be monetized. Culture and facts and analysis are not "improved" by dumping them into the morass of Facebook, Twitter, Reddit, and websites whose content providers generally do not know or care how to create and present carefully reported and researched unbiased information.

Many have argued that the internet and social media, on balance, have wrought tremendous harm to informed discourse, understanding of multiple points of view, democracy, social relations, and psychological well-being. Long ago, in the early 1970s, the demise of *Look* and *Life* were harbingers of the destruction of quality information and discourse that is so apparent today. This is a bigger story, which we will return to, one that few saw when an often brilliant, sometimes tawdry magazine was forced to shut down in October 1971.

Look went into the red in 1969, in part because of the *Suffolk Sun*. Rumors of its impending doom were spreading on Madison Avenue. In 1970 Cowles sold *Family Circle*, the Florida newspapers, his company's book division, and a Memphis TV station, mostly to the *New York Times* for 2.6 million shares of *Times* stock and the *Times*' assumption of $15 million of *Look*'s debt. Despite these and other ominous signs—including the fact that three of *Look*'s last stars—Attwood, Leonard, and Carbine—bailed in 1970, Cowles was publicly bullish on *Look*. In 1970 he told *Newsweek*: "My heart is in *Look*. It's my baby. I founded the magazine and would sell everything to keep it going." Yet, by the summer of 1971, the masthead had few familiar names from the magazine's glory days. Writers like Ira Mothner, Jack Star, Leonard Gross, Christopher Wren, and Leonard Shecter were still there, as were photographers like James Karales, Stanley Tretick, Paul Fusco, and Hansen—but the others were gone.[52]

Less than a year later, after talking to his top executives on the evening of September 15, 1971, Mike Cowles publicly announced the next morning that *Look* would cease publication with its October 19 issue. He cited declining advertising revenues as well as a controversial 142 percent increase in magazine postal rates that the Nixon Administration had put into effect. Claiming that his "heart said, 'keep it going,'" and that reader interest remained high, Cowles said that wasn't enough to insure its financial survival.[53]

"We knew there were difficulties, but this news came as a total shock," photographer Douglas Kirkland said. His wife, Francoise, recalled: "He was white as a sheet when he hung up the phone. It was as if God died."[54]

"There is hardly any way to describe how the photographers and writers felt," Pat Sayer Fusco, Paul Fusco's wife, remembered. "Imagine going to bed one night and waking up to learn the magazine was no more. There was no advance warning." For Fusco who had never worked anywhere else, "it had been his home and his family and career," she added.[55]

Well over one thousand employees were fired, although CCI tried to place many former staff. At 488 Madison, staffers drank Bloody Marys made the night before in huge pots with ladles, cracked jokes, cried, and kissed longtime associates goodbye. Some blamed Cowles or Shepard for the lack of editorial direction after Mich died. William F. Buckley Jr. wrote a trenchant article that week asking why readers couldn't absorb the higher costs, noting that a subscription to *Look* was a fraction of the cost of a hamburger.[56]

One of several sad and bizarre codas to the history of *Look* occurred when—days after *Look* folded—*Vogue* ran an eight-page spread on how Cowles and his wife remodeled their lavish Manhattan apartment for a million dollars.[57]

Several years later, two publishers made an ill-fated attempt to revive *Look*. Daniel Filipacchi, the publisher of *Paris Match* and the French edition of *Playboy*, announced in 1977 that he would bring back *Look*. Shortly after it hit the newsstands in February 1979, Jann Wenner, the thirty-three-year-old founder of *Rolling Stone*, was brought in to run the new monthly magazine. The first 128-page issue reported on the Jonestown massacre in Guyana and the newly installed Chinese leader Deng Xiaoping and naturally threw in a little Marilyn. Wenner blamed Filipacchi for not pouring in more dollars, but the European publisher was losing money hand over first and shut down the magazine within a year.[58]

Look had made Cowles and his family enormously wealthy, and despite the losses of the magazine's last years, he owned one-quarter of the *New York Times* when he had to give up his directorship in 1974 because he had turned seventy. CCI was dissolved in 1978 and finally liquidated assets in 1982, when Cowles was seventy-nine years old. Most of its assets were in *New York Times* common stock, and most of the proceeds went to the Cowles family. Nine years after Mike Cowles died in 1985, *Forbes'* list of family fortunes put the collective worth of seventy Cowles heirs at $525 million (the equivalent of $1.3 billion in 2021).[59]

While *Look* made Mike Cowles rich, it also made the United States a much richer country, culturally and politically. Despite his blunders, Cowles created a magazine of immeasurable value—a medium that, in many ways, is worth emulating in an internet-poisoned America where more people are ill-informed and unwilling to hear others' views.

The next chapter will look at the people who made *Look* a great magazine and a force in mid-twentieth-century America. The following chapters will describe and analyze the magazine's content, highlighting its unique contributions, influence, and approach.

4

The People Who Made *Look*

"*Look* was put out by editors and writers who were young in years or young in spirit, or both. They held strong opinions and were encouraged to express them," Cowles wrote after the magazine folded.[1]

Many writers, editors, photographers, art directors, and others played key roles at *Look* throughout its history. Several *Look* staff members stayed with the magazine from beginning to end, while many others had ten- to twenty-year careers there. Virtually all were politically liberal or farther left. In addition to the stars, there were many other editorial, advertising, promotion, and circulation personnel who helped *Look* succeed.

Former staff members recall a spirit of adventure, camaraderie, and fun. They were relatively well paid, with good benefits. Although payroll records show that men generally got bigger paychecks than women, Cowles and Mich prided themselves on hiring and promoting women and African Americans. Cowles also liked younger writers and photographers.[2]

During *Look*'s halcyon days in the quarter century after World War II, Daniel Mich, who was with *Look* from 1937 to 1950, and again from 1954 until his death at age sixty in 1965, was the most influential editor in shaping the magazine. Whereas Cowles loved the high life, hobnobbing with the famous and powerful, Mich was more introverted.

Mich joined *Look* in 1937, when Cowles hired him away from the *Wisconsin State Journal*. *Collier's* described him as "a man with a self-made split personality, [both] a successful editor and a struggling writer." An outspoken defender of a free press, he once wrote: "With apathy, and sometimes with its assistance, the press has allowed its freedoms to be whittled away by politicians, government administrators, and commercial interests." He was "very progressive" and "so focused on exposing and doing away with racism," according to Carbine. Staff writer Laura Bergquist also praised him for supporting female journalists: "There are men who really like women or who think of women as equals, with ability . . . Dan Mich, was like that. [To him,] whether you are male or female, it doesn't matter so long as you do the job."[3]

Called by his staff "Mich," he was more interested in compelling yet informative stories. He was named managing editor under Vernon Pope in 1940 and executive editor in 1942, after Harlan Logan dismissed Pope. Four years later, he succeeded the more intellectual Logan as top editor. He left in 1950, because of his clash with Fleur over *Look*'s content and his belief that publishing *Quick* and *Flair* diverted resources from *Look*, and became editorial director at *McCall's*. He returned to *Look* in 1954, as Fleur disappeared after she and Cowles divorced. "Dan Mich as editorial director was an awesome figure," Poppy recalled. "He was not unkind but gruff." Photographer Andrew St. George said that he "had the appearance of a Renaissance archbishop and wielded approximately the same power." Mich was also hot-tempered, had a bad leg, and was married to Isabella Taves, an accomplished fiction writer.[4]

Executive editor Woody Wirsig and managing editor Leslie Midgley took over from Mich during the Fleur years (which happened to coincide with the height of McCarthyism). Midgley introduced a four-page "*Look* Reports" news section, and made assignments and decisions on story ideas. Assistant managing editor William Arthur would supervise picture stories and layouts. In the early 1950s, the managing editor, William Lowe, would schedule and edit each story before it went to the copy chief, Frank Latham. By the end of 1953, Lowe, Wirsig, and Midgley all resigned.[5]

Harlan Logan served as top editor prior to Mich, from 1939 to 1946. He brought "a kind of professionalism that was sorely needed," Cowles recalled. "Logan was a teacher at heart [who wanted to show] readers how to live better lives." Cowles also credited him with pushing the publisher to "think big" and not be too "cost conscious."[6]

Logan had big ideas for *Look*, launching a short-lived book division (one of several started by *Look* over the years) and an editorial art research department. He introduced newsreels and wanted the magazine to be involved with television, at a time when there were fewer than ten thousand TV sets in America. Logan led an experimental effort with General Electric that turned *Look*'s "Photocrime" and "Photo Quiz" features into TV content that aired only in Schenectady, New York. He also sought to develop a "Magazine X" to compete with *Reader's Digest*. At *Look*, he wanted to "improve" readers with features like "*Look*'s Personality Clinic," written by a psychiatrist; "Strictly Personal"; and stories on such topics as how to manage your money, be a good father, and know if you were in the right job.

Logan based his hiring decisions on how many academic degrees a candidate had, according to Cowles. While Logan made *Look* respectable, Cowles felt that his patriotic coverage of World War II was "often dull and boring." Logan clashed with Pope, firing him in 1942. After also clashing with Mich, Cowles fired Logan in 1946.[7]

In 1936 Vernon Pope helped Cowles put together dummies for *Look* before the first issue came out, and he edited the magazine from New York at the very beginning. He developed a photogravure section and the picture-sequence technique while at the *Register* and *Tribune*, which would be important to *Look* throughout its history. He left the magazine in 1942 for a career in public relations and later was elected to the New Hampshire House of Representatives, becoming the majority leader in 1969.[8]

Mich was succeeded by William Arthur and Pat Carbine, who led the magazine in its last years. Arthur spanned much of the *Look* era, coming to the magazine from the *Louisville Courier-Journal* in 1946 to be a Washington correspondent. Mich promoted him to assistant managing editor in 1949, and he became *Look*'s "Editor" during the magazine's last six years. Politically "left of center," according to Poppy, Arthur enabled *Look* to pursue a more radical path in the late 1960s.[9]

Like her predecessors, Carbine played a major role in deciding what to cover and the tone of the coverage. Kirkland called her the magazine's "Mother Superior." Fusco described her as "quiet, tough, soft, confident, and really funny." She joined *Look* in 1953 at age twenty-two and stayed with the magazine for seventeen years. Mich named Carbine and Robert Meskill, whom she was dating, assistant managing editors in 1959. Her politics were progressive; she wrote about subjects like poverty and, as executive editor, gave the green light to the "'70s" issue, which was devoted to fairly radical politics and psychology and grand visions of the world's future. When Carbine left in 1970, she, Steinem, and several other leading feminists started *Ms.* magazine, which hit the newsstands two months after *Look* folded. Carbine later served as editor of *McCall's*, publisher of *Ms.*, and chairman of the Advertising Council.[10]

Meskill was with *Look* from 1957 until his death in 1970 at age fifty-one. He briefly headed Cowles Book Company. Cowles said that he "understood the responsibilities of word power and was passionately concerned that the power should be used carefully to inspire and motivate man." As assistant managing editor, he was especially engaged with writers.[11]

George Leonard, one of *Look*'s most legendary and colorful figures, also joined the magazine in 1953 and stayed until 1970. He headed the San Francisco bureau for many years, beginning in 1956. He wrote about cutting-edge issues—often with cutting-edge opinions—including race, education, the changing family, the counterculture, the Cold War, and education. Leonard's many stories about education and the need for reform began with an award-winning piece on "What Is a Teacher?" that the National Education Association reprinted and sold 1.5 million copies. His ideas and his writing, always liberal and often prophetic, moved much farther to the left in the late 1960s.

He hailed California as a "window into the future," ventured through the Soviet satellite states with Fusco, and put together the "'70s" issue. He was a big believer in technology and the limitless possibilities it opened up.

Many of his prognostications turned out to be true. Leonard won eleven national awards for his articles on education; three 1968 pieces became his book *Education and Ecstasy*. He became involved with the Esalen Institute, becoming its president after *Look* folded, and is credited with coining the term, the "human potential movement." Like Mich, his wife briefly worked for *Look*.[12]

Poppy, who was born in prewar Czechoslovakia and graduated from Harvard, spent the 1960s with *Look*, worked with Leonard and married his sister. He covered student protests at Berkeley, rock musicians, and the counterculture. He coined the term "generation gap" in a 1967 story and wrote as a freelancer for *Esquire* and other magazines after *Look*.[13]

Twenty-five-year-old William Hedgepeth, "a madcap writer" who wore an eye patch, told America about the hippies who had come to San Francisco for the 1967 "Summer of Love" (and whose article inspired many more to come). Fifty years later, he recalled: "I took drugs on that assignment, . . . but figured I was doing so on behalf of the American people."[14]

Laura Bergquist was another liberal, fearless reporter for *Look*, from 1954 until 1971. She had early access to Fidel Castro and Che Guevara and won eight national awards for her reporting on Cuba and Latin America. Berg- quist became *Look*'s leading Kennedy correspondent and confidante, writing about JFK the man, the husband, the father, and his illustrious extended family. She published a 1965 book on JFK, and wrote that Kennedy was "very sexually oriented" and made many sexual comments to her. In addition to politicians, she had extraordinarily wide-ranging contacts—from writers Arthur Miller and Carlos Fuentes to Eleanor Roosevelt, anthropologist Bruno Bettelheim, and Lucille Ball. A feminist, she waited until she was forty-seven to marry *Look* political writer and novelist, Fletcher Knebel. Bergquist committed suicide in 1982 at their home in Princeton.[15]

Although almost all *Look* staff wrote about U.S. politics in one form or another, it had a number of dedicated writers who focused on it. Like other staffers, they were objective, but their points of view were usually clear.

Fletcher Knebel covered presidents and the Washington scene for two decades, while writing a syndicated column, "Potomac Fever," from 1951 to 1964. He also wrote fifteen political novels and other books, one of which,

Seven Days in May (1962), was made into a successful motion picture. A liberal, he described himself as being "suspicious of the size and power of the American military." Like his wife, he covered the Kennedys, among many other leading figures of the mid-twentieth century. Knebel committed suicide eleven years after Bergquist did, in 1982.[16]

Knebel was preceded by Jack Wilson, who wrote the "Washington Roundup" column for *Look* in the late 1940s and early 1950s. Wilson later covered the space race and wrote the "Potomac Fever" column after Knebel. Warren Rogers was named chief Washington correspondent in 1966.[17]

Richard Wilson, who worked for the Cowles family for nearly half a century, started with the *Des Moines Register* in 1926 and worked for the *Register* and *Look* until 1970, as well as John Cowles's *Minneapolis Star-Tribune and Register* until 1975. He served as chief Washington correspondent beginning in 1950, writing about Nixon's fitness for office in 1953 and again in 1970, and won a Pulitzer Prize in 1954 for his reporting on the FBI.[18]

Ernest Dunbar, the pioneering Black journalist, wrote for *Look* from 1954 until 1971. He mostly covered civil rights, Black America, and Africa. He also wrote on racial politics and introduced America to Jesse Jackson. Dunbar served as an advisor on Africa for President Kennedy while on a leave from *Look*, and published two books, *The Black Expatriates* (1968) and *Nigeria* (1974). He became Exxon's top editor for publications after *Look* folded.[19]

T. George Harris, who had fought in the Battle of the Bulge and was in the same class at Yale as William F. Buckley Jr., covered business, politics, and civil rights for *Look* in the 1960s. He was the first journalist to ask a presidential candidate, George Romney in 1968, for his tax returns, setting a precedent. Harris later became editor of *Psychology Today*.[20]

Leo Rosten, *Look*'s Polish-born jack-of-all-trades, wrote not only on art, religion, politics, and the luminaries who "made our world" but also on democracy and late 1960s radicals. "An author of academic bent is rarely given such freedom to act as gadfly, critic, . . . or such freedom to write," Rosten said. Poppy called him the "house intellectual," and Cowles called him "one of the most brilliantly creative people I have ever known." Having worked with Cowles in the Office of War Information, the publisher hired him in 1949, and his tenure with *Look* lasted until 1971. Rosten had a PhD in political science, was a screenwriter for a number of 1940s and 1950s Hollywood movies, wrote short stories for the *New Yorker* under a pseudonym, and wrote *The Joys of Yiddish* (1968).[21]

Patricia (Pat) Coffin, who had started at *Look* in 1942 and spent twenty-nine years with the magazine, succeeded Fleur Cowles as head of the Women's Department in 1955. She turned the department into a creative and wide-ranging "Special Features" division, which subsequently became "Modern Living." She oversaw *Look*'s travel stories, wrote regional features, and successfully pushed for more quasi-sociological stories like "Meet a Real Parisienne" and "Meet an Italian Career Woman." She put together a fifty-page package of stories on the status of American women in 1966, although her views on women were more traditional than Carbine's or Bergquist's. She was also a poet, a painter, and author of several children's books.[22]

Thomas Morgan—who reported as a staffer and freelancer on subjects from Appalachian poverty and the American Jewish community to a student exchange in India—created *Look*'s San Francisco-based "Ideas Group." He went on to become editor of the *Village Voice*, tried to buy the *Nation*, and married Nelson Rockefeller's daughter, Mary.[23]

William Attwood, *Look*'s French-born star foreign correspondent, joined the magazine in 1951 and was its Paris-based European editor until 1954. He accompanied Adlai Stevenson on his 1953 round-the-world trip, spent four hours on Fidel Castro's private plane interviewing the Cuban leader, wrote *Look*'s memorial tribute after Kennedy was assassinated, and drove six thousand miles through Eastern Europe with his wife, Simone, taking photos for a major story on the Soviet satellite states. When they came back from Europe in 1955, as a way to rediscover America, they drove across the United States in an Austin-Healey with red French license plates. He became JFK's ambassador to Guinea and LBJ's to Kenya in the early 1960s and wrote a book about Africa, *The Reds and the Blacks* (1967). He received multiple awards for foreign reporting and wrote six other books. Returning to *Look* in 1966, after his stints in government, he consulted Supreme Court chief justice Earl Warren about the appropriateness of an essay on whether freedom was dying in America. After leaving the magazine in 1970, he succeeded Bill Moyers as publisher of *Newsday*.[24]

Edward Korry succeeded Attwood as chief European correspondent, from 1954 to 1960. President Kennedy named him ambassador to Ethiopia. Later, as ambassador to Chile, he witnessed the 1973 coup that overthrew President Salvador Allende.[25]

Leonard Gross was *Look*'s next man in Paris, during the 1960s. During his twelve years with the magazine, he also covered Latin America and the West Coast. He authored and ghost-wrote more than twenty nonfiction and fiction books, including *The Last Jews in Berlin* (1981) and *The Memoirs of JFK* (2013), a novel imagining that Kennedy had survived Dallas.[26]

J. Robert Moskin, a historian who spent nineteen years with *Look* and coauthored a 1958 book on *The Decline of the American Male* with George Leonard, became foreign editor in 1966. He reported from hot spots like the Middle East, Vietnam, and Eastern Europe.[27]

Edmund Stevens, a Pulitzer Prize winner who the *New York Times* called "the dean of the Moscow press corps," covered the Soviet Union from 1950 for the *Christian Science Monitor*, through the *Look* years, until Mikhail Gorbachev's late 1980s reforms. He became the magazine's Moscow correspondent in 1956, and was the first American journalist for a major publication to report from Communist China, going to the country for *Look* later that year, despite State Department warnings. Stevens and his Russian wife were among the very few Americans to own a house in the USSR. During his many decades in the Soviet Union, he also wrote for *Time* and *Life*.[28]

Other writers covering international affairs included Christopher Wren and Joseph Roddy. After ten years with *Look*, Wren went to *Newsweek* before spending twenty-eight years with the *New York Times*. Jack Shepherd— who wrote for *Look* on subjects such as youth and working women—had gone to college with Wren at Dartmouth. Roddy went from *Look* to *Life* and back to *Look* between 1948 and 1970. Sam Castan, a daring foreign correspondent, was with the magazine from 1957 until he was killed in Vietnam at age thirty-one while reporting a story.[29]

Ira Mothner spent fifteen years with *Look*, covering Kennedy and Johnson-era policies, but also taking a yearly month-long sojourn in Hollywood to write celebrity profiles. He and Morgan worked for New York mayor

John Lindsay after the magazine folded. He devoted the rest of his life to drug-abuse issues, working with Phoenix House, a national substance-abuse treatment organization, cowriting books like *Drugs, Parents, and Children* (1972). He also wrote the well-regarded 1967 book *Among the Anti-Americans*.[30]

Jack Star, who was with *Look* from 1951 to 1971 and headed its Chicago bureau, wrote on topics ranging from abortion to the impact of computers on society. Frank Trippett was another *Look* writer who covered a little bit of everything during the 1960s—from Vice President Spiro Agnew and the beauty of Hawaii to sexual privacy and the popularity of German novelist Herman Hesse. Dan Fowler, who was hired in 1944, covered politics as well as subjects like unwed mothers, organized crime in Las Vegas, and Mexican braceros in the late 1940s and 1950s. Chandler Brossard, who wrote for *Look* between 1956 and 1967, was a novelist associated with Beat writers. The best known of his fifteen books, *Who Walk in Darkness* (1952), was appreciated by French critics as a "new wave," existential novel.[31]

Roland Berg was an award-winning writer who covered science and medicine from 1954 until it closed. John Osmundsen also wrote about science for *Look* and the *New York Times*.[32]

Sports was the province of Tim Cohane, who wrote some five hundred articles for *Look*, many on college football, between 1944 to 1967. Leonard Shecter, who was on staff during *Look*'s last years, coauthored the bestselling baseball expose *Ball Four* (1970). His reporting and book broke the longstanding sports-writing etiquette of not reporting what happened off the field.[33]

Jean Herrick, who had served in World War I at age fifteen, was *Look*'s Hollywood correspondent from the 1940s to 1967. Having started at the *Register*, he reported on the movie industry and its stars, and launched *Look*'s annual movie awards at the Cathay Theater in Los Angeles. Initially called "Achievement Awards," they ran from 1947 to 1967, and the first went to Gregory Peck and Jennifer Jones. The large Hollywood bureau that he supervised included writers Teme Brenner, Dan Fowler, and Marcia Reed, and photographers Maurice Terrell, Earl Theisen, and Sprague Talbott. Jack Hamilton was a later entertainment writer.[34]

Look's editorial research department and library were headed by William

J. Burke. Many writers, including Carbine, Dunbar, and Roddy began as researchers. The department did exploratory research to determine if a subject was story worthy, provided detailed background reports for writers, and was in constant communication with editors and writers "to carefully determine the slant, nature, and specific research requirements of the story," Cowles said. In addition to a library, the magazine had four to six fact-checkers in its later years—including Morton Hunt, later an award-winning science writer, psychologist, and author of twenty-one books—which resulted in extremely few mistakes.[35]

Assistant managing editors Myrick Land, a historian, and Martin Goldman and book reviewer Peter Prescott were among other notable editorial staff members. The many editorial and picture researchers; darkroom staff; and copy editors, like Martin Foldman, were out of the limelight, but key to *Look*'s success. Martha Stephens was Cowles's secretary from 1952 to 1985 and helped organize *Look* reunions after the magazine folded.[36]

The Art Department

The Art department was headed by three talented men, first Merle Armitage, then Allen Hurlburt from 1953 to 1967, and Will Hopkins from 1967 to 1971. Armitage and Hurlburt turned *Look* into one of America's best-designed magazines. Armitage was fifty-five years old when Cowles hired him in 1948 to head the department. Seen as an iconoclast, he brought new verve to the magazine, transforming it from the rag of the late 1930s into a glossy magazine acclaimed for its layouts. He restyled the covers and typography and made the color in *Look* the best in publishing, using both photogravure and letter-press, together with a new paper-coating process. He had already made his fortune as an opera and theater impresario and founder of the Los Angeles Grand Opera and had turned to designing and writing books on American artists.[37]

Hurlburt succeeded Armitage in 1953, making *Look* more visually appealing and elegant, improving the color with the Look-Kromatic printing process introduced in 1960, and creating a special issue at the beginning of each year. He focused on how text and images interacted, with the goal of maximum visual impact. Hurlburt conceived *Look*'s "Story Behind the

Painting" series, and won more than fifty art and design awards. After *Look*, Hurlburt wrote many books on design and founded *American Photographer* magazine.[38]

When Hurlburt was named art director for all of Cowles Communications in 1967, Hopkins succeeded him at *Look*, supervising a staff of about thirteen. "He was absolutely essential to the success of the look of the book," Fusco recalled. He "went a long way toward creating layouts that were revolutionary." Hopkins later headed a Minneapolis design firm.[39]

In 1963 Cowles lured artist Norman Rockwell to leave the *Saturday Evening Post*, where he was known for his largely celebratory images of American life, to do more "muckraking" painting for *Look*. In 1964 Rockwell created images of three slain civil-rights workers and of a Black girl who desegregated New Orleans' schools. Among the thirty paintings that Rockwell did for *Look* were a Soviet classroom, LBJ and Barry Goldwater during the 1964 presidential campaign, and a 1966 cover image of Peace Corps workers in a Bogota shantytown. Reflecting on how his work changed when he came to *Look*, Rockwell said: "For 47 years, I portrayed the best of all possible worlds—grandfathers, puppy dogs—things like that. That kind of stuff is dead now, and I think it's about time."[40]

Photographers

Just as Dan Mich was the leading figure behind *Look*'s editorial achievements, Arthur Rothstein was the "master of the lens" shaping the magazine's photographic success and mentoring many a photographer. He was hired by Cowles in 1940, after his time with the FSA, and stayed until *Look* folded in 1971, with a break to do photography for the army during World War II. Photos by early FSA photographers were published in *Look* during the last years of the Depression. Rothstein, who developed the six-stage photo essay process, won thirty-five awards. He published seven photojournalism books; organized a 1957–59 traveling exhibition of *Look* photos, "People in Pictures: *Look* at America"; worked with the Museum of Modern Art on photo exhibitions; and taught at Syracuse and Columbia Universities. The legendary director of photography was "very friendly and easy to work with, very helpful," Fusco said. "You could get to him and ask for help." Similarly, Kirkland praised him as "my champion and mentor, who helped me navigate a new editorial world." Many photographers praised Rothstein and Mich for letting them have considerable input about stories and layouts, which was quite different from *Life*.[41]

By the late 1940s, the magazine had about eight staff photographers, a picture research division, and a stable of freelancers. *Look*'s first photographers in the late 1930s and early 1940s included Marion Pease, Earl Theisen, and Frank Bauman. Other early photographers included Maurice Terrell, who played a *Look* photographer in *The Barkleys of Broadway*, and Sprague Talbott in Hollywood. Earl Theisen, Phillip Harrington, Robert Sandberg, Kenneth Eide, and a very young Stanley Kubrick were hired in the 1940s as New York-based staff photographers. James Hansen, a former bank clerk, covered the North African and Sicilian fronts during World War II. Michael (Tony) Vaccaro, who began his career as a photographer by taking photos while serving as an army infantry scout in the Second World War, spent two-and-a-half decades with the magazine, photographing celebrities, including artists like Pablo Picasso, Georgia O'Keefe, and Jackson Pollock.[42]

Kubrick, who became the renowned director of films such as *Dr. Strangelove* and *2001: A Space Odyssey*, started selling photos to the magazine as a teenager during World War II. He was hired in 1946 by picture editor Helen O'Brian, stayed for about five years, and shot about fifteen thousand images. His best-known *Look* photo, a man at a newsstand reading of FDR's death, was published when he was sixteen years old. Before embarking on his long cinematic career, he covered Sen. Robert Taft's 1948 presidential campaign, worked on a travel story on Portugal, and photographed political and entertainment-industry celebrities.[43]

In the 1950s and 1960s, noted staff photographers included Fusco, Karales, Tretick, Vachon, Charlotte Brooks, Doug Jones, Bob Lerner, Robert Vose, Milton Greene, Leonard Freed, Kirkland, Harrington, Theisen, and Terrell. At any given time, *Look* had about a dozen photographers on staff and contracted many freelancers.[44]

Karales, who joined *Look* in 1960, was one of the greatest visual chroniclers of the civil rights movement. He shot arguably the best-known photo of the movement—of the 1965 Selma to Montgomery march—as well as a stereotype-defying 1960 story of a Black speech therapist teaching white children in rural Iowa. He was given unequaled access to Martin Luther King Jr., with one photo showing King telling his seven-year-old daughter that they couldn't go to an amusement park. Andrew Young, Martin Luther King Jr.'s aide and, later, mayor of Atlanta, said that Karales captured the "complexity of emotions intertwined with the hopes and hardships of the struggle." Karales, the son of Greek immigrants, later covered the war in Vietnam. His photos had "the weight of history and the grace of art," *Village Voice* critic Vince Aletti said.[45]

Fusco, another star photographer who went to Ohio State with Karales and had been a combat photographer in Korea, was with the magazine from 1957 to 1971. Recalling a Cuban rally at which Che Guevara was to speak, he was told he didn't need permission to take photos but was hauled away and jailed for two days for taking some shots. He rode Bobby Kennedy's funeral train and took an extraordinary series of photos as the train slowly passed mourning track-side crowds from New York to Washington. He was close with George Leonard and accompanied him to Esalen and photographed the Korean and Iraq wars before and after his years with *Look*. With Jack Fox and Doug Jones, Fusco also published a 1967 photo book on the era's youth rebellion, *Youth Quake*. As his wife Pat said, "The stories that meant the most to Paul were always those that involved social change, or the lack of it."[46]

Tretick, whose famous photographs of John Kennedy's three-year-old son playing under the Resolute desk in the Oval Office and of JFK and his advisors during the Cuban Missile Crisis, was once called "President Kennedy's Boswell." A marine during World War II who became a photographer for UPI, he joined *Look* in 1961. His photos were included in Bergquist's 1965 book, *A Very Special President*. Tretick photographed every president from Truman to George H. W. Bush, and published two books on Richard Nixon. After his *Look* years, he helped found *People* magazine and later turned down President Jimmy Carter's request to be his personal photographer. Leonard Freed also took many photos of the civil rights movement for *Look*.[47]

Vachon—like Rothstein came from the FSA, documenting Depression-era hardship throughout the country. He spent twenty-three years with the magazine, shooting images of poverty, race, and war as well as the first photo of Joe DiMaggio with Marilyn Monroe. Harrington shot Mao's China in 1956, did a pioneering photo essay on developmentally disabled children, and covered Africa and Vietnam. Sandberg produced a photo essay on Hiroshima a decade after the bombing. Brooks, *Look*'s first female photographer—only a handful of other women were staff photographers in the 1940s and 1950s—was originally pigeonholed to do photos of women's issues but went on to contribute to 450 features during her nineteen years with the magazine. These included features on the integration of Little Rock's Central High School in 1957 and Taiwan. She was also president of *Look*'s Newspaper Guild bargaining unit. Kirkland, who was with *Look* from 1960 to 1970, was one of the most renowned celebrity photographers, taking an iconic photo of Marilyn Monroe wrapped in silky white sheets and spending three weeks photographing Judy Garland. Hungarian-born photographer Andrew St. George frequently contributed to *Look*, and his best-known images were of Castro before and after the revolution. Milton Greene was hired as a fashion photographer in 1953.[48]

Photographers were not typecast; instead, they were assigned entertainment stories one month and ones about poverty another. They would carry knapsacks, camera bags, and shoulder slings, typically with four to six cameras—Nikons, Hasselblads, Rolleiflexes, and large-format eight-by-tens, a dozen lenses, many filters, lights, tripods, clamps, and dozens of rolls of film. These would come back to the cavernous, well-staffed darkroom long headed by Seymour Silow. Photos by some of the twentieth century's best photographers, including Art Kane, Richard Avedon, Cal Bernstein, Arnold Newman, Irving Penn, Archie Lieberman, and Susan Greenberg-Wood were also published in *Look* on a freelance basis. Irving Penn produced a twelve-page spread of photos of Paris in 1966.[49]

The photo research department also pulled off some extraordinary coups. In 1957 Betty Leavitt, *Look*'s picture research director, and Dorothea Penizek, of the Special Editorial department, went to Munich to meet with the daughter of Hitler's personal photographer, Heinrich Hoffmann. They convinced her to turn over 215 photos that had been buried in a Bavarian forest for use in a twelve-page 1958 spread, "The Insane World of Adolf Hitler." Despite Cowles's closeness to Eisenhower, Kay Summersby—reputedly Ike's mistress—gave Mich photos of the two on a beach, which *Look* published.[50]

Illustrious Contributors

A number of other notable figures passed through *Look* during their journalism careers. These included sociologist William H. Whyte, Joseph Heller (who spent two years in the advertising department many years before writing *Catch* 22), and student radical Jesse Kornbluth. *Look*'s many freelancers who wrote essays and opinion pieces significantly added to readers' understanding and perspectives on America and the world.

The many noted freelancers that *Look* commissioned in the 1950s, who were paid handsomely, included labor leader Walter Reuther, anthropologist Margaret Mead, Supreme Court justice William O. Douglas, historians Henry Steele Commager and Arnold Toynbee, presidential advisor Bernard Baruch, philosopher Bertrand Russell, Republican leader Robert Taft, future Canadian prime minister Lester Pearson, columnist Walter Lippmann, business leader Paul Hoffman (who called for a "Supreme Council of Peace" to be co-equal with the joint chiefs of staff), writer Edgar Snow, and Hollywood gossip columnist Hedda Hopper. Russell wrote four articles between 1953 and 1958, and Lippmann wrote five between 1953 and 1961.[51]

Its 1960s and early 1970s the roster of illustrious contributors included Eugene O'Neill, foreign policy expert George Kennan, Harry Truman, economist Paul Samuelson, Eric Sevareid, William F. Buckley Jr., Stalin's daughter Svetlana Alliluyeva, General Omar Bradley, Martin Luther King Jr., Henry Kissinger, Richard Nixon, and writers Pearl S. Buck, Norman Mailer, Gore Vidal, Italian journalist Oriana Fallaci, Philip Roth, Leo Litwak, and James Michener. The magazine launched the careers of many well-known journalists such as Carl Rowan and film and TV critic Gene Shalit.[52]

Other academics, political commentators, and noted journalists who wrote for *Look* were also overwhelmingly liberal or farther left. These included William Hodding Carter II, Saul Alinsky, Daniel Boorstin, David Brinkley, Allen Drury, Nat Hentoff, John Gardner, Russell Baker, Marquis

Childs, Gloria Steinem, and Dick Gregory. Buckley, whose "Ivy League voice, . . . masklike face, cuff-shooting elegance, and jaunty irreverence" were cleverly described in an article about his wife, was a rare conservative to write for *Look*.[53]

They typically wrote erudite, big-picture essays like Boorstin's meditation on "the end of the two-party world." Childs discussed the 1969 Strategic Arms Limitation Treaty as one essential step to prevent "nuclear Armageddon." Hentoff wrote about censorship in an article on the Smothers Brothers TV show. Jesse Jackson, George Wallace, Bella Abzug, and others wrote about "America's unfinished business" in one of *Look*'s last issues. Ted Kennedy called for greater political autonomy for American Indians.[54]

On the Business Side

Cowles had a number of key right-hand men (they were virtually all men) over the years. None was more important than Marvin Whatmore, who was with *Look* from beginning to end. He served in many roles—as general manager, vice president, president, and chairman of Cowles Communications, and his daughter married Cowles's son.[55]

Donald Perkins, who also worked for *Look* for most of its history, was advertising director and executive vice president. From the eleventh floor of the *Look* building, he presided over regional advertising offices in Chicago, Detroit, Boston, San Francisco, and Los Angeles. Alan Waxenberg, who headed the Detroit office, recalled that Perkins was "a demanding guy who expected quality and performance, and he got it." Merrill Clough, another loyal executive from 1937 to 1971, was business manager and controller.[56]

Vernon Myers rose from advertising manager to become publisher and president of CCI's *Look* division during its last years. He joined *Look* in 1938 and opened the magazine's first offices outside Des Moines—in New York, Hollywood, and Washington.[57]

James Milloy, who was with *Look* from 1941 to 1968 and had extensive contacts in Washington, became Cowles's "fixer" and lobbyist. The Des Moines-based circulation department was headed by Samuel ("Shap") Shapiro, who was a twenty-three-year *Look* veteran. He led the long-running circulation war with *Life* as *Look* and CCI's circulation director.[58]

Other executives included subscription manager Lester Suhler; Alan Waxenberg, central advertising director from 1958 on; and Gilbert Maurer, an advertising manager who headed many divisions of Cowles Communications and was publisher of its short-lived *Venture* magazine. Joseph Bayard, who spent two and half decades with the magazine, rose to become head of advertising sales. Les Doyle, later a founder of ad agency Doyle Dane Bernbach, was also on *Look*'s staff in 1937.[59]

Joel Harnett was the longtime head of marketing and sales promotion, which occupied the twelfth floor. His team conducted research to support advertising staff and developed ad campaigns for *Look*. Thomas R. Shepard Jr., who became *Look*'s last publisher in 1965, was a conservative who condemned the "liberal press" to advertisers, much to the consternation of the editorial staff who was part of the "liberal press."[60]

It is notable that, in addition to Cowles, Mich, Perkins, Whatmore, Myers, Herrick, Suhler, and others were from the Midwest. Even after it moved to New York, *Look* had a whiff of a Midwestern, populist sensibility.[61]

5

Singing the Praises of
Postwar Prosperity

As post–World War II economic growth transformed America and vastly expanded the middle class, *Look* was a leader of the chorus that not only celebrated this ever-more-prosperous era but also linked it with American greatness and supremacy. Despite widespread fears of a postwar depression, accelerating economic growth in the late 1940s led politicians, economists, business leaders, academics, and journalists to marvel at America's increasing prosperity.

Leon Keyserling, President Truman's economic advisor, wrote in 1949 about the nation's "unparalleled prosperity" and argued that economic growth was the "new organizing principle for the United States." In 1945 the United Auto Workers (UAW) published the pamphlet *Purchasing Power for Prosperity*. The Committee for Economic Development (CED), with its roster of leaders in business, academia, media, and government, spoke of how a mixed economy—with business, government, and labor working together—was the recipe for growth and abundance for all.[1]

The Advertising Council's 1948 *Miracle of America* booklet, which waxed rhapsodic about the wealth being created by America's free-enterprise system, was reprinted in *Look*. The council—a liberal business group that, like the CED, favored a mixed economy—played a major role in shaping postwar America's image of itself as a bounteous country, unprecedented in history and clearly superior to the nation's archenemy, the Soviet Union. With its "Selling Our Free Enterprise System" campaign in the late 1940s and its "Future of America" and "People's Capitalism" campaigns in the mid-1950s, *The Miracle of America* was not only a jubilant celebration of U.S. economic supremacy but it also espoused a politics that has not existed in the United States since at least the 1970s: government, business, and labor would work collaboratively to drive economic growth, whose fruits would be relatively equitably divided. It outlined an agenda of increasing "productivity, . . . protection for the individual, . . . and recognition of human values as a prerequisite to better living." The council blanketed the country with ads, billboards, and school curricula.[2]

Journalists became the herald of this euphoric view of the American economy. Magazines such as *Look, Fortune, Life*, the *Saturday Evening Post*, and others published story after story about how the booming economy was bringing higher wages, houses with "labor-saving" appliances, and cars and TVs to the vast majority of Americans. *Look* published stories like "I Predict We'll Have Greater Prosperity," by Eisenhower's commerce secretary Sinclair Weeks, with side-by-side forecasts by government leaders of good times ahead as far as the eye could see. The era's extraordinary fascination with prosperity was well expressed in a lengthy 1960 story that declared: "No people in history ever had it as easy, or so good," adding that Americans would enjoy a "plentiful existence right through the Sixties and maybe forever."[3]

Look's nearly thirty-five-year history almost perfectly coincided with America's long economic boom, from the end of World War II to the late 1960s. Yearly economic growth averaged about 4 percent during this twenty-year period, real wages nearly tripled, home ownership increased by 50 percent, and inequality declined. As John Kennedy memorably said, "a rising tide" was lifting all boats.

Look, naturally, covered this story, and did so in a number of ways. There were staff-written articles and essays by prominent figures that told—and touted—the sheer economic facts of abundance. Some of these pieces focused on mass prosperity, growing equality, and the apparent withering of social classes. Other stories examined economic policy, showing support for a mixed economy and Keynesian demand management—the prevailing views among policymakers from FDR to Nixon. Most *Look* prosperity articles were written to show how abundance touched everyday Americans. These articles portrayed and shaped a view of the United States as the economic wonder of world history and of most Americans as incomparably fortunate.

This chapter will focus on how *Look* lavishly acclaimed the American economy during the go-go years between the 1940s and mid-1960s, although it will also address the growing recognition of a dark underbelly to a society obsessed with economic growth—poverty, alienation, and pollution. It will highlight articles and ideas that shaped economic and sociological debate, as well as public policy. For example, *Look* published leading economists who influenced postwar policies and extensively praised President Johnson's war on poverty.

There were frequent articles about consumption—which was seen as a purely good thing until the last years of the magazine. Stories about technological, medical, and other scientific advances usually conveyed the message that Americans were not only richer but could lead better lives than those of prior generations or people elsewhere in the world. (See chapter 6.)

The magazine, which was obsessed with cars, and whose pages were always filled with automaker ads, published a 1939 article, "The Auto Industry Looks 20 Years Ahead," hinting at the magazine's grand postwar economic coverage: "Increase automobile ownership, say Detroit's economists, and you increase standards of living all along the line—in home building, in household equipment, in every other field."[4]

The torrent of stories about America's world-beating wealth began as World War II was ending. The tone was set by guest columns by three of the era's most influential liberal businessmen—Henry Kaiser, whose Kaiser Shipyard built warships at lightning speed and whose Kaiser Permanente became a model for top-notch employer-provided health care; Eric Johnston, the longtime president of the U.S. Chamber of Commerce who urged cooperation with both of the nation's two big union confederations, the American Federation of Labor (AFL) and the more progressive Congress of Industrial Organizations (CIO); and Paul Hoffman, the Studebaker president who oversaw implementation of the Marshall Plan, led the Ford Foundation, and became the first administrator of the United Nations Development Program.

In early 1945 Kaiser wrote of his "new hobby—it's planning a peaceful, prosperous world" based on tripartite cooperation between business, government, and labor. Two articles by Johnston and Hoffman in December 1946 and August 1947 were emblematic of *Look*'s rapturous economic reporting and analysis. Both men expressed supreme confidence, using data, economic theory, and rhetorical flourishes to paint a picture of the glorious years ahead.[5]

"Your standard of living can be doubled in 20 years, if labor and management will get together and produce," Johnston wrote. Telling readers how "more output means more wealth," he said that America's prodigious economy could "make every man a capitalist." He equally reprimanded management for "feather-nesting" and labor for "feather-bedding" with a sort of balance that would be unheard of from future presidents of the Chamber of Commerce. "Planning" was not a dirty word, as Johnston—like other business leaders, economists, and politicians—called for a "20-year plan" to ensure prosperity.[6]

Hoffman reminded *Look*'s readers of how the standard workweek had been cut from sixty to forty hours in half a century, and promised that living standards would continue to grow. "In all economic history, there is no record of wealth production to match that of the United States in the last century." Hoffman, also a leader of the CED, argued the economic benefits of free trade and was among those who began to equate American greatness with its economic prowess.[7]

Financier Bernard Baruch argued in 1951 in *Look* for greater state control of the economy, and oil magnate J. Paul Getty authored a surprising essay on how "free and honest labor unions helped us create this way of life."[8]

While these supremely optimistic business leaders were highlighting the beginnings of postwar abundance, *Look*'s own writers and editors began to describe the emerging boom with considerable statistical detail, drawing on the new precepts of national income accounting and economic recordkeeping. Accurately describing America's growing and more equal distribution of national income in words and charts, a 1946 article reported that national income had increased by 93 percent between 1929 and 1946, while wages had grown by 107 percent and corporate dividends had declined by 14 percent. "Since 1929, labor has received an increasing share of national income, while the owners . . . have received a declining share," *Look* wrote, sounding more like a happy social democrat than a defender of big business.

Preaching the popular new gospel of consumer-driven growth, the article went on: "Vast amounts of goods and services cannot be consumed by a few wealthy people." Delving into the history of economic theory, *Look* derided the 1930s idea of a "mature" economy that would no longer grow. Reporting that economists now believed in an "expanding economy," it echoed Hoffman in concluding: "It is no accident that the American worker has the highest standards of living in the world and in the history of the world."[9]

These kinds of statistical/historical articles, larded with superlatives were particularly common during the Truman years. The appetite for statistics was astonishing for the time. "We Are Living Better in 1949," which *Look* published that May, not only put forth the axiom that "more goods means better living for more people," but it also demonstrated the principle of rising productivity with a chart showing that it only took ten minutes of work to buy a gallon of milk, compared to fifteen minutes twenty years earlier. In 1951, sixteen "top economists" predicted that low-paid workers would earn more money, as GNP would grow by 10 percent that year; the actual figure that year was just 2 percentage points lower.[10]

The notion of "people's capitalism" was conveyed in the 1952 story "Wall Street Works for Main Street." A photo of a friendly stockbroker with a young couple was accompanied by the assertion that "the big investors in today's stock market are average Americans." This sort of liberal populism also could be found in a 1949 article called "USA Opportunity Unlimited" that described how immigrants and others—like David Sarnoff of RCA, Charles Edward Wilson of GE,[11] and William Knudsen of GM—could go from humble beginnings to leadership of major corporations.[12]

During the Eisenhower Administration, the macroeconomic cheerleading continued, but *Look*'s articles on economic growth and abundance were increasingly told through stories about the everyday lives of newly prosperous Americans and their communities. In 1951 the magazine displayed the wonders of supermarkets, where any food could be found. A nine-page photo essay in 1953 showed TV host Bert Parks with a housewife gazing dreamily at a cornucopia of consumer goods. Children's growing stock of toys and kitchens with miraculous new appliances were part of this new normal. A 1957 article suggested that second homes were within reach of the average middle-class family and could even be built with do-it-yourself kits. A tongue-in-cheek pictorial treatise even touted the high living standards of American cats.[13]

New housing for the rapidly expanding middle class was yet another symbol of the nation's wealth. *Look* spoke of America's "utopian suburbs." The magazine even touted its own postwar house design. The three massive suburban Levittowns built before 1960 were often covered by *Look*. A 1948 story on the new Levittown development on Long Island included photos by John Vachon of couples in one of the six thousand homes that sold for as little as $8,000 each. With the GI Bill and government housing subsidies, many families realized the American Dream of becoming a homeowner for even less money.[14]

Five years later, *Look* wrote about families in Levittown, Pennsylvania, who now had the desire and money to build home additions like porches and to enclose carports. A photo of smiling "add-a-room" specialist Daniel O'Reilly holding models of a sunporch and bedroom was accompanied by Bob Lerner's photos of the Hunter family enjoying their new room with knotty pine paneling and chintz decor. Even Black families could move to Levittown, *Look* reported in 1958. Despite initial neighborly racism, a family the magazine profiled was ultimately welcomed.[15]

In 1960 *Look* returned to Levittown, Long Island, in a story marveling at its "instant houses" for the middle class, with photos by Karales of two industrial designers in front of a model house. Three years later, *Look* and Lerner turned their attention to the New Jersey Levittown to once again celebrate affordable home ownership. The story focused on Ralph and Gerd Switzer and their children happily ensconced in their first home. Paradise for America's expanding middle class was depicted in articles on booming suburbs, like one in Florida where happy residents were shown boating on Lake Suwanee.[16]

Look imparted the idea that home ownership was a great investment and key to prosperity. "The housing market, with its long-term rise in values, has done far more than the stock market, with its limited group of customers, to turn the American majority toward capitalist-minded affluence," the magazine accurately said.[17]

In *Look* and other print media of the time, the American consumer was the gloriously happy antithesis of the Soviet Union's Stakhanovite worker. As early as 1946, *Look* published a short-lived feature called "Primer on Better Living." The first column focused on how "shopping is going to be made easier," with more goods and round-the clock hours. This theme continued throughout most of the magazine's history.[18]

"The great American automobile" was "a symbol of prosperity that is the envy of the world," reported George Koether, *Look*'s auto editor, in 1956. Amid pages of color photos of shiny new cars, he marveled that 71 percent of the world's passenger cars were owned by Americans. Aside from being a status symbol, cars "determine(d) to a large degree how much prosperity America will enjoy," another article declared.[19]

Look published lavish, full-color displays of each year's new models in the late 1950s and 1960s. Its pages were filled with a plethora of other car stories by Koether and staffer Siler Freeman. Among color ads for GM, Ford, Chrysler, and Studebaker in virtually every issue, one early 1950s Ford ad captured the nexus between prosperity, technology, progress, and the good life with the headline "The American Road": "We believe that America can keep traveling on it toward an ever better life for all."

There were "custom cars for everyone" and cars that needed no care. The new gas turbine Firebird, high-horsepower engines, William Ford's new Continental, and auto racing were among many car-related stories in 1954 alone. Auto "stylist" Virgil Exner, who brought an aerodynamic look to cars and helped popularize tail fins, was profiled. Despite the fetish with new cars, *Look* made used cars respectable in a story that same year. In 1956 sixty years of automotive history were chronicled by Koether, with a six-page photo spread.[20]

Leisure was an especially popular subject, as economists and politicians began to predict and worry Americans that—with automation and rising prosperity—work weeks would continue to shorten and people wouldn't know what to do with all their free time. Accompanied by an overhead photo of a besuited man, two women in bathing suits, and two dressed women in lounge chairs, a 1955 article surveyed how Americans spent their three thousand free waking hours per year on entertainment, sports, clothes, food, furniture, instruments, equipment, and "gimmicks." This photo story also showed a dance party, a tennis player serving, and a young man and two women playing water polo. A 1956 piece by Pat Coffin on "The Great American Weekend" was accompanied by color drawings and photos of picnics and casual clothes, telling readers that "our abounding prosperity means mass recreation on a staggering scale." Other forms of recreation for the middle class included backyard swimming pools and vacation homes. Retirement was depicted as the easy life, with "pensions made bigger and bigger."[21]

More evidence of America's bountiful economy, buoyed by new paid vacations, was the growth of holiday travel. A 1954 story showed a Minneapolis secretary—"any energetic American working girl who can save $1,000"—visiting London, Paris, Rome, and the Amalfi Coast on a three-week vacation. The idea that "any American" could enjoy exotic vacations was reprised in many stories, including a 1958 report on a schoolteacher's African safari. Other "dream vacations" and travel feature stories, decked out with color photos of destinations from Seattle and New York to Paris and Africa, appeared with increasing frequency in the mid-to-late 1950s. A fourteen-page section on the 1960 outlook for travel in Europe was followed by travel stories on the Pacific Northwest, New England, Florence, Japan, and Portugal, among others, during the next few years.[22]

Other magazines published similar encomia to the U.S. economy, yet few reached the massive audience that *Look* had or relied so much on tell-ing the story of growing prosperity by showing individuals and families experiencing their new affluence. Henry Luce's lavishly produced *Fortune* turned several of its series into books like *USA: The Permanent Revolution* (1951), playing off Leon Trotsky's theory of the same name, and *The Fabu-lous Future* (1956). *Life* hailed "extra luxuries for families" and "the luckiest generation" in a 1954 "special issue" on "U.S. Growth: Our Biggest Year ... and the Basis for a Bigger Future." In an editorial in *Life*, Luce proclaimed: "The American Business Economy, in a tacit deal with government, has licked the most serious problem of the economic cycle, namely real want in the midst of plenty." The *New York Times* also published lengthy annual "reviews" detailing the marvels of the economy.[23]

The big-picture articles on American prosperity may have reached their apogee with five long stories in the mid-1950s. In the first *Look* issue of 1955, a package of articles gloated about the country's record income and employment, low inflation, dazzling research, worker skills, natural resources, and wise government economic policies. Ike's commerce secretary, Sin-clair Weeks, described how all was right with the U.S. economy, and Sen. Hubert Humphrey (D-MN) wrote how government action could make this the best year in the nation's economic history. In the very next issue, Fletcher Knebel wrote a paean to the welfare state, citing the many ways in which government benefits so many Americans and how Republicans have expanded Social Security, Unemployment Insurance, and policies to increase home ownership. Writing in *Look*, Geoffrey Crowther, editor of the *Economist*, wondered whether the historic cycle of booms and busts might be over since "governments accept the duty of flattening out fluctuations."[24]

Mike Cowles—who was chairman of the CED's Information Committee in the late 1950s—also wrote approvingly of 1955 survey results that found only 16 percent of Americans saying that big business and big government were "bad." This effusiveness was repeated in many of Cowles's speeches. Addressing the Screen Directors Guild in 1951, he predicted that the United States would "enjoy [its] greatest prosperity in the next half dozen years."[25]

Attwood wrote a remarkably upbeat mid-1955 article based on his ten-thousand-mile, twenty-eight-state driving tour. Not only were Americans "acquiring at 35 the things they used to work for until they were 65," but the culture was also rapidly changing for the better. Television "has made people more sophisticated," he wrote. And the "battle for [racial] equality is almost won," with "the white-supremacy diehards" beating their retreat.[26]

Ben Duffy, president of the BBDO advertising agency, summed up the stunning nature of the U.S. economy and the great changes it was bringing for most Americans, in a 1956 article:

> For many of us, the next few years may be so economically fruitful that we will be identifying ourselves with another income group, living in another neighborhood, and leading fuller and more meaningful lives....
>
> We are discovering new places for travel, putting together personal record collections, building dream houses and doing the things we were planning and promising ourselves years ago we would do ... Not only are Americans earning more, but it takes them fewer hours to earn it....
> The workweek is shrinking, while real earnings are steadily going up....
> One of the amazing things about the American standard of living is the availability of time for people to do the many and varied things that they desire or are required to do.... There are more Americans than ever before in the middle-income group.... [America's] outpouring of goods provides the wide choices in cars, washing machines, hair sprays, lawn mowers, toothbrushes and in almost anything else Americans set out to buy.[27]

The Soaring Sixties or the Dark Sides of Prosperity

Look became more ambivalent about prosperity in the 1960s, even though the economy thrived and most Americans were getting richer. The magazine's writers, photographers, and editors depicted a more nuanced, less upbeat picture of abundance, consumerism, the mixed economy, big business, unions, and economic prospects and devoted much more attention to the realities of poverty and environmental pollution. The sixties were a decade of considerable tumult—about not only civil rights and the Vietnam War but also these economic issues. Like the 1950s these were also years when images and articles in mass media like *Look* had a dramatic effect on readers' beliefs—exposing people to new facts and ideas, and often changing how they thought about many aspects of American life.

The overwhelmingly bullish first issue of the decade was "The Soaring Sixties." It included a five-page Attwood article as well as stories of seven middle-class or more well-to-do people. Drawing on one of Gallup's polls, the article reported that Americans expected greater prosperity but also wanted more spent on the country's needs. It depicted a comfortable country in which 78 percent were optimistic. Describing the populace in terms that would seem ludicrous a generation later, he wrote: "Taxes are accepted as inevitable. . . . And big government is no longer resented or feared. In fact, government is trusted to an alarming degree." In short, the country was a "pond of calm and contentment."[28]

That same issue expressed a tinge of ambivalence about economic development and urban renewal. In an article about New York—"Culture City"—photos showing where the grand Lincoln Center performing-arts complex was to be built also hinted at the toll that progress would take: a neighborhood of two-to-five-story brownstones and neighborhood small businesses would disappear.[29]

Nonetheless, the happy story of U.S. wealth continued in the early 1960s. John Gunther wrote in 1962 and 1965 about "a society that spreads its multifarious benefits widely" in "an age of limitless abundance." Another article, by George Leonard, said that American youth had been "reared during a time of unprecedented prosperity, [and] a majority of them take a rising standard of living for granted."[30]

In 1964 *Look* reported that average family income had doubled in less than twenty years and that more people became homeowners during that period than in the entire preceding history of the United States. (The home ownership rate was only two percentage points higher by 2020.) The following year, another article spoke effusively of how the country was "riding history's highest flood tide" of plenty, musing again about whether the economic cycle had come to an end.[31]

The last of the magazine's grand tributes to American prosperity came in a 116-page package of stories in 1966 called "California: The First Mass Aristocracy Anytime, Anywhere." Using the backdrop of thriving Californians whose high school graduates went to college at an unprecedented rate, T. George Harris wrote about the "wealthy masses," who poets would lyrically lionize one day. He concluded that "the overriding reality is abundance widely shared, and multiplied, through an interwoven public and private economy." Leonard called the issue a "manifesto," saying that what was happening in the state was "a new game with new rules"; many readers saw it as a putdown of the East and the Establishment. Earlier, Harris and Leonard had put together a 1962 issue on California, describing it as "a vast laboratory of social change," a harbinger of "tomorrow's hopes and tomorrow's headaches," a month before *Life* published a less inspiring issue.[32]

The Affluent Society?

Harvard economist John Kenneth Galbraith had written in 1958 that America was a nation of "private opulence and public squalor." Despite the prevailing hoopla, *Look* did not ignore the rougher edges of the economy and was periodically critical of big business.[33]

Before *Look*'s first edition, Cowles contacted photographer Roy Stryker, asking if he could send photos of the worst conditions in the South; a feature on sharecroppers was published in its March 1937 edition. The 1950s also saw articles on the fate of the Okies and the hard lives of migrant laborers. The 1952 article by Socialist Norman Thomas damned the 1 percent of corporations that owned 74 percent of corporate assets and called for greater economic planning.[34]

Look took a hard look at poverty in America in July 1959. It was the same month that Michael Harrington published the first of his articles in *Commentary* magazine that later became *The Other America* (1962), credited with galvanizing the War on Poverty. Carbine's words and Fusco's photos shined a light on coal miners in Harlan County, Kentucky, for the magazine's millions of readers. "In a time of plenty throughout most of the nation, some people in mid-USA are suffering acute privation," she wrote. "Our economy has never enjoyed a higher level, yet thousands don't know where their next dime will come from."[35]

Look also covered poverty and hardship throughout the world from its earliest days. The postwar food crisis in Europe, deep poverty in Africa and India, and lower living standards in the Soviet bloc were all familiar to the magazine's readers.[36]

The magazine described the plight of unemployed middle-aged men and the white-collar "rat race," a term coined in the mid-1950s. In 1958 Attwood called it "the price in stress that Americans are paying for their material abundance."[37]

Knebel called poverty—"want amid plenty"—a "puzzle" in "an era of growing national abundance." Harrington wrote about poverty for *Look* in 1964. A fifteen-page section in 1967 praised President Lyndon Johnson's War on Poverty, describing "the American economy [as] a long line of shiny slot machines. Most of them are rigged to pay off. . . . It's a great game: Almost everybody wins. But some machines are busted . . . [and] they gobble down hope." Even the California issue included an article on poverty in Watts, where riots had broken out the year before.[38]

Lord C. P. Snow, the British chemist, novelist, and government official, wrote in *Look* that it was a "delusion" that America would always be the world's richest country, and Gunnar Myrdal authored a grim article about a "stiffening class structure" and a potential "unemployment economy" as the demand for unskilled labor declines. "The problem will get bleaker" for high-school dropouts, two articles reported. As early as 1961, *Look* worried that automation, while increasing production and leisure, might lead to the end of "a working wage with which to buy" goods. All a far cry from the prevailing mantra of "abundance for all."[39]

The magazine posed the question of whether abundance was responsible for growing avarice and immorality in a 1960 issue, with articles by Walter Lippmann, Lionel Trilling, Attwood, and others. Prompted by congressional hearings in the wake of the 1959 "Payola" scandal involving a TV game show, Lippmann posited that the reason "we accept cheating" was because this was "a self-indulgent generation" guided by "the everlasting pursuit of the ever-fleeting object of desire." Attwood bluntly asked if "our moral standards [have] been destroyed by the pursuit of the dollar," adding that a business "deal once considered questionable would now be considered shrewd." "Has money become God?" was emblazoned on the cover of a 1963 issue titled "Morality U.S.A."[40]

The twin concerns that Americans were consuming much more than what they really needed and that there was limited oversight of consumer product safety increased in the 1960s. Ralph Nader's expose of preventable dangers in car design reinforced these ideas that many businesses were putting profit ahead of consumer well-being. Nader's revelations about the lack of auto safety in his 1965 book, *Unsafe at Any Speed*, sparked several *Look* articles between 1965 and 1967. Al Rothenberg, who succeeded Siler Freeman as business editor in 1963, wrote that the "car is fast becoming an abbreviation for carnage." A result of Nader's book and such reporting led President Johnson to create a National Transportation Safety Agency in 1966—whose head, William Haddon, was profiled in *Look*. LBJ also convinced Congress to establish a Cabinet-level Department of Transportation.[41]

In response, Elisha Gray II, the chairman of the newly formed Council of Better Business Bureaus, promised *Look*'s readers that business would police itself to "ensure consumer satisfaction." Recognizing that many consumers "accuse business of bad faith," he pledged that effective self-regulation would ensure that "our consumers are the best informed in the world, and our businessmen the most responsive to their needs."[42]

Picking up the language of the New Left on worker alienation, Chandler Brossard described even the well-educated American man discovering that "his degree bears no real relation to his job or to his survival or meaning." "Often he has a job that is so disengaged from his dignity that, in order to keep it, he has to become a surrealist," he wrote in 1967. Another article wrote of long-term unemployed skilled workers who once would have been "snapped up immediately"; now, they might be "lost to themselves and the nation."[43]

Look, like the country, was somewhat slow to make the link between prosperity and environmental problems, although Sen. Abraham Ribicoff (D-CT) wrote an early, 1963 article on the dangers of air pollution, calling for passage of his proposed Clean Air Act, and Leo Rosten also reported on air pollution that year. Frank Trippett wrote that "the counterpart of increasing opulence will be deepening filth." In an eight-page article in early 1971, a year before the Club of Rome's *Limits to Growth*—the hugely influential book on the environmental implications of prosperity—William Hedgepeth questioned the once conventional wisdom that growth is an unmitigated good.[44]

Ultimately Optimism

Despite its hard-hitting stories and grim depictions of a country whose wealth no longer meant unalloyed good lives for all, *Look* generally returned to the optimistic spirit that guided it from its earliest days.

Eric Sevareid, in one of five articles he wrote for *Look*, denounced naysayers calling America a "sick society" just weeks after Martin Luther King Jr.'s assassination in April 1968 sparked riots in more than one hundred cities. Sevareid, a CBS newsman, predicted that Americans' incomes would soar by the year 2000. As a result of a coming "second scientific-industrial revolution," he confidently spoke of a "guarantee" of a "great lifting of . . . the ordinary people."[45]

A strange 1970 article by Soviet futurist Nikolai Amosoff forecast a society in which "abundance has eliminated class and social strife" by 1991. Even the article about long-term unemployment saw an end to the problem in a forthcoming "computer job-matching service," and its stories about the environment frequently promised that solutions were around the corner. During the magazine's last months in 1971, Ira Mothner expected employee benefits to continue to expand, and Alabama governor George Wallace predicted: "We can reach new industrial heights in five years."[46]

The overarching economic story during the magazine's thirty-five years was that most Americans were becoming richer. *Look* helped them see the ways in which abundance touched their lives, with just enough data—as well as human stories and much commentary—to reinforce this story line. This optimism was buoyed by the parallel story of scientific and technological progress. When poverty, pollution, or other clouds appeared, *Look* reassured its readers that the nation had the capacity to solve any problem. As John Poppy later said: "Hopefulness was key to the pieces in *Look*. It didn't aim to show how awful things are, but rather, here are what people are doing to build a better America."[47]

6

Anything Is Possible

The Boons (and Banes) of Technology

The heroic tale of America's mighty postwar economy and the good life that it brought most Americans went hand in hand with the story of new scientific and technological marvels. Technology was a gateway to unimaginable, exciting new frontiers. It was another spark lighting the stunning optimism of mid-twentieth-century America. It is here where this story intersects with *Look*. Technological progress loomed large for a magazine whose philosophy was "tough-minded optimism," undergirded by the belief that there would always be solutions to the country's problems. Mike Cowles frequently included "optimism" in the titles of his speeches. In one of his many talks to business leaders, he said: "The American people are fantastically optimistic today," adding that optimism helps insure prosperity.[1]

As *Look* told its readers, factors other than technology were at least as crucial for the nation's wondrous, growing economy—enlightened public policies, physical and human capital investment, unions, pent-up demand from the Depression, the global postwar recovery, the housing boom, the belief in a strong middle class, and business-government (and, sometimes, labor) cooperation.

However, scientific discoveries, new technological innovations, consumer "gadgets" (as they were called), and advances in medicine, transportation, engineering, and other forms of applied science played a huge role in improving living standards and quality of life. Research and new discoveries and technologies by scientists working for the military, other government agencies, business, and universities were celebrated. The longtime DuPont slogan expressed this spirit: "Better things for better living . . . through chemistry."

This chapter—like the prior one—focuses on the sky-is-the-limit optimism that characterized *Look* and its America. While there were many articles about scientists, inventors, doctors, and people who benefited from their work, real and predicted technological and medical wonders were themselves the story. Just as the blind faith in the primacy of economic growth as a national goal and basis for national pride and identity began to be questioned in the 1960s, so too was the faith in an always-beneficent technology.

Look was hardly the only news medium that breathlessly made and celebrated the connection between science and technology, progress, and optimism about the future. It would have been absurd for journalists, political and business leaders, or intellectuals not to see the transformational breakthroughs that captured the public's imagination: jet travel, TV, nuclear power, the discovery of DNA, computers, global telecommunications, lasers, the polio vaccine, open-heart surgery, stereos, and space exploration.

Vannevar Bush, often called the father of the internet, wrote a remarkable twelve-page essay in *Life* in 1945 that essentially predicted the information age and the internet. A 1954 *Life* cover story, "The Star-Studded Reaches of Measureless Space," depicted a lonely spacecraft on a barren planet looking out on the sun. A portrait of Dr. Christian Barnard, the South African surgeon who performed the first heart transplant, with a heart, veins, and arteries swirling around his head was on the cover of *Time*. Astronauts were all over the news media. Barnard aside, an underlying theme was the supremacy of U.S. science and the benefits it brought. In a 1960 story, chemist and DuPont president Crawford Greenewalt told *Look* that when he graduated from MIT most scientific articles were in German, but now they were mostly by American scientists.[2]

Look did many of these kinds of stories, as well as ones predicting technological wonders that never were to be. The magazine featured thoughtful scientific reporting, accompanied by dazzling photos, such as the first published images inside a human heart, in 1957. Articles were written by staff writers like Roland Berg and Jack Wilson, as well as by expert guest contributors. What particularly distinguished *Look*'s coverage from that of most other magazines was that the magazine discussed many scientific and technological advances in terms of the scientists or the beneficiaries. Thus, innovations in medicine, "labor-saving" devices, transportation, and other advances were shown through the eyes of patients, families, travelers, and consumers. By doing so, it conveyed to readers that these were not remote or abstract developments, but things that could touch their lives. In this sense, *Look* was especially good at instilling and reinforcing Americans' faith in science.[3]

A Miraculous, Revolutionary New World around the Corner

Look published several articles before World War II about ways in which technology would help create a grand new future of spectacular skyscrapers, dazzling homes, and intercontinental jet travel. Five years later, it devoted much of an issue to a postwar future of sleek cars, mass airline travel, advancing medicine, redesigned cities, and military innovations. During the decade or so after the war, the same kind of euphoria that characterized *Look*'s coverage of the U.S. economy also marked the magazine's reportage on science and technology. The words "miracle" and "revolutionary" were used in many a headline.[4]

The first issue of 1946 told readers of "New Miracles Ahead." Just around the corner were facsimile machines that could send documents around the world in minutes, X-rays, synthetic clothing, and supersonic jets that "may be commonplace." Exuding the sort of optimism that all challenges could be overcome, the article made a stunning prediction: "With medical science steadily mobilizing its forces to conquer disease, we may see a world in which illness is unknown." In another piece that year, it confidently declared: "Ahead is the promise of all the labor-saving power mankind has dreamed of—power as free as water and air," thanks to "science [which] has turned a corner into a new world, where peace and plenty can be yours."[5]

Even in *Look*'s earliest years, the magazine touted discoveries, inventions, and technological progress that would improve Americans' lives. In June 1937 *Look* wrote about higher-resolution television, at a time when virtually no one owned a TV set and there were only experimental broadcasters in the United States. Eleven years later, the magazine reported on television's "boom year." Similarly, years before the first commercial transatlantic flights, in 1938, *Look* reported on the Seversky Super Clipper, a plane that would have staterooms and could fly from New York to London overnight. That same year, it confidently predicted that there would be skyscrapers "three to five times as large as" the Empire State Building.[6]

Ultra-modern houses for the middle class and federally financed "ready-to-use houses for low incomes families" were foretold in articles in 1938 and 1939. Cars were another part of this just-around-the-corner technotopia. Within twenty years, tens of millions of Americans would be buying new cars every three years, a 1939 article predicted.[7]

In one of the first of *Look*'s many medical stories, nurse Larraine Day appeared on a 1941 cover for a long story called "Medical Miracles of the Year." It reported on new flu vaccines and syphilis treatments, surgeries and transfusions, and even "a new clue which may help solve the mystery of cancer and prevent it."[8]

However, this was nothing compared to what *Look*'s readers were to learn during the Truman and Eisenhower years. Articles fell into one of two broad categories: technology would revolutionize our lives, homes, and workplaces, and medical breakthroughs would lead to longer, healthier lives. Woven into many stories was the remarkable message that technology would solve the world's problems.

How You Will Live Better

With "New Miracles Ahead" as something of a preface, stories about "our beautiful postwar world" appeared with increasing regularity. In October

1946, *Look* readers were tantalized by a future of "electronic kitchens, dream houses, and sleek plastic autos," as well as improved "old gadgets" like the iron that would be "safer and more efficient." Plastics like Fiberglas—used in pillows, curtains, and blankets—would be "the housewife's delight," and "shopping is going to be made easier" thanks to vending machines.[9]

"Food dreams will come true in 1947" because new frozen and pre-pared foods "mean less work in the kitchen" and could even be ordered by phone, *Look* told its readers. Products like mixes for brownies and teas, instant rice, chicken with more meat per pound, frozen orange juice, and monosodium glutamate "for added flavor" were "tomorrow's foods" that were "here today." Citing "the magic of irradiation to preserve foods," the magazine described the coming "revolution" of foods produced and con-served with atomic energy.[10]

A 1955 article on "The Great American Appliance" declared, with the sort of purple prose that could be found in many a story: "The future is as bright with improvements as the chrome on the latest dishwashers." The wondrous new microwave was celebrated in 1957. That same year, a three-page foldout of seventy-six "modern electrical home appliances" quoted Le Corbusier, a renowned modernist architect, to emphasize that the "home is a machine for living." Indeed, housekeeping was becoming a breeze thanks to new chemical cleaners as well as appliances, *Look* told the "ladies." Readers learned that "air conditioning is no longer a luxury," as a photo showed cooled air being pumped into a car at a Houston drive-in. The hi-fi, playing 33, 45, and 78 rpm records, was the subject of another 1957 story. Then there were particularly silly stories on fabrics that would allow one "to jump in a pool with your clothes on" and four-room "leisure homes" that could be assembled in twenty hours.[11]

When Disneyland opened in 1955, *Look* was there, focusing especially on Tomorrowland. It would be a place where "science and imagination sketch the future world," a mini-metropolis that would give Americans a taste of how they would live in the not-too-distant future.[12]

Of course, television was the most revolutionary new machine for the home—covered not only for its dramas, situation comedies, and their stars but also as a great technological advance and symbol of prosperity.

Between 1950 and 1960, the proportion of households with television sets soared from 9 percent to 89 percent. David Sarnoff, head of RCA, predicted transatlantic broadcasting in *Look* in 1950, and the subject was revisited in 1953, describing coaxial cables and the more fanciful notion of "an express-plane relay." *Look* went on to excitedly report on the coming of color TV in 1955, and pay TV the following year.[13]

Travel was made easier by new and rapidly improving transportation technologies, from the car and jet to even the train and the rocket. *Look* was agog over such developments as "custom cars for everyone" and maintenance-free cars. Aerodynamic vehicles were displayed as another way of showing that a giddy, technology-driven future was coming fast.[14]

Photos of the airplane of the future—including the seats, lounge, and cockpit—were in a late 1945 issue. Maxine and Bud Branham, an average American couple, were able to vacation in Alaska by 1946 because "air travel creates opportunity." An article entitled "How You Will Travel in 1947" told of "sleeper planes," "new planes cruising at 300 miles per hour [that] will clip hours" from flights, and "luxury trains" like the Burlington Zephyr. In the last issue of 1946, a story about the army's XS-1 jet breaking the sound barrier said that its technology would be used for future commercial aircraft. Although the first commercial jet flight did not actually occur until a British Overseas Airways Corporation de Havilland Comet took off in 1952, a single-passenger jet helicopter was shown cruising at seventy miles per hour in a 1951 story.[15]

It may be unfathomable, given the state of American rail travel in the twenty-first century, that the luxuries of train travel were described in several articles. A seven-page photo spread on the Southern Pacific Railroad was published at the end of 1945. A 1948 piece spoke of Vista Domes and club lounges, and a 1952 story described new "Congressional" and "Senator" passenger service from Washington to New York to Boston. The latter not only had drapes, murals, and etched glass, but its dining cars were equipped with new microwaves. Much more futuristic were the GM-designed Aerotrains "that ride on air," described by *Look* shortly before they briefly went into commercial operation in 1956.[16]

If these dreams of postwar transportation weren't enough, *Look* dabbled in even more fantasy-like stories. An "airphibian," a car that could turn into an airplane, was described in 1947 by its inventor Robert Edison Fulton Jr. Atomic Energy Commission chairman Gordon Evans Dean predicted in 1953 that nuclear energy would soon power planes and ships. An especially breathless 1955 story, "San Francisco to New York in 75 Minutes" forecast the advent of a rocket-driven commercial plane, the WRT-72, within a decade. Predicting an even more dazzling rocket-plane that would fly at speeds of up to eight thousand miles per hour, the author asked rhetorically whether it would be feasible, safe, and economical. "The answers to these questions will soon be an emphatic yes," he assured.[17]

Living Longer Thanks to Medical Breakthroughs

The new "luxuries" of the American middle class, typically demonstrated by a housewife in the kitchen, a family on vacation, or extravagant photo spreads on new appliances, clearly were a popular story line during the late 1940s and 1950s. The marvels of medicine received similar coverage. Most of these stories were thoughtful, explaining in easy-to-understand language subjects as diverse as genetics and cardiology, nutrition and birth control. Some veered into tabloid-like sensationalism, as one story suggested that "You may live forever."[18]

Aside from the 1941 "medical miracles" story and a few pieces in the late 1940s, such as one about helping "handicapped children live better lives," it was not until about 1951 that *Look* started publishing articles about medicine at least every few months. With a few exceptions, the news was all good.

A 1951 article on immunology showed lab-coated Dr. Hans Selye teaching medical school students and discussed how "someday, perhaps soon, doctors will be able to adjust diets and inject hormones so that every patient can put up the strongest fight against disease and stress." In "Spare Parts for Humans," in 1953, *Look* described doctors who could "repair worn-out bodies," enabling "children and adults, in the past doomed to die, [to] walk, see, eat, and live longer—all because of a spare part."[19]

William Laurence, a *New York Times* medical reporter, contributed several articles in 1953, including one on how polio, heart disease, and cancer were being "conquered." His longest and most superlative-laden article,

"You May Live Forever," was in that year's March 23 issue, which had the magazine's typical (some might say bizarre) mix of stories about a weight lifter, newsman Edward R. Murrow, Van Gogh, the Chicago White Sox, another piece on cancer treatment, and a "humorous" piece on "How to Handle Women." In one passage, Laurence wrote of "astounding [scientific] progress in its explorations of the very frontiers of life that it at last reached the point where it can promise men and women now living the realization of mankind's greatest dream throughout the ages—the resurrection of the human body." With this suggestion that the culmination of human history was near, he more soberly discussed genetics and embryology. However, the pièce de résistance was talk of "regenerative scar tissue" that could be "kept indefinitely in a state of perfect preservation," making it possible to bring people back to life and clone them. In theory, he said, we could "re-create not one Einstein or Churchill, but many!"[20]

Blasphemous, naïve, or goofy? No. As was evident in story after story, *Look* generally portrayed a country and world where life and health were getting better, giving Americans reasons to believe that anything was possible.

Berg, who joined the magazine in 1954, wrote many cutting-edge medical and scientific stories. As a medical historian later wrote: "*Look* magazine had a circulation of more than 5 million at the time, but just a few surgeons knew the details of the dramatic stories that Berg told." He wrote several articles on heart surgery, telling how patients, who once would have died, could now be saved. In addition to his 1957 story with the first photos "inside a beating heart," a 1954 article included dramatic photos of a catheter in a twelve-year-old girl and the exposed heart of a forty-one-year-old man undergoing surgery. In one particularly moving passage, he wrote:

> A three-week-old child born with a heart defect who once faced death within weeks, a young mother faced with invalidism because of a heart damaged by a long-forgotten childhood attack of rheumatic fever, a middle-aged businessman sternly warned by his doctor that his last heart attack means giving up business "or else"—these are a few of countless thousands who have been restored to full and active lives through recent spectacular advances in heart surgery.[21]

The next year, Berg wrote two stories on eradicating polio and the benefits of the newly introduced Salk vaccine. These undoubtedly gave hope to a nation where polio had been causing more than fifteen thousand cases of paralysis each year in the early 1950s. A 1954 story discussed how new EEG machines could map the brain, and another in 1959 described brain surgery. The latest in "medical electronics," including color X-rays and other technologies in modern hospitals and doctors' offices, were additional life-saving advances portrayed in text and photos.[22]

Although glass contact lenses had existed since the 1920s, Look told its readers about "new micro-lenses that won't fall out or irritate eyes." In the midst of the baby boom, Berg argued that "children have benefited most from medical advances." With birthrates hitting twentieth-century highs during the mid-1950s, Look assured its readers that even "childless couples can have babies," thanks to fertility clinics.[23]

Look bolstered the almost god-like respect accorded doctors. Readers also learned about the profession through such stories as those on the training of medical students, medical ethics, and "women physicians."[24]

However, Look also published a handful of dissonant medical stories. In a six-article package in 1956 on the "State of the Nation's Health," Berg cautioned that extending life expectancy in the near future was "doubtful," and he astutely said that American medicine has been "winning the battle against acute diseases but losing the war against chronic killers." He also urged "a greater appreciation for research," not just to conquer disease but as "a long-term investment in knowledge." Other stories reported on problems in hospitals and the difficulties of "solving" the "problem of the aged." Quite a wake-up call for readers who were accustomed to hearing only about medical miracles.[25]

Enthralled by Outer Space

The era's grandest scientific achievement was the conquest of outer space. As late 1940s and 1950s articles demonstrate, even before the Soviet Union launched Sputnik in 1957 and the first manned rockets lifted off in 1961, the possibilities for space flight fascinated Americans and Look writers. A late 1957 cover story showed a man in a clunky space suit under the headline,

"Man Prepares for Space Travel." The years between 1961 and 1969—from John Kennedy's pledge to land a man on the moon during the sixties and the first moon landing more than five months before his deadline—were magical for most Americans. Television, breathlessly broadcasting every liftoff, made this very real to tens of millions of Americans. Ever more sophisticated spacecraft were launched, tens of millions gathered around TV sets for each takeoff, and popular culture was filled with visions of the future ranging from *The Jetsons* and *Star Trek* to *First Men in the Moon* and *2001: A Space Odyssey*.[26]

In "The Soaring Sixties" issue, Jack Wilson gave readers a "space timetable." In 1962 he reported that NASA expected to have a manned spacecraft circle Mars by 1975 and land on the red planet a decade later. He also wrote that America would have a man in orbit around Venus in the 1970s and that space-based industries would develop by the 1980s. *Look* lionized astronauts, the "men behind" projects like the 1965 Mariner IV unmanned mission to Mars were profiled, satellites and lunar vehicles were explained, and the magazine briefly sponsored a "trophy for achievement in aeronautics."[27]

Not surprisingly, articles and photos of space came fast and furious in the months before and after the 1969 Apollo 11 moon landing. Noted science and science-fiction writer Arthur C. Clarke and C. P. Snow collaborated on an essay about Apollo 8's late December 1968 voyage to orbit the moon. A July 1969 article described eating in space as "no picnic." *Look* again recruited Snow to write about the actual moon landing.[28]

In one of the magazine's great journalistic coups, Cowles commissioned Norman Rockwell to do a series of paintings on aspects of the moon landing. Rockwell, working with the NASA Art Team, created *Longest Steps: Space Suits* in 1965, *Man's First Step on the Moon* in 1966, *Man on the Moon* in 1967, and *Behind Apollo*, a 1969 twenty-eight-by-sixty-six-inch oil painting of everyone who contributed to the Apollo program, which accompanied an article by Clarke in the issue before the first lunar landing. *Man's First Step* hangs in the National Air and Space Museum in Washington DC. Another Rockwell painting, *Final Impossibility: Man's Tracks on the Moon*, was done for *Look*'s 1969 year-end issue.[29]

Back on Earth: The Technological Wonders of the 1960s

Although the equation between technology and better living started to break down during the 1960s, in *Look* and in the American mind, articles still marveled about real or hypothesized technical developments that would usher in a happier, more prosperous future.

In one of the decade's first stories about the auto industry, the magazine described Detroit's projectile-shaped Levicar prototype that would "float on air." Touting its thirteen years of research with Kodak, *Look* presented a 3-D photo insert in 1964 in conjunction with the debut of Cowles's *Venture* travel magazine. While hardly the seventy-five-minute transcontinental flight predicted in 1955, *Look* boosted the supersonic flight program launched by JFK.[30]

The "Next 25 Years" issue displayed a cornucopia of technologies and products that would be available by 1987. There was an article about the "mass mover [that would] carry passengers across oceans and continents" at up to three thousand miles per hour, flying boats, satellite "filling stations" for space travelers, and even the "family jet-powered sedan" that would use a kerosene-like fuel to go five hundred miles per hour, although the article was vague about how and where one could drive such vehicles. There would be "freezer-ovens" that would combine refrigerators and ovens into a single device that could make food in twenty minutes. Another future car was a self-driving pod that would be programmed to go to one's destination, gliding on a cushion of compressed air. Showing Disneyland's famous "House of Tomorrow," as well as a cat perched on an asbestos-cement pipe, *Look* discussed porcelain-enameled steel, heavy plastic, and other building materials of the future. "Mood conditioning," based somehow on free-floating ions, would make us feel better and learn faster, readers learned.[31]

In a preview of the 1964–65 New York World's Fair, the magazine highlighted GM's Futurama pavilion, which showed a manned lunar station, underwater living, "aquacopters," and self-driving cars on "automated highways." The IBM pavilion's "People Wall" showed how "computer programming [will] seem as simple as planning a dinner party." A more modest preview of the Expo 67 world's fair in Montreal described Jacques Cousteau's plans for underwater living, Buckminster Fuller's geodesic dome, and a "brilliant new way of urban living" in the fair's Habitat housing prototype.[32]

Among the more farsighted of *Look*'s predictions were technologies to beam TV images from Mars to Earth, hydroponic agriculture, and the "all-knowing credit card." The magazine was also on the mark in foreseeing some of the ways in which computers would transform people's everyday lives.[33]

The computer and its future uses received increasing play during the latter half of the sixties. Despite fears earlier in the decade that robots and automation would eliminate jobs and that people would become "prisoners in a computerized hell," T. George Harris assured readers that computers are enhancing business efficiency and production. He added: "[We are] moving toward a society in which robots are the slaves," and people will "be transformed by human intelligence and ingenuity into something better than man has ever known." Two years later, Poppy wrote that if the country succeeds "in eliminating industrial drudgery, people of the future will need to know how not to work." *Look* also worked with a mathematician and programmer to use the giant UNIVAC mainframe computer to design the fashions and hairstyles of the future. Computers would also be able to help people find new jobs "right away."[34]

A 1966 article on "Dating by Computer"—some thirty years before Match.com was launched—described a project created by two Harvard undergraduates that had signed up one hundred thousand college students and guaranteed five names of potential dates for everyone on its system. A happy photo of Nikos and Nancy included the caption, "Brought together on an IBM 7094." "The future belongs to the computer," the young founder Jeff Tarr told Gene Shalit, later of *The Today Show*. Tarr, who became a successful financier, predicted networked computing, saying hundreds of devices could "all [be] linked to a centralized mother computer."[35]

In its 1966 issue on California, *Look* wrote about the dawn of computerized banking and how Comsat would "wire the international economy into a complex human unit." Again accurately forecasting the twenty-first century, it added: "To handle all the information we'll need about each other, both government and business will turn into super data processors."[36]

In 1970 Leonard described a "ComNet" communications system much like the internet and also anticipated a future in which people would have "home (computer) consoles" that would enable them to choose products and express political preferences.[37]

More prosaically, the magazine predicted that "highly sophisticated miniaturized films" (i.e., the videocassette) would be coming in the 1970s. Before the Bay Area Rapid Transit and the Washington Metro opened in the 1970s, *Look* previewed the two systems' "computer-controlled cars" with upholstered seats that would depart every two minutes during rush hour.[38]

More Marvels of Medicine: 1960–1971

Early in 1960, *Look* readers learned about the stunning range of biomedical research at the National Institutes of Health. In addition to a story about a cured cancer patient, several articles on psychiatry appeared that year. Characterized in one as "the troubled science," these stories nonetheless showed the field moving ahead to "find the answers . . . to meet the problems of mental illness." Addressing a debate that still rages, *Look* asked whether "the answer is emotional or chemical," and whether a mentally ill patient should "take to the couch or . . . swallow a pill." At a time when Freud was still widely admired, *Look* described him as "brilliant," while juxtaposing him with a photo of a man beside an array of mainframes. The caption read: "The psychiatrist of the future may be an electronic computer that can analyze results of tests and diagnose a patient's illness."[39]

Photos of sleek new devices, happy patients, serious but kindly (white) doctors, and descriptions and photos of surgeries made medical progress very real to readers. One of the most dramatic series of photos was in a 1962 issue showing an embryo's development at day one, week one, and then at each month during pregnancy. *Look* highlighted medical advances by telling stories like one about a Mayo Clinic patient awed at how computers analyzed his medical tests, while salaciously noting the many "blond girls" as nurses.[40]

The "Next 25 Years" issue also offered grand predictions of medical advances—some quite accurate, others sounding like wild science fiction. By 1987 there would be "tiny electronic brains to operate the crippled or diseased organs of your body," ways to make paraplegics walk, and life could be created in a test tube. "Man will master the secret of creation," *Look* concluded. In 1971 the magazine reported on the first test-tube baby and quoted the former president of the American Association for the Advancement of Science, Dr. Bentley Glass, who said that by the end of the twentieth century "a fully formed baby will be 'decanted' from an artificial womb, heralding the unmistakable arrival of the Brave New World."[41]

A 1964 profile of renowned heart surgeon Michael DeBakey discussed pacemakers and valve replacements—both brand new—as well as the likelihood that "an artificial heart will be implanted within five years." Seven years later, Berg described research on triglycerides and cholesterol, alongside five detailed diets to lower cholesterol. The use of lasers and "cryosurgery" were said to be revolutionizing medicine, with the possibility that cancer cells could be destroyed. A seven-page spread in 1967, showing incubators, respirators, X-rays, cathodes, and a bevy or doctors and nurses, reported that brain damage in babies could be prevented. *Look* reported that medicine "is proving that retardation is not unalterable," after discussing and showing the horrors of institutions for the mentally ill or "retarded." A 1970 issue with a baby crawling on its cover described "how to choose your baby's sex." Other stories told of new therapies for leukemia and how ambulances newly equipped with electrocardiograms and defibrillators were saving heart-attack patients. The odd 1970 story by Amosoff, the Soviet futurist, assured readers that by 1991, "gerontology will control the process of aging." One of the rare, ostensibly negative articles on "Side Effects," was still couched in a broader story of progress: "Modern medical science, while curing more of the ills of mankind than ever before has simultaneously become one of the major causes of human illness."[42]

Two years after President Johnson signed Medicare and Medicaid into law in 1965, *Look* dipped its toes into health-care policy in a series of articles in its March 21, 1967, issue. "A patient's pocketbook should not decide the kind of medical care he receives," the magazine declared. "Only high-quality comprehensive care can break the vicious circle of 'the poor get sicker, and the sick get poorer.'" Although the issue presented favorable and unfavorable views of Britain's "socialized medicine," *Look* fell back on the hopeful idea that increasing prosperity would solve America's health-care problems. "'We cannot deliver the highest quality medical care to nearly 200 million people overnight,'" one doctor told Berg. "'But in 10 years we might not even need Medicaid. In an affluent society such as we have, who knows, maybe we won't have medical indigents.'"[43]

Discovering the Downsides of Technology

Look became increasingly conscious of real or possible ill effects of technology during the 1960s and early 1970s. It presented widely divergent scenarios for what the future would bring: either "the most exciting in mankind's 100,000-year adventure on earth," with the world "transformed by human intelligence and ingenuity into something better than man has ever known," or an "earth [that] may have been made intolerable by human stupidity" and "nuclear annihilation."[44]

Nuclear power, automation, industrial expansion, and the computer were increasingly seen as challenges to survival, work, privacy, and morality. While vocal critics of technology began to gain attention in the 1960s, *Look* presented multiple perspectives and brought these issues and concerns into the mainstream in all corners of America.

The otherwise buoyant "Next 25 Years" issue included a series of interviews with historians by Robert Moskin. Will Durant spoke of great advances in science, knowledge, and the economy but also said that America has "retrogressed in morals, art and manners." Arnold Toynbee spoke to widespread fears that atomic energy has put humanity's survival in jeopardy. In an especially dark quote, Harvard's Samuel Eliot Morrison said: "We have got to get used to living without solutions. We have to get used to living in crisis after crisis, hoping for the best, but expecting the worst."[45]

Another Moskin story, in 1963, damned scientists as being "responsible for our moral crisis": "Their discoveries—the computer, the Bomb, the oral contraceptive, the subconscious—have damaged man's traditional sense of responsibility." Liberal journalist Samuel Grafton asked whether machines were diminishing conversation and human interaction. A 1968 story by George Leonard asked whether computer data banks would destroy our freedom and privacy. Frank Trippett went further, picking up ideas from the cultural New Left: "Technology increasingly depersonalizes and dehumanizes our lives.... Technology is sweeping us into an epoch when privacy is becoming quite literally impossible ... [in which] rapidly advancing technical means of surveillance [exist] in a civilization whose societies obviously intend to keep all individuals under constant watch." Many of these predictions came all too true fifty years later.[46]

In another 1968 issue, an image of men trapped in a metaphorical data bank was captioned: "The private lives of 200 million Americans are now being stored in the computer's memory." Describing computers' use by credit bureaus, the FBI, and medical records, Jack Star quoted the dire prediction of a University of Michigan law professor: "'The computer, with its insatiable appetite for information, its image of infallibility, its inability to forget anything that has been put into it, may become the heart of a surveillance system that will turn society into a transparent world in which our home, our finances, our associations, or mental and physical condition are bared to the most casual observer.'"

The article cited another prescient quote from congressional testimony by IBM's chief scientist: "One day a user will probably be able to identify himself to a computer by letting the machine verify his voice or thumbprint or his signature. But in the end, preservation of privacy will still depend on people.... Machines have no morals, no ethics; men have ethics and morals. A machine is an idiot device, and it does what people tell it to do."[47]

Look came relatively late to cover air and water pollution and other environmental threats, although it told readers in 1950 about "the evil Los Angeles smog." The magazine published nothing about Rachel Carson's *Silent Spring* (1962) or President Johnson's 1965 warning about rising carbon dioxide emissions or his administration's passage of the Water Quality and Air Quality Acts. However, during the magazine's last three years, it printed a raft of articles on how Americans were despoiling their country. In 1969 *Look* reported on singer Pete Seeger's efforts to save "the dying Hudson," as he sailed his sloop, the *Clearwater*, to raise awareness. It also published a package of articles on a variety of ecological issues in a November 1969 issue. In David Perlman's story "America the Beautiful?" he wrote of water and air pollution, DDT and other fertilizers damaging the land and health, thermal pollution in the oceans, and the population explosion. A powerful 1969 story was filled with bucolic photos of people basking in nature, while grimly pronouncing: "Our land has been hacked, gouged, littered, poisoned, and burnt—all on the altar of progress." Another article on wildlife conservation was illustrated with a searing photo of a mother seal looking at her bludgeoned baby. Breaking prior codes of decency, the issue also included an Allen Ginsberg poem about "shit-brown haze" in the air.[48]

Pegged to the first Earth Day, *Look* devoted much of its April 21, 1970, issue to articles on the environment, including ones on prominent environmentalists and citizens taking action, endangered salt marshes, and the still-pristine Big Sur coastline. Once again, turning the bigger story into how Americans could make their country better, the package was headlined: "How you can join the ecology crusade to clean up America." Among the five prominent figures writing for the issue, scientist Rene Dubos discussed tolerance for "worse and worse conditions," Margaret Mead pointed to the need to recognize "man's place in the natural world," and Henry Ford II pledged to have "virtually emission-free internal combustion engines by 1975."[49]

For the anniversary of Earth Day, *Look* published six stories focused on the environment, including ones on the newly created Environmental Protection Agency's first administrator, William Ruckelshaus; residents in Modesto, California, who had started a recycling program; new environmental laws; and business efforts to reduce pollution. The introduction to these optimistic stories described how "everyone" jumped on "the Ecology Bandwagon," and how 121 of the 695 bills passed by the Ninety-First Congress were "pro-environment."[50]

Technology, Optimism, and Utopianism

Technology, science, and medicine had brought dazzling progress, as well as looming problems, to the United States during the momentous three and a half decades that *Look* was published. Overall, *Look*'s tone—whether describing hypersonic jets or the end of aging—went far beyond optimism to a vision that was decidedly utopian. This faith was pervasive in the country, echoed, and reinforced by *Look*, particularly until the late 1960s.

During its last years, *Look* often seemed especially radical in its vision of the future. In a 1968 manifesto published in the magazine, Leonard dramatically amplified Cowles's declaration that, "We place ourselves unmistakably on the side of the future." Warning of "timid expectations" for the future, he wrote:

> Most scientists agree that eventually we shall be able to accomplish anything we can think up. Such things as traveling to the planets, controlling weather, conquering disease, and transplanting bodily organs are clear on the horizon. Much more lies just beyond: control of heredity, computers with "intelligence" and "feelings," and more. Already, men are making God-like decisions. . . . [It is] quite possible now to make a fresh start, to turn all the old limitations inside out. Unparalleled power is coming into our hands from science and technology.[51]

It's hard to imagine a news organization or institution that more powerfully expressed and influenced Americans' belief that technology-driven progress would indefinitely be the country's future. *Look* helped make these heady years of the mid-twentieth century even headier.

7

Look's Pioneering Role in Covering Civil Rights

One of *Look*'s stellar achievements was its coverage of and commitment to civil rights. Its role in the long and ongoing fight for racial justice and equity in the United States—from a 1939 story on Black poverty and the Klan through the murders and "terror tactics" of the 1950s and the historic, turbulent civil rights movement and its warnings about renascent racism around 1970—is a little-known story of journalistic courage and excellence.

As Mike Cowles said years after his magazine folded: "I'm very proud of the fact that *Look* devoted pages and pages to trying to improve relations with blacks, which I think is the number 1 problem in the country." Recognizing that *Look*'s positions were controversial, he added: "Few subjects we wrote about elicited the intensity of feeling as civil or human rights. Whenever we published an article about the plight of blacks during the 1950s or even the 1960s, we knew in advance to expect hundreds, even thousands of the most violent letters calling us 'n—— lovers' and everything else you can think of."[1]

Look reported on key events and people and efforts to bring change, but also used its story-telling approach of focusing on the experiences and feelings of individuals and families—Black and white—whose lives were affected by racism and segregation.

Powerful articles and photographs addressed these issues with depth and sensitivity and exposed the racist attitudes, actions, and laws of mid-twentieth-century America. *Look* arguably did more than any other magazine or newspaper to show millions of Americans the nature and extent of racial injustice and hatred, at least until TV started covering the civil rights movement in earnest in the 1960s. As noted, *Look* also stood out as the first mainstream (read: white) American publication to hire a Black man as a reporter, Ernest Dunbar, in 1954, and to publish a photo of a Black fashion model, Bani Yelverton, in October 1958.[2]

"*Look* is the journalistic marvel of the age," declared the liberal *New Republic.* "It has made the best pictorial study of civil liberties in the United States. The pictures make their case convincingly; we salute *Look* for its courage in showing the seamy side of American life as well as for the skill with which it has done the job." Indeed, *Look* was frequently denounced by white supremacists, including in letters to the editor. An Alabama judge even banned the magazine in 1959 for its "infamous distortion of the truth" about segregation.[3]

The postwar decades saw the great successes of the Supreme Court's 1954 *Brown v. Board of Education* decision; Rosa Parks's civil disobedience on a Montgomery, Alabama, bus in 1955; the integration of professional sports in 1947; the early 1960s sit-ins and Freedom Riders; Martin Luther King Jr.'s 1963 March on Washington; the 1964 Civil Rights Act; the 1965 Voting Rights Act; and the election of the first Black U.S. senator since Reconstruction. There were also the horrors and tragedies—the murders of Emmett Till, Medgar Evers, Malcolm X, and Martin Luther King Jr.; the lynchings, police brutality, and other violent attacks on African Americans; the segregationist backlash in the South led by governors of Alabama, Arkansas, and Georgia; the "massive resistance" movement against integration, and the urban riots of the 1960s.

In addition to Dunbar, other staff writers who covered race and civil rights included Morgan, Star, Harris, Korry, Poppy, Leonard, Kocivar, Wren,

Knebel, and George Goodman. Illustrious public figures and journalists ranging from King and Senators Edward Brooke (R-MA) and Robert Kennedy to William Hodding Carter II, the liberal, Pulitzer Prize-winning publisher and editor of the Greenville, Mississippi, newspaper the *Delta Democrat-Times*; author Robert Penn Warren and investigative Southern journalist William Bradford Huie also wrote incisive articles.[4]

This chapter is divided chronologically into three periods: before 1955, 1955–62, and 1963–71. In each, *Look* was in the vanguard of major-media coverage of racial injustices and the pursuit of racial equality. The chapter touches on many *Look* articles and photos to give a sense of the breadth of coverage, while focusing more closely on a few key articles.

Look's Pioneering Coverage before 1955

As early as 1939, a compelling *Look* story, "Trouble in the South," included photos of Klansmen burning a cross and an effigy of a lynched Black man with the words "This N—— Voted" scrawled on it. The piece also informed readers that "the brunt of the South's poverty rests on its 10 million Negroes." A year later the magazine told the story of a young Black man with little hope of escaping poverty and prejudice.[5]

In 1940 it published photos from the "Harlem Document," an unpublished book project by the Photo League, a New York group that focused on racial and economic justice. Jack Manning's "Elks Parade," which showed residents of an overcrowded Harlem tenement huddled on fire escapes to watch a parade, was among six photos in this surprisingly radical article.[6]

Look's 1945 book *One Nation*, written by Wallace Stegner, was a shining call for racial and religious tolerance. It denounced the "insidious illness" of prejudice, segregation as "the shame of democracy," and "the slimy propaganda shoveled out by demagogues." Stegner went on to say: "Prejudice comes with fear.... It has little basis in reason.... If Americans are good enough to die together in war, they're good enough to live together in peace." The 340-page book discussed nine racial, ethnic, and religious groups and their relation to an America that still identified itself as a white, Protestant country. It made clear that the country had been enriched by its many "minorities." Arguing that information can reduce prejudice, he minced no words, concluding: "The world we hope for, where peace and international accord are possible through cooperation and arbitration, seems like a yeasty dream indeed if within the United States, 'conceived in liberty and dedicated to the proposition that all men are created equal,' we cannot achieve a harmony of our races and creeds into a single nation."[7]

Just before V-E Day, *Look* published the first of several thoughtful articles on prejudice, which it called "our postwar battle." In 1946 it took aim at Eugene Talmadge, the three-term Georgia governor who said he had read Hitler's *Mein Kampf* seven times. Comparing "Old Gene" to the Klan, the story warned that a Talmadge victory in the first state election after the poll tax had been repealed would again herald "white supremacy."[8]

Hodding Carter wrote several scorching articles about race and racism. He challenged liberal white Northerners to recognize that racism wasn't confined to the South, juxtaposing the Klan with the poverty of Harlem, in a 1959 piece. Carter continued this theme in "The Negro Problem Moves North," which showed a white mob in Cicero, Illinois, and "A Wave of Terror Threatening the South."[9]

Jackie Robinson, Major League Baseball's first Black player, had a "special relationship with *Look*," as the *New York Times* said. Between 1948 and 1957, Robinson was the hero of many stories and was commissioned to write four others. A 1948 article was illustrated with eighteen photos by Maurice Terrell, showing Robinson as an army lieutenant, with his family, and in two seven-image sequences batting and fielding. Robinson wrote a three-part series in 1955 on his difficult experiences as a Black athlete and announced his retirement not at a press conference but in a 1957 *Look* article. By 1954 the majority of the Dodgers' line-up were people of color, and Robinson told *Look*: "The club wouldn't hesitate to put nine Negroes on the field if they were the best nine available players."[10]

During the 1952 election, one long article analyzed the Black vote and another looked at both presidential candidates' positions on civil rights. *Look* asked a fundamental question that few Americans were willing to consider in a 1952 article: "How far [is America] from slavery?" In nineteen photos across six pages, readers saw signs showing segregated toilets, movie theaters, and cemeteries as well as Black men and women shining shoes, picking cotton, digging ditches, caring for white children, and living in dilapidated housing.[11]

By contrast, in that same election year, *Life* derided "opportunistic liberals" for "making a moral issue of civil rights." *Life* was by no means blind to racism, having published the brilliant 1936 Margaret Bourke-White photo of Black flood victims in Kentucky waiting on a bread line, beneath a billboard showing a smiling white family in a car beside the words "There's no way like the American Way."[12]

In 1954 *Look* published a seven-page feature on a Black air force squadron commander, Daniel ("Chappie") James, who, two decades later, would become a four-star general commanding NORAD, the aerospace defense command. Just weeks before that year's historic *Brown v. Board of Education* decision overturning the doctrine of "separate but equal," *Look* asked "What Happens When Segregation Ends?" in a story following a Black girl who was the first to integrate the Phoenix public schools.[13]

Terror: 1955–1962

The relatively sparse but important early stories on civil rights became a flood tide in 1955—one that was never to subside. Hodding Carter was sent to cover the white "Citizens Councils" in Mississippi that launched a campaign of propaganda and intimidation in the wake of the Supreme Court's order to end segregation. He called the councils an "uptown Ku Klux Klan," and added: "If I were a Negro, a Jew or even a Catholic, I might be even more disturbed, though it is uncomfortable enough to be labeled simply a 'n—— lover.'"[14]

Look suggested what white readers should tell their children about racial discrimination. It also offered a historical lesson by novelist MacKinlay Kantor, author of the Pulitzer Prize-winning novel *Andersonville*, who wrote of this Georgia town where a notorious Confederate prison had been.[15]

Early 1956 brought one of *Look*'s great journalistic coups, one that awakened millions of Americans to the deepest evils of racism. Emmett Till, a fourteen-year-old Black boy from Chicago who was visiting relatives in Mississippi, had been brutally murdered in the summer of 1955. Four months after an all-white jury acquitted the two killers, investigative Southern journalist William Bradford Huie contacted Dan Mich about the idea of interviewing the murderers and getting them to confess. *Look* had the guts to send him to track down the killers, Roy Bryant and J. W. Milam, who accepted $4,000 in exchange for an interview. In the article, titled "The Shocking Story of Approved Killing in Mississippi," they showed no remorse; instead, they bragged about the brutal killing.

In the January 24, 1956, issue, Mich prefaced Huie's article, saying, "In the long history of man's inhumanity to man, racial conflict has produced some of the most horrible examples of brutality." Huie described Bryant, twenty-four; his twenty-one-year-old wife, Carolyn; and their two children as having "no car, no TV," living in poverty in the back of their small store. Milam, Bryant's half brother, was a veteran with a ninth-grade education.

The fatal drama began when a large group of Black teenagers was outside Bryant's store, and Till showed a photo in his wallet of a white girl. The other boys dared him to go into the store and ask Carolyn for a date. He did, and "wolf whistled" at her, according to Carolyn. When Bryant learned what happened, he told Milam, and Carolyn carried a .38 Colt automatic gun to Milam's wife.

The two armed men went to the home of Till's uncle, where the boy was staying. Milam told Huie that he said to Till, "You the n—— who did the talking?" When the boy said, "Yeah," Milam said, "Don't say 'yeah' to me. I'll blow your head off. Get your clothes on." They planned to drive Till seventy-five miles to cross the Tallahatchie River to whip him at an isolated location that Milam called "the scariest place in the Delta." Instead, they took him to Milam's tool house, where both men pistol-whipped the boy. When Till said he wasn't afraid of them, they ordered him back in the truck, drove him to the river, ordered him to take off his clothes, shot him, and dumped his body in the river.

In the course of the interview, as the killers told their story, Milam said what many white Southerners felt: "N—— are gonna stay in their place. N—— ain't gonna vote where I live.... They ain't gonna go to school with my kids. And when a n—— gets close to mentioning sex with a white woman, he's tired of living. I'm likely to kill him."

A year later, Huie wrote another story for *Look* on "what's happened to the Emmett Till killers." John Malone took photos showing Bryant fixing his pickup truck and playing with his children, and his half brother and fellow murderer, J. W. Milam, and his family sitting on their porch. Milam said, "I got letters from all over the country congratulating me on my 'fine Americanism.'" In Huie's damning conclusion, he wrote: "Milam and Bryant won't be tried again; but as landless white men in the Mississippi Delta and bearing the mark of Cain, they will come to regard the dark morning of Aug. 28, 1955, as the most unfortunate of their lives."[16]

Look's initial story shocked the nation, galvanized civil rights leaders to push the Justice Department to intervene when Blacks' civil rights were violated, and spurred Congress to pass the Civil Rights Act of 1957. Bob Dylan's 1962 song "The Death of Emmett Till" follows the story line described in *Look*. When the 1963 March on Washington was held, it was no accident that it was on the anniversary of Till's murder. Civil-rights leader Jesse Jackson called the killing the "big bang" that launched the civil rights movement. After unsuccessful attempts to reopen the case in the early 2000s, in 2017, Carolyn Bryant confessed that she made up the story. The next year, the FBI reopened the case, believing that Milam and Bryant concealed others involved in the killing. In 2020, sixty-five years after Till was murdered, Congress passed the Emmett Till Antilynching bill.[17]

Just months after Huie's initial blockbuster story, *Look* devoted an entire issue to segregation, Jim Crow laws, and civil rights. Black journalist Carl Rowan wrote "What the Negroes Really Want," while Sen. Sam Ervin (D-NC) made "The Case for Segregation." Another Rowan article, "The South vs. the Supreme Court," called out segregation in a Georgia military school and won a top award for distinguished "public service" journalism. A glimmer of progress was shown in a story about the more-or-less successful desegregation of a St. Louis school.[18]

On December 21, 1956, when the Supreme Court declared Montgomery's segregated bus system illegal, a photo shoot of Rosa Parks was staged that resulted in the most famous photo of Parks, looking out a bus window with a white man behind her (actually a UPI reporter). The story behind this photo is murky. Some say that *Look* staffers persuaded Parks to go downtown to board a Cleveland Avenue bus only to find her old foe, bus driver James Blake. Others say that the shot was staged by the NAACP or UPI. The photo was never published in *Look*, but the incident was replayed as the opening scene in the 2002 film *The Rosa Parks Story*.[19]

Look continued the drumbeat on the extent of legal racism and racist attitudes in all parts of the country. "Jim Crow Northern Style" focused on Philadelphia, another story put Chicago in its crosshairs, and one on segregation had the provocative title "Subtle Whip." A Carl Rowan article damned the Democrats for accommodating Southern segregationists. He quoted the head of the NAACP saying that "the liberals in the Democratic Party sold us out" and a Black union official who said, "If I vote Democratic, I'm voting for [Mississippi Senator James] Eastland to head the Senate Judiciary Committee."[20]

A counterfactual essay by MacKinlay Kantor posed the chilling questions: What would America be like, and what would be the status of African Americans if the South had won the Civil War?[21]

In 1957 Dunbar told readers about the NAACP, and a Georgia minister offered his ideas to end racial conflict. But the year's big civil-rights story was the conflict over integrating Little Rock's Central High School. *Look* quoted a local segregationist declaring: "Yankees are violating the customs of the South. When they take away states' rights and have centralized government that can send down paratroopers with bayonets, then we're no better than Russia. Everyone I know feels the way I do." The magazine followed up with a photo essay on the students who were accompanied into the school by 1,200 soldiers from an army airborne division, while white mobs and Arkansas governor Orval Faubus protested. Minnijean Brown, one of the students, told her traumatic story in *Look* in 1958. A few years later, readers were informed that lynching still occurred in the Deep South. A 1957 story showed eight Klansmen in Tennessee.[22]

Civil rights became an even higher priority when Mich joined Frank Stanton, president of CBS, and Turner Catledge, managing editor of the *Times*, to make a public statement in late 1958 that ensuring civil rights should be at the top of the nation's agenda.[23]

An intriguing article that year told the story of the Myers, the first Black family to move into Levittown, Pennsylvania. Residents initially thought they were a housepainter and a maid. When townspeople discovered that the young, college-educated couple were neighbors, hundreds of whites gathered for eight nights "screaming curses and insults," burning crosses on their lawn, putting Confederate flags and large KKK signs on neighbors' houses, and threatening the Myers by phone. The leader of the so-called Levittown Betterment Committee declared, "I don't want to live in a neighborhood with Negroes. . . . Levittown was set up as a white community. Integration of housing can't be jammed down anyone's throat." Charlotte Brooks's photos showed a worried Mrs. Myers holding her baby and saying, "Baby Lynda is still too young to know what we went through."

Nonetheless, the story had a relatively happy ending. The state attorney general stepped in, a Citizens Committee for Levittown defended the Myers, and some homeowners denounced developer William Levitt's comment that "most whites prefer not to live in mixed communities." The writer David Bittan, a Levittown resident, further tarred the racist provocateurs by noting that they had fought for other rightwing causes such as opposing fluoridation of the water and naming a school after J. Robert Oppenheimer. He concluded by quoting the Myers: "Memories have begun to fade, . . . [and] sooner or later, I know we will be accepted for what we are."[24]

Two similar stories told of a Black ophthalmologist in Florida, Dr. John Brown, who was emblematic of "progress" in race relations, and Rick Adams, a speech and hearing therapist who had moved to a small Iowa town after being driven away from three other counties. "The First Negro in Town" was shown happily engaging with his white child patients and speaking to an all-white Rotary Club, saying, "Someday, maybe, I'll be accepted just as a man."[25]

Marie Jahoda, a prominent social psychologist, wrote a long 1960 essay on the psychological and social roots of prejudice, and how it could be overcome. Prejudice is not innate, but learned, she said, because prejudiced people tend to "hate themselves" and be less educated. Reducing prejudice requires role models, public opinion, therapy, and direct personal experience, although laws could also play a role, she argued.[26]

Readers were given another vantage point on American racism in a 1959 story in which Dunbar, Korry, and photographer Bob Sandberg went to six African countries, and Dunbar said that many Africans "were having their first look at an American Negro." Particularly provocative for *Look* readers was a 1966 piece by Robert Kennedy about his sermon, "Suppose God Is Black," to white churchgoers in South Africa:

> I was told the church to which most of the white population belongs teaches apartheid as a moral necessity. A questioner declared that few churches allow black Africans to pray with the white because the Bible says that is the way it should be, because God created Negroes to serve. "But suppose God is black," I replied. "What if we go to heaven and we, all our lives, have treated the Negro as an inferior, and God is there, and we look up and he is not white? What then is our response?"[27]

As the 1960s began, *Look* discussed the Black sit-ins at whites-only lunch counters in Greensboro, North Carolina, which spread to fifty-five cities during early 1960. The newly founded Student Nonviolent Coordinating Committee (SNCC) was the subject of a May 1963 story by Poppy—who had gotten contacts from crusading journalist Margaret Long, George Leonard's aunt—that described how people were trained for sit-ins. He wrote of SNCC's perilous efforts to register Black voters, and later recalled that "the SNCC people, maybe suspicious, were kind and let me hang out with them. They sent me to talk with one of their people in Greenwood, Mississippi. It was kind of scary going into the Black part of town . . . [and] felt like going into alien territory. SNCC's driver told me to lie down in the back of the car." The article, "The War against Negro Votes," created quite a stir because it gave an exclusive look inside one of the more radical civil rights organizations.[28]

Atlanta was the subject of four articles in the April 25, 1961, issue that examined the city's struggles with race. Benjamin Brown, the student president of historically Black Clark College, was shown planning and leading an anti-segregation march to mark the anniversary of the sit-ins. Douglas Kiker, author of *The Southerner* (1957), replayed the gruesome 1864 Battle of Atlanta, while Leonard, a native Atlantan, wrote of a "Second Battle of Atlanta." Lester Maddox—leader of Georgians Unwilling to Surrender and

later, governor—and the Grand Dragon of the Klan were on one side of
the battle lines; Martin Luther King Jr. and *Atlanta Constitution* publisher
Ralph McGill were on the other, with Mayor William Hartsfield—who
dropped charges against King and students who had demonstrated—trying
to broker a truce.[29]

In an eleven-page series on "The Negro in America Today," Dunbar discussed many forms of racial injustice and some small indicators of change.
Sandberg photos showed the first Black stewardess, greeting passengers
and serving meals on TWA, on the beach with her boyfriend, and riding
the New York subway. He also told a less upbeat story of an attempt in
Cleveland to create a "Negro Garden" apart from an existing American
Garden, which he derided, saying, "A Negro is an American." A Little Rock
follow-up piece, focusing on Doris Bell and her ten children, described the
"reverse freedom ride" of ninety Black families who were relocated from
Arkansas to towns in Massachusetts.[30]

Look and the Height of the Civil Rights Movement, 1963–1971

In 1963 *Look* wrote about King, racism, successful integration, and Black
advancement, told through stories about struggles and successes of individual Blacks and how whites responded. Just as JFK granted Stanley Tretick
unparalleled access, King did the same with James Karales. The photographer documented King's work and family, taking intimate photos of the
civil-rights leader playing with his young daughter. *Look* sent Tretick to
photograph the August 1963 March on Washington, with King, labor and
civil-rights leader A. Philip Randolph, Roy Wilkins, John Lewis, Walter
Reuther, and John Kennedy at the Lincoln Memorial. He took about one
thousand photos, but the magazine published none at the time; strangely,
only one, of a white minister at the march, was used in a 1966 story.[31]

Other stories and photos showed efforts to prevent Blacks from voting,
a white girl pouring catsup on a peaceful demonstrator at a Woolworth's
counter, Black despair and the reasons for "revolt," Mississippi riots, and
the "coming showdown in the race crisis." When Medgar Evers, Mississippi
field director for the NAACP and Black comedian Dick Gregory addressed
a rally in Jackson, Mississippi, *Look* showed police confronting those in

attendance. Tom Morgan talked with Evers a week before his murder in 1963, reporting that a Black bellhop had told him and other protesters to "really take care of yourselves." James Meredith, the first Black student to enroll at the University of Mississippi—amid the state's defiance, campus riots, and federal intervention—was shown in his dorm studying during his first semester. Mississippi's governor, Ross Barnett, disparaged *Look*'s coverage, saying that it was one-sided and showed an "irresponsible sloppiness of mind." Despite prepublication criticism by white city officials, Birmingham civil-rights attorney Charles Morgan wrote: "Who killed Birmingham? We all did. Not only the hate-filled demented murderers of four Negro Sunday-school girls, but we 'nice people,' who did nothing to save our city from race hatred."[32]

Dunbar wrote two stinging articles in the December 17, 1963, issue about the harsh psychological effects of racism. "For many a Northern Negro," he wrote, "the gap between the American promise and the painful reality breeds frustration, despair, and, sometimes, whatever escape can be coaxed from the bottle or the needle."[33]

Whereas Dunbar and *Look* pulled no punches when it came to denouncing racism, other publications were more cautious. *Life*, in 1963, while tepidly criticizing prejudice—notably in unions, not the broader society—wrote: "Negroes, of course, must strive to improve their own eligibility for new job openings."[34]

Norman Rockwell's first commissioned painting for *Look* showed besuited U.S. marshals escorting an eight-year-old Black girl in a white dress, Ruby Bridges, to an all-white school in New Orleans, with the word "n——" scrawled above her. The 1964 painting, *The Problem We All Live With*, which filled two pages of the magazine, became an iconic image of the civil-rights era and, decades later, President Obama had it hung in the White House.[35]

Another grim Rockwell painting for *Look* depicted the Klan's murder of three white civil rights workers—Michael Schwerner, James Chaney, and Andrew Goodman—in Philadelphia, Mississippi, on June 21, 1964. The two-page sepia-toned image shows a man standing above a beaten man on a deserted road, with the shadows of three men to their right. The sketch appeared with a short article, "Southern Justice."[36]

Another 1967 painting showed Black and white children looking at each other to illustrate a story on Black families moving into a white neighborhood. Rockwell later recalled that when he was at the *Saturday Evening Post*, he had to remove a Black man from a picture because the magazine's policy was to only show people of color in service jobs.[37]

Soon after Lyndon Johnson became president, he won passage of the landmark 1964 Civil Rights Act, envisioned his Great Society, and declared war on poverty, which Rockwell painted for *Look*. King discussed his complicated relationship with LBJ in his pointed November 1964 article, "It's a Difficult Thing to Teach a President."[38]

Huie returned to *Look* to write about four Black children murdered in Birmingham's Sixteenth Street Baptist Church. "Men infected with race hate differ only in the sort of action they are willing to take to 'protect' what they call 'their way of life,'" he wrote. The long March 24, 1964 article included photos of a happy child, Denise McNair, earlier in childhood, and one of police beside the eleven-year-old's battered body covered with a sheet. Huie wrote of a hypothetical life that Denise could have lived, eating with whites in a cafeteria, creating a story of white and Black children playing together, becoming class president, attending the University of Alabama, and studying medicine. He damned George Wallace for having the same beliefs as the murderer. "Whenever authority shares the fears of a murderer, and condemns only his violent effort to relieve his fears, the murderer is seldom identified, almost never convicted," Huie concluded.[39]

Civil-rights demonstrations became more frequent in the mid-1960s, and *Look* was there to give the movement a human face. It covered protests at the 1964 New York World's Fair; a failed Mississippi strike by tenant farmers; and Freedom Summer in 1964 Mississippi, showing organizer James Forman, and volunteers registering Black voters at a courthouse and a church.[40]

Together with Huie's story about Till's murderers and Rockwell's painting of Ruby Bridges, another of *Look*'s major contributions to the history of the movement was Karales's photo of the 1965 march from Selma to Montgomery to demand voting rights. The marchers were initially beaten back by state troopers wielding whips and nightsticks, but a third attempt, with twenty-five thousand marchers, completed the five-day trek to the Alabama capital. As the sun was setting, Karales captured the marchers silhouetted against a turbulent sky. The march and haunting wide-angle photo—published on May 18, 1965, with a story provocatively titled "Our Churches' Sin against the Negro"—are credited with the rapid passage of the Voting Rights Act. Historian Taylor Branch used Karales's photo for the cover of his book *Parting the Waters: America in the King Years, 1954–1963.* "It may well be the seminal image to come out of the civil rights movement," Branch said. "It's an amazing combination of movement and shadow. It looks like they are marching out of the Red Sea." The article's author, Robert Spike, a theologian and civil-rights activist, was murdered the next year.[41]

Poppy and freelance photographer Bob Adelman spent several weeks in Camden, Alabama, "to find out what Southerners mean when they say they want to hold onto the old ways." Photos showed a Southern farmer and a Black boy on a donkey. In the same November 1965 issue, Stokely Carmichael, who later espoused "black power" as head of SNCC, was introduced to *Look* readers in a story by Jack Shepherd and Doug Gilbert. An article by former UN ambassador Ralph Bunche, issuing a "call to arms" after that summer's Watts riots in Los Angeles, was never published, although two other stories on the riots did make it into *Look*.[42]

The scary cover of the May 3, 1966, issue showed a hooded Klansman holding two flaming torches that ran the full vertical length of the magazine. Inside, Alabama attorney general Richmond Flowers wrote that the Justice Department had backed down on a promise to help investigate the Klan for the murder of forty-year-old white civil rights worker Viola Gregg Liuzzo, said to be the only white woman killed during the movement. Despite an effort by J. Edgar Hoover to discredit Liuzzo for purportedly being involved with a Black teenager and being a bad mother, LBJ ordered an investigation of the Klan. One of the men who had murdered Liuzzo had worked for the FBI.[43]

Tom Morgan asked whether King had been eclipsed or was poised to reassume leadership of the civil rights movement. Visually posing the question, there were photos of King and his Southern Christian Leadership Conference doing community organizing in Chicago and a photo of Black Muslim leader Elijah Muhammad.[44]

Reporting on the "long hot summer" of riots in 1967, Claude Brown, author of *Manchild in the Promised Land*, asked, "Is the Race Problem Insoluble?" After "348 years of nightmarish perdition" since the first slaves were brought to America, Brown extolled "the power of blackness."[45]

Republican senator Edward Brooke, the first Black senator in the chamber since Reconstruction, was at least as forceful in a 1967 piece. Addressing the violence of that summer's riots in Detroit, Newark, and elsewhere, he said that it is "violence to deny children high-quality education and an opportunity to lead meaningful lives." Refuting the idea that Communists were behind the urban upheavals, he added: "Hunger, bad housing, ill health, lack of work and the absence of law enforcement need no allies to create an atmosphere that breeds violence. . . . Black power is a response to white irresponsibility."[46]

In the April 16, 1968, issue that went on sale two days before King was assassinated on April 4, *Look* published a haunting last statement by the civil-rights leader, "Showdown for Nonviolence." King had moved decidedly to the left, writing of the Poor People's Campaign for economic justice that he was organizing. He warned that the nation faced violence and collapse if government did not enact a far-reaching Economic Bill of Rights. Nonetheless, he said: "I plan to stand by nonviolence because I have found it to be a philosophy of life that regulates not only my dealings in the struggle for racial justice but also my dealings with people and with my own self." A *Look* tribute to King a year after his death included a photo of the Poor Peoples March and Resurrection City in Washington.[47]

When rioting broke out across the country after King's assassination, Rockwell began a painting of one dead Black man and one dead white man, their blood flowing together. Art editor Allen Hurlburt asked him to change it into a Vietnam battle scene with the same figures, in uniform, lying dead next to each other. The painting, *Blood Brothers*, never ran.

Huie wrote another investigative series, this time on King's assassin, James

Earl Ray. Reprising what he had done with Till's killers, Huie got *Look* to pay Ray at least $35,000 to tell of his days before and after the assassination. Showing Ray as a racist petty criminal who wanted to make a name for himself, the articles followed him from California to Louisiana, Mexico, Canada, Atlanta, Birmingham, Memphis, to his arrest in London. Huie was arrested for defying an order banning pretrial publicity. The series was turned into the book *He Slew the Dreamer* (1970).[48]

Also in 1968, Claude Brown wrote about Black power and Leonard scathingly denounced Northern liberals' hypocrisy. They sent money to support civil rights in the South, but it was a different matter when it came to Black people moving in next door or marrying their daughters, he wrote. Two years later, Sen. Abraham Ribicoff (D-CT) also criticized his fellow Northerners for "monumental hypocrisy," calling out "de facto segregation" and arguing that "a segregated education is harmful to white children as well."[49]

Look took on racism in organized labor. "For nearly a century, most unions have forced Negroes into Jim Crow locals, given them dirty jobs or refused to admit them at all," Jack Star reported. The AFL-CIO has a "public and a private position on race." As Wallace appealed to white working-class voters in his 1968 presidential run, Star quoted the NAACP's labor director saying that not only unions but "'the white working class is racist.'"[50]

An entire "special issue," "The Blacks and the Whites," was published in January 1969. It was put together by Pat Coffin and George Goodman, who had joined *Look* from *Ebony*, America's leading magazine geared to Blacks. The cover showed a silhouetted Black woman in profile, with the question, "Can we bridge the gap?" Among its fifteen articles, Norman Mailer wrote on Black power, while Dallas Cowboys quarterback Tom Meredith talked about how Black and white players worked together as a true team. There were stories on Black unemployment, churches' reactions to Black power, how Black Americans saw their African heritage, and a six-page spread on Black fashion models that was unfortunately titled "Black Beauty." Stories about individual Blacks included those on businessman Rick Haynes, artist Daniel LaRue Johnson, and the just-elected mayor of Gary, Indiana, Richard Hatcher.

1. *Look* building, 488 Madison Avenue, New York (with St. Patrick's Cathedral in the foreground). Courtesy of Drake University Archives & Special Collections Cowles Library, Des Moines, Iowa.

Finished article must win approval of this editorial board. Harlan Logan holds pointer.

13

2. Editors approving layout with Harlan Logan in the foreground, ca. 1940. Courtesy of Drake University Archives & Special Collections Cowles Library, Des Moines, Iowa.

3. Woman with beach ball and Hitler cover, *Look*, June 6, 1939. Author's collection.

4. Eleanor Roosevelt and Mike Cowles, mid-1950s. Courtesy of Drake University Archives & Special Collections Cowles Library, Des Moines, Iowa.

5. Mike and Fleur Cowles with Judy Garland and Frank Sinatra, ca. 1950. Courtesy of Drake University Archives & Special Collections Cowles Library, Des Moines, Iowa.

Photographer Earl Theisen, a long-time friend of novelist Ernest Hemingway, chats with the famous author in the course of a photo assignment for Look.

6. *Look* photographer Earl Theisen with Ernest Hemingway, September 4, 1956. Photograph by William Atwood. Courtesy of Drake University Archives & Special Collections Cowles Library, Des Moines, Iowa.

7. *Flair* cover, October 1950. Courtesy of Drake University Archives & Special Collections Cowles Library, Des Moines, Iowa.

8. Chevrolet assembly, "GM's Fifty Years of Men, Money and Motors," *Look*, January 7, 1958. Photograph by Phillip Harrington. Courtesy of the Library of Congress, *Look* Magazine Photograph Collection.

9. Young people at a Florida swimming pool, "Florida," *Look*, April 14, 1959. Photograph by Frank Bauman. Courtesy of the Library of Congress, *Look* Magazine Photograph Collection.

10. Bob's Big Boy, "Los Angeles: The Art of Living Bumper to Bumper," *Look*, September 18, 1956. Photograph by Maurice Terrell. Courtesy of the Library of Congress, *Look* Magazine Photograph Collection.

11. Mexican farmworkers in California, "New Deal for the Mexican Worker," *Look*, September 29, 1959. Photograph by Earl Theisen. Courtesy of the Library of Congress, *Look* Magazine Photograph Collection.

A predic

San Francisco to *New York in 75 minutes*

by ROCKET TRANSPO

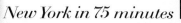

12. Commuters at a train station, "All-America Cities—Park Forest, IL," *Look*, February 9, 1954. Photograph by Bob Sandberg or Jack Star. Courtesy of the Library of Congress, *Look* Magazine Photograph Collection.

13. "San Francisco to New York in 75 Minutes," *Look*, January 11, 1955. Author's collection.

THE COMPUTER DATA BANK:

WILL IT KILL YOUR FREEDOM?

All around the U. S.,
computer centers
may be talking too
much about
everybody and
everything

BY JACK STAR LOOK SENIOR EDITOR

around the country. But now, for the first time, in this age of computers, it is becoming possible for any snooper to get such information quickly and cheaply, without leaving his office chair.

Since the early 1950's, tens of thousands of computers have gone into service in America. Some keep track of payrolls and others mail out bills or help an architect design a skyscraper. Increasingly, hundreds of computers serve as data banks: electronic file

development as the early railroads and the first tele phone companies, which took a number of years to link themselves together in a nationwide network Welfare departments, credit bureaus, hospitals, police departments and dozens of other institutions are put ting their files into hundreds of relatively small data centers. No matter what you call them, they're stil data centers, and they can be linked."

What bothers Representative Gallagher and Sen continued

PHOTOGRAPH BY
PHILLIP HARRINGTON

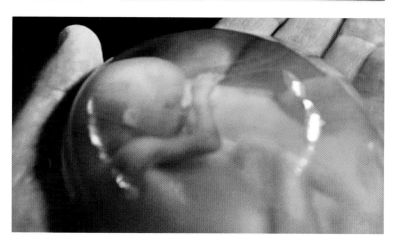

14. "The Computer Data Bank: Will It Kill Your Freedom?" *Look*, June 25, 1968. Photograph by Phillip Harrington. Author's collection.

15. Early image of a fetus, "Dramatic Photos of Babies before Birth," *Look*, June 5, 1962. Author's collection.

16. Housewife and vacuum cleaner, "Great American Appliance," *Look*, May 3, 1955. Photograph by Charlotte Brooks. Courtesy of the Library of Congress, *Look* Magazine Photograph Collection.

17. *Man's First Step on the Moon*, Norman Rockwell, *Look*, December 30, 1969. Norman Rockwell Museum.

18. "A Chance to Begin the Highest Human Adventure," "70's" issue, *Look*, January 13, 1970. Photograph by Paul Fusco. Author's collection.

19. *The Problem We All Live With*, Norman Rockwell, *Look*, January 14, 1964. Norman Rockwell Museum.

the white ministers, priests, rabbis and nuns, who had jetted vast distances to reinforce the march, found a new statement of faith.

TURNING POINT FOR

20. Selma to Montgomery March, "Our Churches' Sin against the Negro," *Look*, May 18, 1965. Photograph by James Karales. Author's collection. © Estate of James Karales. Courtesy of Howard Greenberg Gallery, New York.

21. J. W. Milam (one of Emmett Till's murderers) and family, "The Shocking Story of an Approved Killing in Mississippi," *Look*, January 24, 1956. Photograph by John Vachon. Courtesy of the Library of Congress, *Look* Magazine Photograph Collection.

jackets and helmets of federalized Alabama
National Guardsmen along U.S. Highway 80.

King, "have too often been the taillight
rather than the headlight" of civil rights.
continued

HE CHURCH

22. "White" and "Colored" restrooms, "Segregation—How Far from Slavery?" *Look*, January 15, 1952. Photograph by John Vachon. Courtesy of the Library of Congress, *Look* Magazine Photograph Collection.

23. Black girl and boy by dilapidated house, "Segregation—How Far from Slavery?" *Look*, January 15, 1952. Photograph by John Vachon. Courtesy of the Library of Congress, *Look* Magazine Photograph Collection.

24. Grand Dragon of the South Carolina Ku Klux Klan (James H. Bickley), "Eight Klans Bring Terror to the South," *Look*, April 30, 1957. Photograph by Don Cravens. Courtesy of the Library of Congress, *Look* Magazine Photograph Collection.

25. Jackie Robinson as a rookie, "Baseball's First Negro: The Dodgers Sign Jackie Robinson—First Breach in Game's Racial Barrier," *Look*, November 27, 1945. Photograph by Maurice Terrell. Courtesy of the Library of Congress, *Look* Magazine Photograph Collection.

26. Postwar family in Park Forest, Illinois, "All-America Cities—Park Forest, IL," *Look*, July 27, 1954. Photograph by Robert Sandberg or Jack Star. Courtesy of the Library of Congress, *Look* Magazine Photograph Collection.

27. Dr. Benjamin Spock towers over a toddler, "Visit with Dr. Spock," *Look*, July 21, 1959. Photograph by James Hansen. Courtesy of the Library of Congress, *Look* Magazine Photograph Collection.

28. Robert Frost in a classroom with sixth graders, Hialeah, Florida, "Visit with Robert L. Frost," *Look*, March 31, 1959. Photograph by Robert Lerner. Courtesy of the Library of Congress, *Look* Magazine Photograph Collection.

29. Bell telephone ad. Author's collection.

30. "Husbands: The New Servant Class," *Look*, December 14, 1954. Author's collection.

More radical were articles on interracial marriage and Black Panther leader Eldridge Cleaver. Hedgepeth counterposed Cleaver with white supremacist Roy V. Harris, calling the Panther leader "the hottest piece of Black merchandise on the market," and Harris a "disarmingly amiable old radical with kindly eyes." Harris asserted that Blacks had "lower IQs" and that "the highest ambition of every Negro is to be a white man." Cleaver called for a "Yankee Doodle Dandy form of socialism" to redistribute wealth and for Blacks to have "an equal and proportionate share" in American life. The portrait of Cleaver was more balanced—if occasionally naïve—than a damning article in the *Nation* and a spate of other 1968 media coverage calling the Panthers communist, "neo-Nazis," and in league with Mao Zedong.[51]

Throughout the mid-to-late sixties, *Look* told more stories of successful individual Blacks and a culture that was opening up to them. A 1963 piece showed an attractive twenty-five-year-old Black woman, Joan Murray, who had an apartment on Manhattan's Upper East Side and a good job working for Allen Funt, the creator of the TV show *Candid Camera*. *Look* also reported that year on "greater openness" to Blacks in the workplace, although one anecdote was about a white man inviting a Black man to dinner but never following through.[52]

In an unusually personal piece for *Look*, George Leonard wrote of his childhood in Georgia where "black hands had held me, bathed me, fed me." Moving from his grandfather's antipathy toward Blacks to his "elation" over the Birmingham riots, he wrote: "The Negro has grievances. They are real and pressing. Setting them right will cause pain and maladjustment in the South and North alike. But pretending they are not real will not make them go away. Voting for George Wallace of Alabama will not make them go away. Waiting for everyone to be 'ready' will not make them go away."[53]

The stories kept on coming. Another 1964 piece showed a white couple with its adopted Black children enjoying Disneyland. Former JFK speechwriter Sidney Hyman wrote about Washington's Black elite. Poppy reported on Sigma Chi at Stanford, the first historically white fraternity to pledge a Black student. The five-page story showed a smiling Ken Washington and his Black girlfriend on a double date with a white couple, but reported that his "cool, relaxed manner covers a tautness." In a story on Julian Bond, a Black state legislator in Georgia, Knebel wrote optimistically, "Race still dominates all else in Southern politics, but the very violence of its explosion signals its demise."[54]

In 1969 *Look* interviewed Malcolm X's widow, Betty Shabazz; Leonard described a San Francisco "encounter session" involving Black and white college students; and Knebel authored a story on the psychological burdens that Black women bore.[55]

When Thurgood Marshall, the legendary civil-rights attorney in the 1954 *Brown* case, was sworn in as the Supreme Court's first Black justice in 1967, the story focused more on his life than his jurisprudence, taking the reader to a haunt from Marshall's youth, Ethel's Fish Fry, in the backwater town of Scotlandville, Louisiana.[56]

Look profiled Medgar Evers's brother, Charles, an activist, disc jockey, and mayor of Fayette, Mississippi. The "sassy" mayor spoke of "rosin-chewing, tobacco-spitting red-necks," called Aretha Franklin and B. B. King psychiatrists for "poor black folks," and said that he was waiting for the day when "white folks grow up and act like adults." In *Look*'s last year, Dunbar wrote about Whitney Young, the dynamic executive director of the National Urban League, and Black actors on TV.[57]

Although *Look* wrote fewer stories on race, prejudice, and the status of Blacks during its last two years, its radical "'70s" issue included Buckley's extraordinary essay calling for a Black president. Buckley made his case using several arguments, appealing to traditional conservatives as well as liberals. "The outstanding charge against America is hypocrisy," he wrote. "Where the Negroes are concerned, the practice of inequality directly belies the vision of equality of opportunity." He praised a new generation of Black leaders "harassed by racists," and said that electing a Black to the White House would be "a considerable tonic for the white soul," and "not exactly [a form] of white expiation, but I would not dismiss this."

He derided Black militants, but attacked the notion that any race or group is smarter or more capable than others, and praised the election of Carl Stokes as the first Black mayor of one of America's ten largest cities (Cleveland) and moderate Black leaders in Los Angeles who are "brilliant, ingenious, tough, graceful, irresistible."

Buckley concluded on a rousing note: when an African American is elected, Americans "will celebrate his achievement of the highest office in the world as a personal celebration of the ideals of a country that by this act alone would reassert its idealism."[58]

*

A central theme of this book is that *Look* was not the milquetoast mouth-piece of middle America or a bland copy of *Life*. Nowhere was this more true than in its coverage of white racism, the status of Blacks, and the struggle for civil rights. It broke stories and reported on many topics that other mainstream news media did not—at least until after *Look* did. Its principle of presenting balanced coverage generally broke down when it came to civil rights, for which it became an often angry, forceful advocate for change. By telling stories of Black families, individuals, and children facing discrimination and hardship as well as achieving success, it helped white readers to empathize and turn public opinion and politicians in ways that led to greater tolerance and legislative change.

Cowles, Mich, and *Look*'s writers were outspoken about the evils of racial injustice and the need, as Buckley put it, for an America that was true to its ideals. Leo Rosten later said of Mike Cowles—which could also have been said about his brother John, publisher of the *Minneapolis Star and Tribune*—"He detested injustice. He gave no quarter to race prejudice." Raising hackles, forcing America to confront racial injustice, and—as always—trying to see the path toward progress were what Cowles and *Look* were all about.[59]

8

Changing Families, Changing Roles

As "America's Family Magazine"—a slogan *Look* adopted in 1945—it reported on the many varieties of American families and households, and how family norms changed during its thirty-five-year publishing run. Initially, *Look* celebrated marriage and the postwar nuclear family, with a working father, a stay-at-home mother, and a batch of children. The postwar family was founded on the pillars of the "family wage" won by unions in a booming economy and the "cult of domesticity," which slotted women into the role of homemakers. Most families in *Look* were white and suburban, but—given the magazine's commitment to civil rights—Black families also appeared.[1]

Look discovered and (usually) nonjudgmentally reported on a number of other household configurations, divorce, and the evolving status of mothers and fathers, women and men more generally, and the baby boom and the youth rebellion. Despite the normative nuclear family, *Look* showed its readers the worlds of single men and women, affluent teenagers, and counterculture youth. Even tougher topics like special-needs children, adoption, working women, feminism, sexuality, and gay men were also subjects of articles. *Look*'s liberal staffers wrote most pieces, although many pieces by conservative and liberal guest contributors also appeared.

Look was often ahead of the curve in showing Americans how beliefs and behavior were changing, and it played a crucial role in helping the country adapt to change and begin to shatter taboos. Once again defying later memories of the magazine as a pillar of traditional, Middle American values, *Look* preached tolerance and acceptance of cultural change.

The three following chapters will show how *Look* reported on the transformation of many aspects of the family and marriage, how ideas about the roles of women and men changed, how the baby boom and youth reshaped America, and how its stories differed from those of other publications. These clusters of topics overlap to a large degree, but together illustrate how *Look* changed and influenced the nation.

Marriage and Divorce

The harmonious nuclear family was a given for roughly two decades after World War II, and this ideal was repeatedly portrayed in *Look*. Despite its celebration of working women during the war, *Look* provided a clear definition of what the "Postwar American Family" should look like. In August 1955 the magazine opined: "The American Way of Life is ... you get out of school, you get engaged to the prettiest girl in town, [and] all you want to do is take care of her and make a decent living."[2]

"When people say 'family' nowadays, they generally mean parents and unmarried children only," George Leonard explained in a 1960 article. "This is quite a change from the day when 'family' meant a whole clan of relatives." While there were cracks in this picture that the magazine reported, it was not until the mid-1960s that this normative family structure was seriously questioned.[3]

Typical were several stories in a 1956 issue on "the American woman." One proclaimed that "marriage is still a woman's main goal." Another affirmed that "many young women today take new delight in homemaking." Photos showed a housewife surrounded by a plethora of appliances, happily scrubbing the floor, changing diapers, and taking a break for lunch. This good wife told *Look* that her husband "is boss, [and] that's the way I like it." Another article approvingly described college courses in the basics of being good housewives: "Women learn household skills ... [and] men are expected to learn how to make a living."[4]

Throughout the baby boom years of the 1950s and early 1960s, the great migration to the suburbs was on. *Look* photo essays showed families moving into new homes, enjoying their back yards, buying enticing new "labor-saving" devices, participating in Little League, and taking vacations.[5]

Look frequently outlined the ingredients of successful marriages. A 1945 story instructed young men on "how to hold a wife," with a cover photo of a marine in uniform holding close his young, blond wife. Norman Vincent Peale often addressed subjects like this in his mid-to-late 1950s column, answering questions from readers on how to make their marriages work. Perhaps his most controversial column was one in 1956 about interracial marriage, in which he wrote: "Heaven is completely unsegregated." One of the benefits of marriage, a 1951 article accurately proclaimed, was that married women live longer. Husbands were supposed to work hard—as one story showed a father working six days a week at the gas station while going to school five nights a week to support the couple and its first baby: "He takes care of her and makes a decent living." Wholesome marriages and families were also shown in stories about TV series like *The Adventures of Ozzie and Harriet* and *Dennis the Menace*.[6]

A 1960 survey found most couples saying "they would certainly marry the same person again," and that "very few girls—or boys—think that anyone should remain unmarried after 25." A 1960 article profiling a Palo Alto couple and their three kids reported that half of new marriages were couples under twenty.[7]

Children and Parenting

Because children were an essential ingredient for a successful marriage, it's not surprising that *Look* covered the children of the baby boom in countless articles, from its 1948 story on the "bumper baby crop" to a 1960 story that reported that 43 percent of girls wanted at least four children. The magazine informed readers that "more children equal less divorce," a message that was not lost on teenage girls.[8]

Already, during World War II, *Look* suggested that Americans should have more children, after the drop in birth rates during the Depression and the war. "Marriage may begin with romantic love; but children give abiding strength . . . [and] meaning to the relationship." As childbearing increased during the postwar years, there were frequent stories on parenting—from childrearing tips and findings from studies of child development to home life, the effects of TV violence, and the need for greater father involvement. Happy photo essays showed moms with kids frolicking in blow-up pools and with young daughters in beauty pageants. Two articles provided gender-stereotyped versions of "what little girls" and "little boys are made of." Boys were shown with toy guns, dressing in their fathers' clothes, and playing in the mud, but *Look* tenderly opined: "They're made of what we can pass on to them from the experience of our years."[9]

In 1957 the magazine bragged that "it's no accident that *Look* publishes so many stories of children—more, perhaps, than any other publication." Dr. Benjamin Spock and other childrearing experts like psychologists Peter Blos, Albert Bandura, and Lois Murphy were often published or cited. *Look* translated research into tips on "ways to be a good parent." These included a Vassar study's top ten pieces of parenting advice, what to expect of babies and toddlers during the first years of life, why babies cry, how to integrate a second baby into the family, and a Child Study Association of America primer on how to talk with children about sex. It counseled, "Knowledge won't make a child sex-crazed; lack of knowledge [is] more likely to." *Look* published a series of stories on developmental stages, with articles on the current state of knowledge about babies, toddlers, children in mid-childhood, and adolescents. The magazine also provided advice on such varied topics as how to properly feed children, what toys were beneficial for healthy development, and how to watch out for mental illness.[10]

Although the focus was on couples having children, *Look* addressed adoption in at least eight articles between 1948 and 1959. Reflecting the country's baby-mania and worries about unwed mothers, it reported in 1951 on "a million childless couples" seeking to adopt, with only seventy-five thousand babies legally up for adoption. Touching photos of babies in foundling hospitals and with new families were accompanied by stories about the shortage of potential adoptees. The magazine repeatedly warned about adopting on the "black market." Calling this "traffic in human flesh," *Look* also sounded the alarm about international adoptions. Robert Moskin and Jim Hansen produced a seven-page 1959 story with a dozen photos bringing the good news that agencies were making more very young babies available for adoption. Pleading the case for children needing to be loved, by the late 1960s, *Look* spoke positively of both a California law enabling unmarried women to take in some of the nation's more than three hundred thousand foster children and quoted writer Pearl S. Buck, an adoptive parent, saying: "'It is the loveless man and woman who threaten our national life and culture.'" In one of its last issues, on August 24, 1971, John Poppy profiled a California woman who had adopted fourteen multiracial children from Vietnam, Biafra, a Sioux reservation, and elsewhere.[11]

In a trenchant 1960 essay, author and literary critic Diana Trilling described the current "generation that goes in for so much larger families than was our recent custom, and that eats, sleeps, and breathes nothing but babies and child care." She asked rhetorically, "When have we ever [before] mobilized all our professional skills the way we do today to persuade ourselves that the closely knit family is the be-all and end-all of existence?"[12]

One way that the magazine backhandedly demonstrated the benefits of marriage and family was to examine the scourge of divorce. Six months after it began publishing, *Look* spent nine pages on the "causes of divorce," including "sexual maladjustments." Photos showed a child "torn from his mother's arms" and quickie divorces in Reno. Two years later came a story on "America's misfits"—divorced women—who were to be pitied because they were a "fifth wheel," have to do "manly chores," and whose children are plunged into conflicts of loyalty. The magazine even addressed the topic of soldiers' infidelity during World War II.[13]

Divorce was a frequent topic after the war, with many postwar marriages dissolving, and again in the 1960s, as marital breakups began to rise significantly. Just after V-E Day, sociologist and *Look* contributor Ernest Groves predicted that half of marriages would end in divorce by 1965, telling readers to give troubled marriages more of a chance and spouses a break, because divorce leads to "loneliness, frustration, regret." The same message was conveyed in 1947, urging couples to have "liberal doses of patience, tolerance, and mutual respect," while photos showed the tragedies of a man taking a swing at his wife and a husband having his children taken away by his ex-wife.[14]

Between 1948 and 1950, the dangers lurking behind divorce were the subject of at least nine articles by Jacques Bacal, author of *The ABC's of Divorce* (1947). Bacal and coauthor Louise Sloane urged marriage training and offered "eight rules" for the first, "most dangerous year of marriage." Another article reported on the church's role in preserving marriages. Misogyny crept into one 1949 piece that blamed wives for husbands' infidelity, which Bacal called "a symptom, not a cause" of a bad marriage. Another piece faulted housewives for becoming "mentally lazy" and letting their appearance go, while yet another scolded a wife for not accepting her husband's apology when he kissed another woman, calling jealousy a "morbid, irrational illness." While women—not men—played the principal role in keeping the family intact, their other role was to please their husbands. Men—whom "society . . . taught . . . to act" superior—were never blamed for, or treated as the losers from, divorce.[15]

Divorce more or less vanished from the pages of *Look* during the 1950s, after a 1951 story happily proclaimed "The Family's Coming Back," although the topic returned with a vengeance in the sixties. Articles of the decade talked about couples being resigned to each other, and the difficult road from marriage counselors to separation to lawyers. *Look* repeated the tropes that divorced women were losers, children suffered by not living with two parents, and marital breakups signaled a decline in morality. In one article, a child of a divorced mother who was dating plaintively said: "Thanks for buying me a daddy." As late as 1967, divorce was characterized as a recipe for loneliness, particularly for women.[16]

Betty Rollin, who briefly wrote for *Look* and later became a well-known NBC correspondent, must have shocked many *Look* readers by reporting that most women and men who remarried were happier. Even more shocking, she quoted futurist Alvin Toffler, who said, "Serial marriage is cut to order for the Age of Transience in which all man's relationships . . . shrink in duration."[17]

With the question, "Is the Family Obsolete?" emblazoned on a 1971 cover, a recently radicalized Pat Coffin told readers: "This disintegration of the home is a worldwide phenomenon, but the symptoms are most acute in our own materialist-militarist society." Anthropologist Margaret Mead declared: "What Americans think is the American family is really the post–World War II suburban family: totally isolated, desperately autonomous, unable to tolerate adolescent children at home, pushing its children out into matrimony as soon as possible, no grandparents, no cousins, no neighbors, no nothing—moving from place to place." A Harvard Medical School student living in a commune also situated the "traditional" family in the years between the war and the late 1960s: "Affluence, suburbanization, mobility zapped the old extended family to shreds, and now something new [is] emerging."[18]

Feminist Betty Friedan said that the traditional family was "too confining a mold for the needs of people." Other articles in this issue spoke approvingly of unmarried couples living together and a "radical family" living in a commune. William Hedgepeth wrote about communes where men and women flocked "to cleanse themselves of the impurities of urban life." Anthropologist Bruno Bettelheim also gave a nod to communes as well as working mothers, saying that America needs an equivalent of the kibbutz and childcare "for the sake of millions of American women who have a right to jobs."[19]

With a photo on the cover of a young couple with their faces touching a newborn, the issue suggested that both fathers and mothers should be involved parents. Thoughts on how to be a parent in this new age were offered by child-development experts Benjamin Spock and Urie Bronfenbrenner.

A few years earlier, Leonard and Marshall McLuhan offered their own radical take: "Marriage and the family are shifting into new dimensions. What it will mean to be boy or girl, man or woman, husband or wife, male or female may come as one of the great surprises the future holds for us." Unlike advances in science, Leonard declared in another article, "Marriage is only a scrap of what it could be." Indeed, by the late 1960s, the nuclear family was fast giving way to singles, couples cohabiting, and remarriage.[20]

Out of the Mainstream

Despite the apparent idyll of the postwar family, *Look* reported that not all children or parents were thriving, and not all families were nuclear, suburban ones.

From the children of migrant workers to those suffering from mental illness, readers were occasionally shown another America through sensitive prose, damning facts, and heart-rending photos. A 1951 story about a million migrant children included photos of a little boy sleeping in a truck and a nine-year-old girl hauling water to wash clothes. Six years later, *Look* medical writer Roland Berg wrote about the relatively new awareness that "children can be crippled by emotional storms," but therapies could help. These sympathetic articles helped pave the way for public support of efforts to reduce poverty and help children in need.[21]

Not surprisingly, *Look* published a number of articles on Black families. As we have seen, these included poor families, affluent Washingtonians, and Black households isolated in white suburbs. Interracial marriages were discussed in several late 1960s articles, including the boldly headlined Poppy article in 1969, "Can a N—— Love a Honky?" Another called for legalizing marriage between Blacks and whites.[22]

Look's most influential story on the Black family was "The Discarded Third," by Daniel Patrick Moynihan, then an LBJ advisor. Reprising his controversial 1965 report on "The Negro Family" a year later in *Look*, he pointed to the growing absence of fathers, "overburdened" women having to play both mother and father, and "children doomed at birth" to increased risks, poorer academic outcomes, and often, failed lives. Despite much criticism from civil-rights leaders and liberal magazines like the *Nation*, Moynihan did say that the United States has "an unmistakable responsibility . . . to help provide Negro Americans with the basic conditions of family stability: full employment, decent housing, . . . better than average education [and] a family income." To emphasize Moynihan's point, Ernest Dunbar wrote about a fatherless Harlem boy, whose mother and seven siblings lived in a four-room apartment. "Dope addiction eats at the neighborhood," he wrote. "The lack of a male figure in the home makes it difficult for many children to accept the discipline of the school."[23]

Singles

By the 1960s, the poor "lady loners" started to vie with happy single women and happy bachelors in their twenties and beyond. Another sign that marriage was no longer the ultimate goal were the sympathetic stories in *Look*'s later years on unmarried couples who lived together.[24]

Look introduced readers to the world of singles bars, singles ads, singles apartment buildings, singles parties, and groups for those who were divorced. The new hedonism of singles life was captured in one man's quote: "New York is a single man's paradise. It doesn't pay to get married. There are too many temptations, too many divorces." A similar tone was found in a spoof about the Upper East Side's pioneering and thriving singles bars Maxwell's Plum and TGI Fridays. A Manhattan bartender told *Look*: "They come in here just to pick up a man and go home with him." Even before Harvard students figured out how to introduce single young men and women by computer, *Look* described an experimental organization called the Scientific Marriage Foundation that paired men and women on an IBM mainframe.[25]

Look's Revolutionary Turn on Homosexuality

Look's coverage of homosexuality followed a similar arc from normative damnation to remarkable acceptance for its time. In the first of four articles on gay men, Jack Star spoke at length about "the sad gay life." Describing gay neighborhoods, bars, and steam baths on the Upper West Side of Manhattan and in Chicago and San Francisco, he wrote that gay men were "preoccupied by sex" and "place no great premium on fidelity." Citing the Kinsey Institute, Star reported that 4 percent of white men are gay for life, but 37 percent have had some homosexual experience. Psychiatrists said that homosexuality stems from hatred or fear of fathers, but 25 percent could be "treated." Even Marshall McLuhan suggested that: "Homosexuality may fade out." Star more sympathetically noted how anti-gay prejudice "resembles prejudice toward Negroes and Jews," and argued that ostracism and punishment were no solution; rather, "perhaps better understanding is." Poppy had attempted to write a piece on homosexuality in 1962 that was not published.[26]

A 1969 *Look* article about the gay-themed play *The Boys in the Band* was paired with a Star piece that quoted gay men saying that "life is improving" and police raids on gay bars were decreasing, although one man wished he could take a pill to make him straight. He noted that Connecticut would become the second state where homosexuality would not be a crime. The article elicited much reader mail, and the magazine published six letters. Although two spoke of "perversion" and need for "self-control," one praised *Look* for helping "clear the air of hostile feelings," another was from a gay man who said "the new homosexual looks and feels no different from the rest of American youth," and a third was from a man who led a religious gay group called the Vineyard.[27]

A 1970 Presbyterian Church report on sex, summarized in *Look*, spoke of "aggravated suffering and grievous injustice for homosexual persons," and called for repealing laws criminalizing homosexuality, yet said that "homosexual behavior is essentially incomplete." A Berkeley psychiatrist went further: "Happiness for the homosexual can be as possible as for the heterosexual when he recognizes that sexual relationships are only a small component of a total relationship."[28]

Finally, in one of *Look*'s most noteworthy articles, Star wrote of two twenty-eight-year-old Minnesota men, Jack Baker and Michael McConnell, who had been secretly married by a Methodist minister after legal battles that went to the Supreme Court. He reported that the couple's "household is like that of any young marrieds, except that there is no male-female role-playing." Photos showed the clean-cut young men holding hands and going to church. Forty-two years later, when the Supreme Court legalized gay marriage, the couple was "discovered" by the *New York Times* and many other U.S. and international media. In 1971, when the overwhelming majority of Americans believed that homosexuality itself was a sad, sinful aberration, the magazine once again demonstrated its radicalism on cultural issues. Cowles, whose niece was gay, had no qualms about hiring photographer Charlotte Brooks, who also was gay.[29]

Long before ideas about gender fluidity, Roland Berg discussed transsexuals in a 1970 article. Photos by Doug Jones showed a couple, Danny and Viki, preparing for their marriage, and a transsexual stripper.[30]

Life never went so far. In 1964 it compared homosexuals to communists who "intend to bury us" and called a sympathetic report by the New York Academy of Medicine "dead wrong." Even in 1971, the magazine tried to simply quote scientists regarding whether or not homosexuality was normal, didn't talk to gay men or women, and called those supporting gay rights "homosexual militants."[31]

Sex in the Pages of *Look*

Sex was a complicated topic throughout *Look*'s history because it touched on strongly held values, longstanding norms, and intimate behaviors. The magazine also published many articles on the need for wider dissemination of birth control—an issue that Cowles strongly supported, which led Ireland to briefly ban the magazine. Although there were traces of puritanism—particularly in guest-written articles—*Look* presented strikingly open and increasingly progressive attitudes toward sexuality, sex education, and contraception. From its straightforward discussion of the first Kinsey Report in a 1947 article, "Toward a Saner Sex Life," to Leonard's and others' more radical writings, the magazine undoubtedly helped change Americans' views about sexuality.[32]

Margaret Sanger, the founder of organizations that became Planned Parenthood, was a particular favorite of Cowles. *Look* published articles by Sanger in 1938 and 1939, with an opposing viewpoint by a Catholic priest, and favorable stories on her work in 1942 and 1947. Accompanied by photos from her documentary *Why Let Them Die?* she wrote: there are "8,000 who die each year at the hands of the abortionist because they are ignorant of family planning." She also pointed out that many families fall into poverty because of unplanned babies. One of *Look*'s very rare editorial comments, in 1939, said: "*Look* does think there is something to be said for 'planned families.'" Nearly forty-five years later, Cowles said, "I'm proud that *Look* was first among national magazines to come out for birth control."[33]

In the 1960s, as birth control and abortion became hot political issues, *Look* ramped up its advocacy. There were pieces by Planned Parenthood president Alan Guttmacher discussing the importance of birth control for the poor, a Dunbar article on vasectomies—"a simple 15-minute operation

[that] is putting the pleasure back in marital relations," and an article by Estelle Griswold, a later president of Planned Parenthood, explaining why her organization intentionally violated a Connecticut law banning birth control.[34]

There was more: the "lady doctor who defied her church" was a Kentucky physician trying to fight poverty by making birth control available to women and sterilization for men. To put the issue in perspective, *Look* compared attitudes, practices, and laws regarding birth control in Latin America, Japan, poor Mecklenburg County, North Carolina, and a well-heeled Connecticut town. American policy and Catholic teachings were criticized. John D. Rockefeller III, in an essay about overpopulation, urged wide dissemination of birth control.[35]

A Jack Star piece that won the American Medical Association's award for the best medical journalism spoke of the "tragedy of illegal abortion." *Look* also revealed how a million women each year were "denied by the law the right to a hospital abortion." A suburban abortionist was profiled, and a dissident Catholic priest called for women's right to choice.[36]

The magazine introduced the subject of sex education in 1943 and presented opposing positions in a 1949 educational film with actor Eddie Albert. In 1954 *Look* offered advice to parents on how to talk with their children about sex. By the 1960s *Look* was outspoken in calling for more instruction in schools. "Young Americans—more than two million of them a year—get in serious trouble because they do not know or will not face one of life's fundamental facts, that sexual intercourse causes babies," bluntly began a 1970 piece. Discussing the "explosion of illegitimate pregnancy among young people," it reported that knowledge of contraception is poor, called for parents and schools to increase sex education, and condemned "the prohibitory approach of traditional morality [that] may be contributing to our tragic annual toll of illegitimacy"[37]

A 1958 article by Moskin and Gelolo McHugh, a Duke University professor who developed a "Sex Knowledge Inventory," called on Americans "to unlearn the idea that sex is evil." An intriguing 1955 story discussed how divorced women were not oblivious to their desires. Psychologist Albert Bandura suggested the country's sexual mores were out of date. In a 1963 cover story on "Morality USA," Moskin suggested that "Christian morality of sexual life" was outdated, as a new, freer sexual code was emerging among young people.[38]

Sexual liberation increasingly made it into the pages of *Look*, as in American society, in the late 1960s. Although most middle-class Americans did not reject traditional family patterns, these stories did open some minds about very different ways to live. In a March 1966 issue, Leonard Gross reported that "morals have flipped since World War II," and a sex educator wrote: "'We need new values to establish when and how we should have sexual experiences.... Sex is not just something you do in marriage, in bed, in the dark, in one position." If this was not enough to shock *Look* readers, *Playboy* founder Hugh Hefner gave his own take on sexual ethics in the first issue of 1967.[39]

A half year later, in Leonard and McLuhan's "The Future of Sex," they took the revolutionary position that "sex as we now know it may be dead. Sexual concepts, ideals and practices already are being altered beyond recognition." *Look* reported that "Human Sexual Behavior" had become a college course. "One thing is sure," Knebel wrote, "the boy-girl sexual revolution is deep and wide, and Puritan America is gone forever."[40]

The revolution was on when George Leonard offered his opinions on "Why We Need a New Sexuality." "Swapping bed partners does not work, but sexual exclusivity shouldn't mean (as it now does) emotional and sensual exclusivity.... We need a world where people can trust their good feelings, where members of the same sex can touch and caress each other without fear of homosexuality, [and] where members of the opposite sex can touch and caress without fear of seductiveness."[41]

A 1970 article reported that even the Presbyterians were on board: "No sexual behavior should be forbidden unless it offends one's partner." The church also gave a green light to sex before marriage, criticized the "medical myths" that masturbation was harmful, and put communal living on the table for discussion. The once-unspoken topic of sex among the elderly was broached in an article quoting sexologists William H. Masters and Virginia E. Johnson, who told *Look* that people in their eighties could have good sex. Rollin reported on Dr. David Reuben's 1969 bestseller, *Everything You*

Always Wanted to Know about Sex, citing his advice on topics that included how women can have better orgasms. Getting a bit carried away, *Look* told of "widespread orgies" and "public sex" becoming more common, with the latter described as "the wave of the future."[42]

*

The radical turn in "America's family magazine" was abundantly evident when Leonard wrote in January 1970:

> We need bigger, less well-defined "families." ... We need groups of friends and neighbors who are willing to share the strongest feelings, to share responsibility for the emotional needs of all the children in the group. Thus, no one will be childless, no one will lack affection, and no one will be deprived of a rich and varied emotional and sensual life. . . . The new sexuality leads eventually to the creation of a family as wide as all mankind, that can weep together, laugh together, and share the common ecstasy.[43]

A far cry, indeed, from *Look*'s views and America's conception of the family during the fifteen to twenty years after World War II.

9

Changing Ideas about Women and Men

During its first decades, *Look* mostly reinforced popular norms about women and men's proper roles, but later it took on and opened minds about alternatives to traditional sex roles. It portrayed how these norms and roles were changing, often implicitly telling its readers that the country needed to accept these changes.

Women in *Look*

It is impossible to discuss how *Look* and Americans viewed the family without examining the magazine's complex, changing portrayal of women and their roles. As noted, during much of the 1940s and 1950s, white women were either shown as happy housewives/mothers, unfortunate divorcees, or—as if they were a different species—gorgeous Hollywood stars.

Look's Women's Department assigned stories that largely cubbyholed women in these categories. When Pat Coffin succeeded Fleur Cowles as head of the department, the focus shifted somewhat from fashion to family. Female photographers like Brooks were sent to cover these "women's" matters.

Mothers were mostly angels who were the most important parent and smilingly raised the kids and cooked the dinners. Yet, Bacal and Philip Wylie, who sneered at "momism" in his 1942 book, *Generation of Vipers*, suggested that wives could be irrationally jealous and mothers could be "jerks." Several Wylie pieces were examples of how chauvinism was second-nature in the era.[1]

This unusual bile aside, readers were told in the 1950s that marriage and motherhood were what women most wanted and that women "long to be cherished, protected, and dependent on man's superior strength." Leonard spoke of the "wife's domestic duties" but also noted a 50 percent increase in working wives during this decade of presumed domesticity. *Look* was hardly alone in celebrating the moms of postwar America.[2]

Some pre-1960s stories showed another side of womanhood in America. Two articles before World War II called for equality for women and praised "career women." During the war, *Look* criticized those opposed to working wives as prejudiced, yet derisively said that "only 1 percent of wives in America have sufficient artistic or business talent to follow what is termed a career." A 1943 article highlighted nearly twenty women in "essential" jobs ranging from weatherwoman to lumberjack. An especially prescient 1942 article by Dorothy Thompson warned of "relegation to the kitchen" after the war. Two years later, *Look* asked six women, "Will you quit your job after the war?" Coffin painted a sympathetic profile of a single working mother in 1950. Two other postwar articles profiled women doctors and physicist Leona Marshall, who managed to be successful as a scientist, wife, and mother. A 1949 "Look Applauds" column featured ten professional women. Eleanor Roosevelt was presented as a hero. However, she and the doctors and physicists were outliers, women bucking the prevailing norms. Black professionals were also outliers, but, for *Look* in the 1950s, Black success was more aspirational than women's success. The tone changed in the 1960s, as *Look* did many more stories on working mothers and career women (often in "male" professions like medicine, science, and politics), women who liked being single, Black women, and feminists earnestly striving for equality.[3]

Life was somewhat more likely to focus on the problems supposedly inherent in women working. The caption on a 1948 cover read, "Career Girl:

Her Life and Her Problems," and, in 1954, *Life* described the "achievements and struggles" of working women.[4]

Eleanor Harris—screenwriter for the 1948 movie *Every Girl Should Be Married*—showed the ambivalence of *Look* and American culture in a 1960 article on "manless women." Although 70 percent of American women were married by age twenty-four, she reported that "many do not want marriage" and want to "enjoy a man-free life." This was despite the "world-wide and historic conviction that every woman wants to be married," and that normal young women go on "the man hunt."[5]

A 1966 issue with fifty pages of articles devoted to "the American woman" continued this on-the-one-hand-on-the-other-hand approach in more than a dozen articles. Coffin led by characterizing women as "frustrated single girls, disillusioned divorcees, embattled daughters, and even happy housewives," while emphasizing the difficulty of both working and being a mother. She urged women not to "try to equal men" and "go back to being women," and derided many career and single women as "self-centered drags." Yet, she also discussed Catalyst, a new organization designed to help women balance work and home, and quoted Betty Friedan, who said that women have "a moral obligation to get out of their homes."[6]

Rollin, in a piece reporting that divorce had become "culturally accepted," added: "Despite the current advances toward self-reliance, a woman without a man is, more often than not, a woman who wants a man—probably to marry." However, she astutely noted that feminism was an elite movement, with many women, men, and children "left behind."[7]

Look was certainly moving toward a less restricted notion of what women should be. A working mother wrote that she liked her job, despite the disapproval of her children, psychiatrists, and society at large. She told *Look*'s readers that eight million of the twenty-three million working women in the country were mothers. After quoting a psychiatrist who wondered if a working woman could truly be a mother, she concluded more defiantly, "The working mother situation obviously has its perils, but then so does the opposite situation. It is about time that society stopped denigrating the working mother." A 1967 story turned the miserable divorcee trope on its head, with a forty-two-year-old California woman engaging in the "painful and exhilarating task of creating her own life" by getting a job, volunteering, and joining the recently formed Parents without Partners.[8]

Two of *Look*'s most prominent women writers—Pat Coffin and Laura Bergquist—provided dueling ideas of womanhood. Coffin was more the traditionalist, whereas Bergquist, in her writing and life, was anything but. Coffin wrote of the "happiness of a baby's laugh" and a "jeepful of kids." She talked about a "woman's place" and said that college women were deluded to think that a degree would help them in the job market. For these young women, a BA is only valuable to "succeed with the college man," the only job is to be a secretary, and "boredom ranks with the manhunt as a prime reason for quitting." Several other stories in the 1966 "American Woman" issue harped on the loneliness of unmarried women. Five more articles, including one by *Vogue* editor Diana Vreeland, focused on traditional feminine concerns like beauty, fashion, and cooking. A Norman Rockwell image depicted a more staid mother and daughter looking at a John Singer Sargent painting, while a young, next-generation woman in jeans looked at a Picasso on a different wall of a gallery. Photos also conveyed *Look*'s ambivalence about who a woman should be, as several showed young women in "skimpy" bikinis shimmering in the water and men leeringly watching a burlesque show.[9]

The tide was truly turning when Bergquist wrote a powerful, semi-autobiographical defense of unmarried working women over age twenty-seven. She told how she went from the University of Chicago to become a social worker in the city's slums and campaign for politicians before joining *Look*. She described seeing Hollywood "in its heyday," working for four years in Mexico, and knowing "an infinite variety of men—as friends, more-than-friends, and working colleagues." Rhetorically asking, "Was it worth it to give up domesticity to see Castro's Cuba, Khrushchev's Moscow, and Kennedy's White House? For me, yes." She married at the almost unheard-of age of forty and, fortunately for *Look*, continued her career.[10]

Liberal satirist Jules Feiffer derided "Aunt Toms," traditional women peddling marriage, as "sexual McCarthyism." The emerging critique of old female roles "indicate[s] that something is moving," he wrote. Calling women "the most submerged of minority groups," he said that many were building a "new identity."[11]

John D. Rockefeller III did not disapprove of "young women who pursue activities and careers outside the home, and worry less about proving their femininity." An "executive mother" emphatically denied that there was any conflict between being a businesswoman and a mother.[12]

Look covered "women's lib" more or less sympathetically when it became a major movement in the late 1960s. Psychologist Richard Farson, later president of Esalen, told readers in 1969 that women were underpaid, barred from major jobs, and "often find home a prison from which there is no escape." He predicted that "a new woman may emerge," which could be good for men and the world, as she would "no longer tolerate war" and would be an advocate for endangered children.[13]

Look played a significant role in elevating Gloria Steinem, publishing a profile of the young feminist in 1968 and contracting her to write two stories, including her call for a woman president. In the other, she wrote that women, "uncorrupted by power," could "understand the dispossessed enough to keep the country together," whereas men had to prove their masculinity through war and brinkmanship. Readers must have been astonished by her approvingly quoting Friedrich Engels on "the authoritarian family system" and her identification as a Phi Beta Kappa from Smith College who "used to wonder ... why editors assigned her stories about lipstick."[14]

Rollin wrote the 1970 cover story "Motherhood: Who Needs It." Attacking the "motherhood cult," she wrote that mothers tend to be more unhappy than single women, their creativity is "squelched" by staying home with children, and she quoted a New York psychiatrist, who said, "Women don't need to be mothers any more than they need spaghetti." Margaret Mead told Rollin that "mothering," her term for caring for children, could be "a good occupation for either sex."[15]

Rollin also reported on the early backlash. One opponent told her that libbers were "a bunch of frustrated hags," and described a housewife as "a perfectly adjusted American female." She described two "anti-lib" groups, the Pussycats, who believed in equal pay but opposed the libbers' militancy, and Fascinating Womanhood, "the John Birchiest of all backlash groups," which believed that "man must be the unconditional leader, and that the woman should strive to be an unconditional follower."[16]

In *Look*'s penultimate issue, readers learned of a husband in Virginia who did most of the diapers and housekeeping and supported the "50/50 marriage." The lesson was clear: "Men and women can and ought to share equally the joys and tasks of home and parenthood as well as the thrill of professional development."[17]

Life was less than sympathetic to leading feminists, calling Friedan an "angry battler" in 1963 and Kate Millett a "furious young philosopher" whose feminism stemmed "at least partly [from] private hurts." It published a package of articles and photos on women's liberation shortly after the nationwide marches in 1970, to mark the fiftieth anniversary of women's right to vote. The articles were more sympathetic, noting the "painful record of little progress," but suggested that the movement was "jarring" for most Americans.[18]

In a long, generally positive story about "female liberation" published in the aftermath of the 1969 Miss America pageant, *Life* discussed feminist groups, the history of women's rights, and quoted radicals who said that "marriage means lifelong slavery." Yet, the writer interjected: "What had led these women to the point where they could coldly dismiss feeling and touching, sex and love?" She reported that libbers "retain many female character traits" and added the strange comment that "overexposure to women's liberation leads, I found, to headaches, depression, and a fierce case of the shakes."[19]

The American Man

Look's depiction of men followed a mostly similar trajectory. The explicit assumption from the 1940s to the early 1960s was that men were the breadwinners, masculine, masters of the household, and the parents who played second fiddle to moms. Arthur Lynes, the managing editor of *Harper's*, wrote that in marriages "a man has the last word." Photos of actors reinforced the masculine ideal of the "he-man," strong and debonair. Sports stories and photos—with sports almost exclusively the domain of men—showed tough competitors. Men were the dominant, strong, and rugged sex—whether the "Father in Charge" or "The Fighter" who is "winning our war in Vietnam."

Depictions of men in the 1960s changed more subtly than those of women. Some men were shown as involved fathers, some actors were less hyper-masculine, counterculture men had long hair, and gay men could be happy.[20]

At the same time, several articles in the 1950s decried the supposed emasculation of men. Wylie dished up as acerbic a put-down of men as he had done of women. Fathers don't "associate much with [their] kids" and model "cheating [and] hypocrisy." Calling dads "moral slackers" and "slobs," he added that "pops" are as "ethically dependable as a minefield." Lynes also argued that husbands were becoming a "servant class" "with aprons and safety pins and dishpan hands." An accompanying drawing showed a woman holding an open-mouthed, upside-down man looking like a vacuum cleaner. Even the notion of male superiority took a hit when Bacal wrote that it was only based on "what society taught us."[21]

Articles by Leonard, William Attwood, Robert Moskin, and Diana Trilling in 1958 and 1959 sounded the alarm about "the decline of the American male." Attwood's piece is considered one of the best popular analyses of 1950s American masculinity. *Look* expanded these articles into a partly humorous book with a cover drawing of a woman holding a marionette of a frog-like man and essays ranging from "Why Is He Afraid to Be Different?" to "Why Do Women Dominate Him?" The 1966 Bergquist article on "the American woman" had a more sophisticated take, saying that affluence had caused men to lose their identity and become depressed. Coffin chimed in to say that men are pushed around by women, refuse to grow up, and can be "desexed."[22]

These long-running themes of man the master and woe is man largely continued in a 1967 issue devoted to "the American man." One story began by talking about the good, involved father who is still "teaching his boy to be a man." Being a man "is not easy" and being a father "is even harder," *Look* said. Not surprisingly Coffin urged men to "return to [be] head of your family soonest," denouncing "woman-dominated men."[23]

Chandler Brossard lamented, "In all of history, no life has been more difficult than that of the contemporary American man: father, husband or bachelor. . . . No man has ever been lonelier than today's man, a fact that is rarely talked about." Rollin wrote that divorce is "grim" for fathers as well as mothers, as "Sunday daddies" either hurt at the loss of their children or "remarry . . . [and] just stop showing up."[24]

Although women were generally treated as the real victims of divorce, Eleanor Harris reported on men's loneliness, debunking the *Playboy* image of America's eighteen million unmarried men as "happy, well adjusted bachelors." She also told readers that most men want sex more than companionship. Within a few years, notions of "happy" bachelors, like "lady loners," had mostly disappeared.[25]

As early as 1940, *Look* showed photos of men changing diapers and learning how to bathe a baby. It proclaimed, rather prematurely, that "the old attitude of the male . . . that a father's responsibility ended with earning a living—is as outmoded as the stork." By the late 1950s, the magazine featured loving dads with their sons (rarely daughters), and happily said that "love is the warmth and wonder of fatherhood." "Foster daddies" taking in children from orphanages were praised in 1957. Yet it was not until Leonard's 1960 article that the idea of husbands and wives both being providers was broached. Eleven years later, he attacked "rigid" sexual identities and damned "outmoded ideals of 'manliness'. . . . Their manly upbringing deprived them of emotions, so they are unable to feel the suffering they cause."[26]

In the late sixties, the good father was portrayed in a profile of a New Hampshire lumberman who said that he was "very involved" with his children, unlike his own father who "never changed a diaper." Another story about a middle-class Black "family man" painted a flattering portrait of a father who was close to his son. Just as new images of women started to flood the culture and the pages of *Look*, the magazine started publishing stories on counterculture and activist young men. Rockefeller wrote of "a blurring of male and female roles" and "young men [who] increasingly are against the warrior role. They are not afraid of domestic chores, feeling less need to prove their virility in elaborate ways." Rollin wrote that "husbands, especially those who are young and well-educated, are helping their wives 'a great deal more' with housework." The Farson piece on women's lib astutely suggested that the movement could liberate men too.[27]

10

Baby Boomers

The sharp rise in childbearing during the two decades after World War II, coinciding with America's great economic expansion, made the seventy-eight million baby boomers darlings of the news media from the late 1940s through the 1960s (and well into the twenty-first century). *Look*'s articles on the nuclear family and childrearing were only part of its coverage of this charmed generation. While the joys and gentle tribulations of middle-class children were told and retold, the magazine also devoted considerable attention to teenagers and youth born before the boom began in 1946. *Look* followed the earliest members of this generation to college in the 1960s, as higher education rapidly expanded, and it assiduously covered the youth of the counterculture and antiwar movement.

The many sides of 1950s adolescents were presented in text and photographs. On the one hand, teen parties were clean, teen girls sewed, and "sweet sixteen" was a "wonderful age to be." A beautifully presented eight-page photo gallery opened with a brooding girl looking out a window and ended with her in her first party dress and dad smiling in the background. Good girls modeled dresses and their clean-cut male counterparts wore their hair short.[1]

Yet, an edgier and sometimes darker side came to the fore with those who turned to sex, rock and roll, and youth deemed juvenile delinquents. A 1951 piece on teen "sex problems" and violence reported on "non-virgin clubs" in some small towns. The "JD" scare was partly fostered by reports like those in Look. Two 1953 articles by Dan Fowler spotlighted teen murderers and talked of "taming" teenagers. "Teen-age terror" was discussed in an article about the 1955 movie Blackboard Jungle. Look took readers "inside" a teen gang and a juvenile detention center, and showed wild teens in Philadelphia as a backdrop for a 1956 story calling for a 10:30 p.m. curfew.[2]

These variants of teenage America were juxtaposed in a 1956 story with photos of well-dressed adolescents at a high school dance and a wild teen gyrating to the rock music of Bill Haley. That same year, Elvis Presley burst onto the scene, and rock music became a symbol of rebellious teens and youth.[3]

"Why have we become so preoccupied with teenagers," Look asked, knowing that mass media like it were a big part of the answer. "They've had more opportunities and more advice than any other generation." Yet, despite all the worries, the magazine was sanguine that they would turn out well.[4]

A July 1957 cover story on "How American Teen-agers Live" showed a smiling young mainstream couple, accompanied by the sub-headline: "Why they go steady. Why they go wild. Why they don't listen." Six articles provided an overview of teen subcultures and explained teens' love, slang, parents, and troubles, and the "importance of not being square."[5]

The subjects and tone changed in the 1960s, from the frivolities and dangers of adolescence to what Diana Vreeland called the "youthquake."[6] Another issue devoted to teens was published in 1961, leading with a ten-page George Leonard story on the "Explosive Generation." "Members of the New Generation have looked at the world their elders have made.... They do not like what they see. They are moving fast and hard to change it." The article, which focused on high-achieving youth, included results from a Look survey that found that most wanted to be great teachers, scientists, or politicians.

Teen problems remained, and a powerful story bylined "Anonymous Father" recounted how the man's fifteen-year-old son and his friends were picked up by a patrol car and taken to jail for having illegally bought beer. Other sides of the young generation were shown in stories about high-school science students, teenage marriage, youth listening to the folk music of the Kingston Trio, and others (mostly a bit older) joining civil-rights sit-ins. The teen marriage article noted that nearly half the women married in 1958 were between fifteen and nineteen years old. Two international pieces described the "far less restrictive view of sex" in Sweden and the "disdain" among Hungarian youth toward their communist government. By contrast, the *Saturday Evening Post* a year later showed clean-cut, young white people on its cover and predicted that youth would "settle for low success" and have "little spirit of adventure."[7]

The "Explosive Generation" was rechristened the "Tense Generation" in another cover story and package of articles in 1963. Photos showed sullen adolescents, a young couple on the hood of a car, and motorcycles whizzing by. The topics were decidedly troubling: "Why they steal. Why they destroy property. Why they take dope. Why they have declared war on society." Readers learned of teenage boys failing in school and work, smashing car windows, mooning, having sex, and becoming "the excess baggage of society." *Look* sent writers and photographers to six communities from Westchester County, New York, and Boston, to St. Louis and California. They explained these problems by pointing to a changing economy in which automation was destroying menial jobs for a million teenage boys, widespread "tension and boredom," lack of communication with parents, and deteriorating morals.[8]

"Affluence itself is part of the problem," one article declared. "Even washing dishes used to offer an hour of communion between mother and daughter, as hauling out the coal ashes was a daily or weekly contact between father and son." According to a rabbi in upper-middle class Larchmont, New York, "Once normal middle-class values are relaxed, the descent is rapid."[9]

Look's big 1963 story on morality, "based on [its] three month study," asked: "Do we need a new code to solve our crisis of immorality? Have our churches failed? Has money become God? Is sexual morality gone?" But *Look* wisely saw "immorality" extending far beyond teenagers: "Its bitter fruits are all around us: the beatnik, the racist, the wild kid, the price-rigging executive, the pregnant high school girl, the dope addict, the vandal, the bribed athlete, the uncared-for aged, the poor, the criminal." Liberal theologians William Sloane Coffin and Paul Tillich, as well as Martin Luther King Jr. blamed the profit motive and an unjust economy, "failing" churches, racial segregation, parents who can't say "no," and scientists who developed the bomb and computers and posited the existence of a subconscious where the Id ran free.[10]

These themes returned in a 1966 issue on the "Open Generation," as rebellion was in the air. "Kids are very discontented with life in the United States," an Arizona teen told Jack Shepherd. "Something is definitely missing, and I think we're out to find it." Another said: "I don't think adults value and seek anything. They just live." Results from a *Look* poll of youth undoubtedly stunned many readers. Seventy-five percent hailed a new sexual morality. Seventy percent wanted American society to change, 33 percent believed that the country was no longer a democracy, and 42 percent saw the police as unfair. Although the dire tone was leavened by a look at "mod" fashions and 301 million record players, *Look* also published "six conversations that parents don't want to hear." The magazine showed that youth rebellion was global: Paul Fusco showed a boy with an electric guitar in front of the Kremlin under the headline, "Cool Communists." In a more soothing and approving tone, *Look* declared: "Most kids won't chuck the affluent life," but they are more idealistic and want personal happiness rather than making a lot of money. Even with boomers and their immediate forebears appearing to turn the nation topsy-turvy, *Look* emphasized the positives and was optimistic.[11]

In 1965 *Look* brought together thirteen young men and women between the ages of eighteen and twenty-five to talk about "what they expect, fear, accept, resist, dream of or dread." Most were critical of the present society, yet some were idealistic. A twenty-two-year-old woman who called herself "old-fashioned enough to believe in God," nonetheless said, "We have not been just pampered, but spiritually impoverished. I don't want to live in the poverty of affluence." A young man also spoke of the privileges of prosperity, while describing America as a "society that spends most of its time on arms, entertainment and therapy." A twenty-year-old female college student hopefully said, "The time will come when racial and religious discrimination will end, and when all people will work together for a better world."[12]

College students were another part of the youth story, as enrollments in colleges and universities soared. *Look* reported less on institutional expansion than on students—coeds at Wellesley, the "perils" of fraternities, radicals at Reed, pressures to have sex, and big demonstrations at Berkeley from the mid-sixties through the 1970 nationwide student strike. "The multiversity is so obedient to its economy and society that it cannot truly educate its graduates," John Poppy wrote of the Berkeley student uprising. "Free speech spearheaded their protest, but a powerful moral disquiet motivates it.... They are asking an old, respectable question, 'Just what do you think an education is *for*?'" Fifty-five years later, Poppy recalled how he and Fusco blended into the crowd of demonstrators and found a math grad student who was a leader of the Free Speech Movement they profiled.[13]

The late 1960s quest among many youths for a "higher consciousness" propounded by nonmainstream psychologists like Abraham Maslow, Fritz Perls, and Mike Murphy was given considerable play in *Look*, in large part thanks to George Leonard's connections with Esalen. Describing the "generation gap" in 1967, Poppy explained that the chasm emerging between many youths and their elders was "not defined by their chronological age but by how they look at themselves and the world." A young man accused an older generation of being "'blind to reality, unconscious to love, and deaf to all the crying.'" Poppy warned readers to "pay attention," for this "signals an explosive widening of the old gulf between parent and child." *Life* used his term for a 1968 cover story.[14]

Runaways, drugs, and hippies were on the cover during the summer of 1967. Echoing the Beatles' lyrics in "She's Leaving Home," a tearful parent of a runaway said, "He was never deprived of anything." *Look* reported on a half million kids in "unwashed defiance of their parents" and "potheads in Missouri." Timothy Leary—already familiar to readers from a 1963 story by the erstwhile Harvard professor's former student and mescaline proponent

Andrew Weil—urged the young to "turn on," in an interview with Leonard in his sixty-room Gothic mansion in upstate New York; quasi-psychedelic photos by Karales accompanied the story. Leonard tried LSD with Leary, only to denounce the drug.[15]

William Hedgepeth lived in a Haight-Asbury "pad" during San Francisco's 1967 Summer of Love, telling readers that "the generation gap yawns widest here." He grew a beard to blend in with the "shaggy" hippies in their "communal families," and must have shocked many readers with his descriptions of "dopers," "acid rock," drugs that "blow people's minds," dancing to the Grateful Dead in Golden Gate Park, and characters with names like Rabbit and Kathy With Glasses. During a Sunday "happening" in the Panhandle, the loud rock music "blanks the mind, stuns the senses, and forcibly reaches out and commandeers all the nerve fibers and viscera of the body, so that you find yourself leaping and twitching to the contagious drum-thump-twang rhythm with total and unconscious abandon." A more sober and balanced article appeared in *Life* a few months earlier based on the writer's "brief contact" with them. Again, a contrast between iconoclast and Establishment.[16]

Life writer Loudon Wainwright Jr. wrote a more sociological, albeit negative, account. He too visited a hippie group home, but focused on the "squalor," soaring crime in Haight-Asbury, a middle-class girl becoming an "accomplished panhandler," and parents "who were looking for these young people or . . . [had] given them up."[17]

11

When Government and
Politicians Were Respected

Two overarching qualities are especially noteworthy about *Look*'s coverage
of politics and government from the New Deal to Nixon: First, the magazine's efforts to present a wide range of viewpoints and its commitment
to a fundamentally progress-oriented liberalism that had less to do with
political parties than a belief that public action could make the United
States a better nation for all of its people. Second, *Look*'s longstanding belief
that government could be a force for good—a belief that most Americans
shared at least until the late 1960s. Although many print and broadcast
media over the years have discussed the need for greater civic engagement,
Look was a proselytizer. These characteristics have all but vanished in twenty-
first-century journalism.

Today, a handful of publications present both "progressive" and "conservative" viewpoints in their opinion pages, but the overwhelming majority
of print, broadcast, cable, online, and social media have adopted party-line
positions on the right or left, with others occupying positions on the center-
left or center-right. These dueling points of view essentially echo those of

the Democratic and Republican Parties (or at least wings of each). It was one thing in the mid-twentieth century to have opinion magazines like the *National Review* or the *Nation*, but these were clearly different from publications like *Look* that tried pretty successfully to uphold standards of nonpartisan, objective journalism. In the *New York Times* or *Washington Post*, which try to provide balance on their op-ed pages, their political allegiances are easily discernible. News media with broader, more nuanced outlooks are hard to find.

As discussed earlier, *Look*'s political philosophy is hard to comprehend given today's strident left-right polarization. As Leo Rosten said of Cowles: he was "a lifelong Republican and liberal to his fingertips." John Poppy described the magazine's editors as "not flamingly liberal, but they were open to points of view of writers that were consistently left of center and pro-underdog." They extolled a politics of government intervention and furtherance of the civil and socioeconomic rights of all Americans that would be to the left of most of the Democratic Party since the 1970s.[1]

This brings us back to the postwar "liberal consensus," which embraced all but the far left and far-right segregationists and John Birchers. The belief that government worked for the interests of the American people, and that it was key in building an ever-better society and facilitating social and economic progress was a given for *Look*'s publisher, writers, and photographers, at least until the Vietnam War. As Attwood reported in 1960, the vast majority of Americans agreed about most issues "to an alarming degree," in part due to reporting by *Look*. Other mass print media of the time fostered and believed in a "consensus," but Henry Luce's ideas of what that consensus was differed from the ideas of Mike Cowles or Dan Mich. *Look*'s idea of the "consensus" was central not only to the optimism and public-spiritedness of the magazine but also was something that united Americans in both major parties, across most of the political spectrum.[2]

This chapter illustrates how *Look* was fundamentally progressive, populist, and generally optimistic. Because of its belief in government being a force for good and its admiration for prominent liberals, this chapter differs from others in that politicians—not the "common man"—played a larger role in the magazine's stories.

The generally beneficial nature of the federal government was a recurrent theme, with the exception of scandals during the Truman and Eisenhower Administrations and the Vietnam War. *Look*'s belief in public service and the ideals underlying it were evident in article after article. Fletcher Knebel commended civil servants, Rosten described ten central ideas that make "democracy work," and Eric Sevareid quoted Voltaire to argue the need for vigilance about free speech.[3]

Look was deeply committed to participatory, grassroots democracy, as demonstrated in its long annual feature on "All-America Cities." The series, which was published each February or March for about twenty years, highlighted eleven small, medium-sized, and large cities that had problems but "met them squarely" through civic action. They were places where citizens identified a wrong and worked to right it—be it the need for better governance, supporting the arts or building low-cost housing. Typically, more than ten times the number of winners applied each year. Initially overseen by Vernon Myers and written by Jack Star and others, this *Look* series asked: "Is your city a good place to live? Hundreds of American cities are not. They are being strangled by corruption, inefficient government, poor schools and crime. And paralyzing apathy among their citizens promises no improvement." The magazine's editors warned that "when citizens remain indifferent, almost anything can happen—streets deteriorate, crime syndicates flourish, population booms threaten blight, bumbling administrators fail to administrate—even bankruptcy may impend."[4]

Cities and towns were cited for their civic progress and municipal reform through "courageous and intelligent citizen effort," in the words of Ben Kocivar. Celebrating civic spirit, a 1957 article on Brattleboro, Vermont, described how twelve thousand citizens worked to create a fifty-three-acre park with a ski area, a pool, and a skating rink. In 1964, when Rosedale, California, was one of the winners, photos by Earl Theisen showed residents in front of bundles labeled "Ideas" and men with golf clubs showing projects for which they would raise money. Winners were chosen by twelve leaders in government, education, business, and civic affairs, with George Gallup chairing the selection committee. The awards were jointly sponsored with the National Municipal League, and the announcement of winners came with the fanfare of public awards dinners around the country. Gallup described the awards' purpose as being "not for good government, efficient municipal administration, or a specific improvement," but rather for the "continuous intelligent citizen participation [that] is needed to make self-government effective and forward-looking." The awards have continued into the 2020s under the aegis of the National Civic League, whose website says nothing about *Look*'s longtime role.[5]

Similarly, *Look* bestowed Community Home Achievement Awards to cities in 1956 and 1957. For one story Jim Hansen traveled the country, capturing on film the Women's Chamber of Commerce in Little Rock, inspecting deteriorating housing in a Black neighborhood, and teenagers in Chicago demonstrating for the city's South Shore redevelopment.[6]

Time and *Life*, which presented much more extensive coverage of U.S. politics, hewed more closely to the conservatism of Henry Luce. Although Luce shared some of Cowles's beliefs, such as the importance of a welfare state, Luce was more enamored of politicians like Eisenhower and unlikely to be effusively positive about men like Adlai Stevenson or Hubert Humphrey.

American Politics, Presidents, Politicians, and Government

Look gave Americans insight into its leaders, dissected major issues and political trends, and provided trenchant and provocative analyses and opinions by leading intellectual lights. It devoted much attention to America's six presidents during its thirty-five-year run, as well as to political leaders in both parties whom it particularly admired, unsavory political figures and movements almost exclusively on the right, and the radical movements of the late 1960s. Although its stories were typically built around politicians, *Look* also discussed major political and policy issues.

Presidential elections were covered largely through stories about and by candidates, often including Gallup's polls, which continued from the late 1930s to the 1960s. These were initially an intriguing novelty to readers who had never before seen the pages of charts first displayed in a 1939 article on Americans' opinions about a possible third term for Roosevelt. Gallup polls, which set the standard for polling on elections and issues, addressed topics including "big government," McCarthyism, the Cold War, and American optimism. Trumpeting the influence of its opinion research in a 1947 pitch to advertisers, *Look* said that its national survey about the Taft-Hartley legislation influenced public opinion and the Congress.[7]

Since *Look* began publishing during the midst of the Depression, when FDR was starting his second term, he was the subject of many articles on what made him tick. During the late 1930s, stories ranged from "A Psychologist Reveals the Secret of Roosevelt's Popularity," in the magazine's second tabloid issue in 1937, to articles by Drew Pearson and Robert S. Allen, coauthors of the long-running syndicated column "Washington Merry-Go-Round." They called FDR "the nation's loneliest man," speculated on a post-presidency career as a potential editor of the *New York Post*, discussed his relationship with reporters, and predicted that he would win a third term after Nazi "waves of steel rumbled into Poland" in September 1939. By 1943 he was the "War President" in an issue whose cover depicted the profile of a thoughtful leader. The part of Pearson's storied career that he spent with *Look* ended when the columnist criticized FDR's handling of World War II. FDR called him a "chronic liar," and the magazine itself attacked Pearson for having "peddled more than his share of absurdities."[8]

Look published six articles on Wendell Willkie, FDR's 1940 challenger and Cowles's favorite, in five consecutive issues between September 10 and November 5, 1940 (following two earlier issues that summer), telling readers: "Willkie is a dynamic political figure. He has new ideas." *Look* called him the "Republican Roosevelt" and included two cover stories that he wrote, "I Challenge Roosevelt on These Issues" and "If I Become President." Mike and his brother John met Willkie that spring and became de facto advisors to his campaign, with one journalist later suggesting that there was talk of the brothers joining the Cabinet if Willkie won. In 1943, with his picture on the cover, Willkie mused about the Republicans' chances for winning the 1944 election.[9]

Flying on a converted C-87 bomber, Willkie and Cowles took their seven-week world tour on FDR's behalf in 1942, which Cowles called his "most unforgettable" experience. Willkie wrote about their meetings with Stalin in the Kremlin during the German assault on the Soviet Union,

General Bernard Montgomery in El-Alamein, Charles de Gaulle in Beirut, and Madame Chiang Kai-Shek in China. Cowles said that Willkie's ideas for a global organization and a postwar united Europe came out of the trip, and he claimed to have helped Willkie write his 1943 bestseller, *One World*. There was talk of Willkie running again in 1944, becoming FDR's vice-presidential running mate, or being named by Roosevelt to become the first secretary-general of the United Nations, but Willkie died of a series of heart attacks in October 1944.[10]

In FDR's third term, *Look* published highly favorable articles on "Dr. Win the War" and his Cabinet. Vice President Henry Wallace, a progressive, was described as "Roosevelt's choice for president." Years after FDR's death in 1945, *Look* published stories like "Five Ways FDR Changed Your Life," journalist and historian Gerald W. Johnson's comprehensive remembrance, and John Gunther's lengthy, positive assessment of FDR serialized in five successive 1950 issues.[11]

Cowles and *Look* were great admirers of Eleanor Roosevelt, publishing articles about and by her, from the 1937 "They Lead the Women of America" and a 1941 piece on "What's Wrong with the Draft" to her 1961 piece envisioning "the world of 1987" and a highly praiseworthy obituary in 1962. Shortly after her husband's death, she explained to *Look* readers why she would not run for president: "Men and women both are not yet enough accustomed to following a woman and looking to her for leadership." In the late 1940s and 1950s, she wrote three pieces on the Soviet Union, and she was offered $10,000 to accompany Attwood to the USSR for a trip and article that never materialized. America's most admired woman was also the subject of a 1948 photo spread and one of three 1956 articles reflecting on the Roosevelt years.[12]

Look had a penchant for liberal Republicans like Fiorello LaGuardia (R-NY), Wayne Morse (R-OR), Leverett Saltonstall (R-MA), Harold Stassen (R-MN), Earl Warren (R-CA), Thomas Dewey (R-NY), and Raymond Baldwin (R-CT). During the 1950s and 1960s, *Look*'s favored Republicans included Margaret Chase Smith (R-ME), Charles Percy (R-IL), George Romney (R-MI), and Donald Riegle (R-MI). New York governor Nelson Rockefeller, Massachusetts senator Edward Brooke, and New York mayor John Lindsay wrote for the magazine. Conservatives like Robert Taft (R-OH), moderates like Everett Dirksen (R-IL), and Republicans further right were also given play.

Morse, whom *Look* called the "bad boy of the Senate" in a 1946 article, was a "believer in free trade and 'One World', . . . and a champion of organized labor." Smith was praised for her early opposition to Sen. Joseph McCarthy's fearmongering. Staffer Gerald Astor called New York mayor Lindsay a "maverick" with a "most liberal Republican creed," and *Look* commended Lindsay for his anti-poverty and public-housing policies in 1967. That same year, after the "long hot summer" of urban riots, Brooke condemned systemic racism in a piece responding to the violence. Just a few months later, after George Romney's controversial statement about being "brainwashed" in Vietnam by the U.S. military, *Look* lauded the former chairman of American Motors for working with UAW leaders Walter and Victor Reuther, for calling the GOP's constant praise of "rugged individualism" a "political banner to cover greed," and for having "spent his life rousing workers, consumers, Negroes, Republicans, and ordinary citizens to break out of the passive-masses trap."[13]

In addition to Stevenson, the magazine published many articles by and about liberal Democrats such as Senators Humphrey (D-MN), James Murray (D-MT), Paul Douglas (D-IL), Abraham Ribicoff (D-CT), Eugene McCarthy (D-MN), and Daniel Patrick Moynihan (D-NY), and Representative Bella Abzug (D-NY). John, Robert, and Edward Kennedy authored many stories for *Look*. Ribicoff's daughter briefly worked for *Look*.[14]

If Willkie was Cowles's biggest idol, not far behind were Humphrey and Stevenson, the Democratic governor of Illinois and two-time presidential candidate. In 1956 Humphrey spoke to Black *Look* contributor Carl Rowan about the importance of securing Black voting rights. Humphrey's 1962 article on "big business" attacked anticompetitive practices and strongly touted the benefits of a mixed economy. Three years later, *Look* described Humphrey as a Midwestern optimist, much as Cowles described himself. When Humphrey became Lyndon Johnson's vice president, Knebel called him the "prophet of cornucopia, evangel of economic growth, disciple of goodwill, the gleaming herald of the Great Society." He was an ideas man, the radical who called for a civil-rights plank in the 1948

Democratic platform, and the optimist who found "the present stirring and the future dazzling." Before the Democrats' disastrous 1968 Convention, *Look* published thirty-six pages on politics, with a seven-page spread on Humphrey, including a portrait by Rockwell, crediting his 1949 health-care proposals as the basis for Medicare. Weeks later he wrote that he was running for president to advance racial "reconciliation" and "increasing opportunity for all."[15]

The day after Stevenson lost to Eisenhower in 1952, Cowles gave the liberal Democrat the assignment to spend ten weeks crisscrossing the globe. He produced erudite, often lengthy articles about Western Europe, the Soviet Union, the Balkans, Israel, India, Southeast Asia, and East Asia. Stevenson asked "Must We Have War?" and wrote about decolonization in Africa in two 1955 stories. He also explored America's troubled relationship with Latin America in 1960, eloquently described the UN, NATO, and the Marshall Plan as "stunning achievements," and called for a global peacekeeping force in an article that appeared a few weeks after his fatal 1965 heart attack: "We shall not keep the peace in a world mired by misery, hunger and despair.... To suppose that our world can continue half-affluent and half-desperate is to assume a patience on the part of the needy for which—to put it mildly—history gives us no warrant."[16]

Few men received more praise in the pages of *Look* than Stevenson. He was lauded in a 1952 article by actress Lauren Bacall, again by Attwood in 1953, in four stories before his second run for president in 1956, and in another after JFK named him ambassador to the United Nations. Knebel authored a 1959 article about a possible third run for the presidency, and Sevareid wrote a powerful obituary that began, "I loved Adlai Stevenson, unreservedly." His son, "Adlai III," was described as a potential new star of Illinois politics in two articles by Jack Star in 1966 and 1970.[17]

Southern Democrats and segregationists like Eugene Talmadge (D-GA), Lester Maddox (D-GA), and George Wallace (D-AL) were attacked as white supremacists, racists, and neo-Confederates. In 1966 Wallace called *Look*—along with the *Times, Time,* and the *Saturday Evening Post*—one of the liberal media who was most hostile toward him. Wallace was right: among the many awards that the NAACP presented to *Look*, a 1959 one praised the "contributions of Cowles publications to the general cause of individual liberty and human dignity."[18]

Truman was given mixed reviews, as *Look* hailed the Marshall Plan and elements of his far-reaching, but unsuccessful, Economic Bill of Rights. A year after he was thrust into the presidency by FDR's death, *Look* published a highly favorable piece, with a full-page color photo by staffer Frank Bauman. A 1949 story showed him as a loving father, drawing with his daughter Margaret, and noted that "he's won more in Congress than most people think."

Truman advocated for health insurance for all Americans in 1947, saying that "as a nation we should not reserve good health and long productive life for the well-to-do only, but should strive to make good health equally available to all citizens." Senators Murray and Robert Wagner and Representative John Dingell (D-MI) introduced the National Health Insurance and Public Health Act, which Murray defended as a call for "socialized medicine" in an article paired with a rebuttal by the president of the American Medical Association.[19]

However, *Look* also called Truman a "failure," "belligerent," and in league with the heirs of the Kansas City Democratic machine of boss Tom Pendergast. One article referred to his "scandalous years" as president, yet the magazine published an essay by Henry Steele Commager called "A Few Kind Words for Harry Truman" as well as Truman's meditation on his own presidency.[20]

Eisenhower and Johnson also received mixed reviews in *Look*. During the war Ike was portrayed heroically, with a 1942 story calling him a "one-man general staff" and a 1944 cover that showed him in uniform, head cocked and binoculars in hand. A 1947 story—with Ike and his daughter on the cover—reported that he had "no political ambitions," but in 1950 *Look* told readers that he was "open to a draft" and, if that wasn't feasible, he was considering organizing a new third party. Ike was cited for giving "the boot to all the reactionary, negative elements" in his party. During his first presidential campaign, Walter Lippmann wrote, "Eisenhower is, I believe, the only American in the past 100 years, in fact the only American since Washington, of whom it is really and literally true that he is the preferred choice of the masses of the voters of both parties." During his eight years in office, Dewey, syndicated columnist Marquis Childs, and *Look*'s Washington correspondent Richard Wilson wrote generally positive stories about the thirty-fourth president.[21]

The magazine tepidly endorsed Ike in 1952, even though less than a year before Gunther wrote of the "lack of definition" in his views and his tenure as president of Columbia University being "less than a success." General Douglas MacArthur, ever a loose cannon, called Ike "about as naïve about anything outside his one profession as anyone I know." Stevenson wrote "Memo to the President: Let's Make Our Two-Party System Work" in a 1955 issue whose cover read "Ike's Big Failures." The 1958 story "Must We Always Have a Mess in Washington?" catalogued the many ethical transgressions of Eisenhower Administration officials.[22]

In addition, *Look* published a four-part, nearly tell-all series on Eisenhower in 1948 in which the general's wartime secretary and reputed mistress Kay Summersby told of "smears" on her reputation, but coyly acknowledged: "I undoubtedly had more than my share of male attention, which, in turn, begets female attention."[23]

Domestic Anti-Communism and McCarthyism

Despite *Look*'s courage in other areas, it was quiet during most of Sen. Joseph McCarthy's reckless attacks on civil liberties in the early 1950s. From about 1946 to 1953, the peak years of the House Un-American Activities Committee's (HUAC) anti-communist crusade, *Look* toed the line. It warned of the domestic dangers of "reds," as hysteria was stoked by Richard Nixon, J. Edgar Hoover, HUAC, and McCarthy.

A strange, staged photo essay about communists seizing Detroit in 1948 showed snipers, police pinned to the floor, and a gun to the head of the city's mayor. "Killers could strike during darkness to spread confusion throughout a terror-gripped city," a caption proclaimed. The scare-mongering purple prose concluded that anyone who "tried to give an alarm or who disobeyed orders could expect death at the hands of the raiding squads."[24]

A 1950 article described the process of investigating a fictional communist,

John Jones. Harold Ickes, FDR's longtime interior secretary, warned in 1953 that "we are moving toward a society of modified communism."[25]

J. Alvin Kugelmass, whose articles became the basis for the film *The Two-Headed Spy* (1958), asserted that the Soviet Union was only able to develop a hydrogen bomb by stealing from the Americans. J. Robert Oppenheimer, who had led efforts to develop the U.S. atomic bomb at the Los Alamos laboratory, was wrongly accused by Hoover and HUAC of being among a cabal of U.S. scientists who had helped the Russians.[26]

Morris Ernst, the longtime general counsel for the American Civil Liberties Union, took a more moderate tone in a March 1953 piece suggesting that "we" could "help people quit being REDS." Outlawing and even ostracizing the party would be the wrong tactic, he argued; rather, the country should help the "many who want to quit," especially those emotionally unstable young people who needed to mature.[27]

Just months after the Ernst article, *Look* dramatically changed its tune. In its June 16 issue, the magazine put a close-up of McCarthy accompanied by a dark shadow of the demagogue on its cover. The five-page article—which appeared nine months before the Senate hearings convened that led to McCarthy's downfall—reported on the "unbelievably savage attacks he makes on others," as well as his penchant for "parties and pretty women." Hemingway, after surviving two plane crashes while on safari in Africa, also wrote about his dream of meeting the demagogue:

> I wished that Sen. Joseph McCarthy of Wisconsin had been with us at the crash of both aircraft. . . . I wondered if without his senatorial immunity he would be vulnerable to various beasts with whom we had been keeping company. This thought held my disordered mind . . . I must confess with a certain degree of enjoyment. Then . . . I wondered if anything was wrong with Sen. Joseph McCarthy of Wisconsin which a .577 solid would not cure.[28]

By the spring 1954 Army-McCarthy hearings, the magazine praised Sen. Margaret Chase Smith and CBS newsman Edward R. Murrow as "McCarthy fighters." A Gallup poll showed the "myth of McCarthy's strength."

Rosten denounced McCarthyism's attack on free speech in the essay "Is Fear Destroying Our Freedom?" But he also praised red-baiting J. Edgar Hoover—who claimed to "safeguard civil rights"—and Eisenhower for not joining the "book burners," without noting Ike's hesitancy in challenging McCarthy.[29]

Nine months earlier, as the red scare was cresting with one of America's most controversial trials, Julius and Ethel Rosenberg were convicted on charges that they had helped provide the Soviet Union the know-how to develop an atomic bomb and were executed on June 19, 1953. Given much public consternation about the verdict, Eisenhower's Justice Department investigated and prepared a report that "*Look* was given access to [its] extensive data." This led to a very long 1957 article that reads like a detective story, in which Bill Davidson wrote that "a powerful chain of interlinking testimony—backed by strong circumstantial evidence—would be unassailable in any court of the world." After *Look* had come around to denouncing McCarthy, it is hard to understand why it published this account of the Rosenbergs' alleged treachery.[30]

The 1960s

Despite these mixed messages, *Look* started to devote a fair amount of attention to the rising right wing in the Republican Party in the early 1960s. An extensive 1962 article by Knebel exposed the ugliness of the John Birch Society, the Rev. Billy Hargis, and Fred C. Schwartz's Christian Anti-Communist Crusade. Speaking of "the Rightist revival that began to smolder 18 months ago and now sweeps like a prairie fire through the South and West," he wrote of their ties to large companies like Schick, Technicolor, and Richfield Oil. Birch Society leader Robert Welch was quoted calling Eisenhower a "conscious agent of the Communist conspiracy." Three issues later, after William F. Buckley Jr. denounced the Birchers, *Look*'s readers learned of the "hard right's attack on churches," ministers' homes being bombed, its anti-Semitism, and Hargis's wild assertion that the National Council of Churches was "communist and treasonous." The piece, by UPI religion writer Louis Cassels, portrayed the far right as dangerous and crazy. When Sen. Barry Goldwater (R-AZ) was preparing to run for the presidency, T. George Harris raised alarms about "the rampant right invading the GOP"—the party that *Look* had prematurely praised for expunging the far right fifteen years earlier. On the eve of the 1964 election, the magazine published three more articles on the "extremist" right's influence in the Republican Party. *Look* reported that the far right believed that concerns about mental health were "communist-inspired." The extremist can be found everywhere, Leonard wrote: "in an Alabama shack, a California housing development, a New York penthouse.... He is on the move. He is the elusive, yet powerful, force in a new U.S. political climate in which the central conflict may not be so much liberal vs. conservative as extremist vs. moderate."[31]

Even after LBJ defeated Goldwater in a landslide, undoubtedly with some help from these stories, Harris warned that "a major populist revolt" still loomed. This was fueled by men and women with "an aching doubt—what does he matter to his neighbors, his state, his country? ... Millions of us bump up hard against the larger need for a meaningful role among fellow men. Without it, we are fat beasts caged in ranch houses." Similarly, liberal senator Frank Church (D-ID) said that the "fever has not been overcome.... These are angry people, but they suffer more from folly than hatred."[32]

Ronald Reagan was introduced to readers by David Broder, who was to become a longtime *Washington Post* columnist, as someone who "has a hold on conservatives that is awesome to see." Reagan was on the cover of a 1966 issue in the last days of California's bitter gubernatorial race. Comparing him to his opponent, Gov. Pat Brown, Joseph Roddy reported that the "old star" had been the "evangelist" for a far-right challenger to an incumbent Republican senator in 1962, and that he would not repudiate the John Birch Society. It also noted the curiosity that California's other senator, actor George Murphy, had played the father of the character that Reagan portrayed in the movie *This Is the Army*.[33]

Look gave Americans a first impression of LBJ as a masterful Senate majority leader with "tremendous masculine appeal to the female voter" in two 1959 articles by Davidson. Four months into his presidency, in five articles on March 10, 1964, he was described as harder working than John Kennedy and hailed for his persuasive ability to get things done. Alan Lomax, a Black writer, said that, after initial apprehensions, "a confluence of the times and his own personal commitment to racial justice will fashion Johnson into the most effective civil-rights advocate ever to occupy the White House." After his 1964 landslide, *Look* cited his "swelling list of accomplishments" and said: "His administration could become the success of the century." A 1965 piece on LBJ's bold plans to eliminate poverty was illustrated with a Rockwell painting *Hope for the Poor, Achievement for Yourself, Greatness for the Nation*, showing a hand from above clasping one from below, with other outstretched hands below, against a backdrop of grim faces of the poor. Two years later, *Look* published a fifteen-page series of stories on the War on Poverty, lauding Johnson's grand efforts. In an editorial, the magazine declared: "Everyone has the right to be free of want, just as he has the right to adequate medical care."[34]

More ominously, in the same April 1965 issue after Johnson's election, war correspondent Sam Castan warned that "time has run out for our hope of victory" in Vietnam. A piece the following year spoke of the "Vietnam cloud" hanging over the midterm elections. The next year, the magazine compared Johnson's "credibility gap" over Vietnam to Eisenhower's "anti-intellectualism" and Truman's "cronyism." As *Look* said, he was "bigger than life in both faults and virtues." *Look* gave a mouthpiece to LBJ's Democratic challenger Eugene McCarthy—whom Rockwell painted for *Look*—who told readers, after the 1968 New Hampshire primary, that he had consistently opposed the "indefensible" Vietnam War since early 1966, that he opposed LBJ because of the president's "indifference to the functions and divisions of authority," and that Americans needed to have their belief in politics and government "restored."[35]

Dunbar took a swing at LBJ, claiming that he did not understand Black Americans. Another damning piece opened with a joke about "how to tell when Lyndon Johnson is telling the truth," calling the president "devious" and "obsessed with secrecy," and Defense Secretary Robert McNamara a "pioneer of [the] credibility gap." The tragedy of losing the Great Society to the Vietnam War was thoughtfully discussed by both Sevareid and Arnold Toynbee. As the CBS correspondent wrote: "If not for the War, LBJ would be one of the most vigorously humanitarian Presidents America has had." In a more sad and salacious two-part series after Johnson left office, his brother Sam told of LBJ's "'miserable' years as vice president, his feud with Bobby Kennedy, his agony over Vietnam, [and] his isolation from his daughters."[36]

After Johnson announced in March 1968 that he would not run for reelection—a difficult decision that Drew Pearson described for Look— Humphrey seemed to be coasting to the presidency against the still shadowy Richard Nixon. But violence in the streets of Chicago, just outside the Democratic Convention, destroyed the chances of the "happy warrior." During the tumultuous convention, Look's team was in a nearby TV studio where ABC had brought together liberal Gore Vidal and conservative William F. Buckley Jr. for commentary. The first night degenerated into an ugly verbal (and almost physical) fight, but the format became the model for the cable TV shout fests that began decades later.[37]

Among labor leaders, Look portrayed the firebrand CIO leader John L. Lewis as dangerous, publishing a half-page, menacing-looking photo of Lewis in 1946 and declaring that he wanted "to be the czar of all labor." Even Saul Alinsky, the progressive community activist, wrote of "the hates of" Lewis. Conversely, Walter Reuther was commended for being a great champion of civil rights and the poor in an August 1965 article, and conservative AFL-CIO leader George Meany was criticized for "featherbedding" and his lack of support for the 1963 March on Washington. After its early support for a tripartite division of power between government, business, and labor, Look—like the country—began to turn against labor as investigations into union corruption began in the 1950s.[38]

Similarly, despite the magazine's broad support for the welfare state, Look ran stories attacking "welfare chiseling," "the shiftless, cheats and criminals" on welfare rolls, and noted "the wave of resentment . . . across the land against the rackets and abuses that plague the vast, ever-growing American welfare programs." Yet, even this 1961 article, as well as one the following year, hopefully concluded that reforms—whether by Kennedy's Health Education and Welfare (HEW) secretary, Ribicoff, or by on-the-ground caseworkers like those cited in St. Paul—could make welfare succeed.[39]

Although Look ceased publication before Watergate, it reported that Nixon had been disliked by Eisenhower. He was called uninspiring and a "hustler," his fitness for the presidency was questioned, and Rockwell depicted him in a 1968 painting called *The Two Faces of Richard Nixon*. Radical comedian Dick Gregory put Nixon in the same moral camp as George Wallace and Chicago mayor Richard Daley. Leonard spoke of the "forces of repression" growing "bolder," and Commager damned Nixon and Vice President Agnew for their efforts to silence the press. Frank Trippett wrote that Agnew saw people who disagreed with him in three ways: "as sick, enemies, or loathsome objects."[40]

New York Times humorist Russell Baker jested about the impostor in the White House, and the president's emotional instability was not so subtly portrayed in a 1969 piece by Nixon's longtime psychiatrist Arnold Hutschnecker. Given the antipathy between young protesters and Nixon, a 1970 article provided the surprising news that aides H. R. Haldeman and John Ehrlichman were the "happy-byproduct" of having young people on staff "to keep in touch with the age group most associated with change, with dissent." Rep. Donald Riegle Jr. (R-MI) called for "dumping" Nixon in 1971 because of his "policy of blood and brutality" in Vietnam and his administration's "benign neglect" of domestic problems and lack of a "discernible moral purpose." Even when the president called a White House conference on hunger and nutrition, *Look*'s headline was "Let Them Eat Words." The distaste was mutual, as Stanley Tretick recalled Nixon's press secretary, Ron Ziegler, reputedly saying, "We have a shit list of magazines in the White House, and I want you to know that *Look* ranks above *Ramparts*," the New Left magazine, regarding "the lifestyle stuff."[41]

Despite the mostly relentless criticism, *Look* hopefully said in 1959 that Nixon was "growing" as vice president. Moynihan wrote that he defied labels of "conservative and liberal" and offered a long argument for social welfare policies during the Nixon Administration. Richard Wilson, who had written the 1953 article "Is Nixon Fit to Be President?," asked the same question in 1970, but wrote that Nixon sought "the middle ground of reason and moderation." In *Look*'s final issue, Pulitzer Prize winner Allen Drury described the president as "shy, lonely, much-wounded, ambitious, courageous and deeply patriotic." A photo showed Nixon, back to the camera, standing alone by a White House window.[42]

The Kennedys

Without a doubt, *Look*'s greatest political obsession was the Kennedy family. Approximately 120 articles on the Kennedys were published between 1959 and 1971, with a handful before, going back to a 1946 story of JFK's first run for Congress. There were countless cover stories; dramatic photographs; articles by John, Robert, Edward, and Jackie Kennedy; book excerpts; remembrances; reports on Jackie, the Kennedy children, and extended family; and profiles of a next generation of Kennedy politicians.[43]

JFK's byline appeared on seven articles for *Look*, including four during his brief presidency. He attacked "labor racketeers" in 1959 and described his experience winning the Democratic nomination in 1960. As president, he contributed to the 1962 "Next 25 Years" issue, wrote about the importance of the arts, his administration's stand on communism, and the need for improved physical fitness. In 1964 *Look* also published a posthumous "memoir."[44]

Bobby Kennedy wrote seven *Look* articles, one while attorney general, and several thoughtful pieces between 1964 and his assassination in 1968. Two were tributes to his brother and two were impassioned calls for equality for Blacks and ending the "agony" of Vietnam. Teddy Kennedy, who was elected senator at age thirty in 1962, called for "a new humanitarian force" to spur Southeast Asia's economic development in a 1966 article.[45]

JFK embodied *Look*'s optimism and America's post-Eisenhower panache. Already in 1953 there was a lavish photo spread on the senator's wedding to twenty-four-year-old Jacqueline Bouvier. The stage for the Kennedy dynasty was set with 1957 pieces on "The Rise of the Brothers Kennedy" and a 1959 photo of the "three husky brothers" in the surf at Hyannis Port. Readers heard a lot about Jack Kennedy in the year before the 1960 election, in articles on "the Kennedy family machine" and the significance of a Catholic president, and in a seven-page photo essay with Jackie on the cover and five other smiling, well-coiffed "Kennedy women" sitting in a row. Three years before the 1960 election, *Look* compared Kennedy and Nixon, and photos told the story: Kennedy was in casual dress, walking on the beach with Jackie, playing tennis and going boating, whereas Nixon was shown in a suit, posing stiffly in his living room with his family.[46]

During his one-thousand-day presidency, it was hard to go many months without a story on Kennedy. His policy decisions were explained, his family life was given a warm glow, his love of the arts and sports was emphasized, his Irish origins were explored, his staff members were profiled, and his political difficulties were analyzed. Laura Bergquist and Knebel, as well as authors James Michener and Alfred Kazin, wrote many personal and political stories about the president.

Bergquist, one of very few reporters whom Kennedy trusted, had mixed opinions when she first met him in the late 1950s. She called him "terribly bright and very witty, well-informed and outspoken," but said of a possible Kennedy presidency, "Are you kidding?" She also alleged that Kennedy met her in his underwear and was jealous of Che Guevara, whom she interviewed twice.[47]

A January 1962 issue included Tretick photos of JFK and eight Kennedy children and ten articles about "Life on the New Frontier." Another iconic photo showed Kennedy with his advisers—Robert McNamara, Paul Nitze, and General Maxwell Taylor—trying to pull the world back from the brink during the Cuban Missile Crisis. Tretick, whose access to the Kennedy family was unparalleled, brought five-year-old Caroline Kennedy's "wonderful summer" to life and showed readers her younger brother, John Jr., playing in the Oval Office, on the tarmac with his father beside Air Force 1, and watching a meeting with Soviet ambassador Andrei Gromyko, Secretary of State Dean Rusk, and others.[48]

Hailing the new spirit in Washington, *Look* wrote: "During the Eisenhower era, the White House projected a sort of remote grandeur, affecting the capital with a certain stuffiness," whereas Kennedy was "a vital, visible 'decisionmaker' who would get things moving again." Kazin called the president a man with "the naturalness of a newspaperman and as much savvy as a Harvard professor."[49]

By 1963 *Look* reported on "trouble in the New Frontier," as Kennedy failed to get Congress to pass "great measures to move us forward." A *Look* poll found that Americans praised JFK as a "family man [and] a politician above politics," but they were less impressed by him as a "philosopher, legislator and military strategist."[50]

After Kennedy's death, *Look* played a major role in establishing the Kennedy legend. Within weeks of his assassination, *Look* published the paperback *Kennedy and His Family in Pictures: With Exclusive Pictures from the Files of Look.* "Here is the President under pressure, and the family man relaxed," it began. "Here are his children, his friends and some were his foes; the happy times and the crises." Before proceeding to page upon page of stunning photos, the editors lamented, "He is missed. Things will be different." There were full-page, double-page, and smaller photos in color and black-and-white of JFK with his son, addressing a Massachusetts crowd from atop a car; Jackie; "her father's darling," Caroline, on a pier at Hyannis Port; and his two children, his wife, and Bobby in front of his casket. Many were by Tretick, although ten other photographers—including Frank Bauman and Bob Sandberg—were credited.[51]

Soon after Attwood praised JFK's "cool," his friendliness, and commitment to civil rights, came Bobby Kennedy's tribute, a Jack Star piece describing the emerging "Kennedy legend," and a Rockwell painting. *Look*'s most fulsome encomium to JFK was a memorial issue with sixteen articles published nearly a year after his death that included ones by Martin Luther King Jr., Cardinal Cushing, Supreme Court justice Arthur Goldberg, and economist Walter Heller. Amid scores of photos, the martyred president was praised for "restoring confidence" and his "moral insight." Bergquist and Tretick also published their own photo book on JFK in 1965.[52]

Look serialized *If Kennedy Had Lived,* the 1965 book by Theodore Sorensen, JFK's speechwriter. The five-part series gave an insider's view of the Cuban Missile Crisis and the Bay of Pigs fiasco, for which Kennedy took the blame. Sorenson also recounted that Kennedy "told me, at times in caustic tones, of other 'fathers of defeat' who had let him down"—meaning advisers in the Pentagon and CIA. However, there was not a whiff of failure in the idyllic painting by Bernie Fuchs of JFK sailing.[53]

Look's most ambitious work on JFK was its four-issue, 80,000-word serialization of William Manchester's 380,000-word book, *The Death of a President,* in 1967. Based on more than one thousand interviews, Manchester gave a detailed insiders' account of six November 1963 days from a Kennedy White House reception through the assassination to the funeral, dedicating the book to "all in whose hearts he still lives—a watchman of honor who never sleeps." After a bidding war with *Life*, *Look* paid Manchester $665,000, then the largest sum ever paid for a magazine series. The first issue on January 24, 1967, was a sensation, as *Look* attained its highest-ever sales. It claimed that the four issues, printed on newsprint, were read by seventy million Americans. The series' backstory, which received extensive news coverage, was at least as dramatic. Although Bobby initially supported publication, Jackie filed an injunction against *Look* and Harper & Row, the book's publisher. She flew Cowles and his lawyer to Hyannis Port on her private plane, *Caroline*, to tearfully implore him not to publish and offer him $1 million to halt the serialization. An unhappy Jackie settled when Cowles agreed to reduce the number of stories from seven to four and cut 1,061 words. After the series concluded, *Look* published Manchester's story about the ordeal.[54]

Look paid ample attention to Jackie, first as a symbol of elegance, then as a figure of tragedy. She was called "the new American beauty" with "French cousins." Stories in 1962 described how she redecorated the White House and inspired the stylish "new international look." After the assassination, Bergquist wrote several articles about Jackie's "valiance" and loneliness, her children, and how her style and "breathless little-girl voice" were being copied by millions of women. She remained very much in the public eye, as the magazine reported on her marriage to Greek shipping magnate Aristotle Onassis.[55]

Robert Kennedy was introduced in a 1955 story on the nation's "promising young men." His "ambitions" were described in August 1964, and a half year later, Oriana Fallaci wrote that he was secretive, cold, and stiff, yet "magnetic," which was evident when he went to Harlem and "people risked suffocation just to hear him speak." Three years later, he was "cool and confident" and in tune with the young. When he announced his presidential candidacy, *Look* put him on the cover and commissioned a Rockwell painting. Staff writer Warren Rogers, a friend of RFK, rode in the ambulance the night he was assassinated in June 1968. *Look* subsequently published only a few of Paul Fusco's extraordinary photos of people lining the train tracks from New York to Washington as RFK's funeral train passed. Fusco recalled:

There were people everywhere. It was solemn and quiet. No yelling. I stood in the same spot on the train until it got dark and I photographed everything I saw on the track that day.... My favorite photograph [was of] the father and son standing and saluting in front of a small foot bridge, with the mother standing nearby on a dirt road.... They're poor and have had hard lives, but are proud of what they have accomplished and grateful for the commitment and hope Bobby nurtured in the legions of the poor, the blacks, and countless other forgotten Americans.[56]

The matriarch, the "indomitable Rose Kennedy," was shown in a ten-page photo spread in 1968. Bobby's wife, Ethel, was on the cover of an ill-timed issue that had closed just before his assassination and was published just after.[57]

Teddy joined the pantheon in February 1963, weeks after becoming a senator, when his twenty-six-year-old wife, Joan, was put on the cover. The magazine reported on his growing prominence in the Senate, and he was featured in two 1969 stories months before his Chappaquiddick accident that killed a young aide. In 1971 *Look* speculated whether he would run for president, even though it declared that "Camelot was in ruins."[58]

Look's Move to the Left

By the late 1960s, the magazine had taken to heart Bob Dylan's words that "there's a battle outside and it is ragin'. It'll soon shake your windows and rattle your walls, for the times they are a-changin." Dunbar, Leonard, and others wrote many an article whose radicalism went well beyond pro-civil-rights and anti–Vietnam War sentiments. As early as 1962, Poppy wrote of gadfly Albert Burke, who "excoriated John Q. Public for being lazy, ignorant, and letting democracy die.... He said, unless we all wake up, we are committing national suicide." The final issue of 1969 included two generally pro-youth-movement pieces—an article by Eugene McCarthy and an editorial that declared: "[We] envied them their revolt against hypocrisy, the euphoric devotion to rock music and their mystic unity."[59]

Writing of "a nameless malaise born of the feeling among students that their personal destinies are caught up in forces they cannot influence,"

Dunbar told *Look*'s readers in early 1968: Some may see the student movement as "an aimless nihilism, a pointless lashing out, . . . but the thrashing about is often the outward symptom of a highly idealistic youth in age when realpolitik dictates the suspension of ideals; when morality is a puzzle wrapped in platitudes; and the 'national interest' is invoked to novocaine obvious contradictions." Later that year, he approvingly described the leftist Students for a Democratic Society (SDS) representing "an effort by a key minority of the Nuclear Generation to break out of a political and moral maze built by their elders." William Hedgepeth went even further to warn that the old order could resort to imprisoning protesters under the 1950 Internal Security Act in what he called potential "concentration camps."[60]

Most stunning was Leonard's long May 1968 "New Liberal Manifesto," calling old liberals "reactionary," telling of the benefits of "militant protest," and pronouncing that "the old social forms are crumbling." He also spoke the emerging language of psychological "openness and encounter" and suggested expanded research into psychedelic drugs. He offered a hypercharged version of the old *Look* mantra that prosperity and technology could make anything possible—from electric cars and controlling heredity to interplanetary travel and "computers with intelligence and feelings." Leonard concluded, "We have at hand the resources, the energy and the talent to make each American city a festival, to make the entire country a garden, to find new ways for each individual to develop his capacities to the fullest."[61]

Look's forgotten leftism could be found in other late 1960s articles calling for dramatic education reform, defending the Miranda decision against those calling for "law and order," and describing the merits of a negative income tax and a guaranteed income. Ronald Goldfarb, who later became one of the nation's most prominent liberal attorneys—urged reform of America's "inhumane" prison and criminal-justice system. The wardens he talked with believed that only 10 to 15 percent of prisoners needed to be incarcerated to protect society. Many writers denounced "American militarism" and America's chemical and biological weapons program in a package of thirteen articles in two August 1969 issues. One cover depicted an officer and a businessman happily dancing with each other. *Look* writers

Knebel and George Zimmerman warned of the dangers of "money in politics," and former HEW secretary and Common Cause founder John Gardner called for strong lobbying laws. Dan Fowler's profile of Cesar Chavez described his farmworkers' movement as being "a revolution of mind and heart, not only of economics." A series of five articles on American Indians sympathetic to their plight and their new militancy included one by Teddy Kennedy, two by Hedgepeth, and two on the pro-Indian Western, *Little Big Man*. Hedgepeth's piece on the Bureau of Indian Affairs was provocatively titled "America's Colonial Service." Given the growing public distrust of government stemming from the Vietnam War, an August 1968 issue included Rockwell's painting *Right to Know*, showing citizens addressing their government.[62]

Seeming to reinforce Nixon's view of *Look* as a hotbed of radicalism, calls for "revolution" or radical change came not only from Leonard but also from novelist Leo Litwak, John Gardner, and Hedgepeth, all within an eight-month period from mid-1969 to January 1970. Writers demanded that many existing policies be jettisoned. Military and corporate power and a government no longer "of the people" were roundly denounced. Commager condemned "broad attacks on freedom" and "popular indifference toward the loss of liberty." His six-page essay concluded by saying that if Americans could not fight for their freedoms, "we may be witnessing, even now, a dissolution of the fabric of freedom that may portend the dissolution of the Republic." Even New York mayor John Lindsay said, "We in this nation appear to be headed for a new period of repression." Author Leonard A. Stevens said that the Pledge of Allegiance should be rewritten because of "its unsupportable claims to national virtues that we have not yet attained." A 1971 illustration showed a speckled American flag whose red stripes read "racism," "power structure," and other needs for the nation to address.[63]

Indeed, a darkness had descended on *Look*'s America. The magazine's typically upbeat perspective took something of a beating. The Vietnam War, race riots, and the beginnings of the environmental and women's movements forced *Look* and America to see a less promising future. John D. Rockefeller III wrote that the population "explosion" "threatens, if not human life itself, then surely life as we want it to be." Despite Medicare and

Medicaid, *Look* told readers that "the state of our health is bad" compared to other countries. In response to the tense, gloomy, frightened, and angry mood of the time, in 1971, *Look* asked sixteen "prominent Americans"—from Sammy Davis Jr. and Duke Ellington to Humphrey, Goldwater, and Hawaii representative Patsy Mink—to advise readers on how to find "peace of mind." Leonard told parents that "school stunts your child." Sen. Gaylord Nelson (D-WI) wrote about the predicted extinction of 75 to 80 percent of species within twenty-five years. Another piece explained "the rage of women."[64]

If revolution was called for, nowhere was this better expressed than in *Look*'s remarkable first issue of 1970, "The Seventies: Mankind's Last, Best Chance," which hit the newsstands on December 30, 1969. This was, perhaps, the most radical document of the twentieth century to reach a broad swath of Americans. Planned by Leonard and Poppy, and given a green light by Cowles and top editors Carbine and Arthur, Leonard not-so-modestly described it as "an issue like no other issue ever published—no food, fashion or sports stories. From beginning to end it would be a document of advocacy and personal revelation. . . . We would reveal our biases. We would serve as advocates, making absolutely no pretense of objectivity. . . . The issue wouldn't be about what we thought the seventies would be but about what it should be."[65]

Arguably one of the best, yet least known manifestos of the left, it not only called for Black and women presidents but also freer sexuality, a new breed of politicians and business leaders, a universal language, higher consciousness, and a changed relationship with the Earth. Sixteen articles, including a long essay by Leonard about "the future of power," heralded political, social, psychological, and technological revolution. He argued for more decentralized power, denouncing "dog-eat-dog capitalism and unbridled individualism," and called for "a more sensitive citizen, one who is more attuned to his own feelings and the feelings of others, one who has learned a new sense of community and oneness with all other individuals of his social organism," including, one day, animals and plants. He challenged the idea that human nature is "immutable," saying, "We will continue to expand our capacities—or go down the drainpipe of history." His crystal ball predicted an internet-like technology that could enable "electronic snooping" and make "centralized tyranny possible on a frightening scale," but also could "increase the options of the individual and, in so doing, may weaken despotic authority."[66]

Hedgepeth extolled "a vision of the human revolution" in which people would no longer "lead a locked-in existence." Another piece railed against consumption of "more of everything" and called for a "new corporate culture that puts its trust in people instead of organization charts." If this weren't enough, readers must have been shocked by Leonard's concluding essay advocating a "Dionysian" revolution, "altered states of consciousness" for a voyage to Mars, and, more prosaically, fuel-efficient cars.[67]

A long photo essay included four pages of grim images of war, police batons, Thalidomide, and an oil-soaked bird, followed by fifteen color photos of a magnificent future—with children in the surf and surrounded by luxuriant ferns, an enlarged microcircuit, and a girl (Paul Fusco's daughter) running through an idyllic field. There were dazzling graphics by art director Will Hopkins, and a two-page painting by Paul David juxtaposing the beards of Che Guevara and Ulysses Grant with a lynching in the lower-right corner. Six pages of surrealistic photos by Art Kane showed yoga practitioners overlooking a Pacific sunset and a stunning image of a nude young woman with long black hair wrapped in an ecologically green U.S. flag. Not surprisingly, the issue was controversial: Some readers called it revolting. An SDS activist saluted Look's "creative, courageous effort." And Coca-Cola found the content so compelling that it decided to increase its advertising.[68]

Undoubtedly, the best remembered essays were the pair by William F. Buckley Jr. on "Why We Need a Black President in 1980" and Gloria Steinem on "Why We Need a Woman President in 1976." (In 1949 Vincent Sheean, the distinguished journalist and National Book Award winner, had called for electing a woman president as "a symbol of peace" that would burnish America's image, albeit with the stereotypical caveat that "no mother wants war.")[69]

In one of several articles about the new women's movement and its opponents, Bella Abzug called for the end of a "middle-aged, middle-class white male power structure . . . so totally unresponsive to the needs of this country for so long." Like Steinem, she hoped that this could come about "within two election cycles."[70]

Although upbeat articles about the United States had become rarer, a 1970 essay by C. P. Snow and his son painted a more hopeful picture. "The basic structures are impregnably strong," they wrote of the country's institutions. Americans had a "deserved reputation for welcoming the rest of the world among themselves." It was inspiring to see "friendly" New York City crowds when the 1969 Mets won the World Series and on Earth Day the following year. Lord Snow said he was "deeply impressed by the way the American people appear to be grappling with the environmental problems, and I am convinced that these will be overcome." Nonetheless, he criticized the nation's "urban mess" and many Americans "channeling their beliefs into semi-digested mysticism." Foreshadowing twenty-first-century political correctness, he added: "I have committed a crime. I have expressed a 'liberal' viewpoint, tinged with optimism."[71]

12

Look's "One World" Internationalism

The world and America's role in it were extraordinarily important to *Look*. Cowles and his editors and writers firmly believed that the magazine's readers—and all Americans—should understand other nations and other peoples and how they lived. The idea that all people were part of "one world," the philosophy that Cowles and Mich shared with Willkie, undergirded *Look*'s international coverage. Trite as it may sound, they believed in a peaceful, united world, scorning bellicosity whether it came out of the Kremlin or the White House. Although the magazine's editors were clearheaded about America's Cold War enemies, they allowed communist leaders to have their say. More importantly, *Look* sought to show that a boy in Russia or a woman in South Africa was a person whose circumstances might be very different from a reader in Iowa or New York, yet had similar needs and hopes and was not simply the ideological slave of an abhorrent regime. As a soft advocate and pedagogue, *Look* aimed to promote tolerance and combat ignorance and prejudice.

Whereas Henry Luce hailed "the American Century" and *Time* and *Life* called for U.S. intervention throughout the world, Cowles and his staff fervently and optimistically believed in "One World." It praised the United Nations and Jean Monnet, the founder of what became the European Union, whom Cowles called one of "the very few great men of this generation."[1]

The magazine published countless foreign stories, including many outstanding ones that other news organizations chose not, or were not able, to do. *Look* dispatched writers and photographers to every corner of the globe to tell stories that no one else was telling.

Unlike most other news media, which focused on leaders and major events, and relied overwhelmingly on official sources, *Look* framed and analyzed big issues, like the post-Stalin liberalization in the Soviet Union and decolonization in Africa and Asia, by telling stories of people. *Look* believed that these "common people" were at least as important as government officials. Most *Look* photos did the same, showing masses of poor Chinese children, a little boy playing beside the Berlin Wall, or women carrying food near a mosque in the Mali desert.

Look was often daring—bucking the State Department to send the first mainstream U.S. journalists into "Red China," antagonizing John Kennedy by interviewing Che Guevara, and going behind enemy lines during the 1968 Tet Offensive in Vietnam. *Look* not only scored the first U.S. media interview with Khrushchev, but it also got the Soviet leader to write about the Sino-Soviet split. Two years before Castro's odd U.S. debut on the set of the *Ed Sullivan Show*, *Look* followed him and his revolutionary band in the Cuban mountains.[2]

With far fewer staff and resources than Time-Life, *Look* was also scooped—by *Life* and other news outlets, especially when it came to interviewing prominent figures like Marshal Tito (by a few months) and Stalin's daughter. However, it bears repeating that this was not *Look*'s métier: it did not cover breaking news or devote much attention to pronouncements by the Pentagon or State Department.[3]

Despite its small but talented staff of foreign correspondents—Attwood, Bergquist, Moskin, Christopher Wren, Korry, Stevens, and others—*Look* used old-fashioned shoe-leather reporting, showing up to talk with Israeli kibbutzim, U.S. infantrymen in Vietnam, or reindeer herders on the Finnish-Soviet border. This was encouraged by editors like Mich, who worked hard with writers and photographers to come up with creative angles to international stories.

Not only did *Look*'s staff line up behind these ideals and journalistic principles, but so did many of the illustrious commentators who wrote for the magazine. Some of its most frequent contributors on international affairs were liberals like Adlai Stevenson, Eleanor Roosevelt, Walter Lippmann, John Gunther, Supreme Court chief justice William O. Douglas, and Eric Sevareid.

In addition, world leaders and foreign policy experts often provided commentary and analysis. These included Israeli prime minister David Ben-Gurion, German chancellor Konrad Adenauer and soon-to-be chancellor Willy Brandt, and Canadian prime minister Lester Pearson. Politicians, diplomats, and military leaders who were also contributors included senators like J. William Fulbright, Jacob Javits, and Kenneth Keating; and diplomats like George Kennan, Averell Harriman, William Bullitt, and Walt Rostow; and five-star general Omar Bradley.

This chapter is intended to be more illustrative than comprehensive, describing and discussing only a very small portion of the thousands of *Look* stories and photographs of the world beyond America's shores. While there will be a nod to other intriguing and important stories, the focus will be on particularly noteworthy or emblematic articles or series from World War II and the Cold War to the post-colonial developing world and postwar Europe. Its stories after the war, as suggested, were often quite different from the who-what-when-where-and-how reporting of most other magazines and newspapers.

World War II

Look began covering Nazism and fascism in its earliest issues. Between September 1941 and the end of 1945, *Look* published hundreds of stories and photos of the war in Europe, the Pacific, and China, with at least one in almost every issue. Most covers were war related. Articles fell into several broad categories: there were stories on battles, generals, and the major combatants' leaders—Roosevelt, Churchill, Stalin, Hitler, Mussolini, and

Tojo. Bombers, tanks, and other matériel were another category. Because it did not have its own on-the-ground correspondents, *Look*'s forte was to tell the stories of individual enlisted men.

Life did a superior job covering the war. Staff correspondent Jack Belden reported from the front lines in China, North Africa, and Europe, often getting close to combat. Robert Capa, originally with *Collier's*, and Bob Landry, both *Life* staff photographers, captured the first waves of Allied soldiers on D-Day, and Eliot Elisofon took battlefield photos from Tunisia. Among American magazines, the only three with accredited war correspondents were *Time*, *Life*, and *Collier's*.[4]

Among *Look*'s many stories about Hitler, none were as audacious, or salacious, as one written by the Fuhrer's twenty-eight-year-old nephew, William Patrick Hitler. Laid out like a photo album with long captions, there were sixteen images, including a photo of Hitler with a little girl, a telegram from "Willy," and William's mother, who had married Hitler's half brother.

William—who moved to the United States in 1939 and joined the U.S. Navy in 1944—described the German dictator's "feminine gestures" and crazed brutality in his private life. Explaining "why I hate my uncle," William told of Hitler's affair with his niece Geli Raubal and her 1931 suicide, with Hitler's revolver beside her body. "Everyone knew that Hitler and she had long been intimate and that she had been expecting a child—a fact that enraged Hitler," he wrote.[5]

William recalled his meetings with uncle Adolf. At one, he "was pacing up and down, wild-eyed and tearful," brandishing a horsehair whip, shouting "insults at my head as if he were delivering a political oration." William told of another incident in 1936 at Berchtesgaden, the Fuhrer's mountaintop hideaway, where "he was entertaining some very beautiful women at tea." Again, he was "slashing his whip," warning William "to never again mention that [he] was his nephew." He said that his uncle's paternal grandfather was a Jewish merchant. The six-page spread included photos of Hitler at his desk and with his niece/lover.

William Hitler, who later changed his name to William Stuart-Houston, had badgered the Fuhrer for a high-ranking job in the Third Reich, threatening to publish the photos that ended up in *Look*. He personally beseeched FDR to let him enlist in the navy, writing in 1942, "Under your masterful leadership men of all creeds and nationalities are waging desperate war to determine, in the last analysis, whether they shall finally serve and live in an ethical society under God or become enslaved by a devilish and pagan regime."[6]

More than forty soldiers, sailors, and airmen were singled out in the magazine's "American Heroes" series. Stories profiled heroic fighting men like a marine ace who shot down twenty-nine enemy planes; a coast guard coxswain who swam ashore on D-Day; the first soldier to win the Congressional Medal of Honor; a counterintelligence officer; members of the Army Corps of Engineers; submariners; and the fabled pilot Eddie Rickenbacker, who survived for twenty-three days on a raft in the Pacific. One marveled at pilot Ed O'Hare shooting down five Japanese planes in five minutes, while another honored Walker Sorrell, who found a route for Allied tanks to break the Nazis' Gustav Line in Italy.[7]

Sergeant Franklin Williams, a "distinguished Negro soldier … who fights with distinction," was hailed by Fowler Harper, deputy chairman of the War Manpower Commission, in a story that included photos by Arthur Rothstein, then serving with the Office of War Information (OWI). Williams was chosen by the OWI as a "model colored soldier" to help convince whites that Blacks were essential for the war effort. Photos showed him training at Fort Bragg, leading a segregated platoon, with his family in Baltimore, and "with his best girl, splitting a soda."[8]

Twenty-six of the "Heroes" stories were collected in a 1943 book, *Our American Heroes: A Pictorial Saga of Gallantry*. Edited by art director Edwin Eberman, it was illustrated by more than fifteen artists, including Carolyn Edmundson, Fred Ludekens, Hardie Gramatky, and John Floherty Jr.[9]

Another series of thirty-four dramatic and engrossing tales of heroism, daring feats, and close calls was compiled in a 1945 book, *My Favorite War Story*. Writers included legendary war reporter Ernie Pyle, Larry Lesueur, Vincent Sheean, and other noted journalists such as Alvin Josephy, Pat Robinson, and Martin Agronsky, with a foreword by Marquis Childs.[10]

In one story, a twenty-one-year-old pilot of a P-51, Captain John E. Meyer of America's "Flying Tigers," was bombing a Japanese shipping depot when a shell hit his plane, blinding him. His wingman, Lieutenant John Egan, miraculously "guided the sightless pilot squarely onto the runway." Although Meyer regained his sight, Egan was killed two days later over Hong Kong. Another story, by twenty-six-year-old Walter Cronkite, described his flight in a Flying Fortress on a 1943 raid over Germany.[11]

Many stories praised women's wartime efforts, showing army nurses, women assembling dive-bombers, and the Women's Army Corps. As early as 1942, Dorothy Thompson, an influential newspaper and radio reporter, worried about whether women's wartime status as valued workers would be lost after the war. "Relegation to the kitchen is one of the first steps away from freedom and democracy," she wrote.[12]

Look seesawed between hope and gloom during the war's first years. One piece explained "why Hitler will fail" and George Bernard Shaw wrote about how to win the war. However, after the Nazis conquered France and the Netherlands and Allied troops were evacuated from Dunkirk in 1940, *Look* worried about what would happen "if Hitler wins," and Drew Pearson asked if "we can keep Hitler out of the Americas." As noted, when FDR asked Cowles and Willkie to report back to him from the European and Pacific fronts, the two men published articles from Moscow, Lebanon, Egypt, and China, interviewing Stalin, de Gaulle, Chiang Kai-shek, and other leaders.[13]

World War II stories frequently appeared during *Look*'s next quarter century—as they did in other publications. The extent of the horrors of Nazi Germany were told in articles on atrocities engineered by Hermann Goering and Ilse Koch, the "mistress of Buchenwald," who had used human skin for lampshades, gloves, and book covers. After Adolf Eichmann, a principal architect of the Holocaust, was caught in Argentina by Israeli agents in 1960, *Look* published two stories on his capture and his life. One included Eichmann's chilling note written shortly before he was caught: "I was not a murderer. I was nothing but a loyal, orderly, efficient soldier. . . . I was a good German. I am a good German, and a good German I shall always be."[14]

The magazine described a Europe reduced to rubble and struck by famine in 1946–47 that killed at least a million people. After General George C. Marshall's 1947 Harvard commencement address calling for aid to rebuild

Europe, *Look* joined a chorus of supportive voices for what became the Marshall Plan. Two 1947 articles explained the structure and goals of the new United Nations, and extolled its virtues.[15]

Beyond the photos of soldiers, generals, and wartime leaders, and the odd photos of "Hitler's girlfriends," *Look* published many powerful photos during the war. As the Wehrmacht overran Poland in September 1939, twenty-six images by daring photojournalist Julien Bryan showed smoky embers of destroyed buildings, apartments in flames, Luftwaffe bombers, refugees carrying sacks out of Warsaw, machine-gunned women's bodies, and retreating Polish troops. As the Battle of Britain raged, *Look* photos in spring 1941 showed Londoners sleeping in bomb shelters, a one-eyed man moving rubble, a warehouse fire, and St. Paul's Cathedral surviving the aerial attacks. That summer *Look* published twenty-two powerful images of Chungking burning after Japanese warplanes strafed China. After the Nazi death camps were liberated, *Look* readers saw horrific photos of mass graves at Dachau, the ovens at the Majdanek concentration camp in Poland, and the Klooga death camp in Estonia.[16]

A number of striking illustrations were also published during the war. A color drawing by Arthur Szyk, a Polish Jew who later created a magnificently illustrated Haggadah, showed maniacal Nazi leaders around a globe with a snake festooned with swastikas and the German words for "Today Europe, Tomorrow the World." A Carolyn Edmundson illustration of a sympathetic, gray-haired Stalin—"a guy named Joe"—graced *Look*'s cover the week that 2.3 million soldiers were deployed to force the Germans out of the Soviet Union. The accompanying story, by British journalist Ralph Parker, told of how the Soviet leader read poetry to children on his knee. Edmundson also drew cover portraits of Eisenhower, General Omar Bradley, General Douglas MacArthur, General Marshall, General George S. Patton, Admiral Chester W. Nimitz, Admiral William Halsey Jr., British general Bernard Montgomery, and Lord Mountbatten.[17]

The Cold War: The USSR

Almost as soon as the war ended, the threat of Russia and the expanding communist world preoccupied *Look* for as long as it published. Even before the Soviet Union extended its de facto rule over Eastern Europe, Cowles toured American-occupied Europe, and *Look* warned that Russia was contributing to "world chaos" and that "the Soviet sphere will stretch all the way to the English Channel." Writers like Sheean, Pearl S. Buck, and Eleanor Roosevelt asked, "Will we have to fight Russia?" And Justice William O. Douglas said the communists were turning "the faces of millions toward atheism," while Soviet propaganda effectively played to "the great burning issues" of poverty, poor health, and lack of education in much of the world.[18]

Look took on almost every angle about the Soviets and communism— slave laborers, "Communism vs. Christianity," Russia's atomic bomb, and U.S. Air Force contingency plans to bomb Russia—and claimed to show Americans the "first pictures of the atom bomb" in 1951. The kindly "guy named Joe" had become a tyrannical and feared foe by 1948, when a *Look* cover showed a menacing photo of Stalin with a red hammer and sickle cutting across his face. "This small man with drooping shoulders tyrannizes one fifth of the world," Louis Fischer wrote.[19]

Look's coverage of, and relationship with, Nikita Khrushchev, is telling both in terms of its somewhat more balanced approach than other publications and the relations that Cowles and his magazine cultivated with the Soviet leader. Lippmann reported a "thaw" in the Cold War after Stalin's death in 1953, notably after Khrushchev denounced his predecessor's dictatorship and personality cult in 1956. Cowles called Khrushchev's speech "a fantastic operation, but cautioned that it was largely for domestic consumption."[20]

Look established a Moscow bureau headed by Edmund Stevens in 1955. Eric Johnston, president of the Motion Picture Association of America and the first American to meet Khrushchev, in 1958, wrote an exclusive profile for *Look*. Johnston also hosted the Soviet leader in Washington DC and California on his first visit to the United States in September 1959.[21]

Changes in Khrushchev's Russia were described in generally positive terms in a far-ranging fifteen-page article by Gunther, based on fifty-one days of reporting: life was better than when he was last there, in 1939; there was more openness; queues at shops had become rare; Moscow was clean;

and the number of newly minted doctors was seven times the number of new doctors in America. Walking by the Kremlin, listening to forbidden jazz, reading Hemingway, and exhibiting a Picasso painting—all prohibited under Stalin—were now possible.[22]

Yet, the life of Russian teenagers was "regimented," and, at "cozy" embassy receptions where Politburo members showed up, it was easy "to forget that this group of men [was] not only probably the most powerful but also the most cynical, sinister, and extravagantly ruthless in the world, and that its chief aim is the conquest of *our* world." Housing and clothing were so "wretched," he quipped, "If Marilyn Monroe should walk down the street with nothing on but shoes, people would stare at her shoes first." Gunther painted detailed portraits of Khrushchev, Bulganin, Molotov, Malenkov, and Zhukov, praising Malenkov for being intellectually "sophisticated" and wanting to expand production and access to consumer goods, whereas Khrushchev "led with a fist" and emphasized heavy industry. Although naivete crept in—especially when he declared that there were no longer political arrests—Gunther's article, accompanied by Harrington's photos, was one of the most comprehensive and thoughtful mid-1950s pieces on the USSR written for a mass U.S. audience. This idea that Russia had achieved some successes but was still a dreary, scary dictatorship was echoed in a 1958 piece by Stevenson and Attwood on "Russia's Two Faces."

After the 1959 "kitchen debate" between Khrushchev and Vice President Nixon, *Look*'s story and photos of the two men hit the wire services before Soviet censors could block it. Nixon reported for *Look* that what he saw in the USSR "raises questions about Khrushchev's boasts that the Soviet Union will soon catch up with the United States industrially and economically."[23]

Other negative stories appeared in the late 1950s: Khrushchev's misconceptions about America, the "myth of Russia's productive power," Soviet anti-Semitism, the dark world of the KGB, the threat posed by Sputnik, and defectors like dancer Rudolf Nureyev.[24]

However, as Cowles befriended Khrushchev, *Look*'s tone changed in the mid-1960s, perhaps influencing efforts by Presidents Johnson and Nixon to seek a measure of détente. His Des Moines newspapers had encouraged good agricultural relations between the United States and Russia. Despite

Cowles's praise of Khrushchev's 1956 denunciation of Stalin, their relationship soured when the publisher pointedly asked the premier during their first meeting, in New York in 1959, to explain the USSR's refusal to let Russians read American print media; Tass, the Soviet news agency, referred to the "notorious *Look* magazine."[25]

In April 1962 Cowles spent three hours interviewing Khrushchev and wrote that the Soviet leader expressed "some glimmers of hope" for a German settlement and said that President Kennedy "left a favorable impression on" him. Cowles described his meeting, in a forty-foot-long office with ears of corn in a cabinet, as "cordial," and the Soviet leader as an "optimist," a "statesman," and "a pragmatist who . . . was willing to listen to other points of view and explore new ways of doing things." Khrushchev paid "tribute to American accomplishments" and "appeared anxious to erase the popular American image of him as a loud-mouthed, unruly, vodka-swilling Communist tyrant," according to Cowles. In contrast to Cowles's friendly but frank one-on-one discussion, the Soviet leader a month later met with a group of American editors, leading to less nuanced stories in which news organizations like the *Wall Street Journal* simply called it a "propaganda forum."[26]

After the Cuban Missile Crisis in October 1962 and before the 1963 U.S.-Soviet nuclear test ban treaty, Cowles had invited Khrushchev to write for *Look*—possibly the only time that a Soviet leader published in a major U.S. publication. The premier denounced Mao Zedong, as tensions between Russia and China had emerged. Cowles almost encountered Khrushchev five years after he was ousted in 1964, when Victor Louis, an intrepid freelance reporter, invited the publisher to dinner at his relatively lavish two-story dacha, just down the road from where Khrushchev lived.[27]

Look published more positive—or, at least neutral—assessments in a massive issue in October 1967 to mark the fiftieth anniversary of the Russian Revolution. A writing team of Leonard Gross, Christopher Wren, Warren Rogers, and Joseph Roddy went to the USSR and wrote seventeen stories on "life in Russia," and Norman Rockwell painted a Soviet classroom. Stories covered the arts, education, tourism, medicine, small-town life, mountain climbing in the Caucasus, and caviar. These everyday-life stories were accompanied by ones on the Russian economy, the KGB, and the new premier, Alexei Kosygin. The issue was expanded into the 1968 book *Red Russia after 50 Years*.[28]

Look also covered the Berlin Wall, erected in 1961, and the Iron Curtain in ways that other news media did not. The magazine first turned this geopolitical flashpoint into a poignant six-page essay on a four-year-old West Berlin boy who "cannot remember life without the Wall." Readers saw little Manfred Stein playing in a desolate field near the wall and watching soldiers on both sides of Checkpoint Charlie. The boy's family "lives at the world's most dangerous corner" on a street that dead-ends at his house, where "a young East Berliner was shot and left dying only yards away.... He knows he must not step over the white line in the middle of the street. But he doesn't know why—that this is where the Communists have drawn their boot heel and warned men not to cross."[29]

The wall was just a tiny stretch of the heavily armed border between the "Free World" and the Communist world that stretched from above the Arctic Circle in Finland south to the Adriatic. So, in late 1961, Mich sent Leonard and Fusco on a month-long, twenty-thousand-mile trip by car, plane, helicopter, truck, motorboat, and foot starting in Ivalo, Finland, along the borders of West Germany, Czechoslovakia, Austria, Hungary, Bulgaria, Rumania, Greece, Turkey, Iran, and Yugoslavia. In a long, richly illustrated 1962 cover story, "Eerie Trip along the Iron Curtain," Leonard vividly described the "deathlike silence [that] hangs over the edge of the Communist world," and areas where "the Communists have cleared and plowed a strip of earth to present an open field for gunfire and reveal tres-passers." In Greece an official told him, "The Bulgarians are moving Greek Communists up to the border." He wrote about young Peter and Rosemarie Evers in a Hamburg refugee camp after escaping East Berlin, where they had been imprisoned for drawing a caricature of East German leader Wal-ter Ulbricht on the side of a ship. A Finnish border guard described how reindeer had to be fenced in so that they wouldn't cross the frontier into Russia. Few, if any, other articles in any publication gave a better picture—at once chilling and humdrum—of life along the Iron Curtain.[30]

About thirty of the hundreds of photos Fusco shot were published, including ones of camera-shy communist police, a watchtower guard before he covered his face, a stretch of weeds under which "the Reds have planted mines," and a West Berlin woman showing her baby to her mother on the other side of the Wall. The fourteen-page spread also showed three scenes of young girls: one on a West German beach that abutted the border, an Iranian man herding cattle near the Russian frontier, and Greek girls playing across the river from the Hungarian border. Trying to explain the madness, Leonard said, "The main purpose of this elaborate barrier is not to guard against outside attack but to imprison those who live inside."

As fears of nuclear war engulfed America in the postwar world, *Look* also took a multifaceted editorial approach. As early as 1946, *Look* published a frightening sixteen-page supplement, "Your Last Chance," showing a huge mushroom cloud above a topographic map of the United States. The first half, which included a horrific illustration of destruction and chaos, laid out a grim scenario in which "your life will be unbearable in a world where atom bombs may fall any hour," while the second argued for "a world organization [that] can finally smash the cycle of war." A 1953 article described how a hydrogen bomb detonated over the U.S. Capitol would bring fiery devastation as far away as Baltimore, and an illustration by artist Chesley Bonestell showed a giant orange-and-white flash above a darkened New York City. *Look* went to the Nevada Proving Grounds, observing and interviewing servicemen used as guinea pigs to gauge the effects of radiation in combat, and to show readers above-ground nuclear tests. The magazine also wrote about Hiroshima and Nagasaki ten, fifteen, and twenty years after the bombs were dropped, showing where buildings once stood and doctors operating on a blast victim. Pages upon pages of searing photos by Sandberg and Fusco grimly illustrated the devastation and residents' lasting illnesses and deformities caused by radiation exposure. *Look* made it clear that there could be no winners in an all-out nuclear war. When many Americans started building backyard fallout shelters, stocked with tins of crackers and water, Knebel watched suburbanites dig those fallout shelters, and he listened to a kerosene-powered radio in one St. Paul couple's shelter. He also talked to men and women transforming an abandoned mineshaft, in Hackettstown, New Jersey, into a shelter, and

Look published a photo of New York governor Nelson Rockefeller bringing a canister of water to a couple in their shelter bunk bed.[31]

China

Look's coverage of China differed from other U.S. news organizations in several significant ways. Although "Red China" was seen as the mysterious, dangerous, and loathsome enemy by American policymakers and citizens, *Look* was once again surprisingly evenhanded—at least to the extent that everything that it wrote did not damn the communists. The magazine also paved the way for other news organizations to go behind the "bamboo curtain."

Cowles, the internationalist, made a point of getting to know China in the 1940s, bankrolling filmstrips urging food aid to the hunger-plagued country and meeting nationalist leader Chiang Kai-shek when he was there with Willkie during the war. After Madame Chiang told Cowles that she wanted to rule half the world, the publisher was undoubtedly gleeful when *Look* reported that "the imperious Madame was taught to mind her manners by the democratic Eleanor Roosevelt." *Look* later denounced Chiang as "a lonely, repudiated man," calling for recognition of the People's Republic. *Look* did not let up, as Kuo-Cheng Wu, a prerevolution mayor of Shanghai and "governor" of Formosa, called Chiang's island a "police state," and Winston Churchill wrote that the Taiwanese leader was "corrupt and inefficient." A very different view was taken by Henry Luce, who insisted before and after the revolution that Chiang was China's only hope.[32]

After Mao proclaimed the People's Republic in 1949, Cowles called for the United States to recognize the new government.[33] Despite some critical stories, this may have been a reason that *Look* received permission in 1956 to become the first major U.S. news organization to report from China since the revolution. The State Department, which banned journalists from going to the People's Republic, condemned the move, as did other news media and both liberals and conservatives. Nonetheless, *Look*'s journalists won the prestigious Polk Award.[34]

Stevens, Harrington, and William Worthy, a Black journalist from Baltimore, were allowed to spend a month touring the country, talking to people and interviewing First Premier Zhou Enlai. In seventeen pages they reported on Chinese living in cities and the countryside, medical care, school children, theatrical performances, outdoor markets, and workers in steel and textile factories. Worthy, who wrote for the *Baltimore Afro-American*, also interviewed American POWs held since the Korean War. Stevens's piece, "Inside Red China," appeared in the issue immediately after Gunther's "Inside Russia," in April 1957.[35]

They painted a mixed picture of a country on the move where life was getting better, but its 600 million citizens lived under the yoke of the Communist Party. Stevens wrote of "China's steadily growing industrial might" and "plentiful" jobs, and that its "living standards, though still low, are rising." The people were friendly, as Chinese they met hammed it up for the camera. Comparing China to the Soviet Union, he wrote that he felt "more at home" in the former, adding, "It didn't take us long to discover that, in temperament and culture and in their fundamental approach to human problems, the Chinese have little in common with the Russians—except communism." On the other hand, he wrote:

Much about the system is hateful: the arbitrariness and brutality of police-state methods; the mental conformity (which is the only way to escape "re-education"—or brainwashing); the monotony of dress, slogans, [and] conversation; the oppressive, puritanical morality that extols toil and frowns on frivolity; the conditions of well-fed slavery under which most industrial workers are forced to live; the lying propaganda about the outside world.... [The unisex blue tunics and trousers] made people look like inmates of a huge reformatory—as indeed they are.

When he interviewed Zhou in his single-story house, the premier expressed his "desire to improve relations" with the United States, and acknowledged "differences" with the Soviet Union. But he firmly declared that his government was committed to the "peaceful liberation" of Taiwan.[36]

Harrington stunned the Chinese with his three cameras, and shot more than thirty-five rolls of black-and-white film and six hundred color slides; nineteen were published. There were photos of a Shanghai man pulling a cart, "doing the work of machines and animals," and an incongruously smiling girl digging a drainage ditch who "like a pack animal transports mud." Children were in many photos, as were dazzling shots of the Forbidden City, the Great Wall, and the Suzhou Gardens. Readers saw acupuncture being practiced, but were told that "modern doctors" say that "traditional medicine contained a large amount of hokum."[37]

A second notable China story was written in 1961 by Edgar Snow, the author of *Red Star Over China* (1937) and a China correspondent for the *Saturday Evening Post* during the 1940s. Snow, who had met Mao and Zhou in the 1930s, as the communists battled the Kuomintang and the Japanese, wrote a controversial fifteen-page "Report from Red China." Zhou wanted better relations with the United States, despite U.S. bases just beyond China's southern border. Diplomatic relations were contingent on resolving the Taiwan issue, but Zhou told Snow that his repeated proposals "demonstrate that the Chinese people and the Chinese Government desire to settle disputes between China and the United States through peaceful means. . . . Our proposal [is] to conclude a peace pact of mutual nonaggression among the countries of Asia and those bordering on the Pacific." Snow's article led to hearings by the Senate Foreign Relations Committee to probe what the new Kennedy Administration's China policy would be. *Look* received considerable criticism, including a Taiwan government statement calling Snow a "fellow traveler."[38]

In a rare case of *Look* disavowing its writer, an editorial preface said that much of what Snow reported was "Red Chinese propaganda." *Look* ran a much more pessimistic piece in the same issue by China scholar A. Doak Barnett asserting that the country "will work steadily to help erode the U.S. position throughout Asia" and aim to make "breakthroughs" causing a domino-like "chain reaction."[39]

Snow, who *Look* paid the then-princely sum of $15,000, at first praised the magazine for its "guts and support," but the relationship soured. After a series of editorial changes to two subsequent pieces, Mich killed the stories, saying, "Frankly, we are now too skeptical of many of the facts and figures, and too concerned about the obvious slant." Snow slyly responded by dedicating his next book to Mao, Zhou, and Gardner Cowles.[40]

Thus, more negative reporting followed in the mid-1960s. When China detonated its first atomic bomb in 1964, *Look*'s December 1 cover displayed a Chinese stone dragon seeming to growl. Tung Chi-Ping, a Chinese diplomat who had defected, warned of China's long-range plans for domination, as photos showed glum-looking city dwellers and peasants carrying baskets. A red-covered issue in 1965 warned of internal strife, and *Look* later published photos capturing the tumultuous Cultural Revolution.[41]

The strangest turn came in 1970, when the magazine took its last look at China through the eyes of Swedish communist Jan Myrdal, with photos by Myrdal's wife, Gun Kessle. Myrdal, who had written a 1965 book about Chinese villagers, returned to the village of Liu Ling and reported, "Down to the smallest village, China is clearly in a period of rapid economic development." In his eight-page article, he hailed the Red Brigades for building "well-constructed stone houses" and the Cultural Revolution for enabling women to become local leaders and giving men "the duty to stay at home and care for the children."

He took issue with the widely held belief that the Cultural Revolution was devastating China and its economy, claiming that "the standard of life has gone up," citing questionable production statistics, and that reforms had brought "a high degree of social security based on collective economy and self-reliance with a minimum of administration." Myrdal extolled the benefits of "self-criticism" under the local brigades, and came down on the side of Mao, who had deposed the revisionist leader Liu Shaoqi. Somewhat comically, he quoted a villager: "Most necessary of all is to study Mao Tse-tung Thought," which he did, "even though I can't read." Myrdal approvingly quoted Mao's gruesomely hypocritical statement: "'People are the most precious, . . . As long as there are people, every kind of miracle can be performed." In the end, Myrdal acknowledged he was "most decidedly partial," but rationalized his happy portrayal as fostering a "better understanding in the United States of China" in order to prevent war. The sixteen published photos showed smiling, no longer uniformly clad, children, women singing in front of a poster of a young Mao, and a toddler holding Mao's *Little Red Book*.[42]

Other journalists, including Harrison Salisbury and Robert Patterson; economist John Kenneth Galbraith; and biologist Arthur Galston also succumbed to the seeming wonders of the Chinese revolution, much like "their illustrious predecessors [who] made fools of themselves fawning over Russia," as *Commentary* opined. Nonetheless, it is noteworthy that *Look*, which had denounced Snow, a much more respected journalist, gave free rein to an apologist for Mao.[43]

The Korean War

Look devoted much ink to the other hot spots of the Cold War, although its coverage of the Korean War paled beside that of its often path-breaking writing about Cuba and powerful stories about Vietnam.

In 1950, when troops from communist North Korea invaded South Korea, *Look* sent writers to cover what was initially described as a "police action." Gunther and Churchill criticized MacArthur's leadership: Gunther called him "a man not overwhelmingly loved," and Churchill wrote that MacArthur had "blundered." A moving photo essay by Earl Theisen showed a U.S. Mobile Army Surgical Hospital (MASH) at work. Shortly before the 1953 ceasefire, Stevenson concluded, "You can shoot Communists, but you can't shoot poverty, ignorance, and communism."[44]

The Korean conflict was one of all too many "proxy wars" between the United States and the Soviet Union in postcolonial and other developing countries. These ranged from the Mau Mau uprising in Kenya and the Congo crisis to U.S. interventions in the Dominican Republic and Thailand.

Cuba

The Cold War came to the Western hemisphere with Fidel Castro and his 1959 revolution, bringing fascination and fear. *Look* contributed to Americans' fascination and fear in several dramatic stories.

Just as Stevens was the first major U.S. journalist in Communist China, Andrew St. George, a frequent *Look* writer, was one of the first to interview Castro in the Sierra Maestra Mountains in 1957. Readers learned how the thirty-year-old revolutionary and a small band of men came together in 1956 to fight the U.S.-supported dictatorship of Fulgencio Batista. Castro came across as sympathetic and reasonable, vehemently denying that his movement was communist inspired and likening it to the failed 1956 anti-communist uprising in Hungary. St. George, a photographer as well as a writer, took photos of Castro's Movimiento 26 de Julio on patrol, visiting villages, firing rifles, and capturing opposition fighters. His photos also appeared in *Life*, but with a mere two hundred words of text, three months later.[45]

"Our Cuban support comes from all classes of society," Castro told him. "The middle class is strongly united in its support of our movement. We even have many wealthy sympathizers. Merchants, industrial executives, young people, workers are sick of the gangsterism that rules Cuba. Actually, the Cuban Communists, as your journalist John Gunther once reported, have never opposed Batista, [with] whom they have seemed to feel a close kinship." Castro added that "the right kind of private investment" is better than nationalization and that he was too young to lead the country. He said that he wanted to meet with U.S. authorities, an idea that Washington rejected.[46]

Look allowed Castro to have his say, whereas *Life*—which only got a correspondent into Cuba's jungles months later—focused on the news story of Raúl Castro's kidnapping of Americans at Guantanamo Naval Base.[47]

St. George and Attwood returned after Castro's victory for one of the stranger interviews in journalistic history. After waiting for weeks, they received a phone call at 4:00 a.m. from *Revolucion*, the government newspaper, telling them to come to the air force headquarters to join Castro on his plane (formerly Batista's), which would circle the Caribbean for four hours. They described Castro as "idealistic, impatient, impulsive, thin-skinned, erratic, and naïve." They criticized other U.S. newspaper and magazine coverage for being "sadly lacking in courage" for instead printing the official U.S. line. The loquacious leader was still enormously popular, and Attwood wrote that "women still react to him as though he combined the qualities of Clark Gable, Elvis Presley, Douglas MacArthur, and Perry Como."

Castro described his government as "provisional," and he again invited Americans to see the depth of his support. He told Attwood that he was "against all dictatorships," open to referendums, very much wanted trade and foreign investment, and that his ideas "[had] nothing to do with communism." Readers saw photos of the Cuban revolutionary, mouth open and pointing his finger at Attwood, the plane's windows behind him, and the *Look* reporter gesticulating back.

Attwood and St. George concluded that Castro was too "impatient" and "confused," and that his "tragedy" ahead was "that he may refuse to listen to hardheaded advice and stubbornly prolong this reckless, hoarse and turbulent spree," making him "the world's likeliest target for an assassin's bullet" by year's end. Thirteen years later, Castro was still in power and his country remained poor when Attwood returned to write about a wave of plane hijackings to Havana.[48]

Bergquist—who *Look* called on its cover "our woman in Havana"— brought Fusco to Cuba in 1960 to interview pro- and anti-Castro Cubans. She found growing disillusionment. "He is a changed man from the mountains," one man told her. "He never smiles anymore. He has become a hater." With a cover close-up of Castro's bearded face and open mouth close to a microphone, Fusco's photos showed the fiery leader, a girl dancing at her graduation party, Bergquist with young soldiers, and workers throwing twenty-six coffins into the sea to mark the expropriation of twenty-six U.S. companies.[49]

For the same issue, Bergquist also interviewed Che Guevara, which she called "a meeting of antagonists." Guevara denied being a communist, opposed Soviet aggression, and said that the revolution had made "errors" and that Cuba's future "depends greatly on the United States. . . . U.S. pressure on Cuba has made necessary the 'radicalization' of the revolution. To know how much further Cuba will go, it will be easier to ask the U.S. government." Bergquist described Guevara as "a scholar and seasoned guerrilla warrior," but also like an "enigmatic Buddha." Fusco showed the two talking, with Guevara grimacing and smiling. When he smiled, Bergquist said that he "has a certain charm." *Look* published twenty-seven photos for her two stories—far more than what movie stars typically warranted. *Look* published Rene Burri's iconic photo of Guevara with a cigar in his mouth, which can be found on posters and T-shirts around the world.[50]

Coverage soon turned darker. In an insightful thirteen-page 1963 piece, "My 28 Days in Communist Cuba," Bergquist—who *Look* also called "the lone Yanqui journalist to move about the country"—reported on the dreary "indoctrination" sessions, and wrote: "Castro isn't the new Bolivar, the savior he grandiosely thinks he is. But in four turbulent years, under the severest U.S. pressures, including an invasion, his regime has made amazing strides—in racial integration, health, housing, and education. The price tag—the loss of civil liberties, the party-line press, the police-state trappings—does not appeal to me, but many Cubans feel otherwise."[51]

Guevara told Bergquist in a second interview why Cuba had turned to the Soviets, and she reported on an American who had fought with the Fidelistas and was about to be executed. *Look* also published an excerpt from a book by Castro's former lover and UN representative, Teresa Casusu, who wrote, "He was pathetically unqualified to be a ruler."[52]

The Tragedy of Vietnam

In all of *Look*'s extensive coverage of Indochina, the deadliest front of the Cold War, one man—Sam Castan—set the magazine apart from other publications. *Look* was early to expose the folly and horrors of an expanding war, largely due to its daring reporting and thoughtful commentary. As early as 1955, Leo Cherne, head of the International Rescue Committee, told readers that America had to win the hearts and minds of the Vietnamese—a goal that was never to be achieved. Castan knew this and questioned the government's upbeat news about the war. Having been assigned to assist sports editor Tim Cohane, he nagged editors to send him to cover Vietnam. They agreed, and he went in 1963, 1965, and 1966.[53]

In the first of a half-dozen searing articles about the Vietnam War, just weeks after JFK's death, Castan began, "The child is dead. She died at dawn last November 6 of a bullet, fired by one of her own countrymen, that ripped into her back and left a fist-sized hole in her chest. Moments later, her father was blown apart by a hand grenade while manning the village's sole machine gun against a Vietcong attack." Shifting scenes, Castan and Karales showed an isolated American Special Forces team in the Mekong Delta, "a wet, sour, rotted expanse of hot mud, mangrove swamps, steamy rice paddies and jungle thickets."[54]

With considerable foresight, Castan added, "To a larger extent than we have admitted, the United States is responsible for Vietnam's agony." He described the coup that toppled Ngo Dinh Diem, interviewing a leader of the new junta, Ton That Dinh, who justified the overthrow because Diem "had promised to institute" freedoms and justice. Karales's photos showed a soldier carrying a child's limp body, a downed soldier clutching his weapon, a mother holding her dead baby, a Huey helicopter with its sixteen rockets ready to be launched, and Dinh grinning with his head tilted. "Thanks in part to our blunders, to our policy of seeing and thinking no evil of anyone who labels himself 'anti-communist,' and to our love of bucking reality, a tired bloody nation is approaching its critical hour," Castan concluded.[55]

Look published this damning assessment of U.S. involvement years before an antiwar movement arose and seven months before the Gulf of Tonkin Resolution authorized military engagement that led to the deaths of fifty-eight thousand Americans and millions of Vietnamese, Cambodians, and Laotians.

Another long Castan-Karales piece described Saigon's people and how Johnson was "changing the war." He also pointedly wrote that he spent most of his time "in the field, because that's where Americans are fighting the war I was sent to cover," unlike reporters who attended daily press briefings and spent "much leisure time" at the bar of Saigon's Caravelle Hotel.[56]

In 1966 Castan, who worshipped the legendary World War II–reporter Ernie Pyle, convinced his editors to give him an especially grim assignment to write about the last thoughts of dying soldiers. His wife and one-year-old daughter were in Hong Kong when Castan accompanied the First Cavalry Division to the Central Highlands to interview soldiers, tape recorder in hand.

He was interviewing a soldier when the Viet Cong burst out of the elephant grass and began firing. Sergeant Robert Kirby gave Castan a .357 Magnum and a handful of bullets. Moments later a bullet shattered Castan's arm and grenade fragments lodged in his back. He returned enough fire to allow others to escape, but Castan learned the thoughts of a man facing death; they were his own. Like Ernie Pyle, an enemy bullet to his left temple killed him. "In his last moments, the correspondent had the courage of a lion," wrote military historian General S. L. A. "Slam" Marshall. His recovered camera contained photos leading up to the firefight and his last moments.

At a memorial service, the chaplain said, "Sam was concerned about the conduct of his colleagues . . . and their responsibility to the public. The true facts, he felt, were often being distorted by the military and the press." Among seventeen American journalists killed during the war, Castan was the first with a major news medium who lost his life.[57]

After Castan's death, between 1967 and 1970, stories about the war started appearing in most issues of *Look*. Bergquist, Moskin, and Wren all reported from Vietnam, and James Hansen, Thomas Koeniges, and Karales captured the death and devastation on film. After LBJ announced he would not run for reelection, *Look* made an impassioned call to end the war in a May 1968 editorial, accompanied by seven pages of particularly gruesome photos by Catherine Leroy. "*Look* publishes these photographs to remind you of some things that many Americans seem to have forgotten. . . . The Vietnam War has been a mistake, destroying something precious in the word 'America.'" More horrific photos by James Hansen accompanied a Moskin story, "Vietnam: Get Out Now," after the first national Moratorium to End the War in October 1969.[58]

Moskin, a former hawk, followed the editorial line, as the country had turned against the war. He spoke of America's "failures" and the limits of its power, declared that it had suffered "defeat," and dismissed the idea that the South Vietnamese alone could successfully fight the war, quoting an American officer saying sardonically, "We'll know we're making progress when we can get a phone call [to the South Vietnamese Army] straight." He concluded with an implausible optimism, "This war may at least mark the end of an era and the beginning of a new, less punitive and more imaginative role in the world for the United States."[59]

Senators J. William Fulbright, Robert Kennedy, and Eugene McCarthy and journalists Eric Sevareid and Norman Cousins were among the luminaries who wrote and opined about the war. Kennedy declared that "bombing of North Vietnamese cities and dikes" would "provoke justified condemnation from the world." Particularly intriguing was an in-print debate among five foreign-policy experts published in 1966 that included Henry Kissinger, Herman Kahn, Hans Morgenthau, and Arthur S. Schlesinger Jr. Both Morgenthau, a leading foreign-policy scholar and a critic of U.S. involvement since the Kennedy Administration, and Schlesinger denounced the "Americanization" of a war that was "unwinnable." Kahn and Kissinger defended the war—as Generals Omar Bradley and George C. Marshall had done in other pieces. In a later piece, Gerald Astor described Kissinger talking in the White House basement about "assured nuclear capacity, ICBMs, and Vietnam," while calling antiwar protesters at Harvard "fascists" bent on "the destruction of all humane values."[60]

Sevareid reported that UN secretary-general U Thant had tried to arrange peace talks in 1964 and Hanoi had accepted the offer, only for the United States to put them off. The State Department, which had denied that any such proposal was made, admitted it after *Look*'s article appeared. Five years later, the magazine revealed that North Vietnamese leader Ho Chi Minh, a week before he died, had written to Nixon that a "bit of goodwill could permit a settlement to take place." Needless to say, the Nixon Administration spurned the olive branch.[61]

Freelancers like Oriana Fallaci interviewed a "Vietcong terrorist" behind enemy lines during the 1968 Tet Offensive, and a soldier who had spent four years in a VC prison, declared that "it's open season on Americans all year round." Murray Helfan, a former army neurosurgeon who had treated the wounded in Vietnam, explained why he resigned his commission in a 1970 "letter to the president," printed in *Look* as if written on a typewriter: "Caring for the wounded is indeed a privilege; but I was never able to convince myself that they had been wounded for any good end.... I had been told that if I waited long enough, perhaps the war would go away. I did wait, but it never seemed to go away at all."[62]

Futility, failure, protest, and defeat were very much in the air. As the military became increasingly reviled and student strikes shut down about five hundred colleges in 1970, *Look* asked, "Who would ever want to go to West Point anymore?" Soldiers openly opposed to the war were interviewed, and a full-page Harrington photo showed a soldier peering out of a tank with the word "peace" emblazoned on his helmet. The same 1970 story by Leonard Gross pointed to U.S. racial tensions and a "hard core of marginal whites painfully aware that they are at the bottom of the Establishment heap."[63]

Look, like other news media, harshly criticized Nixon's pledge to end

U.S. involvement and "Vietnamize" the war. "'Before a man can fight, he's got to believe in what he's fighting for,'" Christopher Wren, a former Green Beret, quoted a U.S. military advisor. "Charlie [the Vietcong] will stand up and fire at a gunship with his AK-47. He knows he'll get killed, but he keeps shooting. [The South Vietnamese] have so little to die for.'" By contrast, the North Vietnamese were described as confident and patriotic in a twelve-page photo essay by French photographer Marc Riboud that included shots of Ho Chi Minh and Premier Pham Van Dong.[64]

When Nixon ordered the bombing and invasion of Laos and Cambodia in 1969, the magazine wrote, "Rather than shortening the war, the move will extend it and make it more dangerous." A photo essay of a U.S. "massacre" in Cambodia, including an image of corpses, their hands behind their backs, floating in the Mekong River, was followed by a piece by *Look*'s David Maxey that described Kissinger telling a Republican congressman the day before the invasion that U.S. involvement would be "limited." When *Look* called Nixon's expansion of the war a victory for the Chinese, the president denounced the magazine and unsuccessfully tried to pressure Cowles to tone down its coverage.[65]

As Sen. Fulbright harshly warned in a late 1969 essay: if America did not avoid another war like Vietnam, "the future can hold nothing for us except endless foreign exertions, chronic warfare, burgeoning expense and the militarization of American life."[66]

Decolonization and the "Third World"

The Cold War was the big global story, but *Look* also gave readers a sense of life, politics, cultures, and troubles throughout the world. It took particular interest in the Middle East; postcolonial countries; and the so-called Non-Aligned movement, led by India's Jawaharlal Nehru, Egypt's Gamal Abdel Nasser, Indonesia's Sukarno, Yugoslavia's Tito, and Ghana's Kwame Nkrumah.

Although the magazine's reporting on Africa and Israel stood out, it also published many stories on Latin America and India. When the United States invaded the Dominican Republic, ostensibly to fight communists, *Look* sent Castan to cover the fighting. In a harrowing story by Fallaci that helped disprove Mexican government denials of a massacre in the capital, she described being shot three times, dragged by her hair, and left for dead in Mexico City during bloody protests on the eve of the 1968 Olympics.[67]

Look sought to foster hope in India, showing not only how "cheap life was"—as other publications did—but also how the country and Prime Minister Nehru were "the last important stronghold of democracy in Asia," in the words of John Cowles. A more personal view, through the eyes of twelve visiting UCLA students, made for an upbeat 1953 story. However, it also gave readers a sense of how the United States was widely perceived in the so-called Third World. "There are two views of the United States in India," an Indian student told Tom Morgan. "One is a noble one. We see America as a broad oak tree whose branches shade all those beneath its leafy limbs. The other view is ignoble. Some see America as an octopus whose tentacles squeeze the life out of all who are caught in them."[68]

In an extensive 1966 issue devoted to India, Dunbar compared the lives of an extremely rich and an extremely poor family. Fourteen photos by John Vachon showed the Thackerseys dining in their wealthy compound in Mumbai and the Narans and their village in drought-stricken Rajasthan. Despite the poverty and inequality, *Look* concluded: India is "too poor to be effective and too big to be ignored."[69]

Israel and the Middle East

Look took great interest in Israel and the Middle East, publishing at least thirty articles about the Jewish state, in part because of the Cowles-like idealism in creating a new state, in part to combat anti-Semitism at home, and in part out of Cowles's and Mich's deep desire to achieve world peace. The magazine's writers and photographers roamed the Middle East, showing how people lived in much of the Muslim world—from Iran, Iraq, Syria, and Lebanon, to Saudi Arabia, Egypt, and the Sahel—and interviewed leaders, laborers, shepherds, and guerrilla fighters. Beyond the profiles of Prime Ministers Ben-Gurion and Golda Meir, photos by Vachon and others portrayed a "young" nation of happy kibbutz dwellers, sunbathers and high rises in Tel Aviv, fishermen on the Sea of Galilee, and—like the boy at the Berlin Wall—a boy walking along the Jerusalem border.[70]

Look carried out its own shuttle diplomacy in the mid- to late 1950s. Attwood interviewed both Ben-Gurion and Nasser several times, trying to broker a peaceful coexistence. The Egyptian leader said that he wanted peace but blamed Israel for invading his country in 1956. A settlement had to address the four million refugees, he said. In 1954 Nasser blamed communists for "stirring up disorder and hate," but by 1957 he was singing a different tune, accepting Soviet military aid and, eleven years later, their support to build the Aswan High Dam. "'We certainly feel more friendly with the Russians than the West, but we are still nonaligned,'" he told Attwood.[71]

Ben-Gurion replied that an intermediary had proposed talks between the two countries several years before, but Nasser had refused. Despite Nasser's "ambition to be the dominating leader in Africa and the Moslem world," Ben-Gurion added, he would "not hesitate to negotiate with him man to man." Responding to Arab claims and UN condemnations that Israel was the aggressor and wanted to overthrow Nasser, he said that Israeli raids in Gaza were in response to fedayeen killing Israeli farmers. He wrote of his desire for peace and attributed the UN resolutions to Soviet support for the Arabs. Nonetheless, Deputy Prime Minister Abba Eban said that international institutions were important: "If the United Nations roof collapses over the head of more than 100 nations today, a chain of aggravated tension will be the most probable outcome." In a pricklier exchange, Ben-Gurion compared Jewish "men with university degrees creating settlements out of a wasteland," with "the Arabs [who] have never done this, [and] have turned prosperous countries into deserts."[72]

Hopes for peace were gone by the time of Israel's lightning victory in the 1967 Six-Day War. Look reported on Palestinian refugees and guerrilla leaders, young, rightwing Israelis who "don't believe in peace," and "Israel's darkening image" among American Jews. James Michener wrote that Nasser and Arabs would become even more hostile, adding that "fantasy is hard to eradicate if one's whole society is structured around the perpetuation of the Arabian Nights." A New York rabbi told staff writer Gerald Astor, "We need two declarations of independence. American Jewry must acknowledge Israel as sovereign over itself, not governed by U.S. Jews. And Israel must acknowledge the independence and integrity of American Jewry."[73]

Africa

Look distinguished itself from other publications in its reporting on Africa, telling of dramatic decolonization movements in the late 1950s and early 1960s, while using the continent as a foil for discussing civil rights in America. This was largely due to Ernest Dunbar's reporting, which had the strong support of Dan Mich.

Dunbar compared the injustices in Africa to those in America, noting that many Africans asked him about U.S. race relations. Black Americans' growing interest in Africa was the subject of several late 1960s *Look* articles. Dunbar used one man's story to try to explain, in 1967, why "an American Negro returns to Africa," and Jack Shepherd two years later told the story of a group of poor Black American youth going to Africa to seek their identity.[74]

In 1959 Dunbar, Korry, and two photographers traveled seven thousand miles across Africa, reporting from Nigeria, the Belgian Congo, Ghana, Ivory Coast, and South Africa. "A trip through Africa is like a quick tour through the history of mankind," Dunbar wrote. Readers learned that Africans wanted modernization, yet also sought to "retain some traditional foothold in a constantly shifting society." They described the "small elite of Western-educated men ... [in] Continental-cut suits waving from [their] Mercedes-Benz" uneasily coexisting with "the illiterate masses." *Look* juxtaposed photos by Harrington and Sandberg of Mau Mau leader Tom Mboya and a white farmer with four thousand acres of land, both in Kenya. Dunbar praised Nkrumah, who faced "many problems: a high illiteracy rate, a one-crop (cocoa) economy, poor port facilities, and a shortage of trained people in every field." Although "he has tackled them with a dedicated, and sometimes ruthless energy," Dunbar said that his undemocratic actions "have alarmed African nationalists in the still-colonial areas, who fear that his example may furnish substance to the argument that 'they're not ready to run their own affairs.'" He described the mineral riches of Congo, undermined by "bloody rioting"—the beginning of sixty years of violence. These problems were compounded, he said, because "America's efforts to help Africa do not amount to much." The never-ending Congolese war was also covered in two additional stories in the 1960s.[75]

Since Dunbar was unwelcome in South Africa because he was Black, Korry reported on a country of whites' "sun-drenched creature comforts" and millions of Blacks "working in white enterprises [who] will continue to be deprived of all significant rights." He warned: "Sooner or later, if [Prime Minister Hendrik] Verwoerd and his like remain in power, . . . it could result in the worst racial catastrophe in white history." Robert Kennedy described the cruel stupidity of apartheid in 1966, saying that if Black South Africans did not carry an employer-endorsed passbook they could be imprisoned or exiled.[76]

Dunbar returned to the continent to write several of the eight stories in a 1961 issue on "the challenge of Africa." He reported on life in the Portuguese colony of Angola, the little-discussed rise of Islam, and an American couple working in Nigeria as teachers. Readers again were told that Africa was a low U.S. foreign-policy priority.[77]

Look's interest in Africa brought Cowles there in 1966, giving a personal report to President Johnson at the White House. A year later, when civil war broke out in Nigeria, Jack Shepherd reported on the government's massacre of eight thousand Ibo civilians and its brutality toward breakaway Biafra, where millions were starving.[78]

Dunbar left *Look* briefly to accompany JFK advisor Averell Harriman on a fact-finding trip to Africa before the 1960 election, and to conduct seminars for seventy-five African journalists in 1964. JFK also appointed Attwood ambassador to Guinea, which he described in *Look*, followed by a stint as ambassador to Kenya.[79]

The First World

Much of *Look*'s coverage of Europe and East Asia was about the Second World War and the Cold War, as we have seen. The magazine reflected the nation's worries about "creeping" communism, and—like other publications—also increasingly treated Europe and Japan as travel destinations and Europe as a center of fashion for newly prosperous Americans.

In Japan, on the one hand, this could be seen in devastating critiques of General Douglas MacArthur by Adlai Stevenson and *New York Times* reporter Hallett Abend, who wrote in *Look*: "General MacArthur ignores the fact that the Japanese people today are a disillusioned and bitter people—pauperized by our failure to make them self-supporting. . . . He has lulled us into a false sense of security about the perilous situation in the Far East. He has misled the American people." Businessman Eric Johnston told readers that it was unclear whether Japan was a "problem or partner?"[80]

On the other hand, *Look* wrote of "mystic Japan," with a cover photo of Mt. Fuji, and told surprisingly lighthearted stories about impresario Ed Sullivan and Casey Stengel visiting a country that loved baseball; teenage idol Junko Kano; Japanese-style Beatniks; kimonos; sushi; and very young children learning to play the violin using the Suzuki method.[81]

Much the same was true of Europe, although memories of the Holocaust and the Nazi devastation of Western Europe loomed large. Nonetheless, *Look* helped Americans understand a continent rapidly recovering from history's worst war.

Swirling around the pages of *Look* were the very difficult questions of whether "Germany could be forgiven," as one American rabbi put it, and the "problem" that Willy Brandt described of a divide between middle-age Germans who always "carry the burden of the Hitler period" and younger Germans who say, "'What have we to do about the sins of our fathers and grandfathers?'" Yet, there were also more hopeful stories of the German economic comeback—the Wirtschaftswunder. *Look* put a human face on the country's rapid economic growth in a story about a Dusseldorf businessman, Carl Siebel, who was shown at his office, on his bustling factory floor, and with his family.[82]

Domestic U.S. debates about socialized medicine and communism were reflected in stories about the merits and demerits of Britain's National Health Service and an Attwood story trying to explain "why . . . a man vote[s] Communist" in France.[83]

Travel stories in the 1960s helped Americans think about Europe as something other than a place haunted by Nazi carnage or Soviet threats. *Look* highlighted the glories of Paris, Provence, and French food. In Italy, it published an "ode to Venice" and wrote about Florence, "the birthplace of modern beauty," and how "living is easy in Portofino." Readers also discovered Europe as the center of high fashion, with stories on Yves St.

Laurent, Emilio Pucci, and Coco Chanel. Cliches abounded in stories about the "pagan beauty" of Sweden, "fabulous feudal Portugal," "cutting-edge London," the "proud land" of Canada, and an Australia that was more than just kangaroos.[84]

       *

So, what did *Look*'s coverage of the world mean to its American readers? Whereas there was only one side to the story in World War II, the magazine's writing on the Cold War was nuanced: the communists ran dictatorial countries that threatened the West, but the people of the USSR, China, and elsewhere were trying to make the best of their lives—as people everywhere were. So too were the people on the Western side of the Iron Curtain and in the troubled Middle East and Africa. In this sense *Look* humanized the Cold War, while most news media generally focused on more abstract geopolitical threats. By looking at non-Americans as individuals and fam-ilies—as it did in the United States—the magazine also helped American readers relate to people in other countries. Photos of children around the world did the same. Perhaps, especially given *Look*'s unique access to both major communist powers, this kind of reporting helped dial down tensions enough to keep the Cold War from turning irrevocably hot. Although not blind to the horrors of Stalinism, starvation, and proxy wars, *Look* tried to be optimistic about the future and committed to the idea that the Earth's many countries and cultures were all part of "one world."

13

Covers, Special Features, and Popular Culture

Beyond the Cold War, civil rights, youth, and other topics discussed in previous chapters, *Look* also filled its pages with many other types of content. There were its more high-minded series like All-America cities, and its professorial ones on history's great philosophers and artists and the nation's religions. Celebrities frequently graced the pages of *Look*, and its coverage reflected and reinforced changing tastes in popular culture. The covers are a story in themselves. There were also many stories about movies, sports, and popular music. A 1959 content analysis found that *Look* wrote about sports, fashion, and food more than competitors like *Life*, the *Saturday Evening Post*, and *Time*. That changed in the 1960s.[1]

This chapter offers a quick tour d'horizon of these quirkier and lighter features and stories.

The Covers

Covers, of course, were the first things that readers or those browsing newsstands saw. Although *Look* would feature an occasional politician or social issue (like "the American family" or "the Negro in America") on its covers, it was more likely to show movie stars and glamour than to highlight the profound, path-breaking stories and essays inside the magazine. Perhaps this was partly a function of Cowles's coziness with Hollywood or, more likely, simply a way to sell magazines.

For example, a 1939 issue with a lengthy article about Hitler had an extremely incongruous cover depicting a smiling young woman in a swimsuit holding a beach ball, with the cover of a book titled *Adolf Hitler* glancing off her leg and arm. The 1948 issue with Gunther's essay "Inside the Soviet Union" and Kay Summersby's reminiscences about Eisenhower featured a red-lipsticked woman in a straw hat. Two fashion models were on the cover of the 1956 issue with Huie's story about Emmett Till's murderers. In 1958 about one-third of its twenty-six covers were close-ups of actresses and other women. By contrast, only seven of *Life*'s fifty-two issues that year had attractive women on their covers; instead, most showed the likes of Lyndon Johnson, Anne Frank, the Pope, riots in Venezuela, and a high-voltage X-ray machine for cancer patients. A 1965 *Look* cover showed a Marilyn-Monroe look-alike under "Mussolini" in large type, alerting readers to a story about the fascist leader's last days and all but hiding the dramatic story and photos of the Selma-to-Montgomery march inside the issue. And a July 1970 issue had probing articles on Fayette Mississippi's Black mayor, Charles Evers; torture in Brazil; and the Commager essay, "Is Freedom Dying in America," yet its cover story, ostensibly about water pollution, had a life-size photo of an alluring blond, blue-eyed woman in a clear, idyllic pond.[2]

Movie stars were definitely a favorite. In 1940, as the war raged in Europe, *Look* readers found Judy Garland, Rita Hayworth, Joan Crawford, Ginger Rogers, and Vivien Leigh on five covers. A decade later, the roster included Lana Turner, Esther Williams, June Allyson, Janet Simms, Jack Benny, and Bing Crosby. The pattern hardly let up in the 1960s. Julie Christie, her hair blowing in the wind, and Catherine Deneuve, her thick blond hair framing her face, were on 1966 and 1968 covers. And *Look*'s early 1970 covers featured Raquel Welch, Samantha Jones, Steve McQueen, Glen Campbell, sixty-five-year-old Greta Garbo, Dustin Hoffman, and Richard Burton with Elizabeth Taylor, who had appeared on many covers since the 1950s.

World War II covers tended to show individual soldiers, officers, and commanding generals, as well as members of the Women's Army Corps. *Look*'s 1962 story "Along the Iron Curtain" showed a glum boy clasping a barbed-wire fence, with another layer of wire slicing through the red-lettered headline. Despite many photos of the Vietnam War inside issues, the only cover story showed Ho Chi Minh, his hand raised as if to make a point. Palestinian guerrilla fighters, pointing their AK-47s skyward, were pictured in a 1969 cover.[3]

Sports stars were also a favorite. Tennis player Kay Stammers, in a knee-length dress, swung her racket on the cover of a 1937 issue. A University of Maryland football player, arm around his girlfriend, was on a 1954 cover. A year later, a cover showed Willie Mays, his bat on his shoulder.[4]

One of *Look*'s most dramatic covers was a red-and-purple psychedelic image of John Lennon by photographer Richard Avedon, in 1968. A photo of Elvis, eyes closed, clutching his microphone, belting out a song, and a Tretick close-up of Kris Kristofferson, with an inset showing country musicians, were on covers during *Look*'s last year.[5]

Every president during the *Look* years was on at least one cover, although JFK and his family were much more frequent subjects. Covers with astronauts, cars, and babies celebrated America's technological progress, wealth, and families.

There were a number of more conceptual covers, like a 1948 cover on the baby boom, with multiple images of the same boy and girl walking to school, and the grim face of a Black man for a 1965 cover on "The Negro Now." Artist Frank McMahon depicted cascading cartoon drawings of candidates and political buttons and banners on a cover before the 1968 Democratic Convention. A giant LP with a rock performer at its center and an extreme close-up of a young mother and father kissing their baby for an issue on "The American Family" were on later covers.

Lessons about Religion

During the 1950s, *Look* published two major series, with more than thirty articles, that explained Americans' religions. There were no such series in *Life* or other magazines, but these were very much in keeping with Cowles and Mich's beliefs about promoting tolerance, understanding, and respect, and that no nation, religion, race, or ethnic group was superior to others.

The first eighteen-part series of "question-and-answer"-style articles, such as "What Is a Baptist?" was published between 1952 and 1955 and turned into a book, *A Guide to Religions in America*, which Leo Rosten updated in 1975. The underlying premise was that one of America's virtues and strengths was its embrace of many religions. As one reviewer put it, "The cause of understanding and goodwill among various religious groups has been well served."

"The Story of Religions in America" came next, between 1957 and 1960. Most were written by Hartzell Spence, who was paid the then-enormous sum of $3,000 per article, with photos by Fusco and Jim Hansen. This influential series highlighted the good in each faith and talked about their histories, members, and travails, with stories and quotes from prominent members, past and present. The fourteen long articles profiled Episcopalians, Jews, Methodists, Baptists, Presbyterians, Christian Scientists, Mormons, Catholics, Congregationalists, Seventh Day Adventists, Quakers, Disciples of Christ, Eastern Orthodox, and even agnostics. There was no article on Muslims. Rosten said that it was intended "to answer the kind of questions which an ordinary man might ask of a religious body to which he did not belong or of which he knew not much." Seven million people wrote to *Look* for reprints, which sold for fifteen cents apiece.

Spence described Episcopalians as historically "the Ivy League men and women in furs." He told readers that "a Jew believes that life is good, the gift of God, which man should enjoy." Writing that Mormons "have never been understood by their fellow Americans" and whose "members have been labeled a 'strange people,'" he said that they are a "self-reliant society, which distributes the bounty of all its people to any member in need." He praised the Quakers "for worldwide labors in the cause of brotherhood" and Methodists for what Theodore Roosevelt called their "essential democracy."[6]

A more historical article on Catholics frankly discussed how Protestants persecuted them from the earliest days of the Republic. It told readers how different forms of Catholicism from various parts of Europe were melded into an American Catholicism, how the Protestant *Christian Century* magazine alleged that Catholics' loyalty was to the Pope and not America, and the censorship crusade launched by Patrick Joseph Cardinal Hayes.[7]

Look published many other articles about religions; religious figures, like evangelist Billy Graham; and controversial issues like religious intolerance, school prayer, and the conflicts between Christianity and psychiatry. The reverend Eugene Blake of the National Council of Churches worried that the 1950s upsurge in religion was in danger of "becoming a fad." Rabbi Morris Kertzer, author of the 1953 book *What Is a Jew?*, wrote a 1952 article with a photo showing him holding an open prayer book, leading a Passover service for Jewish soldiers who fought in World War II.[8]

Look attacked religious quackery like L. Ron Hubbard's Dianetics and Scientology. In a 1950 article, writer Albert Maisel said that Hubbard "demonstrated once again that Barnum underestimated the sucker birth rate" and cited the American Psychological Association, saying its claims were "not supported by empirical evidence."[9]

The Towering Figures Who "Made Our World"

Among *Look*'s other long-running series were those on history's great men (yes, Euro-American white men) who "made our world" and great artists since the Renaissance. Although Cowles ultimately considered *Look*'s early 1940s editor, Harlan Logan, too academically oriented, he and Mich strongly believed that Americans should have at least a basic knowledge of history and culture.

"They Made Our World" was launched in 1963, at the time of Kennedy's celebration of intellectuals, to describe the lives and thoughts of "the 50 commanding figures of history." Only nineteen were published before the series was scrapped in 1967. Rosten wrote the series, beginning with Socrates, whom he described as "squat, potbellied, bald-headed, with an absurd pug nose and an unkempt beard." After this unflattering physical description, Rosten gave a concise definition of the Socratic method and said that the ancient Greek philosopher believed that "knowledge is virtue" and "morals must be rooted in reason." The article ended with the glowing assessment:

We are, all of us, descended from him—from Saint Paul to Martin Luther to Einstein. The questions he raised dominated philosophy for 2,000 years. The Socratic method of questioning and teaching has never been surpassed. And wherever men today pursue truth, or are ready to die for intellectual freedom, wherever men assert the holy right to think, to argue, to challenge, to debate—in the conviction that life unexamined is indeed not worth living—they are following the example of that ugly saint who never wrote a word. His ideas were immortalized by Plato, who called him "the bravest, wisest, most just man of all we know."[10]

Jefferson, Newton, Columbus, Machiavelli, and Saint Paul were also profiled in 1963. During the next few years, the mélange of philosophers, political leaders, and scientists included Edison, Constantine, Voltaire, Gandhi, Montaigne, Copernicus, Freud, Erasmus, Adam Smith, Julius Caesar, George Washington, and Aristotle. Churchill was its last great man.[11]

These articles were dripping with superlatives but leavened by a little humor, as in the Socrates essay. Aristotle "made science possible." Jefferson was the "conscience" of the American Revolution, and Machiavelli "dared to introduce that detached, non-moralizing way of looking at political forces and political conflicts that was to become modern political science." Churchill "looked like a Toby jug—but he was born to command, to fight, to inspire, to prevail." However, Washington was "not the wintry patriarch of our folklore."[12]

The Great Artists

Look brought Western art history to millions of Americans through its "Story behind the Painting" series. Both *Look*, and *Life*, had done occasional stories on artists before 1955, when Allen Hurlburt suggested to Mich and photo director Arthur Rothstein that the magazine should publish "a regular series of spreads in each or nearly each issue, reproducing an important painting." Each such article described an artist's life and work, focusing on a particular painting that was reproduced in a full-page color format. Intended to include 150 artists, *Look* published more than fifty pieces between 1956 and 1962, written by Rosten, with the help of *Look*'s research department.

They read art journals, consulted scholars, found artists' notebooks and letters, and gathered information in museums in Europe and the United States. There were many "unexpected windfalls," as Rosten said—finding a Degas behind a bedroom door of a farmhouse in Connecticut, a Rouault found in a gallery five blocks from *Look*'s office, a Matisse discovered in a private Swiss collection, and an interview with Renoir's favorite model, then living in California.[13]

Although not quite a course in art history or appreciation, Rosten wrote sophisticated yet accessible eight-hundred-word pieces on each artist. In a 1956 profile of Rembrandt, accompanied by one of the artist's self-portraits, Rosten described the artist at age sixty-two, living in seventeenth-century Amsterdam. The article on "The Laughing Philosopher" had an esthetic refinement that is hard to imagine in a popular twenty-first-century medium:

[Rembrandt] wanted his painting to be viewed from a distance—so that the eye of the beholder would fuse the separated flashes of color, so that the viewer's mind would participate in the making of the magic illusion, so that light and shadow could move and float and play out their drama. He lured the eye into the canvas, seizing its attention with highlights, teasing it with adumbrations of the half-caught, the half-hidden, the half-revealed. He used color with unparalleled richness and splendor. He used shadows like music, somehow enlisting senses other than the visual. He used light like the blast of a trumpet.[14]

In a piece on Monet paired with one of his *Water Lilies* paintings, readers learned that his work is "a monument to a genius so stubborn, yet so lyrical, that it could transform a pond into a timeless mirage." Hokusai, a Japanese artist, was a key influence on the Impressionists whose work "obliterate[ed] the unessential." Trying to unlock the mystery of the *Mona Lisa*'s smile, Rosten drew on a sixteenth-century Italian primer on "the feminine graces," which counseled: "From time to time, close the mouth at the right corner with a suave movement, and open it at the left, as if you were smiling secretly." A piece on Gauguin told of his "torment in paradise," and one about Braque's Cubism spoke of its "cool mood of balance and repose, . . . lucidity and elegance."[15]

Look published many other stories on contemporary art and artists. A 1948 issue surveyed the work of Edward Hopper, Ben Shahn, Lyonel Feininger, and George Grosz. During the next two years the magazine included stories on Toulouse-Lautrec, Braque, and Munch. After a major, 1947 retrospective exhibition of Shahn's work at the Museum of Modern Art, *Look* surveyed museum directors, curators, and art critics, who agreed that he was one of America's ten best artists. Film director Jean Renoir authored a twenty-page feature on his father, Auguste Renoir, replete with many reproductions of his paintings. Picasso was treated almost like Marilyn Monroe, with at least a half-dozen stories about him, including pieces that he wrote in 1967 and 1968. Indeed, one 1952 cover showed a bare-chested Picasso in a box to the right of Marilyn dressed as a cheerleader.[16]

Sports: From Adulation to Critical Examination

In addition to Jackie Robinson and Willie Mays, *Look* profiled many other Black athletes, from the Cleveland Browns' star running back Jim Brown to tennis pro Arthur Ashe. The magazine published stunning photos of Roger Maris's successful quest to beat Babe Ruth's home run record and the Green Bay Packers' victory in the first Super Bowl. The story of *Look* writer Michael McCormick's weeklong attempts to interview Packers coach Vince Lombardi was the subject of a 2010 Broadway play by Eric Simonson. A piece on Los Angeles Dodgers pitcher Sandy Koufax put a spotlight on one of sports' greatest Jewish athletes. "Broadway Joe" Namath, the New York Jets' iconoclastic quarterback, was written about twice, once by his mother.[17]

Muhammad Ali did not make it onto *Look*'s cover, unlike *Life*'s; however, a full-color, full-page photo of the boxer surrounded by fans was juxtaposed with Ali tenderly holding his two-and-a-half-year-old daughter. He was sympathetically portrayed as "a pied piper of people and gregarious to a fault," even as a draft resister. *Look* called Ali "the loneliest exile" until a court restored "his fundamental right to make a living" after boxing commissions "snatched" his title and banned him from the sport. Another piece on Black athletes converting to Islam discussed how basketball great Lew Alcindor became Kareem Abdul-Jabbar.[18]

31. The first gay married couple in Minnesota, "The Homosexual Couple: Jack Baker and Michael McConnell," *Look*, January 26, 1971. Photograph by Charlotte Brooks. Courtesy of the Library of Congress, *Look* Magazine Photograph Collection.

32. Christine Cantin of Fascinating Womanhood, "She Thinks Woman's Lib Is Crazy—Why?" cover, *Look*, March 9, 1971. Photograph by Stanley Tretick. Author's collection.

33. Man in newspaper stand, with headlines announcing the death of President Franklin Roosevelt, "Truman Is a New Dealer, Too," *Look*, June 26, 1945. Photograph by Stanley Kubrick. Courtesy of the Library of Congress, *Look* Magazine Photograph Collection.

34. JFK and John Jr. in the Oval Office, "President and His Son," *Look*, December 3, 1963. Photograph by Stanley Tretick. Courtesy of the Library of Congress, *Look* Magazine Photograph Collection.

35. Joan, Jean, Eunice, Jaqueline, and Ethel Kennedy, "Kennedy Women," *Look*, October 11, 1960. Photograph by Robert Vose. Courtesy of the Library of Congress, *Look* Magazine Photograph Collection.

36. Crowds watching Robert Kennedy's funeral train, June 1968, unpublished. Photograph by Paul Fusco. Courtesy of the Library of Congress, *Look* Magazine Photograph Collection.

37. Mike Cowles with Lyndon Johnson and his aides, ca. 1965. Courtesy of Drake University Archives & Special Collections Cowles Library, Des Moines, Iowa.

38. "Fun in the Water" cover, *Look*, July 14, 1970. Photograph by Douglas Kirkland. Author's collection.

"Madness" is the title of the above cartoon of Goering, Himmler, Hitler and Goebbels, reprinted by courtesy of Collier's, in which it stirred wide interest. It is the work of Arthur Szyk, scathing anti-Axis artist, who has been called "a one-man army." He drew the caricatures on the opposite page especially for LOOK.

HITLER'S BUTCHERS

The Fuehrer depends on expert mass murderers to Nazify occupied Europe

By PIERRE VAN PAASSEN

Distinguished journalist who knows "inside" Germany

Systematically enslaved, the 400,000,000 people of conquered Europe are fighting the supreme battle against Nazification. If they lose and Hitler succeeds in uniting Europe under the swastika, the Allies will have to defeat the entire continent.

To accomplish the enormous task of subjugating the victim peoples—and luring the few who are eligible into joining the Nazi mob—Hitler has carefully chosen proxies or vice-fuehrers to serve as taskmasters in the various countries. Among these ruthless axmen are 18 (one has already been removed by a Czech bomb) who wield the real Nazi power in overrun Europe.

Six of them are depicted on the opposite page. The others are:

Heinrich Himmler (second from left, in cartoon above). The notorious Gestapo boss and sadistic superwarden of all Nazi concentration camps is a cold-blooded killer whose hobby is whipping Gestapo prisoners.

Baldur von Schirach. The "Protector" of Austria and head of the Nazi youth movement is handsome, vain, glib, a personal friend of the Fuehrer.

Manfred von Killinger. The husky, debonair Gauleiter of Rumania believes in assassination as the best "diplomatic" weapon.

Count Hans-Georg Viktor von Mackensen. He is actually Gauleiter of Italy, a suave master of complex intrigues.

Such are the men assigned by Hitler to maintain Europe in terror.

39. "Hitler's Butchers," *Look*, September 8, 1942. Illustration by Arthur Szyk. Courtesy of Drake University Archives & Special Collections Cowles Library, Des Moines, Iowa.

LOOK

ROOSEVELT, CHURCHILL and HITLER
by Dorothy Thompson

NORTH
AMERICA

WHAT WILL HAPPEN TO
CONSCIENTIOUS OBJECTORS?

January 14, 1941 . . . 10¢

PRESIDENT ROOSEVELT

LOOK

NOVEMBER 2, 1943   10¢   13¢ IN CANADA
YEARLY SUBSCRIPTION $3.50

What's Wrong With the Draft?
by MARQUIS W. CHILDS

Roosevelt's Choice for President

U. S. PARATROOPERS
(See page 36)

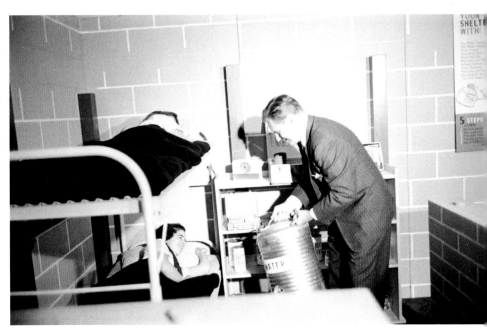

YOUR
SHELTER
WITH:

5 STEPS

LOOK
AMERICA'S FAMILY MAGAZINE

If atomic war comes, your whole country will be a target. In one flaming instant your city, and the thousands of people in it, will disappear as puffs of vapor.

Your
Last
Chance

Never again, so long as war is possible, will your home and hearthside be safe from direct attack. Long-distance aircraft and rockets have placed every square mile of the earth within war's range. The atomic bomb has made it easy to obliterate anything that military experts might consider worth destroying. Our recent enemies would have enslaved or destroyed you had they possessed such weapons. Now victory has brought a breathing spell. You have a last chance to save your civilization . . . and you have the choice of three ways to use that last chance. Few things in your life are more important than which choice you make.

40. "Roosevelt, Churchill and Hitler" cover, *Look*, January 14, 1941. Author's collection.

41. World War II U.S. paratrooper cover, *Look*, November 3, 1942. Author's collection.

42. Nelson Rockefeller and family in fallout shelter, "Great Fall-Out Shelter Panic," *Look*, December 5, 1961. Photograph by Frank Bauman. Courtesy of the Library of Congress, *Look* Magazine Photograph Collection.

43. "Your Last Chance," *Look* reprint pamphlet, 1946. Author's collection.

Stalin: Ally to Adversary

These two *Look* magazine portrayals of Soviet leader Stalin indicate how quickly the Grand Alliance of World War II disintegrated into the superpower confrontation of the Cold War. In the first piece, from mid-1944, correspondent Ralph Parker writes that Stalin spends half his time writing poetry and the other half reading it to the schoolchildren who clamor to sit on his knee. "Stalin," Parker adds, "is undoubtedly among the best-dressed of all world leaders making Churchill in his siren suit look positively shabby." Four years later, Louis Fischer paints a very different picture. "This small man with drooping shoulders tyrannizes one-fifth of the world," Fischer writes of the Soviet leader, adding that neither Hitler nor any Russian czar was as powerful or as menacing as the "Great Red Father." What do these two items suggest about American attitudes toward the outside world? What do they suggest about the role of the press in U.S. society?

"A Guy Named Joe" cover story of Look magazine by Ralph Parker, June 27, 1944

"Life Story of Stalin" by Louis Fischer in Look magazine, June 8, 1948

44. Stalin the ally, "A Guy Named Joe," *Look*, June 27, 1944, and Stalin the enemy, "Life Story of Stalin," *Look*, June 8, 1948. Author's collection.

45. East German border guard, "Eerie Trip along the Iron Curtain," *Look*, January 30, 1962. Photograph by Paul Fusco. Courtesy of the Library of Congress, *Look* Magazine Photograph Collection.

46. Soviet men and billboard, "Russia Today," *Look*, October 3, 1967. Photograph by Douglas Jones. Courtesy of the Library of Congress, *Look* Magazine Photograph Collection.

47. Wounded Korean War soldiers, Pvt. Arthur Nelson and Sgt. Jerry Smith, on Waikiki Beach, "Wounded Fly Home," *Look*, March 11, 1952. Photograph by Earl Theisen. Courtesy of the Library of Congress, *Look* Magazine Photograph Collection.

48. Children on a Chinese street, "Inside Red China," *Look*, April 16, 1957.
Photograph by Phillip Harrington. Courtesy of the Library of Congress, *Look*
Magazine Photograph Collection.

Che Guevara, Cuba's No. 2 man, remembered Laura from their 1960 interview.

49. Che Guevara and Laura Bergquist, "Our Woman in Havana," *Look*, November 8, 1960. Photograph by Paul Fusco. Courtesy of Drake University Archives & Special Collections Cowles Library, Des Moines, Iowa.

50. William Attwood interviewing Fidel Castro on a plane circling the Caribbean, "Tragedy of Fidel Castro," *Look*, September 15, 1959. Photograph by Andrew St. George. Courtesy of the Cowles Family Archives at Drake University.

51. Armed men, "Crisis in the Congo," *Look*, June 23, 1959. Photograph by Phillip Harrington. Courtesy of the Library of Congress, *Look* Magazine Photograph Collection.

52. U.S. soldiers in Vietnam on reconnaissance patrol with writer Christopher Wren, "The Facts behind the Green Beret Myth, Special Forces in Vietnam," *Look*, November 1, 1966. Photograph by Thomas Koeniges. Courtesy of Drake University Archives & Special Collections Cowles Library, Des Moines, Iowa.

53. U.S. soldiers in the Mekong Delta, "Choppers and the New Kind of War," *Look*, April 30, 1968. Photograph by Catherine Leroy. Courtesy of the Library of Congress, *Look* Magazine Photograph Collection.

LOOK

50 CENTS · AUGUST 12, 1969

THE BIG
BUSINESS OF
**AMERICAN
MILITARISM:**
WHO PROFITS?
WHO PAYS?
WHO COMMANDS?
WHO DIES?

With an
introduction
by
Eric Sevareid

**THE
MILLIONAIRE
WHO MADE
"HAIR"**
Pleasure-loving
Michael Butler

**MOST
ELIGIBLE
GIRL
IN THE U.S.**
Charlotte Ford

54. "American Militarism" cover, *Look*, August 12, 1969. Author's collection.

55. Marilyn Monroe, Lauren Bacall, and Betty Grable, "Three D, High, Wide and Handsome," *Look*, June 30, 1953. Photograph by Earl Theisen. Courtesy of the Library of Congress, *Look* Magazine Photograph Collection.

56. *I Love Lucy* cover, *Look*, December 25, 1954. Photograph by Robert Vose. Author's collection.

57. Marilyn Monroe cover, *Look*, May 29, 1956. Photograph by Milton H. Greene. Author's collection.

58. Elvis performing for his fans, "The Great Elvis Presley Industry," *Look*, November 13, 1956. Photograph by Chester Morrison. Courtesy of the Library of Congress, *Look* Magazine Photograph Collection.

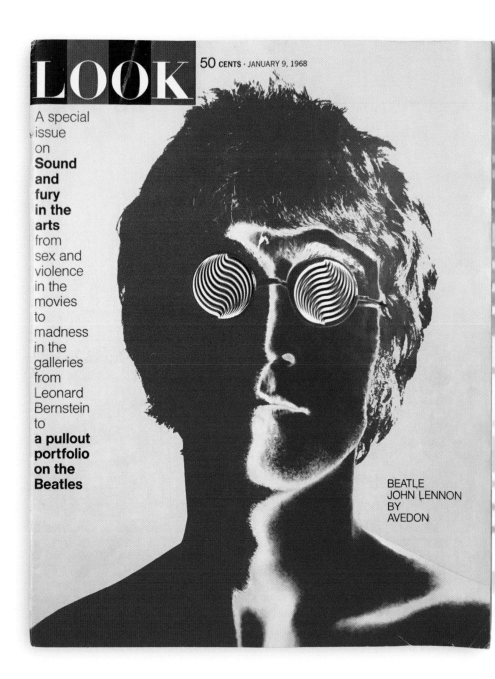

59. Psychedelic John Lennon cover, *Look*, January 9, 1968. Photograph by Richard Avedon. Courtesy of the Richard Avedon Foundation.

60. Sean Connery, "James Bond Conquers All in *Thunderball*," *Look*, July 13, 1965.
Photograph by Earl Theisen. Courtesy of the Library of Congress, *Look* Magazine
Photograph Collection.

61. Joan Baez and Bob Dylan, *Look*, ca. 1964, unpublished. Photograph by Douglas Gilbert. Courtesy of the Library of Congress, *Look* Magazine Photograph Collection.

One of *Look*'s most fascinating sports stories came about when Leonard Shecter approached New York Yankees pitcher Jim Bouton—who had been among the athletes protesting against apartheid during the 1968 Olympics—to write a season-long diary in 1969. This resulted in a 1970 article and Bouton's controversial, best-selling book, *Ball Four*, which has been called one of the greatest sports books of all time. With the book focusing on players' less-than-stellar off-the-field lives, baseball commissioner Bowie Kuhn tried to force Bouton to say that the book was fictional. He didn't, which became the subject of a six-page *Look* article the next year, as well as a follow-up book, *I'm Glad You Didn't Take it Personally*, also coauthored with Shecter. He wrote how the commissioner expected an "easy" recantation and how he "was surprised that I came in their hanging tough."[19]

White St. Louis Cardinals linebacker Dave Meggysey wrote a similarly grim eight-page expose on racism and misogyny in the NFL. Naming names, he blasted fellow players who said that "n—— were generally too dumb to play pro football and only wanted to seduce every white woman." Describing players' "heavily sexual" language, Meggysey quoted one who said, "I'm really going to punish the old lady tonight." He damned his teammates, writing that "even in their orgies [they] were Jim Crow all the way." He also said that "a lot of NFL trainers do more dealing in drugs than the average junkie." The article, excerpted from his book, *Out of Their League*, explained why he quit football due to "the dehumanizing aspect of the game, the emasculating attitude of the coaches, . . . [and] the intimidation and racism."[20]

Food and Fashion

Fashion and food features regularly appeared in the back of the magazine. Initially the province of the "Women's Department," in later years they fell under the purview of Pat Coffin's "Modern Living" section. Fashion pieces—mostly for women, but occasionally for men—were multipage themed photo layouts with brief captions. As in many magazines, these ran the gamut from maternity dresses and slips in the 1950s to French designers and homemade hippie garb in the 1960s. A five-page spread in 1971 on Black fashion designers described their entry into the "fashion establishment" and included full-page chest-up photos of models in African-inspired jewelry. Swimwear, naturally, was a favorite.[21]

Several editors oversaw the food pages, from prolific cookbook author Charlotte Adams, in *Look*'s early days, to Fleur Cowles, in the late 1940s and early 1950s, and Marilyn Kaytor, in the 1960s. Barbecues, pancakes, Caesar salads, and other easy-to-prepare foods were common subjects in the mid-1950s, while the 1960s brought similarly mundane topics like mayonnaise and canned foods as well as the cuisines of Provence, Wales, and Spain. When *Look* gave its readers a primer on wine in 1971, it described "generic" and varietal wines, offered suggestions for which gallon jugs to buy, and quoted British author J. B. Priestley saying, "You Americans have the loveliest wines in the world, but you just don't know it."[22]

Hollywood from Greta Garbo to George Lucas

Look's steady diet of movie stars went well beyond the glamorous actresses who appeared on so many covers. Americans had an enormous appetite for tales of the stars, and there were a host of movie magazines in the 1940s and 1950s, including *Photoplay*, *Modern Screen*, *Motion Picture*, *Hollywood*, *Confidential*, and *Silver Screen*. *Life* also had many cover stories on stars of screen and Broadway. In 1948 alone, these included thirteen covers featuring Sir Laurence Olivier, "grandmother" Marlene Dietrich, Ingrid Bergman, Montgomery Clift, and others.

A 1946 study found that *Look* devoted a much higher percentage of its linage to Hollywood than the more buttoned-down *Life*, by a margin of 22.7 percent to 6.1 percent. By the 1960s, *Life*—with twice the number of annual issues as *Look*—often had at least as many such photo-filled stories. Hollywood was so important to *Look* in the 1940s that there was a separate weekly editorial meeting on Thursdays for movies, stage, fashions, and beauty, after the broader editorial meeting on Wednesdays.[23]

Cowles was fascinated by Hollywood and frequently traveled to meet Daryl Zanuck, Louis B. Mayer, and other studio executives and to attend grand parties. He gleefully recalled when a 20th Century Fox publicity man introduced him to the young Marilyn Monroe on the studio lot in the late 1940s, describing her during a break in a photo shoot "dressed in nothing but bikini panties and shoes [coming] to chat casually." Happy to emphasize his "mutual affection" with Mayer, Cowles said that their fathers had been friends and fellow "die-hard Republicans." Among many other stories, Cowles told of a contentious dinner party during the McCarthy era that included leftwing Charlie Chaplin and rightwing David O. Selznick. He also met Leo Rosten in Hollywood in 1941.[24]

"At the time we began doing Hollywood stories most movie coverage was by fan magazines and was almost uniformly worshipful," Cowles recalled. "But both Jean [Herrick] and I wanted to apply the same sorts of journalistic standards to our Hollywood reporting that we applied to any of the other subjects we covered."[25]

Herrick, who presided over *Look*'s office on Sunset Boulevard, said he took a "frank approach" to the industry. *Look* was one of the first magazines to use candid photos, rather than the staged and retouched photos put out by studio publicity departments. After a 1944 story on "the Selznick girls"—Ingrid Bergman, Joan Fontaine, Janet Leigh, and others—Selznick wrote to Herrick: "This article has nothing to do with me as a producer, and places me in the position of being a flesh peddler." During the late 1940s, *Look* published a ten-part series, "Hollywood Uncensored," with "intimate and sometimes embarrassing details" about stars. One story that mentioned Hedy Lamarr's plastic surgery prompted the actress to sue *Look* for $10 million.[26]

Look had a close relationship with Hollywood in other ways. Two staffers, William Steffens and William Lowe dabbled in screenwriting. Warner Brothers considered a 1947 *Look* story, "The Story of a Teacher," for an adaptation. And Kubrick got his start with *Look*.[27]

Many articles were tied to the release of new films. There was Gloria Swanson in 1950, when Billy Wilder's *Sunset Boulevard* came out, and a young-looking Dustin Hoffman when *The Graduate* was released in 1968, with many more before, in between, and after.[28]

Box-office stars—especially those who were beautiful or handsome, and had colorful love lives and talent—also starred in *Look*. One who spanned the magazine's lifetime was Greta Garbo, from a cover story in 1937—four years before her last movie—to another cover to mark the reclusive actress's sixty-fifth birthday in 1970. Glamorously posed in black-and-white, she was called "the true immortal. Other legends and other goddesses crumble and fade into lovable or laughable antiques; but Garbo miraculously remains."[29]

Vivien Leigh, dressed as Scarlett O'Hara in *Gone with the Wind*, was on the cover of a 1939 issue that described the movie and the Civil War town where the story was supposedly set. Judy Garland, shortly after *The Wizard of Oz*, appeared on two early 1940s covers with frequent costar Mickey Rooney.[30]

Lauren Bacall was in *Look* in 1944 and 1945, following her film debut in *To Have and Have Not*, with Humphrey Bogart. Shortly before their marriage the next year, the two appeared in another story. Rita Hayworth, the popular pin-up girl for American GIs, was on a cover just before the war ended.[31]

Almost no one other than FDR and the Kennedys made the pages of *Look* as often as Elizabeth Taylor and Marilyn Monroe. From the mid-1950s to 1970, Taylor and her many men appeared in photo after photo in at least eight articles. Two of the last stories, by Joseph Roddy, chronicled her "brawl" with husband Richard Burton and their remarriage a few years later.[32]

Marilyn was covered—and, more importantly for many readers, uncovered—in photographs in as many stories as Taylor during the nine years between 1953 and her death at age thirty-six in 1962. Photojournalist Lawrence Schiller was sent to shoot her on the set of *Let's Make Love*, but his nudes did not appear in the magazine. Two 1961 *Look* photos—of her clutching white sheets and partly covered by them—are among the most classic images of Marilyn. Nearly sixty years later, Doug Kirkland, who took these photos, remembered, "It was just me, the camera, and Marilyn. This was, of course, very exciting for me in my young man way." Although she graced the covers of two 1953 issues, a cache of photos by John Vachon—at Canada's Banff National Park, posing in front of Rocky Mountain peaks and in a bikini with crutches were never published—only became public in 2010. A June 1953 cover showed Marilyn beside earlier sex symbols Lauren Bacall and Betty Grable, and a particularly memorable cover in 1956 showed her wrapped in sheets. Marilyn was a darling of most print media, appearing on the cover of *Life* five times. Carl Sandburg, the Pulitzer Prize–winning poet who had befriended America's number one sex symbol, paid homage in a moving essay in *Look* after she died. He described meeting Marilyn in 1960 when her dressing room became his temporary office: "She made a point of coming to introduce herself. It was as if she wanted to see me as much as I wanted to see her."[33]

Other glamorous actresses in *Look* included Lana Turner, Audrey Hepburn, Kim Novak, Gina Lollobrigida, Ava Gardner, Maureen O'Hara, and Jane Russell. Grace Kelly made the cover twice. During the late 1950s, the acting "beauties" of Britain, Italy, and France were also displayed to *Look* readers.[34]

Look hardly ignored leading men. Gary Cooper was called "30 years strong and silent" in a 1955 story, after his classic film *High Noon*. Marlon Brando and Rock Hudson made the cover in the 1950s. After *Rebel without a Cause* showed the dark side of teen culture, star James Dean was pictured on the cover squinting in a Stetson hat and called "the strangest legend since Valentino."[35]

Cary Grant—"of enduring charm," as a 1955 article put it—remained hot, with a 1963 cover showing him almost cheek to cheek with Audrey Hepburn, and one in 1966 with an "exclusive color" story about the actor and his baby. In 1971, thirty-nine years and seventy-two movies after Grant made his Hollywood debut, readers learned of "the new women in [his] life." Shown riding a horse and with his private plane and Rolls Royce, the story is both breathless and touching.[36]

John Wayne, who was on a 1942 *Look* cover, was at the height of his career when he returned in 1960—the ultimate he-man and icon of a West that never existed. The already wizened fifty-three-year-old actor described himself: "I've had three wives, five children, and three grandchildren. I love good whiskey. I still don't understand women, and I don't think there is anyone alive who does."[37]

Look occasionally told stories of celebrities past. For example, it paid $10,000 for the rights to an excerpt of a book by Diana Barrymore, which ran in four installments in March and April 1957 and described her troubled relationship with her father, the acting great John Barrymore.[38]

The focus on stars like Taylor, Grant, Wayne, and Sophia Lauren in the 1950s gave way in the 1960s to less traditional figures. Natalie Wood, a star of *Rebel* and *West Side Story* who was nominated for three Academy Awards before she turned twenty-five, was featured in two early 1960s *Look* stories. Robert Vose photographed her with actor Robert Wagner aboard their yacht in 1958, although the photo essay did not run until 1961.[39]

Julie Andrews, who made it big in *The Sound of Music* and *Mary Poppins*, was on the cover in 1965. In several stories, she was shown in extreme close-up, with her blue eyes and pixie-cut hair, holding her young child on a beach.[40]

Novelist James Baldwin wrote a July 1968 story on Sidney Poitier, who looked out intensely, perhaps angrily, from the cover. A 1971 piece showed Poitier working with Harry Belafonte, both early Black stars, on the film *Buck and the Preacher*, on the set in Durango, Mexico. Writer George Goodman described them as "two wary rivals [who] patch[ed] up to make a movie." In fact, the two had been best friends for seventy years when both actors turned ninety in 2017.[41]

A 1970 story on Ali McGraw—with a two-page color photo of the actress, pensive, with a lush backdrop of bouquets, boots, and rugs—described her personal travails and her acknowledgement that her star vehicle, *Love Story*, has a "plot [that] is thin." Two even more provocative 1971 photos, by Kirkland, showed Britt Ekland's lips filling two pages of the magazine and the actress with her hands, dripping with water, covering her nude midriff.[42]

Sean Connery (aka James Bond) and "his second girlfriend," naturally, were on a beach, lying close together, on the cover of a December 1963 issue. A 1970 cover story about Dustin Hoffman showed two partially overlapping images of the actor, guns drawn and ready for action in the movie *Little Big Man*. The story said that this radical Western delivered "a new experience, the losing of the West." Hoffman, shown in large Ernst Haas action photos, bluntly said, "Indians committed 'massacres,' but white men won 'victories.'" Warren Beatty and Julie Christie, probably the most talked-about couple in Hollywood in the late 1960s and early 1970s, were showcased in connection with another neo-Western, *McCabe and Mrs. Miller*.[43]

The young, then largely unknown directors, Francis Ford Coppola and George Lucas were profiled in 1969. After editors initially balked, Will

Hopkins told Kirkland, "'Okay, do it but you'd better knock my socks off,'" Kirkland recalled. "We shot the two on the roof of the Fairmont Hotel with Alcatraz in the background."[44]

On the cover of a twelve-story issue on "the movies" was a suggestive photo of actress Samantha Jones holding an Academy Award statuette over her breasts, her long hair flowing around it. *Look* writer Frank Botto described the almost overnight change from sexual taboos in film to the advent of those showing "practically every sexual act imaginable." Other articles addressed the perilous state of the industry, movie ratings, mainstream "dirty movies," and a preview of the first videocassette recorders. Orson Welles wrote about how "the great director" was replacing "the old movie star" and hailed the decline of "the studio machine" and the emergence of "very young filmmakers with total control of their own work."[45]

Television Sweeps America

As television swept America in the 1950s, *Look* published many stories on the new medium and its stars. It bestowed annual TV awards from 1951 to 1960. The floodgates really opened in 1953 when a torrent of stories appeared about impresario Ed Sullivan, *Dragnet*, Art Linkletter, *Ozzie and Harriet*, Milton Berle, and Lucille Ball. Lucy was on seven covers between 1953 and 1962, sometimes including Ricky and their "two babies." A 1954 piece showed Walt Disney giving his TV audience a preview of Disneyland.[46]

The late fifties brought coverage of newsmen Edward R. Murrow and Mike Wallace, the new craze for Westerns, and shows for teenagers, like *American Bandstand*, and for children, like *Captain Kangaroo*. In 1957 *Look* asked if TV quiz shows were "fixed," shortly before the *$64,000 Question* scandal led to congressional hearings.[47]

Not every story was a celebration. Sid Caesar, host of the immensely popular variety show *Show of Shows*, wrote in a 1956 story: "On stage, I could hide behind the characters and inanimate objects I created. Off stage, with my real personality for all to see, I was a mess. It was difficult for me to establish a normal, healthy relationship with anyone. I couldn't believe that anyone could like me for myself."[48]

Television after 1960

Look in the 1960s and early 1970s gave its readers talk show hosts Johnny Carson, Jack Paar, and Merv Griffin; goofy shows like *The Flying Nun* and *The Monkees*; comedies like *The Carol Burnett Show*; dramas like *Dr. Kildare*, and Westerns like *Gunsmoke* and *Bonanza*. Poppy recalled that when he wrote about *Bonanza*, TV's most popular show at the time, "the producer was so gratified that his show was taken seriously."[49]

Look's coverage of the spy-spoof *The Man from Uncle* is illustrative of the magazine's conflicting tendencies to appeal to ardent fans and to look behind the surface of the medium. Whereas one 1965 Chandler Brossard story focused on star David McCallum, "a delirium-inspiring, coast-to-coast sex symbol," another by Ira Mothner quoted a writer for the show: "We're putting the audience on.... It's supposed to be melodrama, but there's no menace. It's not high camp or low camp, just an excuse for not knowing how to do better."[50]

A September 1960 piece by longtime *Look* entertainment writer George Eells and Los Angeles bureau chief Stanley Gordon took on some of the more negative aspects of TV. "Creativity was declining and there were fewer specials, as well as more formulaic series," they declared. FCC commissioner Newton Minow, who called TV a "vast wasteland" in 1961, followed up with a more extended assessment in *Look*. The magazine was also one of the first to denounce the "endless exercises in violence" on the big and small screen. A 1969 story asked whether TV was "brutalizing your child."[51]

"So long as the bulk of its air time is bought and produced by advertisers whose motives are understandably more commercial than editorial, television cannot fill the demand for public service journalism," Attwood dismissively added in 1970. The next year, echoing the counterculture's rejection of a bourgeois lifestyle centered on endless TV, *Look* wondered: Is television "a turn-on or turn-off"?[52]

Newsmen like Walter Cronkite, the revered CBS anchor, and Eric Sevareid were both subjects and authors in *Look*. Cronkite warned of the threat of "demagoguery exploiting the public against the free press, of placing elements of suspicion and doubt in the minds of the masses." Herbert Mitgang, who spent forty-seven years with the *New York Times*, talked about

Cronkite's early career as a correspondent during World War II. Sevareid, the renowned CBS reporter hired by Edward R. Murrow before the Second World War, wrote five pieces for *Look* ranging from one on protest movements and "dissent" to two optimistic pieces on America's future shortly after the murders of Martin Luther King Jr. and Bobby Kennedy in 1968. David Brinkley, who spent fifty-four years reporting and commenting on the news, was the subject of several early 1960s stories. One, with his early NBC coanchor Chet Huntley, showed their two faces merged into a single head on the cover of a 1961 issue.[53]

In *Look*'s last few years, it was not only critical of much TV content but also praised more innovative programming. Public television, launched during the Johnson Administration, merited thoughtful articles. Children's TV advocate and *Sesame Street* creator, Joan Ganz Cooney, and Mr. Rogers, the gentle children's television host, were featured in two successive 1969 issues. *Look* described how lovable "dum-dums" Big Bird and Oscar the Grouch always asked questions, teaching children the excitement of learning. Nat Hentoff wrote about the Smothers Brothers, whose TV comedy show's attacks on U.S. policy in Vietnam led to counterattacks by the government. Readers also discovered Dick Cavett, a new kind of intellectual TV talk show host.[54]

Popular Music

From Woody Herman to hit musicals like *Oklahoma*, *Cabaret*, and *Hair*, to the Beatles, *Look* not only celebrated star performers but also told its readers about many musicians out of the pop-music limelight that it believed its readers should know. The latter ranged from Black jazz and Motown musicians and Canadian singer-songwriter Leonard Cohen to classical musicians, like Vladimir Horowitz and Leonard Bernstein, and opera singers, like Maria Callas and Leontyne Price.

After World War II, *Look* thoroughly covered swing and big band performers, like Herman and Stan Kenton, and promoted a swing band contest, with regional competitions each summer. The first winner, Bruce Bybvig, a St. Paul big band leader, brought his troupe to Carnegie Hall for the award, as the magazine self-promotingly declared: "*Look*'s nationwide amateur swing band contest has given these award winners and scores of other outstanding young musicians a boost toward the opportunities in the field of music that they have long dreamed about."[55]

A June 1950 Kubrick photo essay on Dixieland jazz included greats like Louis Armstrong and clarinetist Sidney Bechet. Other shots showed live performances by Eddie Condon, Red Nichols, Phil Napoleon, Muggsy Spanier, and Sharkey Bonano. Duke Ellington, described as a "living legend," was shown as more than a musician in a Charlotte Brooks photo essay that included images of him performing in Florida and traveling through the segregated South, playing baseball with his band in front of their Blacks-only motel, and with civil rights activist and educator Mary McLeod Bethune. Vose took photos of Ella Fitzgerald, America's most popular female jazz singer, at her Beverly Hills home in 1960, and photos of the Newport Jazz Festival appeared in 1959.[56]

George Eells wrote about actor and singer Dean Martin in 1960, and in a 1967 cover story, Martin talked about his work with Frank Sinatra, Bobby Kennedy, the mafia, and women. The partnership between Martin and comedian Jerry Lewis—who was the subject of several late 1950s stories—reportedly ended acrimoniously in 1956 after *Look* cropped Martin out of a cover photo. Sinatra was given his due in four stories in the 1950s and 1960s.[57]

Bing Crosby appeared in *Look* from the magazine's first year to the mid-1960s. The singer/actor was with Bob Hope, both in straw hats, in 1947, with Grace Kelly and his son in 1953, and with his young wife and young sons in 1960 and 1962. In 1958 his brother told readers how he hated being Bing's brother.[58]

Perry Como, another singer and actor out of the big band tradition, was in *Look* three times in the 1950s. Lawrence Welk, who had just begun his fourteen-year run on ABC, played the accordion, his orchestra behind him in a 1957 cover photo by Maurice Terrell. Pat Boone, who recorded sanitized versions of rock hits, was described as an "all-American boy" in a 1958 cover story and shown filming "*Mardi Gras*" in Lexington, Virginia, sending "the town into an uproar."[59]

It's not surprising that George Leonard gave readers a first look at rock and roll. In 1956 he explained, "Music similar to rock 'n' roll has been recorded for decades, but under the 'race' or 'rhythm and blues' labels, intended for the Negro market." With photos of Bill Haley and the Comets, whose "Rock around the Clock" is often called the first (white) rock and roll hit, performing in Hershey, Pennsylvania. Leonard described the scene: "A tenor saxophone tilts backwards and throws insistent, brutal notes into the air.... The melody is simple and repetitious. More important is the beat: it is so firm and strong you can practically walk on it.... [The] audience ... wails, screeches and sometimes dances in the aisle."[60]

Elvis Presley, the avatar who changed American culture, was first profiled in the summer of 1956 when he made his national debut in an article by George Zimmerman, with photos by Phillip Harrington. They followed him as he performed, from Detroit to Cleveland, describing Elvis somewhat disparagingly as "a wild troubadour who wails rock n' roll tunes, flails erratically at a guitar and wriggles like a peep-show dancer."

"Presley's fame is a legend of the 'American Dream' of success that is overshadowed by a nightmare of bad taste," the article continued. "Presley has taken the rock 'n' roll craze to new sales heights. He has also dragged "big beat" music to new lows." Along with photos of his movements while performing, his screaming fans, and the twenty-one-year-old superstar playing pool, *Look* added: "On-stage, his gyrations, his nose wiping, his leers are vulgar. When asked about the sex element in his act, he answers without blinking his big brown eyes: 'Ah don't see anything wrong with it. Ah just act the way ah feel.'" Two more pieces that year focused on the "U.S. entertainment sensation." Tastes were changing, readers were told, as young Americans opted for rock and roll, turning their backs on "languid crooners."[61]

Elvis, whose popularity was waning, was back on the cover in 1971, when *Look* published a fourteen-page, densely written excerpt of Jerry Hopkins's unauthorized biography. Readers learned of Elvis's early life and how manager Colonel Tom Parker launched Presley's career in the mid-1950s, while pocketing a huge portion of the singer's earnings.[62]

Look introduced readers to the new socially conscious folk music coming out of Greenwich Village in a 1963 article by Sam Castan. It included photos of Odetta playing her guitar, Miriam Makeba and Molly Scott performing on the TV show *Hootenanny*, and University of Virginia students listening to a folk concert.[63]

Newly hired twenty-one-year-old photographer Doug Gilbert followed Bob Dylan in 1964, taking photos of the twenty-three-year-old Dylan riding a motorcycle with singer John Sebastian in Woodstock, New York; waving to poet Allen Ginsberg; and lighting a cigarette at the bar of a club in the Village. None were published, as editors deemed Dylan "too scruffy for a family magazine." Two years later, *Look* called the legendary songwriter/ singer a "gifted young man" whose lyrics expressed a "jingle-jangle reality that makes more sense to ["hipsters"] than any square, whitewashed American Dream." Written somewhat naively and safely for its mostly "square" readers, the article nonetheless reinforced *Look*'s drumbeat that the times were a changin.'[64]

The first of *Look*'s many articles on the Beatles focused on their hair, but by 1968 they were featured in what was arguably the most extraordinary and memorable artwork on 1960's rock and roll—a series of solarized photos embellished with DayGlo paint by Richard Avedon. Created as a four-panel poster to be released simultaneously in four countries, they showed John's glasses, Paul's flower power, George's mysticism, and Ringo's peace dove. The images were printed in the January 9, 1968, issue, with Avedon's John on the cover, in the wake of group's 1967 albums, *Sergeant Pepper's Lonely Hearts Club Band* and *Magical Mystery Tour*. *Look* made the 22.5-by-31-inch poster available for sale, for twenty-five cents, as well as a more conventional 14-by-40-inch Avedon photo called *Beatle Banner*. Now in a Museum of Modern Art collection, the original painting for *Look* was bought at auction in 2011 for $722,500. Leonard Gross and Doug Kirkland tracked down the cerebral Beatle in Spain, and Poppy quoted the Beatles' line, "I read the news today, oh boy," in an eight-page essay in the "'70s" issue called "Can We Survive?"[65]

Edgier and politically outspoken figures like the Rolling Stones, "bad boy" Jim Morrison of the Doors, and anti-war Crosby, Still, Nash, and Young never made it into *Look*. (*Life* did cover the Doors.) The magazine didn't write about Woodstock until a year after the 1969 festival, when John Barry argued that nothing like it could happen again.[66]

Despite *Look*'s wariness about the rougher edges of rock, it wrote about many other major late 1960s rock and rollers—Janis Joplin, the Band, Simon and Garfunkel, and the Animals, as well as many Black performers. Movie stars didn't disappear, but in some ways rock stars had eclipsed them.

As "Bridge over Troubled Water" climbed the charts, Gilbert met Simon and Garfunkel in Garfunkel's Manhattan apartment. "While Paul was focused on the interplay of words in his compositions, Art seemed more caught up in the music," he wrote. Joan Baez and her husband, draft resister David Harris, were on a 1970 cover. Baez and Ellington were among sixteen prominent Americans who gave readers their "personal key to peace of mind" in one of *Look*'s last issues.[67]

Using a Beat-like, stream-of-consciousness narrative, Leonard described what undoubtedly seemed strange and threatening about rock and its audiences: "The senses took a beating from flashing strobe lights dazzling film projections electronic rock music taped noises screaming whistles wafting incense couples tried to dance but all the dances got mixed up and people pressed together in clumps reached helplessly upward one girl staged a topless dance another chose to lie motionless while the crowd covered her with confetti."[68]

During San Francisco's 1967 Summer of Love, *Look* wrote about the Jefferson Airplane, showing strobe lights pulsating with the music. "Look into those blue-gray eyes," the magazine said about lead singer Grace Slick. "Hear that voice, that intent, that wailing, uninhibiting grabbing voice."[69]

Leonard Cohen—who had recently been signed by Columbia Records producer John Hammond (who also signed Bob Dylan and Bruce Springsteen)—was the subject of a 1969 Ira Mothner story. Cohen, whose dark, intense songs of love and loss, religion and depression, was later called by photographer Tony Vaccaro "a monument" and "one of the four or five greatest people I have photographed." One black-and-white image showed the Canadian singer staring at the camera outside a weathered wooden building.[70]

In 1970 Carbine asked Poppy, "What do the words 'big pink' mean to you? There's a rock group called the Band, and they are doing another album in L.A.," he recalled. "Go down and spend some time with them," which he did. In his long photo-filled piece for that summer's special issue on music, he wrote, "Their songs hit you like odors remembered from childhood ... plucking a chord of Americanness."[71]

Hendrix was profiled after his intense guitar-burning performance at the 1967 Monterey Pop Festival. He talked about the racism he felt as a teenager when a white schoolteacher told him to stop dating a white girl. Although he dismissed race as an issue in his career, *Look*—which beat *Life* to the story—noted that concert attendance dropped after the conviction of Black Panther leader Huey Newton.[72]

Given *Look*'s focus on civil rights, it generally did a good job highlighting Black performers. Berry Gordy, who founded Motown Records, was pictured outside his modest Detroit office with a sign reading "Hitsville U.S.A." above the door.

Soul music gained attention with a 1968 article on Aretha Franklin, which showed her performing on the *Merv Griffin Show* and at Philharmonic Hall in New York, as well as with her husband, Martin Luther King Jr., and Harry Belafonte. In a piece on Ike and Tina Turner, Dunbar wrote: "[Tina] springs out onstage like a lioness in heat, miniskirt cut to just below her womanhood. As the band cooks behind her, her raspy voice breaks out into a raucous wail that jangles every male in the room. . . . Ostensibly talking about Respect, the heated sexual message comes out undiluted."[73]

Look put James Brown—the soul and funk singer whose "Say It Loud (I'm Black and I'm Proud)" became an anthem of the civil rights movement—on its cover, asking, "Is he the most important black man in America? . . . His stature among American Negroes . . . has become monumental. . . . His constituency dwarfs Stokely Carmichael's and the late Dr. Martin Luther King's." The article argued that Brown had more credibility in the Black community because he never changed his music to appeal to white audiences, as the Supremes and Ray Charles did. A 1971 article profiled blues musician B. B. King who, "after 21 years of bone-grinding one-night stands," had become popular thanks to "hip young whites fast becoming blues scholars."[74]

In the 1970 music special issue with the record album filling its cover, Dunbar wrote of the fortune being made by rock musicians, with a psychedelic two-page collage depicting top record producers and executives.

Another piece included a full-page Doug Jones photo of ten-year-old Michael Jackson's face seeming to float above a blurred array of concert-goers and lights.[75]

Barbra Streisand, the subject of four stories in the late sixties, was pictured on a 1966 cover, her hair black and straight, head on her arm, looking seductively at the reader. Having just starred in the musical *Funny Girl*, Tom Morgan described her "not so funny life"—her father dying before her first birthday and growing up in Brooklyn with a hypercritical mother.[76]

Herb Alpert and the Tijuana Brass, a pop-jazz band, was profiled by Betty Rollin in 1966. The Lennon Sisters were another clean-cut band at a time of wild rock and rollers—dubbed "America's Sweethearts of Song"—that *Look* covered in 1969.[77]

Look produced a twenty-four-page package of stories on country music, which it called "hillbilly no more." This 1969 issue surveyed "country classics," the Grand Ol' Opry, and Merle Haggard, and it also included a lyrical remembrance by journalist David Halberstam of Hank Williams, who had died at age twenty-nine in 1953. Halberstam wrote of the singer's pain and broken life, while being the "rare . . . hillbilly singer with a genuine following among a surprising number of intellectuals." Haggard, who had spent thirty-three months in San Quentin Prison, delivered "a chip-on-the-shoulder swipe at dissent" in songs like "Okie from Muskogee" and was praised by President Nixon. He attacked anti-war protesters, but told Christopher Wren, "'I don't agree with the war.'" Karales photographed him onstage, his foot stomping, and in a car fitted with railroad wheels on desolate train tracks. Wren also wrote about the bluegrass sound of Doc Watson and Johnny Cash's soulful ballads.[78]

Pop culture was more than just the light reading that *Look* knew would appeal to readers. It also was illustrative of the changes in America during the mid-twentieth century. Like its educational series on art, great men, and religion, *Look*'s editors believed that movies and music were part of a complex world Americans should know.

14

The End of *Look*, the
Postwar Consensus, and
America's Golden Age

Although it still had a circulation of 6.5 million in 1971 after cutting its rate base, *Look* was the victim of major changes in journalism, news media, and advertising. As suggested, its demise also reflected and perhaps heralded dramatic changes in the United States that were not to be recognized until many years later.

"Television, particularly network television, cut deeply into our advertising revenues," Cowles said in the press conference announcing that *Look* would cease publication. As *Look* and *Life* raised ad rates during the 1960s, the cost of a four-color ad became as much as a sixty-second spot on network TV, which could reach an even greater audience.[1]

The end of *Look* (and *Life* a year later, on December 29, 1972) marked the end of the mass-circulation, general-interest magazine and the greatest days of photojournalism. News magazines like *Time* and *Newsweek* could still appeal to the nation's opinion leaders and much of middle America, but their content was more limited, and photos were mostly an afterthought. At the same time, special-interest or niche magazines like *Psychology Today* and *Rolling Stone* were beginning to peel away readers. Others—like *People* and *Money*—were waiting in the wings.[2]

By the 1980s cable TV was eating into network TV's viewership. When Walter Cronkite anchored the CBS *Evening News*, 29 million Americans tuned in. Within fifteen to twenty years, the internet started to crush all print, broadcast, and cable media. In the early twenty-first century, the evening news shows of CBS, NBC, and ABC combined had fewer viewers than Cronkite had. In 2020 the three networks news shows together averaged about 24 million viewers, half the number they had in 1980. ABC's *World News Tonight* averaged 9.9 million viewers, a fraction of its 1960s viewership, yet still more than triple the number of viewers of Fox News during primetime. News magazines like *Newsweek* and *US News and World Report* shut down their traditional print editions in the early 2010s, and *Time*, which was sold to a tech billionaire in 2018, was the only current-affairs magazine among the nation's fifty most read periodicals that year.[3]

Daily newspaper circulation fell from more than 60 million between 1964 and 1992 to less than 29 million in 2018, and the number of newsroom jobs was cut in half between 2006 and 2018. Media, which already began to splinter in the 1970s with specialized magazines and cable TV, are now a vast, disorganized library of unedited and largely incoherent content. Partisan and "fake" news abound, particularly for the 250 million Americans who have social media accounts. If facts and news are doled out in decontextualized bytes, ideas inhabit segregated bubbles, and Americans corral themselves into micro-terrains delimited by their Facebook "likes" and Instagram followers—while kidding themselves that they are knowledgeable about the country and the world—nationhood is less of a genuinely shared experience.[4]

The end of *Look* and the fracturing of America's media in subsequent decades may have made it possible for smaller, targeted media to briefly flourish and for millions of voices to be heard on the internet. But it also ended an era when the veracity of writers and photographers' work was subject to stricter editorial control and the quality of information sources mattered. Then, there were editors and editorial meetings, talented reporters, other writers, photographers, research departments, and copy editors. The barriers to entry were much higher. The ideas of public intellectuals and public figures were also brought to a huge audience—not just their Twitter or podcast followers. Thoughtful choices for articles were (usually) made. There wasn't the profusion of social media and self-proclaimed "news" websites that played fast and loose with facts, without accountability. Photographs weren't doctored or taken on smart phones and plastered on the internet. Most importantly, *Look* and other mass media informed people rather than riling them up or gratuitously scaring them. Nonpartisan or multi-partisan sources of information and opinion with huge audiences at the beginning of the 2020s are virtually nonexistent. So too are media that promote the cultural and civic betterment of their readers. Decades after *Look* folded, the unifying effect of mass media—which had presented the same facts, issues, and ideas to a broad swath of the American people and made "common" conversations about national life possible—ended.

Some much smaller media organizations still provide news, analysis, and commentary that has much of the breadth and depth that *Look* offered: the *New York Times*, NPR, the *Economist*, the BBC, PBS *Newshour*, and the *Atlantic*. But these are consumed largely by elites in a tiny number of the nation's forty-three thousand zip codes. These may be carefully read by "influentials," but it is highly unlikely that a *New York Times* or *Economist* would be found in the barbershop or on the kitchen tables of working-class and middle-class America. Sadly, the very idea seems ludicrous. By contrast, *Look* was everywhere.

The End of an Era

When *Look* stopped publishing, it was not just the end of a magazine. Its demise roughly paralleled the end of an era in American history—a time of relative consensus about major issues, comity, and genuine national dialogue. It was also an era of ever-rising living standards, ever-rising expectations, greater respect for others, faith in government and other institutions, and buoyant hopes instead of cynicism and pessimism.

The United States had thrived during *Look*'s heyday—thrived spectacularly, in a way that the country never had before and never did again. The nation's economic growth brought unprecedented abundance to

unprecedented numbers, and more Americans were lifted out of poverty and into the middle class than at any other time since the country's
founding. Its politics and social movements advanced the cause of legal
and economic equality to an extent and at a pace that are remarkable
in hindsight: while full equality is still out of reach for people of color,
women, and others, more progress toward an equitable society was made
politically, economically, and culturally during the *Look* years than at any
time before or after.

Technology dazzled by prolonging lives; making life easier; achieving
unimaginable feats, like manned moon landings; curing once-incurable
diseases; facilitating the mass movement of people; and promising to usher
in a science-fiction-like, utopian future. America's politics largely worked,
as most Americans and their elected representatives, who they generally
admired, agreed on a host of big issues: fighting communism, advancing
civil rights, promoting opportunity for all, supporting science, increasing
home ownership, fostering economic growth that benefited all Americans,
creating a safety net for the poor, providing health care for the elderly,
expanding higher education and access to it, increasing women's rights,
protecting the environment, helping the world's poor, and trying to work
together with other nations.

It was not an accident that *Look* supported these causes. Of course, *Look*
wasn't alone in fostering many of these ideals, but no other mass media was
so zealous in its support of civil rights or internationalism—while generally still sounding so reasonable and moderate. No other major medium
demonstrated its concern for the rights and well-being of Black citizens so
early, before World War II. By its last years, *Look* had no major peers in its
tolerance of—or even support for—what was then radical cultural change,
whether homosexuality or consciousness raising.

What ended was not just a great magazine or a type of journalism but a
faith that America could be made better and that Americans could do so
by working together. This was evident in the business-government-labor
collaboration of the early postwar era or liberal Democrats and moderate
Republicans working together to support space exploration, Keynesian
fiscal policy, broad-based economic growth, and leading the "free world"

in the struggle against communism. Even ideas that originated in fringe movements—such as ending taboos about sex and discussion of mental illness—relatively quickly became mainstream.

Although this period had its share of conflict (think: McCarthyism, civil rights, and Vietnam), compared to twenty-first-century America, postwar Americans' belief in progress and sense that "we're all in this together" were largely true. How did this happen? How did the American people come to share these beliefs and goals to such a great extent? Politicians, business and labor leaders, as well as academics and public intellectuals gave speeches and wrote papers and books. But a pamphlet from the Chamber of Commerce, a book by a prominent professor, and politicians' speeches—which largely were not televised until the 1960s—hardly reached most Americans.

Which brings us back to the role of mass media and *Look*. Newspapers were much more widely read in this era than in the twenty-first century, but their stories and how they were told differed from paper to paper. TV had swept the land in the 1950s, but it was not until 1963 that CBS expanded its evening news to thirty minutes, after which came NBC and ABC. Before and during the critical decades after the war, there were *Life* and *Look* and, to a lesser extent, the news magazines. Articles in *Look* and *Life* were the subjects of office and dinner party conversations, since seemingly everyone had read or heard about their major stories. They brought the country together. *Look* was not a Pollyanna, as its many hard-hitting stories demonstrate, but—as discussed—it believed that even the toughest problems could be solved. And where there was not this "togetherness" or agreement—for example, on issues like the status of Blacks, birth control, and sexuality—*Look* sought to instill greater tolerance and nudge the country toward changed beliefs and values.

As this book has argued, *Look* differed considerably from *Life* in many ways. *Life* was a brilliant magazine, but it spoke from on high, while *Look* portrayed America, its successes and challenges, issues and ideas much more through stories of people with whom readers could identify. *Look* took a broader perspective about what made America what it was and about what issues should matter to the country's people. Both magazines—and others like the *Saturday Evening Post* and *Collier's*—celebrated the country's prosperity, innovation, and popular culture and examined the real or perceived threat of communism. *Look* went beyond these to shed light on racial injustice, changing sex roles, and changing social norms. In addition, *Life* was always subject to Luce's heavy hand, whereas Cowles generally gave pretty free rein to his editors and writers.

Waning Consensus

In October 1971, unknown to its editors and readers, the end of *Look* roughly coincided with the breakdown of consensus, the slow disappearance of common conversation, and the end of unbridled faith in better tomorrows. The tumult of the 1960s and early 1970s shattered both, but *Look* still sought to bring Americans around to the beliefs that racial equality was the true American way and that many of the cultural and political beliefs underlying the youth revolt were largely good for the country.

The era between about 1968 and 1973 marked a critical turning point in U.S. history. The nation did not change so abruptly as the closure of a magazine, but what began to wane were the optimism, the faith in progress and technology, ever-greater abundance, the belief that government and experts generally worked to make life better, and the reassuring stability of the family. In the succeeding half century, the confidence, dynamism, and relative unity of the *Look* era withered. There have been achievements since the 1970s, but the arc of American history—at least in the ways discussed in this book—has been more of a zig-zag.

While there have been sporadic bursts of economic growth since the early 1970s, with the exception of the last Clinton years, it has neither been as fast, sustained, nor as fairly shared as during the *Look* era. The government's safety net no longer expanded, at least before the Biden Administration's response to the Covid-19 pandemic, and in some ways was diminished. At the same time, the private welfare state—of rising wages, employer-provided health insurance, pensions that paid a monthly benefit, paid vacation, shorter work weeks—contracted. There was no new analogue to the 1950 "Treaty of Detroit" between General Motors and the United Auto Workers that signaled a collaborative effort by business, labor, and government to improve all Americans' well-being. The rich grew fantastically richer and the upper middle class prospered, while the middle and working classes saw their living standards stagnate or decline. And the industries historically underlying growth came to be rightly seen as major underlying causes of climate change.

Technology continues to dazzle—sometimes—but the downsides to the internet, smart phones, artificial intelligence, and genetic engineering become ever clearer. Despite many advances that have made life better, there is no longer the postwar burst of big and small technological advances— from frozen foods and "labor-saving" devices to the polio vaccine and the space program. In fact, vocal opposition to science and technology emerged among many Americans, whether about the existential dangers of climate change, threats to privacy, or the need for vaccinations. If anything, the internet has made people more inwardly focused, with shorter attention spans, and able to tune out information they don't want to hear. The United States has become a less attractive model for much of the world, as China and the European Union offer alternatives. During the Covid-19 crisis, some commentators said that the country was no longer loved or hated in the world; rather, it was pitied.[5]

Americans are freer to live lives other than those of the heterosexual nuclear family, and women have become more empowered, but changes in family structure have led to the decline of marriage, an increase in single parenthood—with children a major casualty—and increasing loneliness, as the ranks of unmarried Americans have skyrocketed. It is hard to think of much that's good about politics when hyper-partisanship, gridlock, the influence of big money, and the widespread distrust of, and antipathy toward the federal government have wounded American democracy and unity. Too many Americans don't even seem to want a *United* States.

Americans had been seduced by the idea of progress during the postwar era, abetted by media like *Look*, which is why the widely sensed perception that the country is no longer moving forward has left many Americans let down, angry, and lost. The decline of mass media with thoughtful, balanced content that could reach a family in Topeka and the powerful in Washington or Manhattan is as much a part of the story of America's fall from grace as data showing the failures of the economy, education, the family, and politics.

As we have seen, this consensus itself began to be denounced in the 1950s and 1960s by social critics like David Riesman and Herbert Marcuse as another word for "conformism," "cooptation," or "repressive tolerance." Yes, there was conformity, with organization men in gray flannel suits and an "Establishment" that hewed to a narrow political bandwidth. The leftwing Students for a Democratic Society and rightwing politicians like George Wallace could agree that there was not "a dime's worth of difference" between the major parties. Yes, there was a "middlebrow" culture that seemed to elide Robert Frost or Samuel Beckett with Dick Clark or Pat Boone.[6]

Maybe, the broad mid-twentieth-century consensus on fighting communism, building prosperity, and extending opportunity to all Americans was stultifying to the upper-middle-class hippies of Golden Gate Park and station-wagon radicals "levitating" the Pentagon with Abbie Hoffman. But maybe that "Establishment" of mainstream Americans—moderate Republicans and liberal but hawkish Democrats—got it more or less right in building a growing, increasingly prosperous middle class, expanding rights and opportunities for all Americans, building jumbo jets and highways, transplanting hearts, and literally reaching for the stars. Despite the purported problem of a dumbing down of culture, critics of "middlebrow" culture were wrong that people couldn't easily shift from reading about starlets, learning about great artists, and understanding that racism was wrong and why engagement with the world was right. Moreover, if the culture seemed dumbed down in the 1950s, that was nothing compared to a twenty-first-century culture shaped by social media and narrowcast media with narrow agendas.

That consensus and broad faith in economic and social progress had a cultural and intellectual foundation—a foundation that enabled and encouraged Americans to see multiple points of view and fundamentally agree that "we the people" included Blacks and factory workers, women, and those who pushed the bounds of creativity and science. While that consensus excluded Weathermen, John Birchers, and diehard segregationists, it had few of the harsh, wide, and Manichean ideological, political, economic, and cultural divisions of twenty-first-century America.

What is key is that the forward-looking and increasingly tolerant postwar America didn't just happen. It was founded on shared information, ideas, and values—not the echo-chamber intellectual ghettoes of the internet. While the internet has "democratized" information and taken its control from an exclusively white male elite, it has left us with often biased and unreliable "sources" consumed by tiny segments of the American public. By contrast, *Look* covered the nation and the world with objectivity, honesty, and a human face. Vital building blocks of democracy were bundled in a biweekly cultural package that brought brilliant photos and thoughtful essays, astronauts and Abstract Expressionists, business titans and working-class heroes, Hollywood and Washington, an unknown China, Israeli kibbutzim, and life in newly independent countries together in a medium that could legitimately say, "This is America" and "This is our world."

After *Look*'s last issue, the *Times* said that it was "faithful to the conviction that an alert and informed public is the best insurance for a sound America—a magazine neither complacent nor despairing, but never given to easy tolerance of the intolerable."[7]

Look, with its tens of millions of readers, helped create enough common ground for the vast majority of Americans to rally around, or at least come to terms with, a set of economic, political, and cultural ideas and goals that contributed to the nation's postwar triumphs. It enabled bosses and their workers to have something more than sports that they could talk about together. It made it possible to have the proverbial water-cooler conversations in which individuals with very different backgrounds could talk with each other. It saw Americans as one people, a middle-class nation, and a land of achievement and promise. *Look* also celebrated a civic-minded populace intent on making their communities better places to live and work and who could have a common purpose and strive for the common good.

To see America through the eyes of *Look* is to see a nation with boundless possibilities for being more just, wealthier, more technologically advanced, more civilized, and a with can-do faith in problem-solving. It also sets in stark relief a post-*Look* nation that has lost much of what made the country successful and able to strive for a "more perfect union" during these years that began with World War II.

Correlation is not causation, but there is more than enough to demonstrate that *Look* and a few other mass-circulation media played a significant role in making the United States and its people generally successful, hopeful, happy, and united during a few decades of the mid-twentieth century.

Look is more than an artifact of better days, an unrecoverable era in American life. Although *Look* or something similar will not be revived, it offers valuable lessons about how a certain kind of medium could bring greater understanding, if not unity and hope, to a nation that is so bitterly divided, angry, pessimistic, unequal, and ill-informed.

The United States today could benefit enormously from a modern variant of what started as a little newspaper supplement in Iowa—a magazine that helped Americans to be informed, care for others, open to diverse ideas, and be optimistic. The demand for such media may not be there, but is it impossible to imagine that such demand could be stimulated? Information and ideas are not frills. They are as important to the success of a society as a healthy economy and the rule of law.

What mass-circulation media like *Look* accomplished—mimicking what has long been the underlying principle and modus operandi of schools and liberal-arts education—was to edit, bring coherence to, and deliver a thoughtfully selected wealth of knowledge and ideas to a broad and diverse population. Initially, many on the left and right today would not be eager to hear what the other "side" has to say. Similarly, artists and engineers, business people and scientists initially might not be interested in each other's achievements, but the very idea of being a well-informed, well-rounded, engaged citizen needs to be re-instilled and even become "cool." While differences of opinion are healthy—and very much existed during the postwar era—the American people need to find a new "common core" of shared aspirations and values. Central to this task is the need for media that could once again engage and help Americans discover what unites the country and not just focus on what tears it apart.

Are there lessons that can be gleaned from *Look* for journalism and for America? The United States desperately needs the civic engagement, the informed citizenry, the respect for institutions and opposing beliefs, the hope, and the goal of achieving greater equality and justice for all. Could media with the breadth of coverage and mass audience of *Look* make a difference? Probably, yes.

This is what *Look* did and what a creatively constructed mass medium for the twenty-first century might do. Because too many Americans get their information from social media and screaming commentators, the country needs carrots and sticks, incentives and mandates, to develop new media like *Look*, to pull or push people to consume a twenty-first-century variant of *Look*. Foundations, even government—as it did with the Corporation for Public Broadcasting—could help fund and develop such new media with talented journalists and photographers. Schools and public-awareness campaigns could incubate audiences for such media. Creatively designed internet-based platforms and packaging, and print media, could also go a long way to lure people to them.

The nation could reap enormous benefits if mass-audience media could again bring that rich democracy of broad-based knowledge and perspectives to as many Americans as possible. If we know more about each other and the many dimensions of life within our borders and in the world, we can function more effectively, be more understanding and empathic, and live richer, happier lives. *Look* helped do this, and it is hard to underestimate the importance of what it did.

NOTES

ABBREVIATIONS

CCI   Cowles Communication Inc.
CFADU   Cowles Family Archive, Drake University
DKP   The David Kruidenier Jr. Papers
GCADU   Gardner Cowles Archives at Drake University
GCP   The Gardner Cowles Jr. (Mike) Papers
JCP   The John Cowles Papers
LOC   Library of Congress
LRWHS   *Look* Records, Wisconsin Historical Society

I. A FORGOTTEN, MISUNDERSTOOD MAGAZINE

1. Interview, Alan Waxenberg, Sept. 2, 2020; and "Thomas R. Shepard Jr., *Look* Magazine's Last Publisher, Dies at 96," *New York Times*, May 4, 2015.

2. "*Life* Magazine Archive Now Available on Google Books," Warner Media, Sept. 23, 2009.

3. "*Look* Magazine Photograph Collection," Library of Congress (LOC), https://www.loc.gov/pictures/collection/lmc/.

4. "*Look* Magazine to Stop Publication: Postal Rate Increases Cited as a Major Factor," *Look*, press release, Sept. 16, 1971, "Cost Articles," cabinet 3, drawer 4, folder 9, The John Cowles Papers (JCP), Cowles Family Archive, Drake University (CFADU).

5. "Four Kennedy Issues Set Mark at *Look*," *New York Times*, March 12, 1967; and "Fact Sheet #3," in *"Look*—Demise, 1971–1973," cabinet 3, drawer 4, folder 11, The Gardner Cowles Jr. (Mike) Papers (GCP), CFADU.

6. Gardner Cowles Jr., *Mike Looks Back: The Memoirs of Gardner Cowles, Founder of Look Magazine* (New York: Gardner Cowles, 1985), chap. 1; *"Look*: A New Kind of Family Magazine," 1943, cabinet 4, drawer 2, folder 4, GCP, CFADU; and Cowles Communication Inc. (CCI), executive seminar, Orlando FL, March 9–10, 1970, CFADU.

7. "Records of the *Look* Years," CFADU.

8. Leo Rosten, "Introduction: A View from Inside" (unpublished manuscript, April 11, 1975) CFADU.

9. "Gardner Cowles: A Dignified Passion for a Foreign Policy That Will Win Peace," *Printers' Ink*, April 17, 1959; "Federal Bureau of Investigation," cabinet 3, drawer 1, folder 18, CFADU; "Gardner Cowles, OWI Official, Raps Soviet Baiters in U.S.," *Daily Worker*, March 31, 1943; "Africa," *Look*, Nov. 15, 1955; "U.S. Aid to Others Called Essential," *New York Times*, June 10, 1955; "*Look* Editorial Department, 1946–48," cabinet 4, drawer 1, folder 1, GCP, CFADU; "The U.N. and You," *Look*, Sept. 16, 1947; and Mike Cowles, "An Optimist *Look*s at the World," June 2, 1958, speech at Morningside College, Sioux City IA, "Speeches, 1942–1961," cabinet 1, drawer 4, folder 1, GCP, CFADU.

10. Cowles Jr., *Mike Looks Back*, chap. 3; "Gallup, George," cabinet 1, drawer 2, folder 54, GCP, CFADU; "Lord, Mary," cabinet 1, drawer 2, folder 260, GCP, CFADU; Interview, Gilbert Maurer, Nov. 28, 2016; *"Look* Editorial Department, 1946–48"; "A Documentation of the Power of a Single *Look* Article," GCP, CFADU; and "Creative Editor with a Quest for Insight into World Affairs," *Printers' Ink*, April 10, 1959. Senator Taft sent out two million reprints of *Look*'s article on the legislation.

11. Godfrey Hodgson, *America in Our Time: From World War to Nixon—What Happened and Why* (Garden City NY: Doubleday, 1976).

12. Godfrey Hodgson, *America in Our Time*, 67ff.; and Daniel Bell, *The End of Ideology* (Glencoe IL: Free Press, 1960).

13. Gardner Cowles, "An Optimistic Editor Looks at the Sixties," speech to the Institute of Life Insurance, Waldorf-Astoria Hotel, Dec. 8, 1959, in "Speeches, 1942–1961," GCP, CFADU; *"Look*—Hollywood Office, 1946–47," cabinet 4, drawer 1, folder 12, CFADU; "Federal Bureau of Investigation"; Interview, Herbert Strentz, Oct. 31, 2016; "Baruch, Bernard," cabinet 1, drawer 1, folder 96, CFADU; "Correspondence 1952," cabinet 1, drawer 3, folder 160, CFADU; "Use of Advertising as Club Opposed," *New York Times*, March 6, 1948; *"Look* Editorial: Vietnam a Mistake," *New York Times*, May 14, 1968; Interview, John Poppy, April 12, 2018; Hodgson, *America in Our Time*; and Robert Mason and Iwan Morgan, eds., *The Liberal Consensus Reconsidered: American Politics and Society in the Postwar Era* (Gainesville FL: University Press of Florida, 2017).

14. Herbert Strentz, "Gardner Cowles Jr.," GCP, CFADU; "Editorial Preview," July 7, 1959, "Story of *Look*," cabinet 5, drawer 2, folder 1, GCP, CFADU; and "World Free Press Urged as a Crusade," *New York Times*, Nov. 15, 1943.

15. "Records of the *Look* Years"; and *"Look* Magazine to Stop Publication."
16. "Story of *Look*, 1958–59," cabinet 5, drawers 2 and 3, folder 1, GCP, CFADU; "The Public Will Be Served," ca. 1960, cabinet 4, drawer 2, folder 4, GCP, CFADU; and *"Look* Magazine—Editorial Previews," 1963, cabinet 4, drawer 1, folder 3, GCP, CFADU; a "Records of the *Look* Years"; and "Gardner Cowles: A Dignified Passion."
17. "Germany's Lonely Jews," *Look*, Sept. 23, 1952.
18. CCI, executive seminar; "Germany's Lonely Jews"; and Patricia Carbine, "In the Middle of the USA in Mid-20th Century," *Look*, July 7, 1959.
19. "Daniel Mich Dies, Editor of *Look*, 60," *New York Times*, Nov. 23, 1965.
20. Dan Mich, speech to *Look* Advertising Convention, Key Biscayne FL, May 11, 1960, in *"Look* Magazine—Editorial Department, 1946–1968," cabinet 3, drawer 3, folder 5; and "Records of the *Look* Years."
21. *"Look* Magazine Awards, 1950–1966," cabinet 3, drawer 4, folder 2, GCP, CFADU.
22. *"Look* Magazine—Editorial Previews"; and "Records of the *Look* Years."
23. Interview, Will Hopkins, Nov. 22, 2016; Interview, Douglas Kirkland and Francoise Kirkland, April 13, 2016; and Interview, John Poppy, April 12, 2018.
24. "Obama Tells David Letterman: People No Longer Agree on What Facts Are," *USA Today*, Jan. 12, 2018.
25. George Leonard, *Walking on the Edge of the World: A Memoir of the Sixties and Beyond* (Boston: Houghton Mifflin Harcourt, 1988), 14; and "Fox News Viewership Plummets: First Time Behind CNN and MSNBC in Two Decades," *Forbes*, Jan. 16, 2021.
26. Dwight Macdonald, "Masscult and Midcult," *Partisan Review*, spring 1960, and Dwight Macdonald, *Masscult and Midcult: Essays against the American Grain* (New York: Random House, 1962); and "Obama Calls for 'Common Conversation' to Bridge America's Divide," NBC News, Jan. 13, 2017.
27. Leonard, *Walking on the Edge of the World*, 19.
28. "The Midwest's Nice Monopolists John and Mike Cowles," *Harper's*, June 1963; and Joseph Roddy, "Notes from a Bargain Typewriter," *(MORE): A Journalism Review*, Nov. 1971. *Look*'s few editorials took on subjects like CIA support for overseas U.S. student organizations, increasing funding for medical care for the elderly, and withdrawing from Vietnam.
29. The Editors of *Look*, "The *Look* Years—35 Years of *Look*" (1972).
30. Macdonald, "Mass Cult and Midcult."
31. "Story of *Look*, 1958–59," cabinet 8, drawer 2, folder 2; and Philippe D. Mather, *Stanley Kubrick at Look Magazine: Authorship and Genre in Photojournalism and Film* (Chicago: Intellect Books, 2013).
32. "The Reminiscences of Ira Mothner," Columbia Center for Oral History Research, Aug. 19, 2014.
33. CCI, executive seminar; "Publicity Material," cabinet 4, drawer 4, file 15, GCADU; Mather, *Kubrick at Look Magazine*; and "Vernon Knox Pope, 89, Was Founding Editor of *Look* Magazine," *South Florida Sun Sentinel*, March 6, 1995.

34. *"Look* Magazine Photograph Collection," LOC; Rosten, "Introduction: A View from Inside"; *"Look* Archives to Columbia School of Journalism," cabinet 3, drawer 3, folder 11, GCP, CFADU.
35. "Fact Sheet #3"; and *"Look* Magazine—Editorial Previews," 1963.
36. Rosten, "Introduction: A View from Inside."
37. Interview, Douglas Kirkland and Francoise Kirkland; and Interview, John Poppy.

2. IN THE BEGINNING

1. References to "Cowles" will be about Mike Cowles. Other Cowles family members discussed in this book will be referred to by their full names.
2. "How to Live a Full Life? Just Follow Gardner Cowles," *Miami News*, Jan. 31, 1960.
3. "The Reminiscences of George Gallup," 1962, interviewed by Frank Rounds, p. 17, Oral History Research Office, Columbia University; and Department of Photographs, "Photojournalism and the Picture Press in Germany," in *The Heilbrunn Timeline of Art History*, Metropolitan Museum of Art, Oct. 2004.
4. "No. 3 Nazi and His Family," *Look*, Aug. 2, 1938; "Gardner Cowles: Communications Leader Who Believes Success Is a Journey," *Printers' Ink*, April 3, 1959; "Records of the *Look* Years, 1972," cabinet 4, drawer 2, folders 20 and 23, GCP, CFADU; "Publicity Material," cabinet 4, drawer 4, folder 15, GCP, CFADU; and Gardner Cowles Jr., *Mike Looks Back*, chaps. 2 and 3.
5. Margaret Sanger, "Why Birth Control?," *Look*, Aug. 15, 1939; "This Is War in Spain," Feb. 15, 1938; "Photocrime" and "Confidentially," *Look*, Aug. 29, 1939; "Story of a Famous Pirate," Jan. 18, 1938; "World's Most Beautiful Chinese Girl" and J. Edgar Hoover, "Criminals Are Rats," *Look*, March 1, 1938; "Dogs," *Look*, April 26, 1938; John Gunther, "Josef Stalin: Red Emperor," *Look*, Jan. 2, 1940; and "The Last *Look*," *Time*, Sep. 27, 1971.
6. "The Last *Look*"; *Look* cover, Sept. 12, 1939; "Sex Appeal in Sports," *Look*, Oct. 24, 1939; "Broadway's Most Beautiful Girls," *Look*, Nov. 7, 1939; *Look* cover, Dec. 5, 1939; and Erica Schwiegershausen, "Revisit the Golden Era of *Look*," *The Cut*, Aug. 17, 2014.
7. "Story of *Look*," cabinet 8, drawer 2, folder 1.
8. George Benneyan, "The Story of *Look*," (unpub. ca. 1959); and Cowles Jr., *Mike Looks Back*.
9. "Records of the *Look* Years, 1972"; "The Reminiscences of George Gallup," 1962, interviewed by Frank Rounds, pp. 28–29, Oral History Research Office, Columbia University; Interview, Herbert Strentz, Oct. 31, 2016; Herbert Strentz, "Gardner Cowles Jr.," GCP, CFADU; *"Look*: A New Kind of Family Magazine"; and *"Look* Promotion, 1943, 1946–47," cabinet 4, drawer 2, folder 4, GCP, CFADU.
10. "The Reminiscences of George Gallup," 28–29, 44; *"Look*: A New Kind of Family Magazine"; and Correspondence, Herbert Strentz, Nov. 21, 2016.
11. Herbert Strentz, "John Cowles Sr.," GCP, CFADU; "Cowles Correspondence, 1946–49, 1953–54, 1956, 1961–63, 1967," cabinet 1, drawer 2, folder 17, GCP, CFADU; Interview, Gilbert Maurer, Nov. 28, 2016; William Barry Furlong, "The Midwest's Nice Monopolists John

and Mike Cowles," *Harper's*, June 1963; "How to Live a Full Life? Just Follow Gardner Cowles"; "Des Moines Register and Tribune Washington Bureau, 1947, 1951–52," cabinet 3, drawer 1, folder 5, GCP, CFADU; "Reminiscences of George Gallup," 42; Patricia Dawson, "Cowles Family Publishing Legacy in the Drake University Collections"; and "Gardner Cowles, Publisher, 85, Dies," *New York Times*, March 1, 1946.

12. "Gardner Cowles: Communications Leader"; Cowles Jr., *Mike Looks Back*; "Records of the *Look* Years, 1972"; Cowles, "Cowles Brothers See Crimson Vital Factor in College Life," *Harvard Crimson*, Jan. 30, 1948; and Strentz, "John Cowles Sr."

13. "*Look*—Quick—*Flair*: A Report by Cowles Magazines Inc.," 1950, in "Records of the *Look* Years," CFADU; Strentz, "John Cowles Sr."; "Cowles Genealogy," cabinet 2, drawer 3, folder 17, GCP, CFADU; "*Register*'s 'Mike' Cowles Is Dead of Cancer at Age 82," *Des Moines Register*, July 9, 1985; and Furlong, "The Midwest's Nice Monopolists John and Mike Cowles."

14. Strentz, "Gardner Cowles Jr."; "Two Evening Papers Join in Minneapolis," *New York Times*, Aug. 1, 1939; "The Cowles World," *Time*, Dec. 8, 1958; "LRWHS, 1958–60," box 14, folder 12, *Look* Records, Wisconsin Historical Society (LRWHS), Madison WI; Interview, Chris Mahai, Nov. 21, 2016; "Elizabeth B. Cowles Dies at 76: Founded Planned Parenthood," *New York Times*, Dec. 18, 1976; and "John Cowles Jr., 82, Dies: Led Minneapolis Newspapers," *New York Times*, March 19, 2012.

15. Kenneth Stewart, "*Look*," PM, May 28, 1949, in "Publicity Material," cabinet 4, drawer 4, folder 15, GCP, CFADU; Lawrence Hughes, "Cowles Brothers Build a $50,000,000 Empire," *Advertising Age*, Aug. 1, 1949; "50% of Harper's Sold to Cowles Paper in Minneapolis," *New York Times*, April 29, 1964; "John Cowles Sr. Is Dead at 84," *New York Times*, Feb. 26, 1983; "John Cowles Jr., 82, Dies," *New York Times*, March 20, 2012; and Interview, Chris Mahai.

16. Stewart, "*Look*"; "Gardner Cowles," *Printer's Ink*, April 3, 1959; Interview, Gilbert Maurer; "Federal Bureau of Investigation," cabinet 3, drawer 1, folder 18, GCP, CFADU; "The Midwest's Nice Monopolists"; "Telephone Listings," cabinet 5, drawer 4, folder 18, GCP, CFADU; and N. R. Kleinfield, "Looking Back at *Look*," *New York Times*, Feb. 6, 1983.

17. "Call-Cowles History," cabinet 24, drawer 1, folder 1, The David Kruidenier Jr. Papers (DKP), CFADU; and "Cowles Family—Published Data, 1935–1963," cabinet 24, drawer 1, folder 3, DKP, CFADU; "Cowles Correspondence, 1946–49, 1953–54, 1956, 1961–63, 1967"; Interview, Herbert Strentz; "David Kruidenier Jr.," Cowles Family Publishing Legacy, Drake University, http://www.lib.drake.edu/heritage/GardnerCowlesFamily /DavidKruidenier.html; "David S. Kruidenier, 84, Publisher and Philanthropist, Dies," *New York Times*, Jan. 11, 2006; "Nancy Shepard," obituary, *New York Times*, Oct. 29, 2016; and "Marriage to Gardner Cowles 3d to be Held Here in December," *New York Times*, Sept. 3, 1961.

18. "Morley Ballantine," cabinet 1, drawer 1, folder 85, GCP, CFADU; "Morley and Arthur Ballantine," cabinet 10, drawer 1, folder 2, JCP, CFADU; and "Morley Ballantine," Colorado Women's Hall of Fame, http://www.cogreatwomen.org/project/morley-ballantine/.

19. When *Look* folded in 1971, it was estimated that Cowles had $70 million in *New York Times* common stock, in addition to his other investments and property. In 1994 the Forbes 400 of Family Fortunes estimated that the Cowles family was worth $525 million. Joseph Roddy, "Notes from a Bargain Typewriter," *(MORE): A Journalism Review*, Nov. 1971; and Correspondence with Herbert Strentz, 2016.

20. "The Reminiscences of George Gallup," 46.

21. Cowles Jr., *Mike Looks Back*.

22. Interview, Herbert Strentz.

23. "How to Live a Full Life? Just Follow Gardner Cowles"; "Gardner Cowles: Communications Leader"; "The Reminiscences of George Gallup," 46; and Interview, Gilbert Maurer.

24. Strentz, "Gardner Cowles Jr."; Leo Rosten, "Introduction: A View from Inside," CFADU; "NAACP Warned Fight Is Not Won," *New York Times*, Dec. 7, 1959; Laura Z. Hobson, "A Gentleman's Agreement" (excerpt), *Look*, June 10, 1947; Benneyan, "The Story of *Look*," cabinet 5, drawers 2–3, GCP, CFADU; "Use of Advertising as Club Opposed," *New York Times*, March 6, 1948; "*Look* Magazine—Editorial Department, 1946–1968," cabinet 4, drawer 1, folder 1, GCP, CFADU; "New York Urban League, 1966–67" cabinet 4, drawer 1, folder 6; "Committee for Economic Development, 1959–68," cabinet 2, drawer 1, folder 3, GCP, CFADU; Andrew L. Yarrow, *Measuring America: How Economic Growth Came to Define U.S. Greatness in the Late 20th Century* (Amherst: University of Massachusetts Press, 2010); and Jean Preer, "'Wake Up and Read!' Book Promotion and National Library Week, 1958," *Libraries and the Cultural Record* 45, no. 1: 92–106.

25. "169 Notables Ask for Widening of NATO," *New York Times*, Oct. 4, 1954; "Committee for the Marshall Plan, 1947," cabinet 2, drawer 1, folder 4; "An Interview with Nikita Khrushchev by Gardner Cowles," April 20, 1962; Commencement address, Penn State, 1955, "Speeches," GCP, CFADU; "Federal Bureau of Investigation"; and Editors of *Look*, with an introduction by J. Edgar Hoover, *Story of the FBI: The Official Photographic History of the Federal Bureau of Investigation* (New York: Dutton, 1954).

26. "*Look* Guild 1946," cabinet 4, drawer 1, folder 6; GCP, CFADU; "Gardner Cowles: Communications Leader"; and "The Story of *Look*."

27. "One Thing and Another," *New York Times*, May 28, 1944; N. R. Kleinfield, "Looking Back at *Look*"; and Michael Gross, *740 Park: The Story of the World's Richest Apartment Building* (New York: Crown/Archetype, 2007).

28. "*Register*'s 'Mike' Cowles Is Dead"; Gardner Cowles, "Impressions of a Quick Trip around the World," June, 1947 (reprinted from the *Des Moines Register*), GCP, CFADU; "Bets—1955–62," cabinet 2, drawer 2, folder 16, GCP, CFADU; Interview, Herbert Strentz; Cowles Jr., *Mike Looks Back*; "Willkie to Start Abroad in Three Weeks," *New York Times*, Aug. 21, 1942; "Dewey Aboard Stratocruiser," *New York Times*, April 9, 1949; and "Reminiscences of George Gallup," 49.

29. "Khrushchev Sees Hope on Berlin," *New York Times*, April 21, 1962; "Reminiscences of George Gallup," 46; and Cowles Jr., *Mike Looks Back*, chaps. 4 and 5.

30. Cowles Jr., *Mike Looks Back*, chap. 5; Kleinfield, "Looking Back at *Look*"; Dawson, "Cowles Family Publishing Legacy"; *"Register*'s Mike Cowles Is Dead"; Strentz, "Gardner Cowles Jr."; *"Look* magazine, 1946–1968," cabinet 3, drawer 3, folder 5, GCP, CFADU; "Speeches—1942–1961," cabinet 1, drawer 4, folder 1, GCP, CFADU; "Speeches, 1962–1975," cabinet 2, drawer 1, folder 1, GCP, CFADU; and "Museum Builds Globe," *New York Times*, Sept. 29, 1960.

31. Gardner Cowles Jr. Is Dead at 82: Helped Build Publishing Empire, *New York Times*, July 9, 1985; *"Register*'s 'Mike' Cowles Is Dead"; "Gardner Cowles: Communications Leader"; "Gardner Cowles: A Dignified Passion"; Cowles Jr., *Mike Looks Back*; Patricia Prijatel, "Anatomy of a Failure," in *The Magazine From Cover to Cover*, eds. Patricia Prijatel and Sammye Johnson (Chicago: NTC Publishing Group, 1999); Strentz, "Gardner Cowles Jr."; "Gardner Cowles: Creative Editor with a Quest for Insight into World Affairs," *Printers' Ink*, April 10, 1959; "Fleur Cowles Today: As Creative as Ever," *New York Times*, April 27, 1976; and Gross, *740 Park*. Longtime editor of the *Register* Kenneth MacDonald said: "Hell, we print the news of all Mike's divorces on the front page."

32. Rosten, "Introduction: A View from Inside"; "Gardner Cowles: Communications Leader"; and "Kruidenier Family," cabinet 3, drawer 3, folder 2, GCP, CFADU.

33. "Kruidenier Family," CFADU; Gross, *740 Park*; "How to Live a Full Life?"; Cowles Jr., *Mike Looks Back*; Interview, Patricia Dawson, Oct. 31, 2016; *"Register*'s 'Mike' Cowles Is Dead"; and "Telephone Listings."

34. "Advertising Age," Sept. 27, 1971, in *"Look* Suspension 1971" cabinet 4, drawer 1, folder 14, GCP, CFADU.

35. Reminiscences of George Gallup, 29–30; and Cowles Jr., *Mike Looks Back*, chaps. 3 and 4.

3. *LOOK'S THIRTY-FIVE YEARS*

1. *Reader's Digest* and TV *Guide* had larger circulations, but neither included original journalism.

2. Gardner Cowles Jr., *Mike Looks Back: The Memoirs of Gardner Cowles, Founder of Look Magazine* (New York: Gardner Cowles, 1985), chap. 3; and "Gardner Cowles: Communications Leader Who Believes Success Is a Journey," *Printers' Ink*, April 3, 1959.

3. "Records of the *Look* Years, 1972," cabinet 4, drawer 2, folders 20 and 23, GCP, CFADU; "Aviation: America's Fastest Growing Industry," *Look*, Nov. 22, 1938; "Marijuana Becomes a Major American Problem," *Look*, Nov. 22, 1938; "Hitler's Girlfriends . . . and his Hostesses," *Look*, Nov. 22, 1938; Margaret Sanger, "Why Birth Control?," *Look*, Aug. 15, 1939; "America's Own Refugees," *Look*, Aug. 29, 1939; William A. Mueller, "Coughlin and the Nazi Bund," *Look*, Sept. 26, 1939; and "Special War Feature," "When I Get Out of Prison," "Divorced Women: America's Misfits," and "George White's Scandals," *Look*, Oct. 24, 1939; and Cowles Jr., *Mike Looks Back*, chap. 5.

4. "*Look*: A New Kind of Family Magazine," 1943, cabinet 4, drawer 2, folder 4, GCP, CFADU; "Gardner Cowles: A Dignified Passion for a Foreign Policy That Will Win

Peace," *Printers' Ink*, April 17, 1959; and "Gardner Cowles: Creative Editor with a Quest for Insight into World Affairs," *Printers' Ink*, April 10, 1959.

5. Leo Rosten, "Introduction: A View from the Inside," GCP, CFADU; and Joseph Roddy, "Notes from a Bargain Typewriter," (*MORE*): *A Journalism Review*, Nov. 1971.

6. "How Hitler Fools America," *Look*, Dec. 31, 1940; John Gunther, "Inside South Africa," *Look*, Aug. 26, 1941; and "The Life Story of Stalin," *Look*, June 8, 1942.

7. "White Child in a Negro World," *Look*, Nov. 9, 1948; and James Conaway in association with the Library of Congress, *The Forgotten Fifties: America's Decade from the Archives of Look Magazine* (New York: Skira Rizzoli, n.d), 7.

8. "Publicity Material," cabinet 4, drawer 4, file 15, GCP, CFADU; "*Look*: A New Kind of Family Magazine"; "*Look* Magazine—Editorial Department, 1946–1968," cabinet 4, drawer 1, folder 1, GCP, CFADU; "M. C. Whatmore of Cowles Dead," *New York Times*, April 11, 1985; "Marriage to Gardner Cowles 3d to be Held Here in December," *New York Times*, Sept. 3, 1961; "Records of the *Look* Years, 1972"; "Gardner Cowles: A Dignified Passion"; Cowles Jr., *Mike Looks Back*, chaps. 4 and 5; "Daniel D. Mich Is Elected Vice President of Cowles Magazines," *Look* press release, March 15, 1954; "William Arthur, 83," *New York Times*, Dec. 24, 1997; and "*Look* Executives among Plane Dead," *New York Times*, Oct. 25, 1947.

9. "Records of the *Look* Years, 1972," and "*Look*—Quick—*Flair*: A Report by Cowles Magazines Inc.," 1950, in "Records of the *Look* Years," GCP, CFADU.

10. "Records of the *Look* Years, 1972"; "Pat Coffin," box 3, folder 8, *Look* Records, LRWHS; "Pat Coffin, 1958–60," box 13, folder 24, LRWHS; "Memo from Merle Armitage to Mike Cowles," March 25, 1954; "Dan Mich Executive Correspondence with George Eells, 1954" and "Eells, 1953," box 4, folders 1 and 33, LRWHS.

11. "The Public Will Be Served," ca. 1960, cabinet 4, drawer 2, folder 4, GCP, CFADU; Interview, Douglas Kirkland and Francoise Kirkland, April 13, 2016; and Joe Louis, "My Greatest Fights," *Look*, March 4, 1947.

12. "George Benneyan, 1959," cabinet 2, drawer 2, folder 6, GCP, CFADU; "*Look* Magazine— Editorial Department, 1946–1968"; "*Look*—Quick—*Flair*"; "*Look* Magazine Photograph Collection," LOC; "Gardner Cowles: Creative Editor"; Interviews, Will Hopkins, Nov. 22, 2016, and Jan., 12, 2017.

13. Roddy, "Notes from a Bargain Typewriter"; William Lowe, memo to staff, May 27, 1953, in "Story of *Look*," cabinet 5, drawers 2 and 3, folder 1, GCP, CFADU; Cowles Jr., *Mike Looks Back*, 188; Gary S. Cooperman, "A Historical Study of *Look* Magazine and its Concept of Photojournalism," (master's thesis, University of Missouri-Columbia, 1966), 179; and "*Look* Magazine—Editorial Department, 1946–1968."

14. Interview, John Poppy, Nov. 11, 2020.

15. Rosten, "Introduction: A View from Inside"; "*Look* Promotion, 1943, 1946–47," cabinet 4, drawer 2, folder 4, GCP, CFADU; and Interview, John Poppy, Nov. 11, 2020.

16. "*Look* Guild, 1946," cabinet 4, drawer 1, folder 6, GCP, CFADU.

17. "*Look* Magazine—Editorial Department, 1946–1948"; "*Look*—Women's Department," cabinet 4, drawer 2, folder 19, GCP, CFADU; "Records of the *Look* Years, 1972"; "*Look*—Quick—*Flair*"; Patricia Prijatel, "Fleur's Folly," *Print*, Mach/April 1995, 99–108, 110; "Gardner Cowles: Creative Editor"; Interview, Herbert Strentz, Oct. 31, 2016; Interview, Gilbert Maurer, Nov. 28, 2016; Cowles Jr., *Mike Looks Back*, chap. 4; Dan Piepenbring, "Fleur's *Flair*," *Paris Review*, Jan. 20, 2015; "Employee Attitude Survey—1955," cabinet 4, drawer 1, folder 5. GCP, CFADU; Communication with Herb Strentz, Aug. 28, 2020; and *Look* press release, Oct. 18, 1955.

18. "*Look* Magazine—Advertising, 1946–1968," cabinet 3, drawer 3, folder 5, GCP, CFADU; "Records of the *Look* Years, 1972"; "*Look* Magazine, 1946–1968," cabinet 3, drawer 3, folder 6, GCP, CFADU; "*Look* Circulation, 1945," cabinet 3, drawer 4, folder 5; "*Look* at America," cabinet 4, drawer 1, folder 8, GCP, CFADU; "*Look*—Quick—*Flair*"; "*Look* Magazine—Subscription Department, 1946–1950," cabinet 4, drawer 2, folder 13, GCP, CFADU; "Screen News," *New York Times*, April 9, 1940; Editors of *Look*, *My War Story* (New York: Whittlesey House, 1945); "Lost Hope," *New York Times*, July 16, 1944; and "New York City," *New York Times*, July 25, 1948.

19. "*Look* Magazine—Advertising, 1946–1968"; "Records of the *Look* Years, 1972"; "*Look* magazine, 1946–1968"; "*Look* Circulation, 1945"; "*Look* at America"; "*Look*—Quick—*Flair*," 1950; "*Look* magazine—Subscription Department, 1946–1950"; "Screen News"; Editors of *Look*, *My War Story*; "Lost Hope"; and "New York City."

20. CCI executive seminar, Orlando FL, March 9–10, 1970; "Gardner Cowles: A Dignified Passion"; "Gardner Cowles Leaves Top Jobs," *New York Times*, May 15, 1964; and Interview, Will Hopkins.

21. "*Look*—Quick—*Flair*"; "*Look* Promotion, 1943, 1946–47"; "Liquor Ads," cabinet 4, drawer 1, folder 7, GCP, CFADU.

22. "Personnel—Confidential," box 21, folders 26 and 27, LRWHS; "Personnel Memos 1953," box 6, folder 5, LRWHS; "James Milloy," cabinet 3, drawer 3, folder 3, GCP, CFADU; Cowles Jr., *Mike Looks Back*, chap. 4; and "Payroll 1954," box 6, folder 24, LRWHS.

23. "Nine Floors Rented in 488 Madison," *New York Times*, April 3, 1949; "*Look* Publishers Expand Quarters," *New York Times*, Oct. 18, 1963; Interview, Will Hopkins; "*Look* Building Is Named a Landmark," *New York Times*, July 27, 2010.

24. Philippe D. Mather, *Stanley Kubrick at Look Magazine: Authorship and Genre in Photojournalism and Film* (Chicago: Intellect Books, 2013); and "Editorial Preview," April 28, 1963, in "*Look* Magazine—Editorial Previews, 1963," cabinet 4, drawer 1, folder 3, GCP, CFADU.

25. Interview, Will Hopkins.

26. Philip Wylie, "Mom's to Blame," *Look*, Nov. 21, 1950; Norman Thomas, "A Socialist Taunts the Major Parties," June 22, 1952; and "Wallace Making Press His Target," *Look*, April 15, 1966.

27. "The Beatles," *Look*, Jan. 9, 1968; and Interview, John Poppy.

28. "Elliott Roosevelt in Moscow," *New York Times*, Nov. 13, 1946; Adlai Stevenson, "Will India Turn Communist?," *Look*, July 14, 1953; Adlai Stevenson, "Ballots and Bullets," *Look*, June 2, 1953; "Stevenson, Five Questions about Europe," *Look*, Sept. 8, 1953; Adlai Stevenson, "West Builds Balkan Barrier," *Look*, Aug. 25, 1953; William Attwood, "One Way to See the Biggest Prison in the World," *Look*, Sept. 3, 1958; and William Attwood and Adlai Stevenson, "Russia's Two Faces," *Look*, Nov. 25, 1958.

29. Ernest Dunbar and Ed Korry, "Inside Negro Africa," *Look*, June 23, 1959; and Thomas Morgan, "Ordeal in Antarctica," *Look*, April 1, 1958.

30. "California," *Look*, Sept. 29, 1959; and "*Look* Magazine—Editorial Previews, 1963"; "*Look* at America"; "Andrew H. Hepburn," *New York Times*, July 21, 1975; and Editors of *Look*, *Suburbia: The Good Life in our Exploding Utopia* (New York: Cowles Education Corp., 1968).

31. Cowles Jr., *Mike Looks Back*, 187; "Norman Vincent Peale Answers Your Questions" and "Behind the Scenes—J. M. Flagler," *Look*, July 27, 1966.

32. "*Look*—Demise, 1971–1973," cabinet 3, drawer 4, folder 11, GCP, CFADU; Arthur D. Morse, "While Six Million Died," *Look*, Oct. 31, 1967; and "Observer: This Time, Dr. Freud, You've Gone too Far," *New York Times*, Dec. 1, 1966.

33. "*Look* Magazine to Stop Publication: Postal Rate Increases Cited as Major Factor," *Look* press release, in "*Look*—Demise, 1971–1973."

34. "Records of the *Look* Years, 1972"; "*Look* Magazine—1946–1968, cabinet 3, drawer 3, folder 5, GCP, CFADU; "The Last *Look*," *Time*, Sep. 27, 1971; Cowles Jr., *Mike Looks Back*, 194, 196–97; "*Look* Audience Study 1962," cabinet 3, drawer 4, folder 1, GCP, CFADU; "*Look* Circulation Analysis" and "Comparison of U.S. Circulations of *Look* and *Life*," cabinet 3, drawer 4, folder 8, GCP, CFADU; Memo from Pete Dailey to Bill Arthur, Dec. 20, 1956, William Arthur Papers—General Correspondence, box 6, LRWHS; "Advertising: *Look* Aims for Upper Incomes," *New York Times*," Oct. 9, 1967; Cowles Jr., *Mike Looks Back*, chap. 6; "Gardner Cowles: Communications Leader"; "Gardner Cowles: A Dignified Passion"; "Publisher Drops Nielsen Service," *New York Times*, April 12, 1963; "Number of Households in the U.S. from 1960 to 2016 (in millions)," Statista, https://www.statista.com/statistics/183635/number-of-households-in-the-us/; and U.S. Census Bureau, "Estimates of the Population by Age and States, 1965–1967," series P-25, no. 420, April 17, 1969, https://www.census.gov/prod/1/pop/p25-420.pdf. Not surprisingly, readership numbers were hotly contested, with Nielsen reporting that *Life* still had more readers in the mid-1960s.

35. This is about $643 million in 2020 dollars.

36. "*Look* Magazine to Stop Publication"; "*Look* Magazine—1946–1968," cabinet 3, drawer 3, folder 5, GCP, CFADU; "The Public Will Be Served" brochure (ca. 1960), cabinet 4, drawer 2, GCP, CFADU; "Eels, 1957–60," box 13, folder 33, LRWHS; "CCI press releases 1967–68," cabinet 2, drawer 3, folder 8, GCP, CFADU; "Records of the *Look* Years, 1972"; and "Payroll 1954," box 21, folder 24, LRWHS.

37. "Story of *Look*," cabinet 5, drawer 2, folder 1, GCP, CFADU; "Records of the *Look* Years, 1972"; "*Look* Wins a Medal for Story on the South," *New York Times*, May 5, 1957; "NAACP Warned Fight Is Not Won," *New York Times*, Dec. 7, 1959; "Education Writers Chosen for Awards," *New York Times*, Feb. 19, 1962; Interview, Gilbert Maurer; "Correspondence, 1946–49, 1952," cabinet 1, drawer 2, folders 254–69, GCP, CFADU; "The President," *New York Times*, June 25, 1966; Interview, Will Hopkins; "Career Service Awards," Congressional Record-Senate, 11686, July 3, 1956; "*Look* Suspension 1971," cabinet 4, drawer 2, folder 14, GCP, CFADU; and CCI executive seminar.

38. "*Look*—Quick—*Flair*"; Letters in response to "The South's War against Negro Votes," *Look*, May 21, 1963; and Communication, John Poppy, Nov. 11, 2020.

39. "*Flair*, 1949–1951," cabinet 3, drawer 1, folder 12; Interview, Douglas Kirkland and Francoise Kirkland; "A Look at *Look*," ca. 1959, in "*Look* Magazine—Promotion, 1943–1961," cabinet 2, drawer 2, folder 4, GCP, CFADU; "*Look* Magazine, 1946–1968," cabinet 3, drawer 4, folder 5, GCP, CFADU; "Dublin Bans *Look* Magazine," *New York Times*, April 21, 1951; and "Joe McCarthy: The Man with the Power," *Look*, June 16, 1953.

40. "Screen News," *New York Times*, April 9, 1940.

41. *Flair*, Feb. 1950; "*Flair* Magazine, 1950," cabinet 6, drawer 4, folder 1, GCP, CFADU; "*Flair*, 1949–1951"; Patricia Prijatel, "Anatomy of a Failure," in *The Magazine from Cover to Cover*, eds. Patricia Prijatel and Sammye Johnson (Chicago: NTC Publishing, 1999); Prijatel, "Fleur's Folly"; *Flair*, June 1950; and Katharine Graham, "Magazine Rack," *Washington Post*, Jan. 29, 1950.

42. "Gardner Cowles: A Dignified Passion"; Correspondence, Herbert Strentz; Interview, Patricia Prijatel, Nov. 2, 2016; "*Look*—Quick—*Flair*"; Herbert Strentz, "Gardner Cowles Jr." GCP, CFADU; and "Cowles Magazines Inc., 1950–1960," cabinet 15, drawer 1, folder 2, JCP, CFADU.

43. "Quick, 1949–1952" cabinet 4, drawer 4, folder 5, GCP, CFADU; "Gardner Cowles: A Dignified Passion"; "Correspondence, 1946–49, 1952," cabinet 1, drawer 2, folders 254–69, GCP, CFADU; "Cowles Empire—A Magazine Phenomenon," *Business Week*, Oct. 8, 1949; and Strentz, "Gardner Cowles Jr."

44. "Records of the *Look* Years, 1972"; and "What Finally Crippled the Cowles Empire," *Business Week*, Sept. 25, 1971.

45. "Gardner Cowles Leaves Top Jobs," *New York Times*, May 15, 1964; "Advertising: New Horizon for *Venture*," *New York Times*, July 31, 1966; and Interview, Gilbert Maurer.

46. "The Last *Look*"; "Cowles to Buy *Family Circle*," *New York Times*, Oct. 5, 1962; Cowles Jr., *Mike Looks Back*, 207–11; "New Paper Faces Suffolk Pickets," *New York Times*, Nov. 11, 1966; "What Finally Crippled the Cowles Empire."

47. "New York City"; "Case Presented in Text and Pictures on America's Opportunity," *New York Times*, Sept. 29, 1945; "Books of the Times," *New York Times*, July 15, 1955; "The Strong and Diverse Heart of America," *New York Times*, July 17, 1955; "*Look* Books, 1946," cabinet 3, drawer 4, folder 4, GCP, CFADU; "*Look* Guild 1946"; "Gardner Cowles Leaves Top Jobs"; "The Public Will Be Served"; "Look for Leadership in Health and Medicine,"

brochure, 1961, cabinet 4, drawer 2, folder 4, GCP, CFADU; "*Look* magazine—Promotion, 1943–1961"; Edward A. Hamilton and Charles Preston, eds., *Our Land, Our People: People in Pictures from Look Magazine* (Englewood Cliffs NJ: Prentice-Hall, 1958); "Andrew H. Hepburn"; "Red Russia," *Look*, Oct. 3, 1967. Books published by *Look* included *Parenthood* (1942), with Planned Parenthood; *My Favorite War Story* (1945); *How to Keep Your Family Healthy: From the Pages of Look Magazine—Twenty Authoritative Articles on Health and Home Safety Which Will Help You Live Longer and Enjoy It* (1946); and *Red Russia after 50 Years* (New York: Cowles Education Corp., 1968).

48. *Fortune 500*, 1967; and Cowles Communications, Inc., 1965–1974, cabinet 2, drawer 3, folder 8, GCP, CFADU.

49. "*Look* Magazine—Stock List, 1947," cabinet 4, drawer 2, folder 21, GCP, CFADU; and "Records of the *Look* Years, 1972."

50. "Records of the *Look* Years, 1972"; "Gardner Cowles: A Dignified Passion"; "Thomas R. Shepard Jr., *Look* Magazine's Last Publisher, Dies at 96," *New York Times*, May 4, 2015; "Advertising: *Look* Aims for Upper Incomes"; and Interview, Gilbert Maurer.

51. "Over 2000 American Newspapers Have Closed in Last 15 Years," 24/7wallst.com, July 23, 2019.

52. "The Last *Look*," *Time*, Sept. 27, 1971; CCI executive seminar; Roddy, "Notes from a Bargain Typewriter"; "The Last *Look*," *Newsweek*, Sept. 27, 1971; "Cowles Meeting Told of *Look* Ad Losses," *New York Times*, May 15, 1970; and "*Times* Acquiring *Family Circle* and Six Other Cowles Properties," *New York Times*, Oct. 29, 1970.

53. "*Look* Magazine to Stop Publication," cabinet 3, drawer 4, folder 11, GCP, CFADU; and Cowles Jr., *Mike Looks Back*, chap. 6.

54. Interview, Douglas Kirkland and Francoise Kirkland.

55. Interview, Pat Sayer Fusco, April 12, 2018.

56. "The Last *Look*," *Time*; "*Look* Suspension—Personnel," cabinet 4, drawer 2, folder 14, GCP, CFADU; and "*Look*'s Workers Get Aid from Magazine in Finding Jobs," *New York Times*, Oct. 3, 1971; William F. Buckley Jr., "The End of *Look*," *New York Post*, Sept. 23, 1971; "What Finally Crippled the Cowles Empire"; and Interview, Pat Carbine, Sept. 11, 2020.

57. Roddy, "Notes from a Bargain Typewriter."

58. "A Revival for *Look* Is Scheduled in Fall," *New York Times*, Dec. 13, 1977; "The New *Look* Magazine Is On Sale at Newsstands," *New York Times*, Feb. 6, 1979; "Wenner to Run *Look* as a Monthly," May 8, 1979; "*Look* Magazine Dismisses Staff and Ends Ties to *Rolling Stone*," *New York Times*, July 4, 1979.

59. "Cowles to Liquidate Holdings," *New York Times*, March 30, 1982; Interview, Gilbert Maurer; "Cowles Genealogy, 1911–1985" cabinet 2, drawer 3, folder 17, GCP, CFADU; and "Family Fortunes: The *Forbes* 400," *Forbes*, Oct. 17, 1994.

4. THE PEOPLE WHO MADE *LOOK*

1. "Records of the *Look* Years, 1972," cabinet 4, drawer 2, folders 20 and 23, GCP, CFADU; and "*Look* Magazine to Stop Publication: Postal Rate Increases Cited as a Major Factor," *Look*, press release, Sept. 16, 1971, "Cost Articles," cabinet 3, drawer 4, folder 9, JCP, CFADU.

2. "*Look*—Demise," cabinet 3, drawer 4, folder 11, GCP, CFADU; "Employee Attitude Survey, 1954," cabinet 4, drawer 1, folder 5, GCP, CFADU; and "Jean Herrick, 1952–1953," cabinet 3, drawer 2, folder 5, GCP, CFADU.

3. "Daniel Mich Dies, Editor of *Look*, 60," *New York Times*, Nov. 23, 1965; "*Look* Editorial Staff," cabinet 4, drawer 1, folder 4, GCADU; George Leonard, *Walking on the Edge of the World: A Memoir of the Sixties and Beyond* (Boston: Houghton Mifflin Harcourt, 1988), 20; Interview, Patricia Carbine, Sept. 11, 2020; Gardner Cowles Jr., *Mike Looks Back*; and Interview, John Poppy, April 12, 2018.

4. "Daniel Mich Dies"; "*Look* Editorial Staff"; Leonard, *Walking on the Edge of the World*, 20; Interview, Patricia Carbine; Cowles Jr., *Mike Looks Back*; and Interview, John Poppy.

5. "Gardner Cowles: Communications Leader Who Believes Success Is a Journey," *Printers' Ink*, April 3, 1959; Kenneth Stewart, "*Look*," *PM*, May 28, 1949, in "Publicity Material," cabinet 4, drawer 4, file 15, GCP, CFADU; and Interview, Anthony Fusco with Paul Fusco, April 9, 2018.

6. Cowles Jr., *Mike Looks Back*.

7. Cowles Jr., *Mike Looks Back*, 100.

8. "Vernon Knox Pope, 89, Was Founding Editor of *Look* Magazine," *South Florida Sun-Sentinel*, March 6, 1995; Cowles Jr., *Mike Looks Back*; "Records of the *Look* Years, 1972"; Stewart, "*Look*"; "Gardner Cowles: Communications Leader."

9. "William Arthur, 83," *New York Times*, Dec. 24, 1997; "CCI Press Releases 1967–68," cabinet 2, drawer 3, folder 8, CFADU; and Interview, John Poppy.

10. Interview, Patricia Carbine; "Woman Leaves *Look* to Become Editorial Director at *McCall's*," *New York Times*, Aug. 22, 1970; "Advertising: *Ms.* Magazine Editor to Head Ad Council," *New York Times*, June 22, 1981; Interview, John Poppy; Interview, Douglas Kirkland, April 13, 2016; and Interview, Patricia Carbine.

11. "Robert Meskill," *New York Times*, Jan. 8, 1970; and Interview, John Poppy, Nov. 11, 2020.

12. Leonard, *Walking on the Edge of the World*, 21–22, 85, 111–12, 179, 310–11; and "George Leonard, 1923–1950," Esalen.org.

13. Interviews, John Poppy, April 12, 2018, May 21 and 31, 2018; "The California Uprising," *Look*, Feb. 23, 1965; and "The Generation Gap," *Look*, Feb. 21, 1967.

14. Leonard, *Walking on the Edge of the World*, 277; "Inside the Hippie Revolution," *Look*, Aug. 22, 1957; and "Golden Daze: Fifty Years On from the Summer of Love," *Guardian*, May 21, 2017.

15. "Laura Bergquist Knebel," *New York Times*, Nov. 9, 1982; Laura Bergquist Collection, Boston University Archives; Anna S., "'A Very Special President': The Woman Who Wrote JFK," Nov. 23, 2013, "Paris As a Young Woman," https://parisasayoungwoman.wordpress.com/2013/11/23/a-very-special-president-the-woman-who-wrote-jfk/; "My 28 Days in Communist Cuba," *Look*, April 9, 1963; and "Fletcher Knebel, Writer, 81, Dies, Co-Author of 'Seven Days in May,'" *New York Times*, Feb 28, 1993.

16. "Fletcher Knebel, Writer, 81, Dies"; "Fletcher Knebel; Newspaper Columnist, Novelist," *Los Angeles Times*, Feb. 28, 1993; and Fletcher Knebel, *Dark Horse* (Garden City NY: Doubleday, 1972).

17. "*Look* Reports," cabinet 4, drawer 1, folder 9, CFADU; *Congressional Record-House*, 15093, June 7, 1967; and "Warren Rogers Dies," *Washington Post*, Sept. 2, 2003.

18. "Manuscript Collections: Richard L. Wilson Papers," Herbert S. Hoover Presidential Library and Museum; "*Look* Reports," CFADU; and "*Look*—Quick—*Flair*: A Report by Cowles Magazine Inc.," 1950, in "Records of the *Look* Years," GCP, CFADU.

19. "Ernest Dunbar," *New York Times*, Feb. 13, 2011; "First Black Journalist in Mainstream Media Dies at 83," The-Latest.com, Feb.10, 2011; and "The Rev. Jesse Jackson: A New Black Cat," *Look*, Oct. 5, 1971.

20. "*Look* Magazine—Editorial Previews, 1963," cabinet 4, drawer 1, folder 3, GCP, CFADU.

21. Rosten, "Introduction: A View from Inside," GCP, CFADU; "We Hold These Truths," *Look*, Jan. 15, 1963; "To an Angry Young Man," *Look*, Nov. 12, 1968; "Leo Rosten," Britannica.com; "Leo Rosten, a Writer Who Helped Yiddish Make Its Way into English, Is Dead at 88," *New York Times*, Feb. 20, 1997; Interview, John Poppy, May 31, 2018; and Cowles Jr., *Mike Looks Back*, 191.

22. "*Look* Women's Department, 1947" cabinet 4, drawer 2, folder 19, GCP, CFADU; Rosten, "Introduction: A View from Inside"; "Women's Dept., 1953," box 23, folder 4, LRWHS; "Pat Coffin," box 3, folder 9, LRWHS; "*Look* Appoints Editor of Special Departments," press release, Nov. 17, 1955; "Patricia Coffin, Society Writer, Poet and *Look* Editor, Dies," *New York Times*, May 31, 1974; and "The American Women," *Look*, Jan. 11, 1966.

23. "Ex-Editor of *The Voice* to Buy *The Nation*," *New York Times*, Nov. 29, 1976.

24. Rosten, "Introduction: A View from Inside"; "Editor Named Envoy to Guinea," *New York Times*, Feb. 18, 1961; "Attwood Named to Head *Newsday*," *New York Times*, Sept. 2, 1970; "G. Cowles, Attwood, William 1967," cabinet 2, drawer 2, folder 4, GCP, CFADU; "W. Attwood, Ex-Publisher, Is Dead at 69," *New York Times*, April 16, 1989; Interview, Douglas Kirkland and Francoise Kirkland, April 13, 2016; "A Look at *Look*," ca. 1959, in "*Look* Magazine—Promotion, 1943–1961," cabinet 2, drawer 2, folder 4, GCP, CFADU; "*Look* Magazine, 1946–1968," cabinet 3, drawer 4, folder 5, GCP, CFADU; William Attwood, *Present at the Misconception: Twilight Struggle—Tales of the Cold War* (New York: HarperCollins, 1987); "Editor Named Envoy to Guinea"; and Leonard, *Walking on the Edge of the World*, 361–62.

25. "Edward M. Korry Dies," *Washington Post*, Jan. 30, 2003; and Rosten, "Introduction: A View from Inside."

26. "RIP Leonard Gross," May 1, 2015, lindengross.com; Leonard Gross, *The Last Jews in Berlin* (New York: Basic Books, 1981); and *"Look* Magazine, 1946–1968."

27. J. Robert Moskin, *American Heritage*, https://www.americanheritage.com/users/robert -moskin#:~:text=J.,from%20Harvard%20and%20Columbia%2C%20Mr; "CCI Press Releases 1967–68," cabinet 2, drawer 3, folder 8; "A Look at *Look*"; and *"Look* Magazine, 1946–1968."

28. "Edmund Stevens, 81, a Reporter in Moscow for 40 Years, Is Dead," *New York Times*, May 27, 1992.

29. Christopher S. Wren, *Walking to Vermont: From Times Square into the Green Mountains: A Homeward Adventure* (New York: Simon & Schuster, 2004); Interview, Douglas Kirkland and Francoise Kirkland; and "Joseph Roddy," *New York Times*, May 26, 2002.

30. "Ira Mothner," Aug. 19, 2014, Columbia Center for Oral History Research; *"Look* Magazine, 1946–1968"; and "Thomas B. Morgan, Writer, Editor, and Lindsay Press Aide, Dies at 87," *New York Times*, June 18, 2014.

31. "Jack Star: 1920–2009," *Chicago Tribune*, July 19, 2009; "Frank Trippett, Writer and Editor," *New York Times*, June 22, 1998; "Story of *Look*," cabinet 8, drawer 2, folder 2, GCADU; "Chandler Brossard, Prolific Writer, 71, Was Self-Educated," *New York Times*, Sept. 1, 1993; "Spiro," *Look*, Aug. 27, 1971; and *Dictionary of Literary Biography, Vol. 16: The Beats: Literary Bohemians in Postwar America* (Detroit: Gale, 1983).

32. Cowles Jr., *Mike Looks Back*; *"Look* Magazine—Editorial Previews, 1963"; and "Foundation Gives Three Health Awards," *New York Times*, Apr. 29, 1957.

33. "Tim Cohane, 76," *New York Times*, Jan. 24, 1989; "Leonard Shecter, Sportswriter, *Ball Four* Co-Author Is Dead," *New York Times*, Jan. 20, 1974; and Cowles Jr., *Mike Looks Back*.

34. Cowles Jr., *Mike Looks Back*, chap. 5; *"Look* Editorial Staff"; "Peck Wins Honor," *New York Times*, Feb. 4, 1947; and Interview, Douglas Kirkland and Francoise Kirkland.

35. Cowles Jr., *Mike Looks Back*, chap. 3; "Klein-Lang Ceremony Solemnized," *Minneapolis Morning Tribune*, Dec. 30, 1962; and "Morton Hunt," *New York Times*, March 15, 2016.

36. "George Benneyan, 1959," cabinet 2, drawer 2, folder 6, GCP, CFADU; *"Look* Magazine— Editorial Department, 1946–1968," cabinet 4, drawer 1, folder 1, GCP, CFADU; "*Look*—Quick—*Flair*"; and *"Look* Magazine Photograph Collection," LOC; and Rosten, "Introduction: A View from the Inside."

37. Jay Satterfield, "Merle Armitage: Accent on Taste," University of Iowa, n.d.; "Merle Armitage, 82, Art Publisher, Dies," *New York Times*, March 18, 1975; "The Press: The New *Look*," *Time*, June 7, 1948; "Advertising: Art Director in Starring Role," *New York Times*, April 9, 1967; Leo Rosten, "Introduction: A View from Inside"; "Gardner Cowles: Creative Editor with a Quest for Insight into World Affairs," *Printers' Ink*, April 10, 1959; and Interviews, Will Hopkins, Nov. 22, 2016 and Jan., 12, 2017.

38. Interview, Will Hopkins; Interview, Douglas Kirkland and Francoise Kirkland; and Margret Rhodes, "Allen Hurlburt," American Institute of Graphic Arts, Aug. 14, 2017.

39. Interview, Will Hopkins; and Interview with Pat Sayer Fusco by Anthony Fusco, April 12, 2018.

40. Norman Rockwell, *The Problem We All Live With, Look,* Jan. 14, 1964; Norman Rockwell, *Murder in Mississippi* and "Southern Justice," *Look,* June 29, 1965; "Norman Rockwell, Artist of Americana, Dead at 84," *New York Times,* Nov. 10, 1978; Interview, Gilbert Maurer, Nov. 28, 2016; "The Peace Corps," *Look,* June 14, 1966; "I Paint the Candidates," *Look,* Oct. 20, 1964; Norman Rockwell Museum, "Changing Times: Norman Rockwell's Art for *Look* Magazine," Stockbridge MA, Jan 11–May 1, 2018, https://www.nrm .org/2017/01/Look/; and "Rockwell and Race, 1961–1968," PopHistoryDig.com.

41. "Arthur Rothstein, 70, Is Dead," *New York Times,* Nov. 12, 1985; "Look at America," cabinet 4, drawer 1, folder 8, GCP, CFADU; Arthur Rothstein, *Photojournalism* (New York: Watson-Guptill, 1973); Rosten, "Introduction: A View from Inside"; "Dan Mich Executive Correspondence—Benneyan, 1957–59," box 3, folder 4, LRWHS; Interview, Anthony Fusco with Paul Fusco; Interview, Douglas Kirkland; Philippe D. Mather, *Stanley Kubrick at Look Magazine: Authorship and Genre in Photojournalism and Film* (Chicago: Intellect Books, 2013); and "Camera Notes," *New York Times,* May 5, 1963.

42. "Photographs, 1947–1968," cabinet 6, drawer 2, folder 1; "Story of *Look,*" cabinet 5, drawer 2, folder 3, GCP, CFADU; "*Look* Magazine—Editorial Department, 1946–1968"; "George Benneyan, 1959"; "*Look* Magazine—Editorial Department, 1946–1968"; "*Look*— Quick—*Flair*"; "*Look* Magazine Photograph Collection," LOC; "At 94, Tony Vaccaro *Looks* Back at His Brutal Images of World War II," *Newsday,* June 7, 2017; Interview, Pat Sayer Fusco, April 12, 2018; and Cowles Jr., *Mike Looks Back,* chap. 6.

43. "*Look* Editorial Staff"; "Young Man with Ideas and a Camera," *New York Times,* Jan. 14, 1951; "See a Different Kind of Stanley Kubrick Film," Museum of the City of New York, May 3, 2018; and Mather, *Kubrick at Look Magazine,* 51.

44. "About This Collection," *Look* Magazine Photograph Collection, LOC.

45. "James Karales, Photographer of Social Upheaval, Dies at 71," *New York Times,* April 5, 2002; James H. Karales Photographs, Archive of Documentary Arts, Duke University; Julian Cox with Rebekah Jacob and Monica Karales, *Controversy and Hope: The Civil Rights Photographs of James Karales* (Columbia: University of South Carolina Press, 2013); "James Karales," Rebekah Jacob Gallery, n.d.; "Civil Rights, One Person and One Photo at a Time," *New York Times,* April 22, 2013.

46. Clement Cheroux and Linde Lehtinen, eds., *The Train: RFK's Last Journey* (San Francisco: San Francisco Museum of Modern Art, 2018); "William Arthur, Legal Files," box 16, folder 25, LRWHS; Jack V. Fox, with photos by Paul Fusco and Douglas Jones, *Youth Quake* (New York: Cowles Education Corp., 1967); Nadine Birner, "Email Interview with Paul Fusco," April 26, 2010; and Interviews with Pat Sayer Fusco and Paul Fusco, April 9 and 12, 2018.

47. "Stanley Tretick," *New York Times,* July 20, 1999; "Photographer Stanley Tretick, 77, Dies," *Washington Post,* July 23, 1999; "The President and His Son," *Look,* Dec. 3, 1963;

and Kitty Kelley, *Capturing Camelot: Stanley Tretick's Iconic Images of the Kennedys* (New York: St. Martin's Press, 2012).

48. "John F. Vachon," *New York Times*, April 21, 1975; Thomas Morgan, "John Vachon: A Certain Look," *American Heritage*, February 1989; "Photographs That Speak Quietly of War and Grief," *New York Times*, Dec. 24, 2006; Interview, Douglas Kirkland; and "Charlotte Brooks, 95," *New York Times*, March 25, 2014; "Story of *Look*," cabinet 8, drawer 2, folder 2, CFADU; and Cowles Jr., *Mike Looks Back*, chap. 6.

49. Cowles Jr., *Mike Looks Back*; "Personnel Memos 1953," box 6, folder 5, LRWHS; Interview, Anthony Fusco with Paul Fusco; Interview, Douglas Kirkland and Francoise Kirkland; "Paris by Penn," *Look*, July 26, 1966; and "*Look* Editorial Staff."

50. "Story of *Look*—1958–1959," cabinet 5, drawer 2, folder 1, GCP, CFADU; and Cowles Jr., *Mike Looks Back*, chap. 5.

51. "Committee for Economic Development, 1959–1968," cabinet 2, drawer 3, folder 3, GCP, CFADU; and Rosten, "Introduction: A View from the Inside"; and Interview, Alan Waxenberg, Sept. 1, 2020. "Hemingway Out of the Jungle," *New York Times*, Jan. 26, 1954; and "*Look* Magazine, 1946–1968," cabinet 3, drawer 3, folder 5, GCP, CFADU.

52. "*Look*—Demise, 1971–1973"; Paul G. Hoffman, "Crash Program for Peace," *Look*, Jan. 21, 1958; and "Records of the *Look* Years, 1972."

53. "How Would You Like Your Daughter to Marry William F. Buckley, Jr," *Look*, March 21, 1967.

54. Daniel Boorstin, "The End of Our Two Party World?," *Look*, Aug. 20, 1968; Childs, "Nuclear Talks: Survival or Armageddon?," *Look*, Dec. 30, 1969; Hentoff, "Smothers Brothers: Who Controls TV?," *Look*, June 24, 1969; Jackson, "Unfinished Business of America," *Look*, July 13, 1971; and Edward Kennedy, "Let Indians Run Indian Policy," *Look*, June 2, 1970.

55. "Gardner Cowles: A Dignified Passion for a Foreign Policy That Will Win Peace," *Printers' Ink*, April 17, 1959.

56. "Donald Perkins, an Executive at *Look*, Is Dead," *New York Times*, May 22, 1973; Interview, Gilbert Maurer; and "Advertising: New Horizon for Venture," *New York Times*, July 31, 1966.

57. "Records of the *Look* Years, 1972"; "Myers, 1958–1960," box 14, folder 13, LRWHS; "Advertising," *New York Times*, April 4, 1962; Interview, Alan Waxenberg, Sept. 1 and 2, 2020; and "Organization Chart, 1954–1955" box 21, folders 20–21, LRWHS.

58. "Samuel O. Shapiro, 87," *New York Times*, Sept. 6, 1990; Interview, Alan Waxenberg; and Interview, Gilbert Maurer.

59. Cowles Jr., *Mike Looks Back*, chap. 5; Interview, Gilbert Maurer; Interview, Alan Waxenberg; Correspondence, Herbert Strentz; "Gardner Cowles Leaves Top Jobs," *New York Times*, May 15, 1964 "Cowles Communications Elects Three," *New York Times*, May 13, 1967; and George Benneyan, "The Story of *Look*" (unpub. ca. 1959), GCP, CFADU.

60. "Thomas R. Shepard Jr., *Look* Magazine's Last Publisher, Dies at 96," *New York Times*, May 4, 2015; "Joel Harnett, 80," *New York Times*, Aug. 15, 2006; Interview, Thomas R.

Shepard III, Nov. 22, 2016; Interview, Patricia Carbine; Leonard, *Walking on the Edge of the World*, 352–62; and "Advertising," *New York Times*.

61. Cowles Jr., *Mike Looks Back*.

5. POSTWAR PROSPERITY

1. Council of Economic Advisers, *Economic Report of the President* (Washington DC: Government Printing Office [GPO], 1949), 1, 3, 63; Donald Montgomery, "Purchasing Power for Prosperity" (United Auto Workers [UAW], 1945); Marion B. Folsom, Columbia Oral History Project Memoir, Eisenhower Administration, volumes 55–56, Columbia University Libraries, New York; Committee for Economic Development (CED), "Toward More Production, More Jobs, and More Freedom" (October 1945); Advertising Council, "The American Roundtable Discussions on People's Capitalism" (1957); Pamphlets and leaflets produced between 1953 and 1960, boxes 2 and 8, RG 306-99-008, entry 1252, Records of the United States Information Agency, National Archives and Records Administration (NARA).

2. "The Miracle of America," *Look*, May 25, 1948; Robert Griffith, "The Selling of America: The Advertising Council and American Business, 1942–1960," *Business History Review* 57 (August 1983); and Andrew L. Yarrow, *Measuring America: How Economic Growth Came to Define American Greatness in the Late 20th Century* (Amherst: University of Massachusetts Press), 87.

3. Sinclair Weeks, "I Predict We'll Have Greater Prosperity," *Look*, Jan. 11, 1955: and "How America Feels as It Enters the Soaring Sixties," *Look*, Jan. 5, 1960.

4. "Norman Bel Geddes: He Molds the Future," *Look*, March 31, 1938; "Tomorrow's Houses," *Look*, June 7, 1938; "The Airliner of Tomorrow," *Look* Nov. 22, 1938; and "The Auto Industry Looks 20 Years Ahead," *Look*, Oct. 24, 1939.

5. "Henry Kaiser: The Man Behind the Job," *Look*, Feb. 6, 1945.

6. Eric Johnston, "More Production Means Better Living for You," *Look*, Dec. 10, 1946.

7. Paul G. Hoffman, "More Machines Mean More Wages: Mass Production Raises Living Standards," *Look*, Aug. 19, 1947; and Paul G. Hoffman, "Suicide by Tariff?," *Look*, Feb. 23, 1954.

8. "Baruch Answers," *Look*, July 3, 1951; and J. Paul Getty, "What's Wrong with American Business?," *Look*, Sept. 1, 1959.

9. "Who Gets Our National Income," *Look*, March 16, 1946. See: Lizabeth Cohen, *A Consumers' Republic: The Politics of Mass Consumption in Postwar America* (New York: Vintage, 2003).

10. "We Are Living Better in 1949," *Look*, May 5, 1949; and "16 Top Economists Predict What Your Dollar Will Buy in December," *Look*, Aug. 14, 1951.

11. Charles Edward Wilson of GE was often called "Electric Charlie" to distinguish him from Charles Erwin Wilson, Eisenhower's secretary of defense and a former chairman of General Motors, who was called "Engine Charlie."

12. "Wall Street Works for Main Street," *Look*, May 20, 1952; and "USA Opportunity Unlimited," *Look*, June 7, 1949.

13. "Supermarkets," *Look*, Nov. 6, 1951; "American Dream of Christmas," *Look*, Dec. 1, 1953; "Child's World of Toys," *Look*, Dec. 15, 1953; "The Great American Appliance," *Look*, May 3, 1955; "American Kitchen Takes Off in Two Directions," *Look*, May 1, 1956 "The Fate of Our Economy Rides with 1959 Cars," *Look*, Oct. 28, 1958; "Extra House," *Look* Aug. 20, 1957; and "City Cats," *Look*, Oct. 5, 1954.

14. "The 'LOOK' House," *Look*, Aug. 3, 1948; Editors of *Look*, *Suburbia: The Good Life in Our Exploding Utopia* (New York: Cowles Education Corp., 1968); and "Levittown Houses," *Look*, Oct. 20, 1948.

15. "'Add-a-Room' O'Reilly," *Look*, April 21, 1953; and "Ordeal in Levittown," *Look*, Aug. 19, 1958.

16. "Instant Houses," *Look*, Sept 27, 1960; "Their First Home," *Look*, Jan 14, 1964; and "Expanding Florida" and "Boating on Lake Suwanee," *Look*, April 14, 1959.

17. "A House Is Not Just a Home. It's a Piggy Bank," *Look*, Jan 14, 1964.

18. "Primer on Better Living," *Look*, Nov. 26, 1946.

19. "The Great American Automobile," *Look*, Nov. 27, 1956; "The Fate of Our Economy"; and "1967 Automobile Preview," *Look*, Oct. 18, 1966.

20. "Custom Cars for Everyone," *Look*, Nov. 3, 1953; "First *Look* at the Gas Turbine Car," *Look*, Jan. 26, 1954; and "Case of the Care-less Car," *Look*, May 15, 1956; "High Horsepower," *Look*, Jan. 26, 1954; "Bill Ford Builds the Continental," *Look*, Nov. 16, 1954; "Motor Mayhem," *Look*, July 13, 1954; "In the Automotive Industry, Virgil Exner Is the Stylist on the Spot," *Look*, Nov. 30, 1954; "Automobile Has Many Lives," *Look*, June 1, 1954; and "Great American Automobile, 1896–1957," *Look*, Nov. 27, 1956.

21. "Leisure," *Look*, July 12, 1955; and "How to Retire in Florida on $2,000 a Year," *Look*, March 20, 1956.

22. "*Look* Books, 1946," cabinet 3, drawer 4, folder 4, CFADU; "Andrew H. Hepburn," *New York Times*, July 21, 1975; "Minneapolis Secretary Sees Europe for $1,000," *Look*, June 1, 1954; "Safari for a School Teacher," *Look*, Dec. 9, 1958; "The Great American Weekend," *Look*, July 10, 1956; "America's Dream Vacation," *Look*, June 14, 1955; "Europe 1960," *Look*, Aug. 16, 1960; and "Travel USA," *Look*, May 5, 1964.

23. Editors of *Fortune* in collaboration with Russell W. Davenport, *USA: The Permanent Revolution* (New York: Prentice Hall, 1951); Editors of *Fortune*, *The Fabulous Future* (New York: Fortune, 1956); "U.S. Economy," *Life*, Jan. 4, 1954; and Henry Luce, "Reformation of the World's Economies," *Fortune*, Feb. 1950.

24. "I Predict We'll Have Greater Prosperity," *Look*, Jan. 11, 1955; Fletcher Knebel, "The Welfare State Is Here to Stay," *Look*, Jan. 25, 1955; "CED, 1959–60," cabinet 2, drawer 3, folder 3, GCP, CFADU; and Geoffrey Crowther, "How Long Will World Prosperity Last?," Jan. 24, 1956.

25. Gardner Cowles, "What the Public Thinks about Big Business," *Look*, Feb. 8, 1955; Gardner Cowles, "An Optimistic Editor Looks at the Sixties," speech to the Institute

of Life Insurance, Waldorf-Astoria Hotel, Dec. 8, 1959, in "Speeches, 1942–1961," CFADU; and "Cowles Predicts No All-Out War," *Los Angeles Times*, Feb. 27, 1951.

26. William Attwood, "A New *Look* at Americans," *Look*, July 12, 1955.

27. Ben Duffy, "Why We Buy What We Buy," *Look*, June 12, 1956.

28. William Attwood, "The Soaring Sixties," *Look*, Jan. 5, 1960.

29. "Culture City," *Look*, Jan. 19, 1960.

30. John Gunther, "Quarter Century: Where Has It Left Us," *Look*, Jan. 2, 1962; "Inside the 20th Century," *Look*, Jan. 12, 1965; and "The Explosive Generation," *Look*, Jan. 3, 1961.

31. "How We Live," *Look*, Jan. 14, 1964; and "America's Mood Today," *Look*, June 29, 1965.

32. "California: The First Mass Aristocracy Anytime, Anywhere," *Look*, June 28, 1966; "California: A Promised Land for Millions of Migrating Americans," *Look*, Sept. 25, 1962; George Leonard, *Walking on the Edge of the World: A Memoir of the Sixties and Beyond* (Boston: Houghton Mifflin Harcourt, 1988), 240–48; and "California," *Life*, Oct. 19, 1962.

33. John Kenneth Galbraith, *The Affluent Society* (Boston: Houghton Mifflin, 1958).

34. "What's Become of the Okies," *Look*, Jan. 13, 1953; "Church Work with Migrant Labor," *Look*, July 12, 1955; "Children of Sharecroppers," *Look*, March 1937; Norman Thomas, "A Socialist Taunts the Major Parties," June 22, 1952; and Bernard Baruch, "Baruch Answers," *Look*, July 3, 1951.

35. Patricia Carbine, "In the Middle of the USA in Mid-20th Century," *Look*, July 7, 1959.

36. Charles A. Hill and Marguerite Helmers, eds., *Defining Visual Rhetorics* (Mahwah NJ: Lawrence Erlbaum, 2008).

37. "You Can't Get a Job After 45," *Look*, Nov. 9, 1948; and "Why Does He Work So Hard?," *Look*, March 4, 1958.

38. Fletcher Knebel, "The Scandal of Welfare Chiseling," *Look*, Nov. 7, 1961; Michael Harrington, "Closeup on Poverty," *Look*, Aug. 25, 1964; "War on Poverty," *Look*, June 13, 1967; and "California: The First Mass Aristocracy."

39. C. P. Snow, "Great Delusions," *Look*, Dec. 19, 1961; Gunnar Myrdal, "It's Time to Face the Future," Nov. 19, 1963; "Our Biggest Strike Peril: Fear of Automation," *Look*, April 25, 1961; Chandler Brossard, "A Growing National Problem: Teen-ager without a Job," *Look*, Feb. 27, 1962; "The Tense Generation," *Look*, Aug. 27, 1963; and "George Pleasures Them with Groceries," *Look*, May 5, 1964.

40. Walter Lippmann, "Why We Accept Cheating," *Look*, March 29, 1960; William Attwood, "Payola," *Look*, March 29, 1960; and "Morality U.S.A.," *Look*, Sept. 24, 1963.

41. Gray, "What Business Has to Do about Consumerism," *Look*, March 9, 1971; "Car Safety: Miracles or Mayhem?," *Look*, May 18, 1965; "Advertising," *New York Times*, Jan. 4, 1963; and "LBJ's Safety Boss: Babe in Bureaucracy's Jungle," *Look*, May 30, 1967.

42. Gray, "What Business Has to Do about Consumerism."

43. Chandler Brossard, "Who Says He's a Flop?," *Look*, Jan. 10, 1967; and "Fired at 49," *Look*, Dec. 1, 1970.

44. Abraham Ribicoff, "We Are Poisoning the Air," *Look*, Oct. 22, 1963: Lyndon Johnson, "Special Message to Congress on Conservation and Restoration of Natural Beauty," Feb. 8, 1965; and "Growth," *Look*, Jan. 12, 1971.
45. Eric Sevareid, "The World Still Moves Our Way," *Look*, July 9, 1968.
46. Nikolai Amosoff, "1991," *Look*, July 14, 1970; "Fired at 49"; Ira Mothner, "How Much Is Your Job Really Worth?," *Look*, April 20, 1971; and George Wallace, "Unfinished Business of America," *Look*, July 27, 1971.
47. Interview, John Poppy, April 12, 2018.

6. ANYTHING IS POSSIBLE

1. "Records of the *Look* Years, 1972," cabinet 4, drawer 2, folders 20 and 23, GCP, CFADU; and Gardner Cowles, "An Optimistic Editor *Look*s at the Sixties," speech to the Institute of Life Insurance, Waldorf-Astoria Hotel, Dec. 8, 1959, in "Speeches, 1942–1961," GCP, CFADU.
2. Bush, "As We May Think," *Life*, Sept. 10, 1945; "The Star-Studded Reaches of Measureless Space," *Life*, Dec. 20, 1954; "The Transplanted Heart," *Time*, Dec. 15, 1967; and "Let's Take Pride in American Science," *Look*, Oct. 11, 1960.
3. "Inside a Living Heart," *Look*, April 22, 1952.
4. "After the War—What?," *Look*, May 18, 1943; and "Electric Submarine of the Future," *Look*, Dec. 11, 1945.
5. "New Miracles Ahead," *Look*, Jan. 8, 1946; and "Your Last Chance," *Look*, 1946 (booklet).
6. "How Television Has Improved," *Look*, June 6, 1937; "Television's Boom Year," *Look*, July 20, 1948; "The Airliner of Tomorrow," *Look*, Nov. 22, 1938; and "Norman Bel Geddes: He Molds the Future," *Look*, March 31, 1938.
7. "Tomorrow's Houses," *Look*, June 7, 1938; "Prefabricated Houses," *Look*, March 29, 1939; and "The Auto Industry *Look*s 20 Years Ahead," *Look*, Oct. 24, 1939.
8. "Medical Miracles of the Year," *Look*, Jan. 26, 1941.
9. "Ten Years of *Look*," *Look*, Oct. 29, 1946; "Household Gadgets," *Look*, Oct. 15, 1946; and "Science Forecasts," *Look*, Nov. 26, 1946.
10. "These Food Dreams Will Come True in 1947," *Look*, Jan. 7, 1947; "Tomorrow's Food Here Today," *Look*, May 10, 1949; and "They Live with Atomic Food," *Look*, Feb. 7, 1956.
11. "The Great American Appliance," *Look*, May 3, 1955; "Cooking with Radar," *Look*, Feb. 5, 1957; "Automatic Housekeeping," *Look*, May 14, 1957; "Ladies, Let the Chemicals Do Your Housework," *Look*, Oct. 6, 1953; "How the Nortons Beat the Heat," *Look*, July 23, 1957; "Low Down on Hi-Fi," *Look*, Oct. 15, 1957; "Ever Had the Mad Impulse to Jump in a Pool with Your Clothes On?," *Look*, May 31, 1955; and "Summer Shelters," *Look*, May 20, 1952.
12. "Here's Your First View of Disneyland," *Look*, Nov. 2, 1954.
13. Sarnoff, "Transoceanic TV," Sept. 17, 1950; "Transocean TV Is on its Way," *Look*, Jan. 13, 1953; "I Predict Color Controversy in TV," *Look*, Jan. 11, 1955; and "Let's Give the Public a Chance at Pay TV," *Look*, March 20, 1956.

14. "Custom Cars for Everyone," *Look*, Nov. 3, 1953; "Case of the Care-less Car," *Look*, May 15, 1956; and "In the Automotive Industry, Virgil Exner Is the Stylist on the Spot," *Look*, Nov. 30, 1.

15. "The Future Airplane, the Consolidated Vulture 3," *Look*, Sept. 4, 1945; "Alaska: Air Travel Creates Opportunity," *Look*, Jan. 12, 1946; "How You Will Travel in 1947," *Look*, Jan. 7, 1947; "1,700 Mile-an-Hour Plane," *Look*, Dec. 24, 1946; and "The Jet Helicopter Arrives," *Look*, April 24, 1951.

16. "Southern Pacific—the Railroad Giant," *Look*, Dec. 25, 1945; "New Trains," *Look*, July 20, 1948; "Debut of a Train," June 3, 1952; and "Train That Rides on Air: Y Train," *Look*, June 28, 1955.

17. "Airphibian," *Look*, March 18, 1947; "Atomic Miracles We Will See," *Look*, Aug. 25, 1953; and "San Francisco to New York in 75 Minutes by Rocket," Jan. 11, 1955.

18. "You May Live Forever," *Look*, March 24, 1953.

19. "You Can Live Longer," *Look*, March 27, 1951; "Better Health for Millions," *Look*, Sept. 11, 1951; and "Spare Parts for Humans," *Look*, Jan. 13, 1953.

20. "Science Is Conquering Polio, Heart Disease, Cancer," *Look*, Sept. 8, 1953; and "You May Live Forever."

21. W. Bruce Fye, *Caring for the Heart: Mayo Clinic and the Rise of Specialization* (Oxford: Oxford University Press, 2015), 236; "New Miracles to Save Your Heart," *Look*, Sept. 7, 1954; "My Heart Is Normal Again after a Surgical Miracle," *Look*, Feb. 8, 1955; "First Photos Taken Inside a Beating Heart," *Look*, Oct. 29, 1957; and "Surgery Finds a New Way to Curb the No. 1 Killer," *Look*, April 17, 1956.

22. "Medical Electronics," *Look*, Feb. 22, 1955; "X-Rays in Color," *Look*, May 14, 1957; "Push-Button Hospital," *Look*, Dec. 15, 1953; "I Predict the End of Polio," *Look*, Jan. 11, 1955; "The Truth about the Salk Vaccine," *Look*, July 26, 1955; Centers for Disease Control and Prevention, "Polio Elimination in the United States" 2007; "Now They Can See Your Brain," *Look*, Aug. 10, 1954; and "Exploring the Brain," *Look*, Feb. 17, 1959.

23. "Glasses That Can't Be Seen," *Look*, July 13, 1954; "Children Have Benefited Most from Medical Advances," *Look*, April 17, 1956; and "Childless Couples Can Have Babies," *Look*, Sept. 17, 1957.

24. "The Education of Dr. Fuchs," *Look*, Dec. 27, 1955; "Your Doctor's New Conscience," *Look*, Dec. 11, 1955; and "Violence, Pain, and Compassion," *Look*, Feb. 18, 1958.

25. "State of the Nation's Health," *Look*, April 17, 1956; "A Report on Hospitals," *Look*, Feb. 3, 1959; and "Problem of the Aged Is Still Not Solved," *Look*, May 1, 1956.

26. "Man Prepares for Space Travel," *Look*, Dec. 10, 1957.

27. "Space Timetable for the 1960s," *Look*, Jan. 5, 1960; "Space," *Look*, Jan. 16, 1962; "Our Boys in Space," *Look*, June 19, 1962; "Collier Trophy Given for Atlas," *Look*, Dec. 6, 1960; "The Man Behind Our Mission to Mars," *Look*, July 13, 1965; "Our Secret Eye in Space," *Look*, Nov. 15, 1966; "Longest Step: Space Suits," *Look*, April 20, 1965; and "Man on the Moon," *Look*, Jan. 10, 1967.

28. Arthur C. Clarke and C. P. Snow, "Views from Earth on the Odyssey in Space," *Look*, Feb. 4, 1959; "Moon Landing," *Look*, Aug. 26, 1969; and C. P. Snow, "Eating in Space: It's No Picnic up There," *Look*, July 15, 1969.

29. "Man on the Moon," Jan. 10, 1967; "Behind Apollo," *Look*, July 15, 1969; Arthur C. Clarke, "Apollo and Beyond," *Look*, July 15, 1969; "Final Impossibility: Man's Tracks on the Moon," *Look*, Dec. 30, 1969; Pierre Mion, "Norman Rockwell's Ghost: The Most Artistic Collaboration of the Entire Apollo Program," *Air and Space*, Sept. 2006; and Norman Rockwell Museum.

30. "Inside Detroit," *Look*, Oct. 25, 1960; "3D," *Look*, Feb. 25, 1964; "Supersonic Hot Seat," *Look*, May 5, 1964; and "A Jet-Age Expert Gives Some Blunt Answers," *Look*, Dec. 14, 1965.

31. "The Next 25 Years," "1987 Newsletter," and "How the Next 25 Years Will Change Your Home," *Look*, Jan. 16, 1962.

32. "New York World's Fair Preview Issue," *Look*, Feb. 11, 1964; and "Montreal's Expo '67," *Look*, April 4, 1967.

33. "The Next 25 Years," and "Space," *Look*, Jan. 16, 1962.

34. "Automation," *Look*, Jan. 12, 1965; "The Generation Gap," *Look*, Feb. 21, 1967; "Fashion in 25 Years," Jan. 16, 1962; and "Fired at 49," *Look*, Dec. 1, 1970.

35. Gene Shalit, "The Big College Craze: Dating by Computer," *Look*, Feb. 22, 1969.

36. "California: The First Mass Aristocracy Anytime, Anywhere," *Look*, June 28, 1966.

37. "'70s," "The Future of Power," "Vision of the Human Revolution," "*Look* Symposium: 21 Hours to the Future," Jan. 13, 1970; and Interviews, John Poppy, May 21 and 31, 2018.

38. "Push-Button Movies: The Video-Cassette Revolution," *Look*, Nov. 3, 1970; and "Mass Urban Transit: It's Hell Now, but Help's Coming," *Look*, April 29, 1971.

39. "They're Giving Their Emotions to Science," *Look*, April 26, 1960; "A Cancer Patient Is Cured," *Look*, July 5, 1960; "Psychiatry, the Troubled Science," *Look*, Feb. 2, 1960; and "The Couch vs. the Pill," *Look*, Feb. 2, 1960.

40. "Babies before Birth," *Look*, June 5, 1962; and "My Checkup at Mayo's," March 24, 1964.

41. "The Next 25 Years," "Medical Electronics Will Give New Life to Your Body," "Man Will Master the Secret of Creation," *Look*, Jan. 16, 1962; and "Taking Life in Our Own Hands–A Historic Step: The Test-Tube Baby Is Coming," April 18, 1971.

42. "Medicine's Frontier: Rebuilding the Human Body," *Look*, June 30, 1964; "There's More Than Cholesterol behind Heart Attacks," *Look*, Feb. 9, 1971; "A New World for Surgery," *Look*, May 4, 1965; "Brain Damage Can Be Prevented," *Look*, Sept. 5, 1967; "How to Choose Your Baby's Sex," *Look*, April 21, 1970; "Heart-Saver Squad," *Look*, Feb. 4, 1969; Nikolai Amosoff, "1991," *Look*, July 14, 1970; and "Side Effects," *Look*, Dec. 31, 1963.

43. "The Revolution in Medicine," "Crisis in Britain's Health Plan," "A Doctor Views 19 Years of Socialized Medicine," and "For Us, the Big Change Is Now," *Look*, March 21, 1967.

44. "The Soaring Sixties," *Look*, Jan. 5, 1960.
45. "The Brink of a New Age," *Look*, Jan. 16, 1962.
46. "Morality USA," *Look*, Sept. 24, 1963; "The Tense Generation," *Look*, Aug. 27, 1963; George Leonard "A New Liberal Manifesto," *Look*, May 28, 1968; and "What's Happening to Sexual Privacy?," *Look*, Oct. 20, 1970.
47. "The Computer Data Bank: Will It Kill Our Freedom?," *Look*, June 25, 1968.
48. "That Evil Los Angeles Smog," *Look*, June 20, 1950; Pete Seeger, "To Save the Dying Hudson," *Look*, Aug. 26, 1969; David Perlman, "America the Beautiful?" and "Land Lovers," Lillie Leonard, "Why Must They Die?," and Allen Ginsberg, "By Air—Albany to Baltimore," *Look*, Nov. 4, 1969.
49. "Earth Day: The Fight to Save America Starts Now," "Five Who Care," "Ladies Save the Lakes," and "The Most Beautiful View in the World," *Look*, April 21, 1970.
50. "Fun in the Water" and "Joys of Clear Water," *Look*, July 14, 1970; "Happy Birthday Earth Day!," "Earth Week," "What Have We Done?" "Garbage Power," "Introducing William Ruckelshaus, Who?," and "What Has Business Done," *Look*, May 4, 1971.
51. Cowles, "*Look* to the Future," *Look*, Jan. 10, 1967; and Leonard, "A New Liberal Manifesto."

7. COVERING CIVIL RIGHTS

1. "Cowles, 80, Looks Back on Fabulous Publishing Career," *New York Times*, Feb. 6, 1983; Cowles Jr., *Mike Looks Back*, 204; and "The Public Will Be Served," "Publicity Material," cabinet 4, drawer 4, GCP, GCADU.
2. "Ernest Dunbar," *New York Times*, Feb. 13, 2011; and "Fashion Designer Hires Negro Model," *New York Times*, June 23, 1961.
3. "Publicity Material," cabinet 4, drawer 4, file 15, GCP, GCADU; and "Judge in Alabama Bars *Look* Magazine," *New York Times*, Aug. 23, 1959.
4. "*Look* Magazine—Editorial Previews, 1963," cabinet 4, drawer 1, folder 3, GCP, CFADU; "Leonard Freed," *New York Times*, Dec. 4, 2006; and "Ernest Dunbar," *New York Times*, Feb. 13, 2011.
5. "There Is Trouble in the South," *Look*, Nov. 21, 1939; and "Age: 19, Color: Negro, Occupation: None," *Look*, Dec. 3, 1940.
6. Jack Manning, "Elk's Parade," *Look*, May 21, 1940; Art Simon, "The Photo League's New York," *Cineaste* 37, no. 4 (Fall 2012); "New York's Photo League: Black Lives Mattered before It Was a Movement," Feb. 28, 2017, The Jewish Museum; and "The Photo League: Remembering the Radical New York Collective That Brought a Social Conscience to Street Photos," *Artsy*, Aug. 6, 2013.
7. Wallace Stegner and the editors of *Look*, *One Nation* (Boston: Houghton Mifflin, 1945); "Story of *Look*," cabinet 5, drawer 2, folder 1, GCP, CFADU; "Age: 19, Color: Negro, Occupation: None"; "Prejudice: Our Postwar Battle," *Look*, May 1, 1945; and "Case Presented in Text and Pictures on America's Opportunity," *New York Times*, Sept. 29, 1945.

8. "Prejudice: Our Postwar Battle"; and "Georgia Election: National Test," *Look*, July 9, 1946.
9. Hodding Carter, "A Southerner Tells What's Wrong with the North," *Look*, Aug. 16, 1949, "The Negro Problem—North and South," *Look*, Dec. 6, 1949; "The Negro Problem Moves North," *Look*, Apr 8, 1952; and Hodding Carter, "A Wave of Terror Threatening the South," *Look*, March 22, 1955.
10. "Baseball's First Negro: The Dodgers Sign Jackie Robinson—First Breach in Game's Racial Barrier," *Look*, Nov. 27, 1945; "A Branch Grows in Brooklyn," *Look*, March 19, 1946; "Jackie Robinson," *Look*, Dec. 19, 1950; "U.S. Civil Rights Trail Honors the Jackie Robinson Training Camp," Major League Baseball, n.d.; Jackie Robinson, "Now I Know Why They Boo Me," *Look*, Jan. 25, 1955, Feb. 8 and Feb. 22, 1955; "Why I'm Quitting Baseball," *Look*, Jan. 22, 1957; and "For Jackie Robinson's Centennial, an Exhibition of Rarely Seen Photographs," *New York Times*, Feb. 5, 2019.
11. "The Negro Vote," *Look*, Oct. 7, 1952; "Where the Candidates Stand on Civil Rights," *Look*, Nov. 4, 1952; and Carl T. Rowan, "How Far from Slavery?," *Look*, Jan 15, 1952.
12. "White Supremacy," *Life*, Aug. 4, 1952; and "The Flood Leaves Its Victims on the Bread Line," *Life*, Feb. 15, 1936.
13. "Squadron Commander," *Look*, Oct. 19, 1954; "What Happens When Segregation Ends?," *Look*, May 4, 1954; and "J. Edgar Hoover," *Look*, Sept. 7, 1954.
14. "A Wave of Terror Threatening the South," *Look*, March 22, 1955; and "The South and I," *Look*, June 28, 1955.
15. MacKinlay Kantor, "MacKinlay Kantor and Andersonville," *Look*, Dec. 13, 1955.
16. William Bradford Huie, "The Shocking Story of an Approved Killing in Mississippi," *Look*, Jan. 24, 1956; and William Bradford Huie, "What's Happened to Emmett Till Killers," *Look*, Jan. 22, 1957.
17. Christopher Metress, *The Lynching of Emmett Till: A Documentary Narrative* (Charlottesville: University of Virginia Press, 2002); Bob Dylan, "The Ballad of Emmett Till," 1962; "The Ghost of Emmett Till," *New York Times Magazine*, July 31, 2005; "Emmett Till, Whose Martyrdom Launched the Civil Rights Movement," *New York Times*, Aug. 28, 2016; "U.S. Reopens '55 Murder Case, Flashpoint of Civil Rights Era," *New York Times*, May 11, 2004; "U.S. Reopens Probe into 1955 Killing of Emmett Till," *Wall Street Journal*, July 12, 2018: Devery S. Anderson, *Emmett Till: The Murder That Shocked the World and Propelled the Civil Rights Movement* (Jackson: University of Mississippi Press, 2016); and "Anti-Lynching Bill, Long Sought, Passes in House," *Washington Post*, Feb. 27, 2020.
18. Carl T. Rowan, "What Negroes Really Want," Ervin, "The Case for Segregation," "The South vs. the Supreme Court," and "Is This the Pattern of the Future?," *Look*, April 3, 1956; and "*Look* Wins a Medal for Story on South," *New York Times*, May 5, 1957.
19. Riche Richardson, "Framing Rosa Parks in Reel Time," *Southern Quarterly* 50, no. 3 (Spring 2013); Ruth Ashby, *Rosa Parks: Freedom Rider* (New York: Sterling, 2008); "The Man behind Rosa Parks," *New York Times*, Dec. 7, 2005; and Barry Schwartz, "Collective

Forgetting and the Symbolic Power of Oneness: The Strange Apotheosis of Rosa Parks," *Social Psychology Quarterly* 72, no. 2 (June 2009): 123–42.

20. "Jim Crow Northern Style," *Look*, June 26, 1956; "Subtle Whip," *Look*, June 26, 1956; and Carl T. Rowan, "Who Gets the Negro Vote?," *Look*, Nov. 13, 1956.

21. MacKinlay Kantor, "If the South Had Won the Civil War," *Look*, Nov. 22, 1960.

22. "Inside the NAACP," *Look*, Aug. 6, 1957; "How It Looks from the South," *Look*, May 27, 1958; "Chicago's Segregation Tragedy," *Look*, Sept. 30, 1958; "Georgia Minister Offers a Solution for the South," *Look*, May 28, 1957; "Charlotte Brooks, 95," *New York Times*, March 25, 2014; "The Real Little Rock Story," "Members of the Mob," and "Georgia: Rallying Point of Defiance," *Look*, Nov. 12, 1957; Minnijean Brown, "What They Did to Me in Little Rock," *Look*, June 24, 1958; "Little Rock from the Inside," *Look*, March 17, 1959; "Memo from Mississippi," *Look*, Jan. 19, 1960; and "Eight Klans Bring Terror to the South," *Look*, April 30, 1957.

23. "Civil Rights Put in New Frontier," *New York Times*, Dec. 7, 1958.

24. "Ordeal in Levittown," *Look*, Aug. 19, 1958.

25. "First Negro in Town," *Look*, Dec. 6, 1960; and "The Negro in Florida," *Look*, April 14, 1959.

26. Marie Jahoda, "What Is Prejudice?," *Look*, May 24, 1960.

27. "Inside Negro Arica" and "South Africa: Where the White Man Rules," *Look*, June 23, 1959; "Story of *Look*," cabinet 8, drawer 2, folder 2, GCP, GCADU; and Robert Kennedy, "Suppose God Is Black?," *Look*, Aug. 23, 1966.

28. "Sitdowns: The South's New Time Bomb," *Look*, July 5, 1960; "School for Sit-ins," *Look*, Aug. 30, 1960; "Introduction to a Sit-in," *Look*, Jan. 3, 1961; "The South's War against Negro Votes," *Look*, May 21, 1963; and Interview, John Poppy, April 12, 2018.

29. "The Second Battle of Atlanta" and "A Man's Battle for Freedom," *Look*, April 25, 1961.

30. "The Negro in America Today," *Look*, April 10, 1962; and "From Little Rock to Hyannis: A New Life for the Bells," *Look*, Dec. 18, 1962.

31. "Visit with Martin Luther King," *Look*, Feb. 12, 1963; and "Minister Who's Not Afraid to Fight," *Look*, May 31, 1966.

32. "Look Magazine Attacked Over Mississippi Article," *New York Times*, Dec. 20, 1962; "Five Days in Mississippi," *Look*, July 16, 1963; "*Look* Magazine—Editorial Previews"; James H. Meredith, "I Can't Fight Alone," *Look*, Feb. 6, 1963; and Charles Morgan, "Birmingham: I Saw a City Die," *Look*, Dec. 3, 1963.

33. "When the Negro Faces North" and "A White Man *Looks* at the Negro," *Look*, Dec. 17, 1963.

34. "Civil Rights Yes—But What about Jobs?," *Life*, Nov. 8, 1963.

35. Norman Rockwell, *The Problem We All Live With*, *Look*, Jan. 14, 1964.

36. Norman Rockwell, *Murder in Mississippi* in "Southern Justice," *Look*, June 29, 1965.

37. "Changing Times: Norman Rockwell's Art for *Look* Magazine"; and "New Kids in the Neighborhood," *Look*, May 16, 1967.

38. Martin Luther King Jr., "It's a Difficult Thing to Teach a President," *Look*, Nov. 17, 1964; "The Attorney General of the U.S. Talks," *Look*, June 1, 1965; and Norman Rockwell, *How Goes the War on Poverty*, *Look*, July 27, 1965.

39. William Bradford Huie, "Death of an Innocent," *Look*, March 24, 1964.

40. "Mississippi: Attack on Bigotry," *Look*, Sept. 8, 1964.

41. Robert W. Spike, "Our Churches' Sin Against the Negro," *Look*, May 18, 1965; "James Karales, 71; Photographed Selma March," *Los Angeles Times*, April 8, 2002; and Bob Shamis and Howard Greenberg, eds., *James Karales*, (Gottingen: Steidl Verlag, 2014). George Leonard also wrote a piece on the march that was published in the *Nation*.

42. "Southern Justice"; "Last Summers of a Dreamlike Town," *Look*, Nov. 16, 1965; Interview, John Poppy; "A Worker Hits Freedom Road," *Look*, Nov. 16, 1965; and Stanley Hoffman, "Ralph Bunche: A Man of the World, but Never at Home," *Foreign Affairs*, Jan. 1995.

43. Richmond Flowers, "Southern Plain Talk about the Ku Klux Klan," *Look*, May 3, 1966; "Flowers Says U.S. Refused to Aid Him in Klan Inquiry," *New York Times*, April 19, 1966; and "Viola Gregg Liuzzo," Encyclopedia of Alabama.

44. "Requiem of Revival?," *Look*, June 14, 1966.

45. "A Jolting Turn in Civil Rights," *Look*, June 27, 1967; and Claude Brown, "Is the Race Problem Insoluble?," *Look*, June 27, 1967.

46. Edward Brooke, "Where Do We Go?," *Look*, Sept. 25, 1967.

47. Martin Luther King Jr., "Showdown for Nonviolence," *Look*, April 16, 1968; and "Doctor King, One Year After: He Lives, Man!" *Look*, April 15, 1969.

48. William Bradford Huie, "The Story of James Earl Ray and the Plot to Assassinate Martin Luther King," *Look*, Nov. 12 and 26, 1968; "Why James Earl Ray Murdered Dr. King," *Look*, April 15, 1968; and "Biographer of Ray Arrested over Articles on Dr. King Case," *New York Times*, Feb. 8, 1969.

49. "Word from Black America," *Look*, June 11, 1968; George Leonard, "A New Liberal Manifesto," *Look*, May 28, 1968; and Abraham Ribicoff, "Do Most Americans Really Want Segregation?," *Look*, Sept. 8, 1970.

50. "A National Disgrace: What Unions do to Blacks," *Look*, Nov. 12, 1968.

51. "The Blacks and the Whites"; "Black-White: Can We Bridge the Gap?," Mailer, "Looking for the Meat and Potatoes: Thoughts on Black Power," Cambridge, "Godfrey Cambridge's Open Door Policy," Meredith, "Black and White Cowboys," "Can a N—— Love a Honky?," "Black and White Progress Report," "Black Power Shakes the White Church," "Black Americans' African Heritage," "Black Beauty," "Black Brains for White Business," "Black Artist in a White World," "In Gary, the Man is Black," "Radicals: Are They Poles Apart," *Look*, Jan. 7, 1969; and Jane Rhodes, *Framing the Black Panthers: The Spectacular Rise of a Black Power Icon* (Urbana: University of Illinois Press, 2017).

52. "A New Job for Joan," Oct. 8, 1963; and "Quiet Revolution: Business Backs the Negro Advance," *Look*, Dec. 17, 1963.

53. "Southerner Appeals to the North," *Look*, Aug. 11, 1964.

54. "Negro View: Johnson Can Save the South," *Look*, March 10, 1964; "The Fight in Mississippi, Attack on Bigotry," *Look*, Sept. 8, 1964; "Rare Lesson About Love," *Look*, March 23, 1965; "Washington's Negro Elite," *Look*, April 6, 1965; "What Happens When Sigma Chi Pledges a Negro," *Look*, July 27, 1965; John Poppy, Interview, April 18, 2018; "What They Stood For," *Stanford*, March/April 2014; and "The Changing Face of Southern Politics," *Look*, Nov. 16, 1965.

55. "Visit with the Widow of Malcolm X," *Look*, March 4, 1969; and "Beyond Campus Chaos," and "Identity: The Black Woman's Burden," *Look*, June 10, 1969.

56. "The Man in the Fish Fry Parlor," *Look*, Oct. 17, 1967.

57. "Mississippi Widow," *Look*, June 1, 1965; "Black, Sassy and Still Tryin' to Be Independent," *Look*, July 14, 1970; "American South: Rise of a New Confederacy," *Look*, Nov. 17, 1970; "Lost Black Leader," *Look*, April 20, 1971; and "Black-on-White TV," *Look*, Sept. 7, 1971.

58. William F. Buckley Jr., "Why We Need a Black President," *Look*, Jan. 13, 1970.

59. Rosten, "Introduction: A View from Inside," GCP, CFADU.

8. CHANGING FAMILIES, CHANGING ROLES

1. *Look*, May 1, 1945; Nelson Lichtenstein, *Walter Reuther: The Most Dangerous Man in Detroit* (Urbana: University of Illinois Press, 1997); and Betty Friedan, *The Feminine Mystique* (New York: W. W. Norton & Co., 1963). Both terms predated the postwar period but became prominent ideals in the two decades or so after World War II.

2. "The Postwar American Family," *Look*, Dec. 12, 1944; and "Their First Baby," *Look*, Aug. 9, 1955.

3. "The Changing American Family," *Look*, March 15, 1960.

4. "A New *Look* at the American Woman," *Look*, Oct. 16, 1956; and "Why Don't We Prepare for Marriage?," *Look*, May 11, 1948.

5. "Their First Home," *Look*, Jan. 14, 1964; and "The Well-Prepared Vacation," *Look*, June 25, 1957.

6. "More Children Equal Less Divorce," *Look*, Feb. 13, 1951; "Divorce Suburban Style," *Look*, May 16, 1967; "What's Behind Our Rising Divorce Rate?," *Look*, May 29, 1945; "Their First Baby"; "How to Hold a Wife," *Look*, Oct. 30, 1945; "Norman Vincent Peale Answers Your Questions," "If You're Getting Married," *Look*, June 16, 1953; Peale, "How to Make Marriage Work," *Look*, Sept. 16, 1958; "Heaven 'Unsegregated,' Says New York Pastor," *Philadelphia Tribune*, Sept. 18, 1956; "Married Women Live Longer Than Single Women," *Look*, March 13, 1951; and "Dennis the Menace," *Look*, June 2, 1953.

7. "The Soaring Sixties," *Look*, Jan. 5, 1960; and "The Changing American Family," *Look*, March 15, 1960.

8. "The Soaring Sixties"; and "The Changing American Family."

9. "Parenthood USA," *Look*, June 2, 1942; "Why Have Children?," *Look*, Jan. 23, 1945; "Bumper Baby Crop Now Gets Its First School Clothes," *Look*, Aug. 17, 1948; "Man: Woman's Best Gift Investment," *Look*, Feb. 23, 1954; "Beginning of Responsibility," *Look*,

Aug. 20, 1957; Albert Bandura, "What TV Violence Can Do to Your Child," *Look*, Sept. 24, 1963; and "What Little Boys Are Made Of," *Look*, Nov. 2, 1954.

10. "Between a Boy and His Dad," *Look*, June 25, 1957; "Visit with Dr. Spock," *Look*, July 21, 1959, "10 Ways to Be a Good Parent," May 24, 1949; "Two Is the Age of Curiosity," *Look*, March 5, 1957; "Why Babies Cry," *Look*, Sept. 20, 1955; "Second Baby," *Look*, April 15, 1958; "You Can't Keep Up with a Baby," *Look*, June 10, 1958; "What Should Children Be Told about Sex?," *Look*, Sept. 7, 1954;; "Adolescence: A Time of Trial and Tragedy," *Look*, April 11, 1950; Peter Blos, "How Much Do We Know about Adolescence?," *Look*, June 28 1955; "Are You Feeding Your Child Properly," *Look*, May 28, 1957; "Children and Toys," *Look*, Dec. 31, 1963; and "Children in Search of Sanity," *Look*, May 28, 1957.

11. "The Problem of Unwed Mothers," *Look*, July 19, 1949; "How to Adopt a Baby," *Look*, July 6, 1948; "How to Adopt a Baby Safely," *Look*, April 24, 1951; "Babies, Our One Remaining Black Market," *Look*, Dec. 28, 1954; "The Joy of Adopting a 5-Year-Old," *Look*, Sept. 5, 1955; "Children Who Wait," *Look*, March 20, 1956; "Answer to the Baby Black Market," *Look*, Nov. 27, 1956; "Revolution in Adoption," *Look*, Dec. 8, 1959; "An Unmarried Mother for Mike," *Look*, Feb. 4, 1969; and "What Makes a Super-Mother? 'Selfishness'" *Look*, Aug. 24, 1971.

12. Diana Trilling, "What Ever Became of Romantic Love," *Look*, Feb. 16, 1960.

13. "Causes of Divorce," *Look*, June 22, 1937; "Divorced Women: America's Misfits," *Look*, Oct. 24, 1939; and "Marital Infidelity," *Look*, Dec. 12, 1944.

14. "What's Behind Our Rising Divorce Rate" and Ernest and Gladys Groves, "Divorce Is Not a Cure-All," *Look*, May 29, 1945; and "Divorce: America's Growing Tragedy," *Look*, Feb. 18, 1947.

15. "Why Don't We Prepare for Marriage?"; "Marriage Counsel from the Church," *Look*, July 6, 1948; Bacal, "The Other Woman Is Often the Creation of the Wife," *Look*, Aug. 2, 1949; "Divorce: A Woman's Tragedy," *Look*, Nov. 22, 1949; "The Most Dangerous Year of Marriage," *Look*, Sept. 13, 1949; "Are You the Woman Your Husband Married?," and "The Differences between Men and Women," *Look*, Feb. 28, 1950; Bacal, "How to Quarrel and Stay Married," *Look*, Sept. 12, 1950; Bacal, "Jealousy: A Threat to Marriage," *Look*, Oct. 24, 1950; and "Scientist, Wife, and Mother," *Look*, Oct. 16, 1956.

16. "Divorce Suburban Style," *Look* May 16, 1967; "Men and Women: A Special Report," Dec. 28, 1968; "An Unmarried Mother for Mike"; Harris, "Women without Men," *Look*, July 5, 1960; "Morality USA," *Look*, Sept. 24, 1963; "The Long, Lonely Wait of a Young Divorcee," *Look*, Jan. 11, 1966; and "Sunday Daddy," Jan. 11, 1967.

17. "The American Way of Marriage: Remarriage," *Look*, Sept. 21, 1971.

18. "Is the Family Obsolete?," "The Young Unmarrieds," "The Radical Family," *Look*, Jan. 26, 1971; and "1971 BC," *Look*, Aug. 10, 1971.

19. "Is the Family Obsolete?"

20. "The Future of Sex," *Look*, July 25, 1967; "Man and Woman: A Special Report on How Some Couples Are Learning New Ways to Work," *Look*, Dec. 24, 1968; and "The American Way of Marriage: Remarriage."

21. "A Million Migrants: Children of Misfortune," *Look*, June 19, 1951; and "Children in Search of Sanity," *Look*, May 28, 1957.

22. "Can a N—— Love a Honky?," *Look*, Jan. 7, 1969; and "Presbyterian Debate over Sex," *Look*, Aug. 11, 1970.

23. "Washington's Negro Elite," *Look*, April 6, 1965; "Negro in the Suburbs," *Look*, May 16, 1967; Moynihan, "The Discarded Third," *Look*, May 17, 1966; and "Life without Father," *Look*, May 17, 1966.

24. Harris, "Women without Men."

25. "Young, Single and a Stranger in New York," *Look*, Aug. 23, 1966; "The Big College Craze: Dating by Computer," *Look*, Feb 22, 1966; and Harris, "Men without Women," *Look*, Nov. 22, 1960.

26. "The Sad Gay Life," *Look*, Jan. 10, 1967; "The Future of Sex"; and George Leonard, *Walking on the Edge of the World: A Memoir of the Sixties and Beyond* (Boston: Houghton Mifflin Harcourt, 1988), 129.

27. "The Faces of 'The Boys in the Band,'" *Look*, Dec. 2, 1969; and "Letters," *Look*, Jan. 13, 1970.

28. "A Changing View of Homosexuality?" and "The Presbyterian Debate over Sex."

29. "The Homosexual Couple: Jack Baker and Michael McConnell," *Look*, Jan. 26, 1971, cabinet 3, drawer 2, folder 17, GCP, GCADU; "Jack Baker and Michael McConnell: Gay Americans Who Married in 1971," BBC World Service, July 3, 2013; and Leonard, *Walking on the Edge of the World*, 329, 344; and "Charlotte Brooks, 95," *New York Times*, March 25, 2014.

30. "Trans-sexuals: Male or Female?," *Look*, Jan. 27, 1970.

31. "Homosexuality: Scientists Search for an Answer to a Touchy and Troubling Question—Why?," *Life*, June 26, 1964; and "Is Homosexuality Normal or Not?," *Life*, Dec. 31, 1971.

32. "Toward a Saner Sex Life," *Look*, Dec. 9, 1947; and "Dublin Bans *Look* Magazine," *New York Times*, April 21, 1951.

33. "Looking Back at *Look*," *New York Times*, Feb. 6, 1983; Sanger, "The Case for Birth Control," and Fr. Edward Curran, "The Case against Birth Control," *Look*, Nov. 8, 1938; "Why I Fight for Birth Control," *Look*, Aug. 15, 1939; "New York's Planned Parenthood Clinics," *Look*, June 16, 1942; and "*Look* Articles, 1947," cabinet 3, drawer 3, folder 1, GCP, CFADU.

34. Guttmacher, "Birth Control and the Poor: A Solution," *Look*, April 7, 1964; Griswold, "The Law vs. Birth Control: Contraception and Commotion in Connecticut," *Look*, Jan. 30, 1962; and "For Men Only: Foolproof Birth Control," *Look*, March 9, 1971.

35. "Let's Take Birth Control out of Politics," *Look*, Oct. 10, 1961; "Birth Control: The Problem We Fear to Face," *Look*, Dec. 5, 1961; Griswold, "The Law vs. Birth Control"; "Birth Control in Japan," *Look*, Feb. 26, 1963; Guttmacher, "Birth Control and the Poor: A Solution"; "Latin American Catholics and Birth Control," *Look*, July 14, 1964; "Catholics Take a New Look at the Pill," *Look*, Sept. 8, 1964; John D. Rockefeller, "Hidden Crisis," Feb. 9, 1965; "Lady Doctor Defies Her Church," *Look*, Aug. 10, 1965; "Kentucky Doctor:

One Man's War against Southern Poverty," *Look*, Nov. 16, 1965; "Miss Stephanie Mills vs. Motherhood," *Look*, April 21, 1970; and "For Men Only."

36. "The Growing Tragedy of Illegal Abortion" Oct. 19, 1965, cabinet 3, drawer 4, folder 2, GCP, GCADU; Lawrence Lader, "Non-Hospital Abortions," *Look*, Jan. 21, 1969; "Overheard in Suburbia: Abortionist," *Look*, May 16, 1967; Rev. James Kavanaugh, "Church's Teaching Attacked by Priest," *Look*, May 29, 1969; and "Presbyterian Debate over Sex."

37. "Why Your Child Needs Sex Education," *Look*, Oct. 19, 1943; "Our Daughters Have Too Much Sex Education," *Look*, Aug. 30, 1949; "Sex Education Comes of Age," *Look*, March 8, 1966; "What Should Children Be Told about Sex?," *Look*, Sept. 7, 1954; and "What Kids Still Don't Know about Sex," *Look*, July 28, 1970.

38. "Does Morality Make Sense?," *Look*, Aug. 11, 1953; "Her Sex Life and Marriage," *Look*, Oct. 16, 1956; Kingsley Davis, "How Much Do We Know about Divorce?," *Look*, July 26, 1955; "What Ministers Are Learning about Sex," *Look*, Nov. 11, 1958; Bandura, "Are We as Modern as We Think," *Look*, Jan 3, 1961; and "Morality USA." McHugh and Moskin had published an article in *Collier's* on Nov. 9, 1954 about McHugh's six-year study, which described Americans' "gaps in knowledge" about sex.

39. "The American Woman," "The Open Generation," "Sex Education Comes of Age," *Look*, March 8, 1966; and Hefner: "I Am in the Center of the World," *Look*, Jan. 10, 1967.

40. "The Future of Sex"; Nancy Gay Faber, "Sex for Credit," *Look*, April 1, 1969; and "The Mood of America," *Look*, Nov. 18, 1969.

41. "Why We Need a New Sexuality," *Look*, Jan. 13, 1970.

42. "Presbyterian Debate over Sex"; "Little Dr. Reuben and His Big Sex Book," *Look*, July 14, 1970; "What's Happening to Sexual Privacy," *Look*, Oct. 20, 1970; and "The American Way of Marriage: Remarriage."

43. "Why We Need a New Sexuality."

9. WOMEN AND MEN

1. Bacal, "The Other Woman Is Often the Creation of the Wife," *Look*, Aug. 2, 1949; Bacal, "How to Quarrel and Stay Married," *Look*, Sept. 12, 1950; Bacal, "Jealousy: A Threat to Marriage," *Look*, Oct. 24, 1950; Wylie, "Mom's to Blame," *Look*, Nov. 21, 1950; "*Look* Women's Department," cabinet 4, drawer 2, folder 19, GCP, GCADU; "Charlotte Brooks, 95," *New York Times*, March 25, 2014; and Rosten, "Introduction: A View from Inside," GCP, CFADU.

2. "Sex Life and Marriage," *Look*, Oct. 16, 1956; Diana Trilling, "The Case for the American Woman," *Look*, March 3, 1959; and "The Changing American Family," *Look*, March 15, 1960.

3. *Look*, Aug. 15, 1939; "Wives Who Work," *Look*, April 25 and May 8, 1941; M. F. K. Fisher, "Career Women, 1942 Style," *Look*, July 28, 1942; "Women Replace Men in Unglamorous Everyday Jobs," *Look*, Jan. 26, 1943; Dorothy Thompson, "American Women," *Look*, July 14, 1942; "Will You Quit Your Job after the War?," *Look*, Sept. 5, 1944; "Women Doctors," *Look*, March 1, 1949; "Single Mother," *Look*, May 9, 1950; "Scientist, Wife, and Mother," *Look*, Oct. 10, 1956; and "An Unmarried Mother for Mike," *Look*, Feb. 4, 1969.

4. "Career Girl: Her Life and Problems," May 3, 1948; and "The American Woman," *Life*, Dec. 24, 1956.
5. Harris, "Women without Men," *Look*, July 5, 1960.
6. "Memo to the American Woman," *Look*, Jan. 11, 1960.
7. "The American Way of Marriage: Remarriage," *Look*, Sept. 21, 1971.
8. Marie Torre, "I Am a Working Mother," *Look*, March 13, 1962; and "Divorce Suburban Style," *Look*, May 16, 1967.
9. "Is Someone Kidding the College Girl?," "Happiness Is a Baby's Laugh," "To a Busy Suburban Wife," "That Question," "The Long, Lonely Wait of a Young Divorcee," Norman Rockwell, *Picasso vs Sargent*, "New Skimpy, Backless Bikinis," Vreeland, "What Is Fashion?," *Look*, Jan. 11, 1966.
10. "How Come a Nice Girl Like You Isn't Married," *Look*, Jan. 11, 1966.
11. Feiffer, "Men Really Don't Like Women," *Look*, Jan. 11, 1966.
12. "Young, Single and a Stranger in New York," *Look*, Aug. 23, 1966; Rockefeller, "Youth, Love and Sex: The New Chivalry," *Look*, Oct. 7, 1969; and "Is the Family Obsolete?," *Look*, Jan. 26, 1971.
13. Farson, "The Rage of Women," *Look*, Dec. 16, 1969.
14. "Looking around with Gloria Steinem," *Look*, Nov. 26, 1968; Steinem, "Why We Need a Woman President in 1976," *Look*, Jan. 13, 1970; and Steinem, "What Culture," *Look*, Nov. 26, 1968.
15. "Motherhood: Who Needs It?," *Look*, Sept. 22, 1970.
16. "Backlash against Women's Lib!" *Look*, March 9, 1971; and "The American Way of Marriage: Remarriage."
17. "Maybe It'll Be Different Here," *Look*, March 23, 1971; Bettelheim, "A New Way to Raise Kids," *Look*, Feb. 24, 1970; and "The 50/50 Marriage: Is This What Women Want?," *Look*, Oct. 5, 1971.
18. "Betty Friedan: Angry Battler for Her Sex," *Life*, Nov. 1, 1963; "Angry Author Kate Millett," *Life*, Sept. 4, 1970; and "Women Arise: The Revolution That Will Affect Everyone," *Life*, Sept. 4, 1970.
19. "An 'Oppressed Majority' Demands Its Rights," *Life*, Dec. 12, 1969.
20. Lynes, "Husbands: The New Servant Class," *Look*, Dec. 14, 1954.
21. Bacal, "The Differences between Men and Women," *Look*, Feb. 28, 1950; Wylie, "Pop Is a Moral Slacker," *Look*, July 3, 1951; and Lynes, "Husbands: The New Servant Class."
22. "American Male," *Look*, Feb. 4, 1958; "American Male," *Look*, Feb. 18, 1958; James Gilbert, *Men on the Suburban Frontier: Rethinking Midcentury Masculinity* (Chicago: University of Chicago Press, 2006); Editors of *Look* Magazine, *The Decline of the American Male* (New York: Random House, 1958); Trilling, "The Case for the American Woman," *Look*, March 3, 1959; "How Come a Nice Girl Like You Isn't Married"; and "Message to the American Man," *Look*, Jan. 10, 1967.
23. "The Games Men Play" and "Message to the American Man," *Look*, Jan. 10, 1967.
24. "Who Says He's a Flop?" and "Sunday Daddy," *Look*, Jan. 10, 1967.

25. Harris, "Men without Women," *Look*, Nov. 22, 1960.
26. "The Duties of an Expectant Father," *Look*, June 18, 1940; "Between a Boy and His Dad," *Look*, June 25, 1957; "Weekend Daddies," *Look*, Feb. 9, 1957; "The Changing American Family," *Look*, March 15, 1960; and "Why We Need a New Sexuality," *Look*, Jan. 13, 1971.
27. "A Father in Charge" and "The Two Worlds of Thomas Houman," *Look*, Jan. 10, 196 7; "The Social Dropout," *Look*, Jan. 10, 1967; "The Generation Gap," *Look*, Feb. 21, 1967; "The Hippies," Aug. 22, 1967; Rockefeller, "Youth, Love and Sex"; Farson, "The Rage of Women"; and "The American Way of Marriage: Remarriage."

10. BABY BOOMERS

1. "Teen-age Party," *Look*, Dec. 29, 1953; "*Look* Reports on Teen-Age Sewing," *Look*, Aug. 9, 1955; "It's Still Sweet Sixteen," *Look*, Dec. 14, 1954; and "How American Teenagers Live," *Look*, July 23, 1957.
2. "Teen-age Morals: City vs. Small Town," *Look*, June 19, 1951; "Teen-age Killers," *Look*, Jan. 27, 1953; "How to Tame Teen-agers," *Look*, Aug. 25, 1953; "Blackboard Jungle: A Movie Tackles Teen-Age Terror," *Look*, May 3, 1955; "Teen-age Gang from the Inside," *Look*, Aug. 23, 1955; and "Can Cops Tame Wild Kids," *Look*, Sept. 16, 1958.
3. "Generation in a Searchlight," *Look*, Jan. 24, 1956; "Elvis Presley: He Can't Be, but He Is," *Look*, Aug. 7, 1956; and "Face Is Familiar," Dec. 11, 1956.
4. "Generation in a Searchlight."
5. "How American Teen-agers Live."
6. "How a 52-Year-Old Word Invented by Vogue Editor Diana Vreeland became 2017's Word of the Year," *Vanity Fair*, Dec. 15, 2017.
7. "Explosive Generation," *Look*, Jan. 3, 1961; "We Have Your Son," *Look*, Jan. 3, 1971; and "American Youth/Cool Generation," *Saturday Evening Post*, Dec. 23–30, 1961.
8. "The Tense Generation," *Look*, Aug. 27, 1963.
9. "The Tense Generation."
10. "Morality U.S.A." *Look*, Sept. 24, 1963.
11. "The Open Generation," *Look*, Sept. 20, 1966.
12. "The Faces of the Future," *Look*, Jan. 12, 1965.
13. "Reed College: Portland's Gadfly," *Look*, March 27, 1962; "California's Revolution in Higher Education," *Look*, Sept. 25, 1962; "Wellesley Girl," *Look*, Dec. 2, 1962; "The Perils of Brotherhood," *Look*, March 12, 1963; "What Kids Still Don't Know about Sex," *Look*, July 28, 1970; "Behind the Campus Revolt," *Look*, Feb. 23, 1965; Interview, John Poppy, Nov. 9, 2020; and "Princeton Commitment: A Race against Mace," *Look*, June 16, 1970.
14. "Man and Woman Thing," *Look*, Dec. 24, 1968; "Generation Gap," *Look*, Feb. 21, 1967; Interview, John Poppy, April 12, 2018; and "The Generation Gap," *Life*, May 17, 1968.
15. "Runaways," *Look*, July 25, 1967; "Drugs," *Look*, Aug. 8, 1967; "Strange Case of the Harvard Drug Scandal," *Look*, Nov. 5, 1963; and "The Visions of 'Saint Tim,'" *Look*, Aug. 8, 1967.
16. "Inside the Hippie Revolution," *Look*, Aug. 22, 1967; and "The Strange New Love Land of the Hippies," *Life*, March 31, 1967.

17. "The Strange New Love Land of the Hippies."

II. GOVERNMENT AND POLITICIANS

1. Rosten, "Introduction: A View from the Inside," GCP, CFADU; and Interview, John Poppy, May 21, 2018.
2. William Attwood, "The Soaring Sixties," *Look*, Jan. 5, 1960.
3. "Bureaucrats Are People Too," *Look*, May 14, 1957; "Where We Stand," *Look*, Jan. 15, 1963; and Sevareid, "Dissent or Destruction," *Look*, Sept. 5, 1967.
4. "The National Municipal League and *Look* Salute All-America Cities," *Look*, Jan. 10, 1956; George Leonard, *Walking on the Edge of the World: A Memoir of the Sixties and Beyond* (Boston: Houghton Mifflin Harcourt, 1988), 79–80; and "Myers, 1958–60," box 14, folder 13, LRWHS.
5. "All-America Cities," *Look*, Feb. 10, 1953; "All-America Cities," *Look*, Feb. 9, 1954; "Speeches, 1942–1961," cabinet 1, drawer 4, folder 1, GCP, CFADU; "All America Cities," *Look*, Jan. 22, 1957; "Editorial Preview," *Look*, April 13, 1963, cabinet 4, drawer 1, folder 3, GCP, GCADU; "All-America Cities," National Civic League, https://www.nationalcivicleague .org/america-city-award/; and "All-America City: Rosedale CA," Jan. 13, 1964, *Look* Magazine Photo Collection, LOC.
6. "Community Home Achievement Awards," *Look*, Feb. 21, 1956.
7. "Records of the *Look* Years, 1972," cabinet 4, drawer 2, folders 20 and 23, GCP, CFADU; George Gallup, "What America Thinks about a Third Term," *Look*, Sept. 12, 1939; and "A Documentation of the Power of a Single *Look* Article" (1947), cabinet 2, drawer 2, folder on "Bets," CFADU.
8. "A Psychologist Reveals … the Secrets of Roosevelt's Popularity," *Look*, Feb. 1937; Harold Ickes, "I Want Roosevelt for a Third Term," *Look*, June 20, 1939; Pearson and Allen, "President Roosevelt: The Nation's Loneliest Man," *Look*, Dec. 6, 1938; "Roosevelt after 1940," *Look*, July 4, 1939; "Now Roosevelt Can Win in 1940," *Look*, Oct. 24, 1939; and "Roosevelt's 1940s Troubles," *Look*, Jan. 16, 1940; "Roosevelt: War President," *Look*, Sept. 24, 1943; "U.S. at War: Chronic Liar," *Time*, Sept. 13, 1943; and "Pearson," *Look*, Nov. 26, 1946.
9. Wendell Willkie, "Roosevelt Should Run for a Third Term," *Look*, June 4, 1940; "Willkie … the Roosevelt Republican," *Look*, Aug. 13, 1940; Willkie, "I Challenge Roosevelt on These Issues: National Defense, Business Recovery, War Policy, Social Reform," *Look*, Sept. 10, 1940; "Roosevelt-Willkie Battle," *Look*, Sept. 24, 1940; Alf Landon, "What Willkie Faces," Oct. 8, 1940; "Can Eleanor Roosevelt Stop Willkie?," *Look*, Oct. 8, 1940; Willkie, "If I Become President," *Look*, Oct. 22, 1940; "Roosevelt or Willkie?," *Look*, Nov. 5, 1940; Willkie, "How the Republican Party Can Win in 1944," *Look*, Oct. 5, 1943; Mike Cowles, "A Look at My Life," cabinet 2, drawer 2, folder 9, GCP, CFADU; Herbert Strentz, "Gardner Cowles Jr.," GCP, CFADU; "Gardner Cowles: Creative Editor with a Quest for Insight into World Affairs," *Printers' Ink*, April 10, 1959; Kenneth Stewart, "*Look*," PM, May 28, 1949; and "Publicity Material," cabinet 4, drawer 4, file 15, GCP, CFADU.

10. Gardner Cowles Jr., *Mike Looks Back: The Memoirs of Gardner Cowles, Founder of Look Magazine* (New York: Gardner Cowles, 1985); "Willkie to Start Abroad in Three Weeks," *New York Times*, Aug. 21, 1942; Willkie, "What I Learned about the Nazis from Stalin," *Look*, Dec. 1, 1942; Willkie, "Madame Chiang Kai-Shek," *Look*, Dec. 29, 1942; "Willkie Indicates Intention to Fight for '44 Nomination," *Look*, Sept. 21, 1943; and "Gardner Cowles," *Printers' Ink*, April 10, 1959.

11. "The Ten Most Powerful People in Washington," *Look*, Jan. 26, 1941; "Henry Wallace, Roosevelt's Choice for President," *Look*, Nov. 3, 1942; "Five Ways FDR Changed Your Life," April 12, 1949; Johnson, "How Great Was Roosevelt?," *Look*, July 10, 1945; and "Inside FDR," *Look*, March 14 and 28, April 11 and 25, and May 9, 1950.

12. "They Lead the Women of America," *Look*, Nov. 23, 1937; "The Ten Happiest People in America," *Look*, March 29, 1938; "What's Wrong with the Draft," *Look*, July 15, 1941; Eleanor Roosevelt, "Why I Do Not Choose to Run," *Look*, July 9, 1946; E. Roosevelt, "The Russians Are Tough," *Look*, Feb. 18, 1947; "Eleanor Roosevelt's Life in Pictures," *Look*, Sept. 16, 1947; "E. Roosevelt," *Look*, Nov. 23, 1948; "Eleanor Roosevelt, 1882–1962," *Look*, Dec. 18, 1962; E. Roosevelt, "Christmas Message," *Look*, Dec. 1950; and E. Roosevelt, "Juvenile Delinquency in the USSR," *Look*, Jan. 6, 1959.

13. "Wayne Morse: Bad Boy of the Senate," *Look*, Aug. 6, 1946; "John Lindsay: New GOP Hope," *Look*, April 6, 1965; "John Lindsay: Ringmaster of Fun City?," *Look*, March 21, 1967; Edward Brooke, "Where Do We Go?," *Look* Sept. 25, 1967; and "What Makes Romney Run?," *Look*, Dec. 12, 1967.

14. "*Look* Magazine, 1946–1968," cabinet 3, drawer 3, folder 5, GCP, CFADU; Interview, Patricia Carbine, Sept. 11, 2020; and "Hemingway Out of the Jungle," *New York Times*, Jan. 26, 1954. Lippmann was paid $3,000 for his 1953 story, "Showdown in Germany."

15. Carol Rowan, "Who Gets the Negro Vote?," *Look*, Nov. 13, 1956; Humphrey, "Big Business: Is It Too Big?," *Look*, May 22, 1962; "Hubert Humphrey: Advance Man for the Great Society," *Look*, April 6, 1965; "This Is Humphrey," *Look*, July 9, 1968; and Humphrey, "Why I Want the Job," *Look*, Aug. 20, 1968.

16. Strentz, "Gardner Cowles Jr."; "Stevenson Slates World-Trip Stops," *New York Times*, Feb. 14, 1953; Adlai Stevenson, "Ballots and Bullets," *Look*, June 2, 1953, "Will India Turn Communist?," *Look*, July 14, 1953; "No Peace for Israel," *Look*, Aug. 11, 1953; "World I Saw," *Look*, Sept. 2, 1953; Adlai Stevenson, "Must We Have War?," *Look*, Nov. 16, 1954; "Africa: The Giant Awakens," *Look*, Nov. 15, 1955; "Our Plight in Latin America," *Look*, Nov. 22, 1960; and Adlai Stevenson, "Stevenson Urged New Peace Force," *Look*, Aug. 24, 1965.

17. "*Look* Magazine, 1946–1968," cabinet 3, drawer 3, folder 5e, GCP, CFADU; "What Asia Thinks of Adlai," *Look*, June 30, 1953; "Democrats Look Ahead to Stevenson's Return," *Look*, Aug. 2, 1953; "Can Stevenson Come Back?," *Look*, May 29, 1956; Adlai Stevenson, "Memo to the President: Let's Make Our Two-Party System Work," *Look*, Sept. 20, 1955; "Democratic Fat Cats Still Prefer Adlai," *Look*, Sept. 1, 1959; "Our Man in the Middle,"

Look, Oct. 10, 1961; Eric Sevareid, "The Last Troubled Hours of Adlai Stevenson," *Look*, Nov. 30, 1965; "Adlai III," *Look*, Oct. 6, 1966; and "Adlai III," *Look*, Oct. 4, 1970.

18. "The Public Will Be Served" brochure, ca. 1960, in *"Look* Promotion, 1943–1961," cabinet 4, drawer 2, folder 4, GCP, CFADU; "Wallace Making Press His Target," *New York Times*, April 15, 1966; *Look* Magazine—Awards, 1950–1966," cabinet 3, drawer 4, folder 2, GCP, CFADU; Interview, John Poppy, April 12, 2018; and Kleinfield, "Looking Back at *Look*," *New York Times*, Feb. 6, 1983.

19. "Truman Is a New Dealer Too," *Look*, June 26, 1945; "Is Truman Winning Again?," *Look*, Dec. 6, 1949; "Can We Solve Our Health Problem?," *Look*, Nov. 11, 1947; and Murray, "Socialized Medicine?," *Look*, June 21, 1949.

20. "Truman's First Year—How Big a Failure?," *Look*, April 2, 1946; "Why Harry Truman Needs a Hair Shirt," *Look*, April 26, 1949; "These Scandalous Years in Washington," *Look*, May 22, 1951; Henry Steele Commager, "A Few Kind Words for Harry Truman," *Look*, Aug. 28, 1951; and Harry S. Truman, "My View of the Presidency," *Look*, Nov. 11, 1958.

21. "Eisenhower Is a One-Man General Staff," *Look*, Sept. 8, 1942; "General Eisenhower," *Look*, July 11, 1944; "Why Eisenhower Won't Run," *Look*, March 18, 1947; "Eisenhower Is Open to GOP Draft," *Look*, Jan. 17, 1950; "Elect Eisenhower," *Look*, Nov. 4, 1952; Lippmann, "Elect Ike," April 22, 1952; "Eisenhower," *Look*, April 22, 1952; Dewey, "Eisenhower and the Next Congress," *Look*, Oct. 19, 1954; Merriman Smith, "The Eisenhower I Knew," *Look*, March 8, 1955; Marquis Childs, "Eisenhower," *Look*, July 22, 1958; "President's Office," *Look*, Jan. 22, 1957; and "How Eisenhower Views His Presidency," *Look*, Nov. 8, 1960.

22. "Eisenhower Will Run for President, If—" *Look*, June 5, 1951; "What Can We Expect of Eisenhower," *Look*, Dec. 18, 1951; "Can Ike Save the GOP?," *Look*, Sept. 4, 1956; Adlai Stevenson, "Ike's Big Failures," *Look*, Sept. 20, 1955; "Ike's Second Term Tragedy," *Look*, Jan. 22, 1958; and "Must We Always Have a Mess in Washington?," *Look*, July 22, 1958.

23. Kay Summersby, "Eisenhower at War," *Look*, Sept. 28, 1948; "My Boss: General Eisenhower," *Look*, Oct. 12, 1948; "Eisenhower Had His Troubles in Africa," *Look*, Oct. 26, 1948; "War Was Hell on Eisenhower," *Look*, Nov. 9, 1948; and Summersby, *Past Forgetting: My Love Affair with Dwight D. Eisenhower* (New York: Simon & Schuster, 1975).

24. "Could the Reds Seize Detroit?," *Look*, Aug. 3, 1948.

25. "Is John Jones a Communist? How We Investigate America Loyalty," *Look*, Sept. 12, 1950; and "Harold Ickes Diaries," cabinet 3, drawer 4, folder 1, GCP, GCADU.

26. J. Kugelmass, "How a Double-Cross Gave the Reds the H-Bomb," *Look*, July 13, 1954.

27. Ernst, "New Way to Fight U.S. Communism," *Look*, March 24, 1953.

28. Joe McCarthy, "The Man with the Power," *Look*, June 16, 1953; "Ring around McCarthy," *Look*, Dec. 1, 1953; and Hemingway, "Christmas Gift," *Look*, April 20, 1954.

29. "Daniel Mich Dies, Editor of *Look*, 60," *New York Times*, Nov. 23, 1965; "Murrow: The Man, the Myth, the McCarthy Fighter," *Look*, Aug. 24, 1954; "Myth of McCarthy's Strength," *Look*, June 1, 1954; and "Is Fear Destroying Our Freedom?," *Look*, Sept. 7, 1954.

30. Davidson, "The People Who Stole It from Us," *Look*, Oct. 29, 1957.

31. "Who's on the Far Right?," *Look*, March 13, 1962; Cassels, "The Rightist Crisis in Our Churches," *Look*, April 24, 1962; "The Rampant Right Invades the GOP," *Look*, July 16, 1963; "Extremism," *Look*, Oct. 20, 1964; "A Republican Looks at Extremism," *Look*, Jan. 26, 1965; and Church, "Conspiracy USA," *Look*, Jan. 26, 1965.

32. "A New Conservative Manifesto," *Look*, Dec. 29, 1964; Church, "Conspiracy USA," *Look*, Jan. 26, 1965.

33. Broder, "California's Political Free-for-All," *Look*, July 13, 1965; "California's Bitter Race" and "Ronnie to the Rescue," *Look*, Nov. 1, 1966.

34. Davidson, "Texas Political Powerhouse," *Look*, Aug. 4, 1959, and "Lyndon Johnson: Can a Southerner Be Elected President?," *Look*, Aug. 18, 1959; "Lyndon Johnson: Trained for Power," *Look*, Dec. 31, 1963; LBJ issue, *Look*, March 10, 1964; Lomax, "A Negro View: Johnson Can Save the South," *Look*, March 10, 1964; "Changing Washington," *Look*, April 6, 1965; "War on Poverty," *Look*, June 13, 1967; and "Lyndon Johnson: How Goes the War on Poverty?," *Look*, July 27, 1967.

35. "Vietnam: Washington's Biggest Problem," *Look*, April 6, 1965; "LBJ and the Election: Trouble Ahead," *Look*, Oct. 4, 1966; "The Truth about LBJ's Credibility," *Look*, May 2, 1967; and McCarthy, "Why I'm Battling LBJ," *Look*, Feb. 6, 1968.

36. "A Memo to LBJ," *Look*, April 16, 1968; Sam Houston Johnson, "My Brother Lyndon Johnson," *Look*, Dec. 2 and Dec. 16, 1969; Sevareid, "Dissent or Destruction"; and "Interview with Toynbee," *Look*, March 18, 1969. When Robert Kennedy announced his candidacy two months later, *Look* reported that RFK had pledged to support McCarthy, who reminded readers that Kennedy had been "a Red-baiting aide to Sen. Joseph McCarthy." See: "Bobby's Decision," *Look*, April 16, 1968.

37. "After Chicago, Where Will the Young People Go?," *Look*, Oct. 15, 1968; and Pearson, "The Ghosts that Haunted LBJ," *Look*, July 23, 1968.

38. "John L. Lewis," Jan. 13, 1942; "John L. Lewis' New Drive for Power," *Look*, June 24, 1947; Alinsky, "The Hates of John L. Lewis," *Look*, Nov. 22, 1949; "How Tough Is Walter Reuther?," *Look*, Aug. 10, 1965; "Labor Trouble," *Look*, June 26, 1956; and John F. Kennedy, "Labor Racketeers and Political Pressure," May 12, 1959.

39. "The Scandal of Welfare Chiseling," *Look*, Nov. 7, 1961; and "A Way Out of Our Welfare Dead End," *Look*, May 8, 1962.

40. "Is Nixon Fit to Be President?," *Look*, Feb. 24, 1953; "Eisenhower Doubt on Nixon Alleged," *Look*, Nov. 20, 1962; "The Puzzling Case of Richard Nixon," *Look*, March 5, 1968; "Who Will Control the GOP in 1968," *Look*, Jan. 24, 1967; Dick Gregory, "What George Wallace Means to Me," *Look*, Oct. 29, 1968; Henry Steele Commager, "Is Freedom Dying in America," July 14, 1970; and "Spiro," *Look*, Sept. 7, 1971.

41. Russell Baker, "Who Is the Man in the White House?," *Look*, Dec. 16, 1969; Leonard, *Walking on the Edge of the World*, 329, 344; Arnold A. Hutschnecker, "The Mental Health of Our Leaders," *Look*, July 15, 1969; Riegle, "The Dump Nixon Movement," *Look*, June 1, 1971; "18-Year-Old Vote Could Beat Nixon in 1972," *Look*, July 13, 1971; David Maxey, "Nixon's Youth Corps," *Look*, Feb. 10, 1970; and "Let Them Eat Words," *Look*, Dec. 2, 1969.

42. "Ike's Boy and How He Grew," *Look*, June 23, 1959; "Why Nixon's Liberal Lines Up with Conservatives" and "Odd Alliance: Moynihan and the Robber Barons," *Look*, April 7, 1970; "Do We Owe People a Living? Guaranteed Income, or Negative Income Tax," *Look*, April 30, 1968; "Nixon's Big Gamble," *Look*, May 5, 1970; and Allen Drury, "Inside the White House 1971," *Look*, Oct. 19, 1971.
43. "A Kennedy Runs for Congress," *Look*, June 11, 1946.
44. John F., Kennedy, "Labor Racketeers and Political Pressure"; "Day I'll Remember," *Look*, Sept. 13, 1960; "The Next 25 Years," *Look*, Jan. 16, 1962; "Where We Stand," *Look*, Jan. 15, 1963; "Arts in America," *Look*, Dec. 18, 1962; "Physical Fitness," *Look*, Aug. 13, 1963; and "Memoir," *Look*, Nov. 17, 1964.
45. Robert Kennedy, "Tribute to JFK," *Look*, Feb. 25, 1964; Robert Kennedy, "Suppose God Is Black?," *Look*, Aug. 23, 1966; "What We Can Do to End the Agony of Vietnam," *Look*, Nov. 28, 1967; "To Seek a New World," *Look*, Nov. 14, 1967; and Edward Kennedy, "A Fresh Look at Vietnam" Feb. 15, 1966.
46. *Look*, Sept. 22, 1953; "The Rise of the Brothers Kennedy," *Look*, Aug. 6, 1957; "The Big Change in Richard Nixon," *Look*, Sept. 3, 1957; "Democratic Forecast: A Catholic in 1960," *Look*, March 3, 1959; "Protestant View of a Catholic for President," *Look*, May 10, 1960; "Kennedys: A Family Political Machine," *Look*, July 19, 1960; "Jack Kennedy," *Look*, Oct. 13, 1959; "Other John Kennedy," *Look*, June 7, 1960; and "Kennedy Women," *Look*, Oct. 11, 1960.
47. Anna S., "'A Very Special President': The Woman Who Wrote JFK," Nov. 23, 2013, "Paris As a Young Woman," https://parisasayoungwoman.wordpress.com/2013/11/23/a-very-special-president-the-woman-who-wrote-jfk/.
48. "Caroline's Wonderful Summer," *Look*, Aug. 14, 1962; "President and His Son," *Look*, Dec. 3, 1963; "Stanley Tretick," *New York Times*, July 20, 1999; and Kitty Kelley, *Capturing Camelot: Stanley Tretick's Iconic Images of the Kennedys* (New York: St. Martin's Press, 2012).
49. "The New Frontier," *Look*, Jan. 2, 1962; and "Surprising Aftermath of a Crisis," *Look*, Dec. 4, 1962.
50. "Why We Face a Deadlock in Washington," *Look*, Jan. 29, 1963; "Why There's Trouble on the New Frontier," *Look*, July 2, 1963; and "How the Public Rates JFK," *Look*, Aug. 13, 1963.
51. The Editors of *Look* Magazine, *Kennedy and His Family in Pictures: With Exclusive Pictures from the Files of Look* (New York: Look, 1963).
52. "In Memory of John F. Kennedy," *Look*, Dec. 31, 1963; "Robert Kennedy's Tribute to JFK"; "Kennedy Legend," *Look*, June 30, 1964; "New Kennedy Painting," *Look*, July 14, 1964; "JFK Memorial Issue," *Look*, Nov. 17, 1964; and Laura Bergquist and Stanley Tretick, *A Very Special President* (New York: McGraw-Hill, 1965).
53. Sorensen, "Kennedy's Worst Disaster: Bay of Pigs," *Look*, Aug. 10, 1965; "Kennedy vs. Khrushchev," Sept. 7, 1965; and "Kennedy's Greatest Hour," Sept. 21, 1965.
54. William Manchester, "Death of a President," "Parkland Hospital: Case No. 24740," "Troubled Flight from Dallas," "Jarring Change in Washington," *Look*, Jan. 24, Feb. 7,

Feb. 21, 1967, March 7; William Manchester, *The Death of a President: Nov. 20–25, 1963* (New York: Harper and Row, 1967); "Pressure Denied on Kennedy Book," *New York Times*, Aug. 27, 1966; Mrs. Kennedy Will Seek an Injunction to Block Book about Assassination," *New York Times*, Dec. 15, 1966; "Statements by Mrs. Kennedy and Cowles," *New York Times*, Dec. 22, 1966; "Advertising: What Manchester Did to *Look*," *New York Times*, Jan. 19, 1967; "Four Kennedy Issues Set Mark at *Look*," *New York Times*, March 12, 1967; "Fact Sheet #3, "*Look* Magazine to Stop Publication: Postal Rate Increases Cited as a Major Factor," Sept. 16, 1971, "Cost Articles," cabinet 3, drawer 4, folder 9, GCP, CFADU; "A Clash of Camelots," *Vanity Fair*, Oct. 2009; and "William Manchester's Own Story," *Look*, April 4, 1967.

55. "Jacqueline Kennedy: The New American Beauty," *Look*, July 4, 1961; "Valiant Is the Word for Jackie," *Look*, Jan. 28, 1964; "Kennedy Children," *Look*, Oct. 5, 1965; "Jacqueline Kennedy Goes Public," *Look*, March 22, 1966; and "Jackie's Fabulous Greek," *Look*, June 30, 1970.

56. "*Look* Applauds Ten Top Young Men of the Year," *Look*, Jan. 25, 1955; "Ambitions of Bobby Kennedy," *Look*, Aug. 25, 1964; Fallaci, "Robert Kennedy Answers Some Blunt Questions," *Look*, March 9, 1965; "Bobby's Decision," *Look*, April 16, 1968; "Bob Kennedy We Knew," *Look*, July 9, 1968; "Warren Rogers Dies," *Washington Post*, Sept. 2, 2003; Nadine Birner, "Email Interview with Paul Fusco," April 26, 2010; and Interview, Paul Fusco, April 12, 2018.

57. "Visit with the Indomitable Rose Kennedy," *Look*, Nov. 26, 1968; "Ethel," *Look*, June 25, 1968; and "Magazines Rushing to Change Material after Assassination," *New York Times*, June 8, 1968.

58. "New Mrs. Kennedy in Washington," *Look*, Feb. 26, 1963; "Ted Kennedy on His Own: Coming Up Strong in the Senate," *Look*, July 13, 1965; Kennedy, "A Fresh Look at Vietnam"; "Ted Kennedy Talks about His Past and Future," *Look*, March 4, 1969; "The Rise and Fall of the House of Kennedy," *Look*, Dec. 30, 1969; and "Kennedy's Comeback: Will He or Won't He?," *Look*, Aug. 10, 1971.

59. Interviews, John Poppy, April 12 and May 21, 2018; "Angry American Speaks Out," *Look*, Aug. 1, 1961; "Behind the Campus Revolt: California Uprising," *Look*, Feb. 23, 1965; and "The Sixties: A Special *Look* Bonus—An Unbelievable Decade," *Look*, Dec. 30, 1969.

60. "Campus Mood, Spring, '68," *Look*, April 2, 1968; "America's Concentration Camps: The Rumors and the Realities," *Look*, May 28, 1968; and "Vanguard of the Campus Revolt," *Look*, Oct. 1, 1968.

61. "A New Liberal Manifesto," *Look*, May 28, 1968.

62. Fred Rodell, "Can Nixon's Justices Reverse the Warren Court?," *Look*, Dec. 2, 1969; "A New Liberal Manifesto"; "Do We Owe People a Living?"; "American Militarism: What Is It Doing to Us?," *Look*, Aug. 12, 1969; "American Militarism: The Defense Establishment," *Look*, Aug. 26, 1969; "A Killing Shame," *Look*, Dec. 16, 1969; Ronald Goldfarb, "Why Don't We Tear Down Our Prisons?," *Look*, July 27, 1971; "If You Want to Run for President," *Look*, Aug. 20, 1968; Norman Rockwell, *The Right to Know*, *Look*, Aug. 20,

1968; "Why We Need New Politicians," *Look*, Jan. 13, 1970; and Gardner, "Unfinished Business of America," *Look*, July 13, 1971; "Nonviolence Still Works," *Look*, April 1, 1969; and "America's Indians" and Edward Kennedy, "Let the Indians Run Indian Policy," *Look*, June 2, 1970. As noted, long before the Chavez article, *Look* had published a long, sympathetic story on migrant farmworkers in its June 19, 1951, issue.

63. Litwak, "Why We Need a Revolution," *Look*, May 27, 1969; Gardner, "Message for a Revolutionary Generation: You Can Remake This Society," *Look*, July 15, 1969; "A Vision of the Human Revolution," *Look*, Jan. 13, 1970; Commager, "Is Freedom Dying in America?"; Stevens, "Do We Need a New Pledge of Allegiance?," *Look*, Dec. 1, 1970; and "Unfinished Business of America," *Look* July 13, 1971: six articles—by John Gardner, Bella Abzug, Jesse Jackson, George Wallace, George Wald, and James Gavin—were packaged together in a section of this issue on the country's "unfinished business."

64. Rockefeller, "The Hidden Crisis," *Look*, Feb. 9, 1965; "Peace of Mind," *Look*, July 27, 1971; "For the U.S., the Big Change Is Now!," *Look*, March 21, 1967; "How School Stunts Your Child," *Look*, Sept. 17, 1968; Nelson, "Five Who Care," April 21, 1970; and Farson, "The Rage of Women," *Look*, Dec. 16, 1969.

65. "The Seventies: Mankind's Last, Best Chance," *Look*, Jan. 13, 1970; Interview, John Poppy, April 12, 2018; and Leonard, *Walking on the Edge of the World*, 344–45.

66. "The Future of Power," *Look*, Jan. 13, 1970.

67. "Why We Need a New Sexuality," "A Vision of the Human Revolution," "Why We Need New Businessmen," and "A Place for Snakes as Well as Naked Lovers," *Look*, Jan. 13, 1970.

68. "'70s," *Look*, Jan. 13, 1970; and Leonard, *Walking on the Edge of the World*, 344–50, 354–56.

69. Steinem, "Why We Need a Woman President in 1976," *Look*, Jan. 13, 1970; and Vincent Sheean, "A Woman for President," *Look*, Sept. 27, 1949.

70. Abzug, "Unfinished Business of America," *Look*, July 13, 1971.

71. C. P. Snow and Philip Snow, "Hope for America," *Look*, Dec. 1, 1970.

12. "ONE WORLD" INTERNATIONALISM

1. "Introduction to the First Issue of *Life*," *Life*, Nov. 23, 1936; Henry Luce, "The American Century," *Life*, Feb. 17, 1941; "Mr. Europe at 80," *Look*, Nov. 26, 1968; and "*Look* Editorial Department," cabinet 4, drawer 1, folder 1, GCP, GCADU.

2. "When Fidel Castro Charmed the U.S.," *Smithsonian*, Jan. 24, 2019.

3. "Marshal Tito," *Life*, Sept. 13, 1948; and "Tito," *Look*, Nov. 23, 1948.

4. "German Labor Camps," *Look*, Aug. 31, 1937; "Spain Is Starving," *Look*, Feb. 14, 1939; "Adolf Hitler," *Look*, June 6, 1939; "Goering," *Look*, Feb. 1937; "No. 3 Nazi and His Family," *Look*, Aug. 2, 1938; and "Reich Bans U.S. Magazine: Action against *Look* Is Tied to Goering Taking Offense," *New York Times*, Feb. 27, 1937.

5. William Hitler, "Why I Hate My Uncle," *Look*, July 4, 1939.

6. "William Hitler's Letter to FDR," Warfare History Network, Nov. 21, 2016.

7. "Marine Machine Gunners (18th in American Heroes series)," *Look*, Feb. 23, 1943; and "Walker Sorrell," *Look*, July 11, 1944.

8. Fowler Harper, "Negro Solider, Sergeant Franklin Williams of Baltimore Fights with Distinction," *Look*, Oct. 6, 1942.

9. Editors of *Look*, *Our American Heroes: A Pictorial Saga of Gallantry* (New York: Look, 1943).

10. Editors of *Look*, *My Favorite War Story* (New York: Whittlesey House, 1945); and "My Favorite War Story," *Infantry Journal*, April 1946.

11. Moscrip Miller, "Inter-Plane Radio Saved the Captain, but Not His Buddy," *Look*, May 29, 1945; and Cronkite, "Riding a Fortress over Germany," *Look*, Nov. 16, 1943.

12. Thompson, "American Women," *Look*, July 14, 1942; and Marion K. Sanders, *Dorothy Thompson: A Legend in Her Time* (Boston: Houghton Mifflin, 1973).

13. "Why Hitler's Planes Failed to Beat Britain," *Look*, Dec. 17, 1940; "Winston Churchill and the World Crisis," *Look*, Feb. 25, 1941; and Cowles and Willkie, "The British People Under Fire," *Look*, April 8, 1941; Sheean, "How Hitler Plans to Invade England," *Look*, March 11, 1941; Sheean, "Why Are We Going to War? Practical Reasons," *Look*, May 20, 1941; Freud, "What Bombing Does to British Babies," *Look*, Aug. 26, 1941; "Three Full-Color Pages of Photos of Bombed England," *Look*, July 29, 1941; and Sheean and C. S. Forester, "The Truth about Our English Allies," *Look*, July 28, 1942.

14. "Death Camp Photos," *Look*, May 15, 1945; "Goering Tells How the Nazis Did It," *Look*, Sept. 3, 1946; "Mistress of Buchenwald," *Look*, Jan. 4, 1949; Zwy Aldouby and Ephraim Katz, "Untold Story of Adolf Eichmann," *Look*, Aug. 2, 1960; and "The Agonized American Jews," *Look*, April 20, 1971.

15. "Europe Digs Out from War's Debris," *Look*, April 17, 1945; "Europe's Hunger," *Look*, Nov. 25, 1947; "Getting Europe Back on Her Feet," *Look*, Feb. 3, 1948; "The UN and You," *Look*, Sept. 16, 1947; "The United Nations," *Look*, Sept. 30, 1947; and Abba Eban, "Do We Really Need the UN?," *Look*, June 29, 1965.

16. "The Siege," RKO Pathé Pictures, photographed and described by Julien Bryan, in "Special War Feature Sections," *Look*, Oct. 24, Nov. 7, and Nov. 21, 1939; Cowles and Willkie, "The British People Under Fire"; "22 Color Photos of Burning Chungking," *Look*, Sept. 23, 1941; and "Death Camp Photos."

17. Szyk, "Hitler's Butchers" (story by Pierre Van Paassen), *Look*, Sept. 8, 1942; and Edmundson, "A Guy Named Joe" and "Exclusive Personal Interview" (stories by Ralph Parker), *Look*, June 27, 1944.

18. Sheean, "How Did Russia Get That Way?," *Look*, Sept. 4, 1945 and Oct. 16, 1945; "Will We Have to Fight Russia?," *Look*, Oct. 16, 1945; Buck, "How to Understand the Russians," Sept. 2, 1947; "Cowles Urges a Reunited Germany as a Bar to Soviet Expansion," *New York Times*, May 14, 1946; Cowles, "Impressions of a Quick Trip around the World," *Des Moines Register*, June, 1947 and "Records of the *Look* Years, 1972," cabinet 4, drawer 2, folders 20 and 23, GCP, CFADU; Eleanor Roosevelt, "The Russians Are Tough," *Look*, Feb. 18, 1947; and Douglas, "Soviet Colonialism: Product of Terror," *Look*, Dec. 13, 1955.

NOTES TO PAGES 188–193

19. John Gunther, "Behind the Iron Curtain," *Look*, Nov. 9, 1948; Fischer, "Life Story of Stalin," *Look*, June 8, 1948; "Men around Stalin," *Look*, April 17, 1945; Sheean, "How Did Russia Get That Way?"; "What Stalin Tells the Russians about Us," *Look*, Jan. 21, 1947; and "First Pictures of the Atom Bomb," *Look*, May 8, 1951.

20. Walter Lippmann, "Armistice in the Cold War?," *Look*, Feb. 9, 1954; and "Cowles Urges People to Scan Russ Changes," *Los Angeles Times*, Aug. 28, 1956.

21. "*Look* to Establish Bureau in Moscow," *Look* press release, Dec. 13, 1955; "Edmund Stevens, 81, a Reporter in Moscow, Is Dead," *New York Times*, May 27, 1992; "Mrs. Roosevelt Cancels Planned Visit to Russia," *Washington Post and Times Herald*, July 2, 1954; and Johnston, "At Home with Khrushchev," *Look*, Feb. 17, 1959.

22. John Gunther, "Inside Russia," *Look*, April 2, 1957; and William Attwood and Adlai Stevenson, "Russia's Two Faces," *Look*, Nov. 25, 1958.

23. "Eisenhower in the USSR," *Look*, Sept. 15, 1959; and Richard Nixon, "Roads I've Traveled," *Look*, Oct. 25, 1960.

24. Averell Harriman, "Khrushchev in the USA," *Look*, Sept. 15, 1960; "The Myth of Russia's Productive Power," *Look*, Sept. 27, 1960; Rabbi Joshua Goldberg, "Soviet Anti-Semitism," *Look* Oct. 24, 1961; and "Inside the Soviet Spy System," *Look*, Dec. 10, 1957.

25. "*Register*'s 'Mike' Cowles Is Dead of Cancer at Age 82," *Des Moines Register*, July 9, 1985; and "Khrushchev Still Angry about '57 Coup Attempt," *New York Times*, April 25, 1962.

26. "Editor Reports on Europe and Russia," *Look*, June 5, 1962; "Interview with Khrushchev: He Uses Meeting with American Editors to Pound Home Key Propaganda Points," *Wall Street Journal*, July 17, 1962; and Gardner Cowles Jr., *Mike Looks Back: The Memoirs of Gardner Cowles, Founder of Look Magazine* (New York: Gardner Cowles, 1985), 174–76.

27. Khrushchev, "Behind the Sino-Soviet Split," *Look*, Feb. 12, 1963; and Cowles Jr., *Mike Looks Back*, 176–77.

28. "Russia Today," *Look*, Oct. 3, 1967; and Editors of *Look* Magazine, *Red Russia after 50 Years* (New York: Cowles Education Corp., 1968).

29. "Berlin: Will We Fight for This Tormented City?," *Look*, Feb. 28, 1961; and "Little Boy at the Wall," *Look*, June 18, 1963.

30. "An Eerie Trip along the Iron Curtain" and "The Fence," *Look*, Jan. 30, 1962.

31. "How Hellish Is the Hydrogen Bomb?," *Look*, April 21, 1953; "Your Last Chance," *Look*, 1946; "Flight over the A-Bomb," *Look*, Aug. 13, 1963; "Lest We Forget," *Look*, June 14, 1955; Michihiko Hachiya, "Hiroshima Diary," *Look*, Aug. 9, 1955; "Hiroshima: The Decision That Changed the World," *Look*, June 7, 1960; "Nagasaki" *Look*, Aug. 10, 1965; and "Great Fall-out Shelter Panic," *Look*, Dec. 5, 1961.

32. Cowles, "Impressions of a Quick Trip"; "Records of the *Look* Years, 1972"; "The Cowles World," *Time*, Dec. 8, 1958; "Generalissimo Chiang Kai-shek," *Look*, May 2, 1944; "Behind the Scenes with Chiang Kai-shek," *Look*, July 24, 1945; Adlai Stevenson, "Chiang Kai-shek and Korea's Rhee Still Think Red China Can Be Beaten," *Look*, May 19, 1953; Wu, "Your Money Has Built a Police State in Formosa," *Look*, June 29, 1954; "Wu on Formosa," *Look*, Aug. 10, 1954; Churchill, "Cold Peace and Our Future," *Look*, April 29,

1958; and Steven Ambrose, review of Robert E. Herzstein's *Henry R. Luce: A Political Portrait of the Man Who Created the American Century*, *Foreign Affairs*, May/June 1994.

33. "Records of the *Look* Years, 1972"; and "The Cowles World."

34. "Newsmen in China Penalized by U.S.," *New York Times*, Dec. 29, 1956; "Reporters Cited on Trip to China," *New York Times*, April 16, 1958; and "Worthy Loses Passport Bid," *Chicago Defender*, April 6, 1957.

35. "Inside Red China," *Look*, April 16, 1957; and "William Worthy Dies at 92: Journalist Challenged U.S. Policies," *Los Angeles Times*, May 20, 2014.

36. "Inside Red China."

37. "Red China Clings to Ancient Medicine," *Look*, Oct. 1, 1957.

38. Snow, "A Report from China," *Look*, Jan. 31, 1961.

39. Barnett, "What Chou Enlai's Words Mean to Us," *Look*, Jan. 31, 1961.

40. John Maxwell Hamilton, *Edgar Snow: A Biography* (Bloomington: Indiana University Press, 1988); and "Memorandum of Conversation," U.S. Department of State, Washington DC, Feb. 20, 1961, *Foreign Relations of the United States, 1961–63*, vol. 13, *Western Europe and Canada*.

41. "Chinese Bomb Menace," *Look*, Dec. 1, 1964; "Red China," *Look*, Nov. 2, 1965; Zorza, "Hidden Battle for Power in Red China," *Look*, Aug. 23, 1966; Barnett, "China after Mao," *Look*, Nov. 15, 1966; William Ryan and Sam Summerlin, "The Incredible Story of How China Got the Bomb," *Look*, July 25, 1967; Barnett, "Tensions on the Sino-Soviet Border," *Look*, Oct. 3, 1967; and Alan Whiting, "How We Almost Went to War with China," *Look*, April 29, 1969.

42. Myrdal, "A New *Look* into Mao's China," *Look*, Feb. 10, 1970.

43. Sheila K. Johnson, "To China, with Love," *Commentary*, June 1973.

44. "Wounded Korean War Soldiers," *Look*, Jan. 9, 1952; John Gunther, "How Good Is MacArthur?," *Look*, Oct. 24, 1950; Churchill, "Cold Peace and Our Future"; and Stevenson, "Chiang Kai-shek and Korea's Rhee."

45. "Inside Cuba's Revolution" and "Interview," *Look*, Feb. 4, 1958; and "Castro on Eve," *Life*, April 14, 1958.

46. "Inside Cuba's Revolution" and "Interview." Castro's stated desire to meet with CIA agents was reported more extensively for a front-page article for *New York Times* later that year. This story, which could have changed the course of U.S.-Cuban relations, appeared on December 11 but never made it into the hands of anyone beyond the Times Building because of a 17-day delivery-drivers' strike.

47. "Inside Rebel Cuba with Raul Castro," *Life*, July 21, 1958.

48. "The Tragedy of Fidel Castro," *Look*, April 21, 1959; and "Cuba Revisited: How to See Havana without Getting Hijacked," *Look*, April 7, 1970.

49. "30 Days in Castro's Cuba," *Look*, Nov. 8, 1960.

50. "A 2:30 a.m. Interview with 'Che' Guevara," *Look*, Nov. 8, 1960; "Cuba: A Revisit with 'Che' Guevara," *Look*, April 9, 1963; Johanna Derry, "A Thousand Words: The Smoking

Revolutionary," *Jackal*, Oct. 17, 2017; and "Behind the Image: Che Guevara by Rene Burri," Magnum Photos.

51. "My 28 Days in Communist Cuba"; and "Editorial Previews," cabinet 4, drawer 1, folder 3, GCP, GCADU.

52. "Cuba: A Revisit with 'Che' Guevara"; Derry, "A Thousand Words"; and "Behind the Image: Che Guevara"; "Epitaph for a Big Loser," *Look*, April 25, 1961; and Casusu, "I Saw Castro Change," *Look*, Nov. 21, 1961.

53. Cherne, "To Win in Indochina, We Must Win These People," *Look*, Jan. 25, 1955; Rosten, "Introduction: A View from Inside," GCP, CFADU; and Interview, John Poppy, Nov. 11, 2020.

54. "What Johnson Faces in Vietnam," *Look*, Jan. 28, 1964; and "Vietnam Shellfire Kills a *Look* Senior Editor," *New York Times*, May 22, 1966.

55. "Vietnam's Two Wars," *Look*, Jan. 28, 1964.

56. "Recollections from a Lost Notebook in Vietnam," *Look*, April 6, 1965.

57. S. L. A. Marshall, "Men Facing Death: The Destruction of an American Platoon," *Harpers*, Sept. 1966; Gerald L. Steibel, "Are We Getting the Vietnam War Story?," *American Legion Magazine*, Jan. 1967; John Laurence, *The Cat from Hue: A Vietnam War Story* (New York: Public Affairs, 2002); and "Sam Castan, 1935–1966, *Look* Senior Editor," *Look*, July 12, 1966.

58. Editors of *Look* and Catherine Leroy, "This Is That War," May 14, 1968; and "Vietnam: Get Out Now," *Look*, Nov. 18, 1969.

59. "Vietnam: Get Out Now"; and "Vietnamese GI: Can He Win His Own War?," *Look*, Aug. 11, 1970.

60. Kennedy, "The Agony of Vietnam," *Look*, Nov. 28, 1967; Kissinger, Morgenthau, Kahn, Schlesinger, and Hanson Baldwin, "Vietnam: What Should We Do Now?," *Look*, Aug. 9, 1966; "Schlesinger Warns of Danger of 'Americanization' of War," *New York Times*, July 25, 1966; "Henry Kissinger: Strategist in the White House Basement," *Look*, Aug. 12, 1969; Interview, Will Hopkins, Nov. 22, 2016; Bradley, "My Visit to Vietnam," *Look*, Nov. 14, 1967; *Congressional Record—Senate*, Nov. 8, 1967, 31643; and Marshall, "He's Winning Our War in Vietnam," *Look*, Jan. 10, 1967.

61. Sevareid, "Final Troubled Hours of Adlai Stevenson," *Look*, Nov. 30, 1965; "Vietnam: Dispute over Reported Vietnam Feller," *Los Angeles Times*, Nov. 21, 1965; and "Vietnam: Get Out Now."

62. Fallaci, "Interview with a Vietcong Terrorist," *Look*, April 16, 1968; Master Sgt. Daniel Lee Pitzer, "Animal Called POW: My Four Years in a Vietcong Prison," Feb. 18, 1969; and Helfan, "A Letter to the President," *Look*, July 28, 1970.

63. "Who Would Ever Want to Go Anymore," *Look*, Oct. 6, 1970; and "Our Uptight Troops in Europe," *Look*, Sept. 8, 1970.

64. "Military's New Dilemma: Protest in the Ranks," *Look*, Oct. 18, 1968; "South Vietnamese Army: Can It Replace Our GIs?," *Look*, Dec. 10, 1968; Harriman, "Vietnamization Is Immoral," *Look*, Nov. 17, 1970; "The Vietnamese GI"; and Riboud, "Communist North Vietnam, Cocky and Patriotic," *Look*, Jan. 21, 1969.

65. "Our Asian War Widens," *Look*, May 19, 1970; "How Nixon Decided to Invade Cambodia," *Look*, Aug. 11, 1970; "The Worst Massacre of All," *Look*, June 15, 1971; "Henry Kissinger"; and "From Peking, Sihanouk Talks to Americans," *Look*, Oct. 20, 1970.

66. Fulbright, "Wars in Your Future," *Look*, Dec. 2, 1969.

67. "U.S. Troops in Santo Domingo: Grim Price of Power," *Look*, June 15, 1965; and Fallaci, "The Shooting of Oriana Fallaci," *Look*, Nov. 12, 1968.

68. "Records of the *Look* Years," GCP, GCADU; "Cowles Urges Support of Nehru to Avert a 'Calamitous Blunder,'" *New York Times*, Sept. 25, 1951; "Calcutta: Metropolis of Misery," *Look*, July 10, 1956; "*Look* Applauds 12 UCLA Students," *Look*, March 10, 1953; Morgan, *Friends and Fellow Students: An Adventure in Mutual Understanding* (Cromwell, 1956); and Judith Kerr Graven, *Project India: How College Students Won Friends for America* (Minneapolis MN: Mill City Press, 2014).

69. "India Today," *Look*, July 12, 1966; and "India: Too Poor to Be Effective, Too Big to Be Ignored," *Look*, July 12, 1966.

70. "Ben-Gurion Talks," *Look*, April 15, 1958; "Golda," *Look*, Oct. 7, 1969; "Young Israel in Pictures," *Look*, May 6, 1952; "Israel Today," *Look*, Oct. 11, 1960; and "Israel: Twenty Years of Siege and Struggle," *Look*, April 30, 1968.

71. "Nasser Talks," *Look*, June 25, 1957; Capt. Melvin V. Blixt, "Soviet Objectives in the Eastern Mediterranean," *Naval War College Review*, March 1969; "Soviet Military Aid to the United Arab Republic," CIA, 1969; *Congressional Record—Senate*, April 17, 1958, 6674; and "Nasser Talks," *Look*, May 16, 1968.

72. "Ben-Gurion Talks"; Ben-Gurion, "Ben-Gurion Sees Gradual Democratization of the Soviet Union," *Look*, Jan. 4, 1962; Ben-Gurion, "Why Israel Wants Peace," *Look*, Aug. 27, 1963; and Eban, "Do We Really Need the UN?"

73. "Revolt of the Arab Refugees: We'll Meet in Tel Aviv," *Look*, May 13, 1969; "Hidden Leader of the Arab Guerrillas," *Look*, June 10, 1970; "Israeli Youth: The Coming Explosion," *Look*, June 15, 1971; Michener, "Israel: Nation Too Young to Die," *Look*, Aug. 8, 1967; and "The Agonized American Jews."

74. "Inside Negro Africa," *Look*, June 23, 1959; "When an American Negro Returns to Africa," *Look*, April 4, 1967; "Who am I? Ghetto Students Search for Answers in Black Africa" and "Black America's African Heritage," *Look*, Jan. 7, 1969.

75. "Inside Negro Africa"; "Visit with Tshombe," *Look*, March 9, 1965; and "Report from the Congo—War-Drum Days Ahead," *Look*, Oct. 31, 1967.

76. "Where the White Man Rules," *Look*, June 23, 1959; and Robert Kennedy, "Suppose God Is Black?," *Look*, Aug. 23, 1966.

77. "Inside Negro Africa"; "Is the United States Meeting the Challenge of Africa?," *Look*, March 28, 1961; "Angola," *Look*, March 28, 1961; and "Black America's African Heritage."

78. "The President," *New York Times*, June 25, 1966; and "Memo from Nigeria: Old Headaches for Our New President," *Look* Nov. 26, 1968.

79. Kennedy, "America and Africa," speech, June 4, 1960, John F. Kennedy Presidential Library; "The President," *New York Times*; "Attwood Named to Head Newsday," *New*

York Times, Sept. 2, 1970; and "Three Editors Going to Africa," *New York Times*, June 26, 1964.

80. Abend, "The Strange Case of MacArthur in Japan," *Look*, Jan. 18, 1949; "Adlai Stevenson Reports on His World Tour," *Look*, May 19, 1952; and Johnston, "Japan: Problem or Partner," *Look*, April 5, 1955.

81. "Casey Stengel Dazes Japan," *Look*, Jan. 24, 1956; "Ed Sullivan in Japan," *Look*, July 10, 1956; "Japan's Teen-age Idol," *Look*, June 21, 1960; "There Are Also Zen Beatniks," *Look*, Sept. 10, 1963; "Every Child a Prodigy," *Look*, Nov. 28, 1967; and Art Kane, "Mystic Image of Japan," Richard Okamoto, "Japan," and Edwin Reischauer, "Our Man in Japan," *Look*, Sept. 10, 1963.

82. Joseph Asher, "Rabbi Asks, Is It Time We Forgave the Germans?," *Look*, April 20 1965; Brandt, "Wall Has Cut My City in Half," *Look*, June 18, 1963; Brandt, "Don't Pull the GIs Out of Europe," *Look*, April 21, 1970; and "What's behind the German Comeback," *Look*, Jan. 25, 1954.

83. "Socialized Medicine: Does it Work in Britain?" *Look*, Dec. 20, 1960; and "Why Does a Man Vote Communist," *Look*, July 27, 1954.

84. See, for example: "First Time She Saw Paris," *Look*, July 2, 1963; "Ode to Venice," *Look*, Feb. 4, 1969; "London: The Cutting Edge," *Look*, Sept. 20, 1966; "This Proud Land, This Canada," *Look*, Aug. 22, 1967; "Australia: It's Much More Than Kangaroos," *Look*, Aug. 23, 1966; "Chanel No. 1," *Look*, Oct. 23, 1962; and Interview, John Poppy, May 21, 2018.

13. COVERS, SPECIAL FEATURES, CULTURE

1. "Editorial Analysis 1st 6 months of 1959 by Lloyd H. Hall Co.," cabinet 8, drawer 2, folder 3, GCP, GCADU; "Story of *Look*," cabinet 8, drawer 2, folder 2, GCP, GCADU.

2. *Look*, June 6, 1939; *Look*, May 18, 1965; "Earth Day: The Fight to Save America Starts Now," "Five Who Care," "Ladies Save the Lakes," and "The Most Beautiful View in the World," *Look*, April 21, 1970; and "Fun in the Water," *Look*, July 14, 1970.

3. "Along the Iron Curtain," *Look*, Jan. 30, 1962; "What's Behind Ho?," *Look*, Jan. 21, 1969; and "With the Arab Guerilla Forces," *Look*, May 13, 1969.

4. *Look*, Aug. 17, 1937; *Look*, Nov. 7, 1954; and "The Mystery of Willie Mays," *Look*, May 3, 1955.

5. *Look*, March 9, 1971; *Look*, Sept. 6, 1955; "John Lennon," *Look*, Jan. 9, 1968; "The Hidden Life of Elvis Pressley," *Look*, May 4, 1971; and "Country Music," *Look*, July 13, 1971.

6. "Story of *Look*"; Leo Rosten, ed., *Guide to the Religions of America: The Famous Look Magazine Series on Religion; Plus Facts, Figures, Tables, Charts, Articles, and Comprehensive Reference Material on Churches and Religious Groups in the United States* (New York: Simon & Schuster, 1955); Leo Rosten, *Religions in America: Ferment and Faith in an Age of Crisis* (New York: Simon & Schuster, 1975); Hartzell Spence, *The Story of Religions in America* (New York: Holt Rinehart and Winston, 1960); "Story of *Look*," cabinet 8, drawer 2, folder 2, GCP, GCADU; "William Arthur Executive Correspondence—Mich,

1956–60," box 14, folder 10, LRWHS; "Gardner Cowles: Creative Editor with a Quest for Insight into World Affairs," *Printers' Ink*, April 10, 1959; "The Jews in America," *Look*, May 13, 1958; and *Rotarian*, May 1961.

7. "Roman Catholics," *Look*, Nov. 12, 1957.

8. Blake, "Religious Bodies Growing Rapidly," *Look*, Sept. 6, 1955; and Lila Corman Berwin, *Speaking of Jews: Rabbis, Intellectuals, and the Creation of an American Identity* (Berkeley: University of California Press, 2009).

9. Maisel, "Dianetics: Science or Hoax?," *Look*, Dec. 5, 1950.

10. "Socrates," *Look*, June 18, 1963.

11. Rosten, "Introduction: A View from Inside," GCP, GCADU; and "Socrates."

12. "Aristotle," *Look*, June 14, 1966; "Jefferson," *Look*, July 30, 1963; "Gandhi," *Look*, Aug. 25, 1964; "Machiavelli," *Look*, Nov. 19, 1963; "George Washington," *Look*, March 8, 1966; and "Churchill," *Look*, Feb. 7, 1967.

13. The Editors of *Look*, with text by Leo Rosten, and art direction by Allen Hurlburt, *The Story Behind the Painting* (New York: Cowles Magazines & Broadcasting, distributed by Doubleday, 1962).

14. *The Story Behind the Painting*; and "Laughing Philosopher," *Look*, Dec. 11, 1956.

15. "Monet," *Look*, Nov. 11, 1958; "Hokusai," *Look*, June 11, 1957; "Leonardo," *Look*, June 25, 1957; "Gauguin," *Look*, Jan. 6, 1959; and "Georges Braque," *Look*, Aug. 18, 1959.

16. "Ben Shahn," *Look*, Feb. 3, 1948; Museum of Modern Art, "Ben Shahn," Sept. 30, 1947 to Jan. 4, 1948; Jean Renoir, "Renoir," *Look*, Nov. 6, 1962; *Look*, Sept. 9, 1952; Pablo Picasso and Jacqueline Picasso, "Picasso: The Ninth Decade," *Look*, Dec. 27, 1967; Pablo Picasso, "Picasso," *Look*, Dec. 10, 1968; and "Picasso," *Look*, Sept. 9, 1952.

17. "Cleveland's Jim Brown," *Look*, Nov. 24, 1959: "I'm Only Human," *Look*, Dec. 31, 1963; "Green Bay Coach Reveals His Secrets of Winning Football," *Look*, Sept. 19, 1967; "Lombardi," *New York Theater Guide*, Oct. 1, 2010; Sandy Koufax, "What Baseball Means to Me," *Look*, July 26, 1966; and Rose Szolnoki, "My Son, the Quarterback," *Look*, Sept. 9, 1969.

18. "Fall and Rise of Muhammad Ali," *Look*, March 9, 1971; and "Alone in a Crowd," *Look*, Feb. 21, 1967.

19. Bouton, "My Love/Hate Affair with Baseball," *Look*, June 2, 1970; and "I'm Glad You Didn't Take It Personally," *Look*, June 15, 1971.

20. Dave Meggysey, "Sex and Racism in the NFL," *Look*, Dec. 1, 1970.

21. "Fashion Now: Black Pow!" *Look*, April 20, 1971.

22. "The Grape's the Thing," *Look*, June 15, 1971.

23. Gardner Cowles Jr., *Mike Looks Back: The Memoirs of Gardner Cowles, Founder of Look Magazine* (New York: Gardner Cowles, 1985); "*Look* Magazine, 1946–1968," cabinet 3, drawer 3, folder 5, GCP, GCADU; "*Look* Motion Pictures, 1946," cabinet 4, drawer 1, folder 11, GCP, GCADU; and Kenneth Stewart, "*Look*," PM, May 28, 1949.

24. Cowles Jr., *Mike Looks Back*; and Rosten, "Introduction: A View from Inside."

25. Cowles Jr., *Mike Looks Back.*

26. "*Look* Magazine, 1946–1968"; "*Look* Motion Pictures, 1946"; Stewart, "*Look*"; "The Selznick Girls," *Look,* Jan. 1944; and Thomas Schatz, *The Genius of the System: Hollywood Filmmaking in the Studio Era* (New York: Henry Holt, 1988).

27. "Peck Set for Lead in Baseball Film," *New York Times,* Dec. 23, 1947; and "Young Man with Ideas and a Camera," *New York Times,* Jan. 14, 1951.

28. "Gloria Swanson," *Look,* June 6, 1950; and "Dustin Hoffman: Star of *The Graduate* Turns Bum," *Look,* Sept. 17. 1968.

29. "Garbo," *Look,* Aug. 31, 1937; and John Bainbridge, "Garbo Is 65," *Look,* Sept. 3, 1970.

30. "Gone with the Wind," *Look,* July 18, 1939; "The Private Life of Mickey Rooney," *Look,* May 7, 1940; and "Judy Garland and Mickey Rooney," *Look,* Oct. 5, 1942.

31. "Bacall," *Look,* Nov. 14, 1944; "Bacall and Bogart," *Look,* April 3, 1945; "Bacall Comes Back Big," *Look,* March 22, 1966; and "Rita Hayworth," *Look,* March 6, 1945.

32. "Elizabeth Taylor and Richard Burton, the Night of the Brawl," *Look,* Feb. 8, 1966; and "How Do I Love Thee: Let Me Count the Ways," *Look,* June 18, 1970.

33. Nan Talese and Lawrence Schiller, *Marilyn and Me: A Photographer's Memories* (New York: Doubleday, 2012); "Iconic Marilyn Monroe Photos to Go Up for Auction, Alongside the Camera That Took Them," *Town and Country,* Sept. 19, 2019; "The Lost Marilyn Monroe Photos," *Hollywood Reporter,* Oct. 13, 2010; "Marilyn," *Look,* June 30, 1953; "Marilyn Monroe," Nov. 17, 1953; "Marilyn Monroe," *Look,* May 29, 1956; Interview, Douglas Kirkland, April 13, 2016; and Carl Sandburg, "Tribute to Marilyn from a Friend," *Look,* Sept. 11, 1962.

34. "The Gorgeous Lana Turner," *Look,* June 6, 1950; "Audrey Hepburn," *Look,* Feb. 12, 1952; "Kim Novak," *Look,* May 31, 1955; "Janet Leigh," *Look,* July 27, 1954; Grace Kelly, *Look,* June 15, 1954; "Grace Kelly," *Look,* Jan. 10, 1956; "Gina Lollobrigida Joins the Circus," *Look,* May 15, 1956; "Maureen O'Hara," *Look,* Nov. 20, 1951; "Ava Gardner," Dec. 12, 1951; and "Jane Russell," *Look,* Oct. 9, 1951.

35. "Gary Cooper's Last Trip Home," *Look,* July 18, 1961; "Marlin Brando: The Real Story," *Look,* May 17, 1955; "Rock Hudson," *Look,* March 18, 1958: and "James Dean," *Look,* Oct. 16, 1956.

36. "Cary Grant of Enduring Charm," *Look,* Aug. 23, 1955; "Curious Story behind the New Cary Grant," *Look,* Sept. 1, 1959; "Cary Grant: The Legend and the Ladies," *Look,* Dec. 17, 1963; "Cary Grant and His Baby," *Look,* July 26, 1966; and "The New Women in the Life of Cary Grant," *Look,* Feb. 23, 1971.

37. "John Wayne," *Look,* Oct. 6, 1942; and "John Wayne," *Look,* Aug. 2, 1960.

38. "Memo from Mike Cowles to Dan Mich," Nov. 29, 1956, GCP, CFADU; and Barrymore, "My Battle with My Father," *Look,* March 19, 1957.

39. "Natalie Wood: Beauty and Violence," *Look,* April 11, 1961.

40. "Julie Andrews' Star Rises Higher with *The Sound of Music*," *Look,* Jan. 28, 1965; and "Julie, Baby," *Look,* Dec. 28, 1965.

41. Baldwin, "Sidney Poitier," *Look*, July 23, 1968; "Durango: Poitier Meets Belafonte," *Look*, Aug. 24, 1971; and "Harry and Sidney: Soul Brothers," *New York Times*, Feb. 20, 2017.

42. "Ali McGraw," *Look*, Aug. 11, 1970; and "The Anatomy of a Beauty," *Look*, March 9, 1971.

43. "Secret Agent James Bond's Second Girlfriend," *Look*, Dec. 31, 1963; "The Good Guys Wear Paint," *Look*, Dec. 1, 1970; and "Warren and Julie: Together at Last," *Look*, June 1, 1971.

44. Interview, Douglas Kirkland and Francoise Kirkland, April 13, 2016.

45. "Movies," *Look*, Nov. 3, 1970.

46. "Hollywood Goes TV," *Look*, Aug. 12, 1952; "TV's Boswell," *Look*, July 14, 1953; "Ed Sullivan in Japan: Looking for Talent in the Orient," *Look*, July 10, 1956; "Lucy's Two Babies," *Look*, April 21, 1953; "Desi and Lucy," *Look*, Dec. 25, 1956; and "Here's Your First View of Disneyland," *Look*, Nov. 2, 1954.

47. "Dick Clark Talks to Teenagers," *Look*, Nov. 24, 1959; and "Are TV Quiz Shows Fixed?," *Look*, Aug. 20, 1957.

48. Caesar, "What Psychoanalysis Did to Me," *Look*, Oct. 2, 1956.

49. Interview, John Poppy, April 12, 2018; and "Worldwide Lure of Bonanza," *Look*, Dec. 1, 1964.

50. "U.N.C.L.E.'s Illya: A New Kind of TV Idol," *Look* July 27, 1965; and "Stefanie Powers: The U.N.C.L.E. Doll," *Look* Oct. 18, 1965.

51. "Ten Years of TV: How It's Better, How It's Worse, What's Ahead," *Look*, Sept. 27, 1960; Minow, "A New Look at TV," *Look*, Oct. 9, 1962; and Eliot Daley, "Is TV Brutalizing Your Child?," *Look*, Dec. 2, 1969.

52. CCI executive seminar, Orlando FL, Mar 9–10, 1970, GCP, GCADU; and "TV: Turn-On or Turn-Off," *Look*, Sept. 7, 1971.

53. Fallaci, "What Does Walter Cronkite Really Think?," *Look*, Nov. 11, 1970; Mitgang, "D-Day Plus 20 Years," *Look*, Feb. 25, 1964; "American Dream" and "World Still Moves Our Way," *Look*, July 9, 1968; and "TV News, Its Crisis, Conflict and Change," *Look*, Nov. 7, 1961.

54. "Cooney and the Kids," *Look*, Nov. 18, 1969; "TV's Mr. Rogers: Quality for Kids," *Look*, Dec. 1, 1969; "The Secrets of Sesame Street," *Look*, Sept. 22, 1970; Hentoff, "Smothers Brothers: Who Controls TV?," *Look*, June 24, 1969; "Does Dick Cavett Have It?," *Look*, July 15, 1969; and "What's Different about Public TV?," *Look*, Sept. 7, 1971.

55. "Band of the Year," *Look*, Jan. 1946; "The Woody Herman Band," *Look*, Feb. 5, 1946; and "All American Swing Band," *Look*, Nov. 12, 1946.

56. "Dixieland Jazz Is Hot Again," *Look*, June 6, 1950; Philippe D. Mather, *Authorship and Genre in in Photojournalism and Film* (Bristol, UK: Intellect, 2013); "Duke Ellington: A Living Legend Swings On," *Look*, Aug. 20, 1957; "How *Look* Magazine's Only Female Staff Photographer Covered a Changing World," *Time*, Sept. 28, 2016; "Ella Fitzgerald," *Look*, April 20, 1960; and "Tale of Three Jazz Festivals," *Look*, July 21, 1959.

57. "Dean Martin" and "TV Christmas with the Martins and Sinatras," *Look*, Dec. 26, 1967; "1926–2017: Jerry Lewis," *Hollywood Reporter*, Aug. 23, 2017; "I've Always Been Scared,"

Look, Feb. 5, 1957; "Jerry Lewis," *Look*, Dec. 23, 1958; "Sinatra," *Look*, Sept. 6, 1955; "Sinatra," *Look*, May 14, 1957; and "Sinatra at 50," *Look*, Dec. 14, 1965; and "Working Sinatras," *Look*, Oct. 31, 1967.

58. "Crosby," *Look*, July 6, 1937; "Crosby and Hope in *Road to Rio*," *Look*, Dec. 22, 1947; Bob Crosby, "I Hated Being Bing Crosby's Brother," *Look*, July 22, 1958; "The Crosbys of Hollywood," *Look*, June 7, 1960; "Bing's New Family," *Look*, July 22, 1962; and "Mrs. Bing Crosby: Student Nurse," *Look*, March 12, 1963.

59. "Perry Como," *Look*, Dec. 1953; "Perry Como Party," *Look*, May 12, 1959; "Lawrence Welk: Nobody Likes Him but His Public," *Look*, June 15, 1957; and "Pat Boone," *Look*, Aug. 5, 1958.

60. "The Great Rock 'n' Roll Controversy," *Look*, June 26, 1956.

61. "Elvis, What? Why?," *Look*, Aug 7, 1956; "Great Elvis Presley Industry," *Look*, Nov. 13, 1956; and "Face Is Familiar," *Look*, Dec. 11, 1956.

62. Hopkins, "The Hidden Life of Elvis Presley," *Look*, May 4, 1971.

63. "Folk Singers and Their Fans," *Look*, Aug. 27, 1963.

64. "Once-Rejected Bob Dylan Photos Find Home at Grand Valley State," *Detroit News*, Feb. 7, 2020; and "Folk Rock's Tambourine Man," *Look*, March 8, 1966.

65. Avedon, "Beatles," *Look*, Jan. 9, 1968; Interview, Douglas Kirkland and Francoise Kirkland; "John Lennon: Beatle on His Own," *Look*, Dec. 13, 1966; and "Beyond Survival," *Look*, Jan. 13, 1970.

66. "An Infinity of Jimi's," *Life*, Barry, Oct. 3, 1969; and "Why There Can't Be Another Woodstock," *Look*, Aug. 25, 1970.

67. "Simon and Garfunkel, Young Poets of Folk Rock," *Look*, Nov. 29, 1966; Gilbert, "Simon and Garfunkel," douglasgilbert.com; "Joan Baez and David Harris: A Family Kept Apart by Conscience," *Look*, May 5, 1970; and "Peace of Mind," *Look*, July 27, 1971.

68. "Where the California Game Is Taking Us," *Look*, June 26, 1966.

69. "Jefferson Airplane Loves You," *Look*, May 30, 1967.

70. "Leonard Cohen: Songs Sacred and Profane," *Look*, June 10, 1969; and Allan Showalter, "Tony Vaccaro Talks about His Iconic Leonard Cohen Photographs," Oct. 8, 2019, www .allanshowalter.com.

71. "The Band: Music from Home," *Look*, Aug. 25, 1970; and John Poppy, Interview, April 12, 2018.

72. "Jimi Hendrix Experience: A Black and White Fusion in the Now Music" *Look*, Jan. 7, 1969.

73. "New Soul-Sound," *Look*, Feb. 20, 1968; and "Ike and Tina Turner: They're Too Much," *Look*, Sept. 8, 1970.

74. "The Importance of Being James Brown," *Look*, Feb. 18, 1969; and "B. B. King," *Look*, June 29, 1971.

75. "Music: Where the Big Money Is Now," "Jackson Five," *Look*, Aug. 25, 1970.

76. "Barbra Streisand," *Look*, April 5, 1966.

77. "Small Band, Big Sound, the Tijuana Brass," *Look*, June 14, 1966; and "Tragedy Touches Their Triumph," *Look*, Oct. 21, 1969.

78. "Country Music," *Look*, July 13, 1971; "Hank Williams Remembered," *Look*, July 13, 1971: "Doc Watson: Musicmaker from Appalachia," *Look*, Jan. 23, 1968; and "Restless Ballad of Johnny Cash," *Look*, April 29, 1969.

14. THE END OF *LOOK*

1. "Cowles Closing *Look* Magazine after 34 Years," *New York Times*, Sept. 17, 1971; and "Why the Power Vacuum at Time Inc. Continues," *New York Magazine*, Oct. 23, 1972.

2. "Why the Power Vacuum at Time Inc. Continues."

3. "The Decline of the Major Networks," *Forbes*, July 26, 2009; "Network Evening News," Pew Research Center, March 13, 2006; "Evening News Audiences Surge during Coronavirus," *Variety*, April 15, 2020; "Cable News Ratings Tighten with Big Months for CNN, MSNBC," ABC News, Feb. 2, 2021; and "America's 100 Most Popular Magazines," *Stacker*, Sept. 10, 2018.

4. "Newspapers Fact Sheet," Pew Research Center, July 9, 2019; and "Social Media Usage in the United States," *Statista*, May 19, 2020.

5. "Fintan O'Toole: Donald Trump Has Destroyed the Country He Promised to Make Great Again," *Irish Times*, April 25, 2020.

6. Robert Paul Wolfe, Barrington Moore, and Herbert Marcuse, *Critique of Pure Tolerance* (Boston: Beacon Press, 1965); and Dwight Macdonald, "Masscult and Midcult," *Partisan Review*, 1960.

7. "Requiem for Look," *New York Times*, Sept. 17, 1971; "Memo from Vernon Myers to the *Look* Staff," September 1971, cabinet 3, drawer 4, folder 11; and "*Look*—Demise, 1971–1973," cabinet 3, drawer 4, folder 11, GCP, CFADU.

INDEX

Bunche, Ralph, 120
Burke, William J., 63–64
Bush, Vannevar, 90
business: coverage of, 14, 60, 81–82, 84–86,
  90, 100, 105, 161, 169, 176; leaders, 10,
  69, 76–77, 89, 178; and liberal postwar
  politics, 7–8, 73–77, 81, 238–40; Mike
  Cowles's relationship with, 29, 31

California, 17, 32, 36, 43, 44, 58, 83–85, 100,
  131, 143, 151, 167, 188
Cambodia, 17, 201, 204. *See also* Vietnam War
Cambridge Book Company, 50
cameras, 68
Canada, 69, 183, 210, 222
Capa, Robert, 184
Carbine, Patricia, xx, 7, 43, 52, 56–58, 61, 64,
  84, 178, 231
Carmichael, Stokely, 120, 232
cars, 14, 74, 75, 79–80, 82, 91, 92, 94, 99, 101,
  176, 179, 213
Carson, Johnny, 226
Carson, Rachel, 104
Carter, Hodding, 69, 109–11
Cassels, Louis, 166
Castan, Sam, 62, 168, 200–202, 204, 229. *See
  also* Vietnam War
Castro, Fidel, 59, 61, 68, 144, 182, 197–200.
  See also Cuba
Castro, Raul, 198
Catledge, Turner, 114
CBS, 87, 114, 165, 168, 227, 236, 239
Charisse, Cyd, 36
Che Guevara, 16, 43, 59, 67, 172, 179, 182, 199
Chiang Kai-shek, 16, 31, 37, 186, 193
Chiang Kai-shek, Mme., 31, 193
children. *See* baby boom; family
Childs, Marquis, 69–70, 164, 185
China, 16, 17, 36, 44, 62, 68, 160, 182, 183–84,
  186–87, 190, 193–97, 210, 241, 243. *See also*
  Cold War; communism

Christianity, 47, 139, 188, 214–15
Christian Science Monitor, 62
Church, Frank, 167
Churchill, Winston, 96, 183, 193, 197, 216
Civil Rights Act of 1957, 113
Civil Rights Act of 1964, 108, 119
Clapper, Olive, 38
Clarke, Arthur C., 98
Cleaver, Eldridge, 123
Clemenko, Harold, 38
Clough, Merrill, 70
Cocteau, Jean, 48
Coffin, Patricia, 38, 44, 61, 80, 122, 133,
  141–44, 147, 219
Cohane, Timothy, 38, 63, 200
Cohen, Leonard, 227, 231
Cold War, 3, 7, 9, 43, 58, 159, 181, 183,
  187–204, 208, 210–11
Collier's, 3, 21, 41, 46, 58, 184, 240
Commager, Henry Steele, 69, 163, 170,
  177, 212
Committee for Economic Development,
  73–74, 76, 81
common conversation, xiv, 4, 237, 240
communism, 5, 6, 44, 164–65, 171, 197, 208–
  9, 238–40, 242; and China, 193–97; and
  Cuba, 197–200; and Eastern Europe,
  191–92; and Soviet Union, 188–91. *See
  also* anti-communism; China; Cuba;
  McCarthy, Joseph; Soviet Union
Como, Perry, 198, 228
computer dating, 100, 135
computers, 63, 87, 90, 99, 100–101,
  103–4, 106, 135, 152, 176. *See also* medical
  advances
"Confidentially" issue, 22, 36
Congo, 11, 197, 207
Connery, Sean, 224
counterculture, 43, 58, 59, 127, 147–49,
  153–54, 226. *See also* hippies; New Left
country music, 213, 233

and China, 193; and Mike Cowles, 22, 33; politics of, 81, 156, 158. See also *Life* magazine; Time-Life

Ludekens, Fred, 185

lynchings, 43, 108, 113–14, 179. *See also* racism

MacArthur, Douglas, 164, 187, 197, 208

Maddox, Lester, 116, 162

Magsaysay, Raman, 43

Mailer, Norman, 69, 122

Malcolm X, 108, 124

Manchester, William, 4, 30, 173–74. *See also* Kennedy, Jackie; Kennedy, John F.

Manning, Jack, 109

Mao Zedong, 190, 193, 195–97. *See also* China

March on Washington (1963), 108, 113, 117, 169. *See also* King, Martin Luther, Jr.

marriage, 43, 123, 127–36, 139, 142–44, 146, 151, 174, 241. *See also* divorce; family

Marshall, George C., 186–87, 203

Marshall, Thurgood, 124

Marshall Plan, 76, 162–63, 186–87

Mau Mau, 10, 197, 207

Maurer, Gilbert, xx, 28, 49–50, 71

Mboya, Tom, 207

McCall's, 40

McCarthy, Eugene, 161, 168, 175, 202

McCarthy, Joseph, 9, 29, 43, 48, 56, 159, 161, 164–66, 221, 239

McHugh, Gelolo, 138

McLuhan, Marshall, 133, 135, 139

McMahon, Frank, 213

Mead, Margaret, 69, 105, 133, 145

Medicaid, 102–3, 178

medical advances, 75, 90, 91–92, 95–97, 101–3

Medicare, 102, 162, 177

Meggysey, Dave, 219

Meir, Golda, 205. *See also* Israel

men's roles, 141, 146–48

"Men Who Fascinate Women," 43

Meredith, James, 118

Meredith, Tom, 122

Meskill, Robert, 58

Mich, Dan, 4, 38, 40, 45, 53, 55–59, 65–66, 69, 71, 191, 216; and civil rights, 112, 114, 125; and Mike Cowles, 24, 55–56, 181, 215; and Edgar Snow, 195; editorial approach, 8, 9–10, 35, 56, 183; politics of, 5, 7, 9, 43, 56, 112, 156, 181, 205, 214; and staff, 55–58, 66, 205; wife (Isabella Taves), 56, 59

Michener, James, 69, 172, 205, 206

Middle East, 48, 62, 204, 205–6, 210. *See also* Egypt; Israel

Midgley, Leslie, 56–57

Milloy, James, 51, 70

Minneapolis Star (and *Star-Tribune*), 26, 60, 125

"Miracle of America," 73–74

Mississippi, 109, 111–13, 116–19, 124, 212

Modern Medicine, 50

Monroe, Marilyn, 16, 31, 37, 68, 189, 212, 218, 220–22

moon, 3, 18, 98, 238. *See also* space program

"Morality USA," 139, 151–52

Morgan, Charles, 118

Morgan, Thomas, 44, 61, 62, 108, 118, 120, 205, 233

Morganthau, Hans, 202–3

Moskin, J. Robert, 16, 62, 103, 131, 138–39, 147, 182, 202

mothers, 127, 129, 131–34, 141–45, 148, 151

Mothner, Ira, 15, 52, 62, 87, 226, 231

Motown, 227, 232

Moynihan, Daniel Patrick, 9–10, 134, 161, 170

Ms. magazine, 43, 58. *See also* Carbine, Patricia; Steinem, Gloria

Muhammad, Elijah, 121

Muhammad Ali, 218

194; criticism of *Look*, 48, 191; and Cuba, 199–200; economy of, 74, 79, 85; and Edmund Stevens, 62; Eleanor Roosevelt articles on, 160; George Leonard article on, 58; "Inside the Soviet Union" (Gunther), 188–89, 212; and Joseph Stalin, 187–88; *Look* coverage of, 9–10, 16, 23, 43–44, 58, 61, 182, 187–91, 212; Mike Cowles and, 6, 29, 30–32, 159; and Nikita Khrushchev, 188–90; Norman Rockwell painting of, 65, 190; and nuclear weapons, 165–66; propaganda, 6, 188; proxy wars, 197; space program, 97, 189; Wendell Willkie article on, 159–60; William Attwood article on, 61

space program, 60, 97–98, 241

space travel, 90, 99, 238

Spanier, Muggsy, 228

Spanish Civil War, 23

Spence, Hartzell, 214

Spike, Robert, 120

Spock, Benjamin, 130, 133

Stalin, Joseph, 7, 23, 31, 37, 44, 69, 159, 183, 186, 187–90, 210. *See also* Soviet Union

Stanton, Frank, 114

Star, Jack, 52, 85, 104, 122, 135, 138, 157, 162, 173

Steffens, William, 221

Stegner, Wallace, 50, 109

Steinem, Gloria, 14, 43, 58, 70, 145, 179–80

Stephens, Martha, 64

Stevens, Edmund, 62, 182, 188, 193–94, 197

Stevenson, Adlai, 6, 44, 61, 158, 161–62, 164, 183, 189, 197, 208

St. George, Andrew, 56, 68, 197–99

Stokes, Carl, 124

"The Story Behind the Painting," 17, 50, 64–65, 216–17

The Story of Religions in America, 214–15

Strentz, Herbert, xx, 28, 40

Stryker, Roy, 84

Student Nonviolent Coordinating Committee (SNCC), 116, 120

Suffolk Sun, 50, 52

Suhler, Lester, 71

Summersby, Kay, 69, 164, 212. *See also* Eisenhower, Dwight D.

Supreme Court, 32, 47, 61, 69, 108, 111, 113, 124, 136, 173, 183, 188

Szyk, Arthur, 187

Taft, Howard, 25

Taft, Robert, 66, 69, 159, 161

Taiwan, 10, 68, 193–95

Talbott, Sprague, 63, 66

Talmadge, Eugene, 110, 162

Taves, Isabella, 56

Taylor, Elizabeth, 37, 212, 222–23

Taylor, Maxwell, 172

technology. *See* medical advances

teenagers, 10, 33, 119–20, 127, 129, 131, 149–52, 158, 189, 223, 225

television, 3, 4, 10, 14, 51, 57, 82, 92–94, 98, 225–27, 235

Terrell, Maurice, 63, 66, 110, 228

test-tube babies, 102. *See also* medical advances

Theisen, Earl, 63, 66, 157, 197

"They Made Our World," 17, 215–16

Thomas, Norman, 43, 84

Thompson, Dorothy, 142, 186

Till, Emmett, 108, 111–13, 212. *See also* Huie, William Bradford

Time-Life, xvi, 3, 39, 182

Time magazine, 21, 22, 23, 49, 62, 90, 158, 162, 181, 184, 211, 235, 236

Tito, Marshal Josep Broz, 17, 182, 204

Toynbee, Arnold, 69, 103, 168

travel, 11, 17, 40, 44, 49, 50, 61, 80, 82, 90, 91, 94, 99, 208, 209–10

Tretick, Stanley, 52, 66, 67, 117, 170, 172–73, 213

Trilling, Diana, 131, 147

women's movement, 177, 179. *See also* feminism; *Ms.* magazine

"Women Who Fascinate Men," 43

World's Fairs, 99, 119

World War I, 35, 63

World War II: and Arthur Rothstein, 65, 185; and enlisted men, 9; era beginning with, xiv, 1, 7, 48; and families, 130–31; and Holocaust, 186; and James Hansen, 66; *Look* coverage of, 9, 36–37, 57, 159, 183–87; *Look* covers, 37, 187, 213; *Look* newsreels, 41, 48; military leaders, 187; *My Favorite War Story*, 41, 185–86; *Our American Heroes*, 41, 185; and Stanley Tretick, 67; and Tony Vaccaro, 66. *See also* Hiroshima; Nazis; Roosevelt, Franklin D.

Worthy, William, 193–94

Wren, Christopher, 52, 62, 108, 182, 190, 202, 204, 233

Wylie, Philip, 142, 147

Yelverton, Bani, 108

Young, Whitney, 124

youth movement. *See* baby boom

Zhou En-lai, 10, 194–95